P9-DMF-340

COLONEL THEODORE ROOSEVELT OF THE 'ROUGH RIDERS'

WALTER MILLIS

* * * * * * * * *

THE
MARTIAL SPIRIT

* * * * * * * * *

WITH TWENTY-FIVE ILLUSTRATIONS

THE LITERARY GUILD OF AMERICA
1931

The Riverside Press
CAMBRIDGE · MASSACHUSETTS
PRINTED IN THE U.S.A.

TO
ELIZABETH SEMMES DESSEZ

War of itself cannot be the great evil; the evil is in the horrors, many of which are not necessarily concomitant. . . . The war now beginning between the United States and Spain was one in which these greater horrors were largely to be absent.

— *Admiral* CHADWICK

CONTENTS

ILLUSTRATIONS

THE MARTIAL SPIRIT

THE MARTIAL SPIRIT

CHAPTER I

THE SETTING OF THE STAGE

I

ON the morning of February 28, 1895, the newspaper readers of the United States were apprised of the fact that an insurrection against the decaying authority of Spain had broken out in the Island of Cuba. The despatch was brief, but it was accompanied by those official assurances of its unimportance which subsequent experience with revolution has taught us to recognize as the infallible signs of trouble. The Spanish Minister at Washington declared that the insurrectionists (and it has a strangely familiar ring) were mere bandits who were already in flight; 'the whole movement had collapsed.' Havana was equally prompt in reporting that the 'rioters' were either dispersed or offering to negotiate for a promise of clemency, and even the leaders of the Cuban home-rule party itself, it was declared, condemned them as 'brigands,' or at best as misguided patriots engaged upon a hopeless and ill-timed attempt.

The large Cuban colonies in New Orleans and other American seaports, however, were observed to be in a state of unusual excitement. A reporter visiting the offices of *El Porvenir* in New York discovered them filled with swarthy and gesticulating expatriates, the air heavy with cigar-smoke and the war fever. He was assured that this was no casual riot but war in earnest, opened upon a prearranged schedule, and a war 'for which every detail had been prepared with the most minute attention.' That evening there was an interesting mass meeting in Nineteenth Street, just off Fifth Avenue, with martial speeches and a collection; while telegrams from Washington made it quite clear that, notwithstanding the official collapse of the movement, two whole provinces, Matanzas and Santiago de Cuba, had been formally declared under martial law. The news, it seemed evident, was important; and night editors gave it front-page prominence. As they did so, they were in fact opening a new chapter in the history of the American people. For properly speaking, it marked the beginning of our War with Spain.

It was to be a war brief in duration and small in scale which was nevertheless to have a profound influence upon the whole tenor of our national life. Immense consequences were to flow from it, and even now the full effects of this remarkable episode are scarcely calculable. Yet it is a war which has hardly been reëxamined since the first victorious rush to the printing-presses thirty years ago; today, if it is remembered at all, it is remembered through the patriotic enthusiasms of an already distant age. We see it mainly through the eyes of its contemporary historians (always a trifle uncertain as to whether they were recording a rather badly managed skirmish or one of the world's decisive struggles) and the effect is a little odd. We still think of an event which was to mark a new rhythm in American history as having begun with the complete irrelevance of a boiler explosion, as having been conducted (though upon the highest moral plane) like an absent-minded comic opera, and as having left us in the end with a colonial empire acquired (for so President McKinley, in a famous passage, assured posterity) only under explicit instructions vouchsafed in response to prayer. One has the disturbing impression that the nation was launched upon the present stage of its development by a pleasant, but strangely unstatesmanlike, combination of sheer accident and direct revelation. It seems hardly just.

Nor is it. Though we accept Mr. McKinley's word that the war was terminated under divine guidance, the matter of its origins and conduct still offers a fascinating field for study in more strictly human elements.

II

The psychological background against which the news of insurrection in Cuba arrived was, as fate would have it, a peculiar and a pregnant one. In 1895 the seeds of a new unity in American life were actively germinating, fertilized by the chaotic débris of the past which still overlaid and concealed them. The Civil War, the last great outpouring of the national energies upon a national scale, was already thirty years away; it was seen down the same time perspective as that in which we view the Spanish War today, or in which the generation of 1950 will see the war in Europe. Its great figures had all passed into retirement or the grave, and a new, a post-war, generation had grown up into the seats of power or their immediate anterooms. Its history had been written and read; its passions were fading, and its pains, especially, had been forgotten.

Between the Civil War and the nineties there had stretched a complex and vaguely unsatisfactory period which even today we find it difficult either to remember or to interpret. It was a period, as one of its historians has said, which lacked 'definiteness either of purpose or of progress; there was no unanimity of opinion as to the facts of economic life or as to national policy. Old political platforms were not applicable to new problems. Party politics became confused and shrewd political leaders were at a loss which way to turn. The result was uncertainty, vacillation, and inconsistency.'

Perhaps little else could be expected of a time whose extraordinary achievement it was to combine a frontier conquest with an industrial revolution. Somewhere in those tangled (though strangely complacent) years we see, for example, a youthful William Jennings Bryan who was yet to learn that he was a free silverite, and a certain Major McKinley from whom the fact that he was born to be a pillar of honest money was still, unfortunately, concealed. We see a Mr. M. A. Hanna, a business man of Cleveland, as yet only casually interested in politics, and politicians everywhere only dimly cognizant of the great forces of business which were making the political world over under their very feet. We watch the westward sweep of the frontier, and in the East the rise of 'the Interests' and of 'Wall Street' and of the great city slums, where a horrid shadow called anarchism moved suddenly at times, to the panic-stricken indignation of all the best people. We witness the appearance of those dreadful and clearly un-American institutions, the labor unions, and we catch a hurried glimpse of brickbats and volley firing as the militia are called out to suppress them and maintain 'law and order.'

It was a period in which our foreign policy followed the inescapable logic of internal conditions; it was practically non-existent. The West was still the untamed West, and ample to our energies. Foreign nations could have little influence upon the great conquest which we were achieving, and the American people paid little attention to them — a circumstance profoundly vexatious to those more cultured souls who modeled themselves upon European examples and blushed to belong to a nation so vulgar as to be without even a diplomacy. The Navy was allowed to dwindle gently away until it was somewhat doubtful, even as late as 1891, whether we should win the war which threatened in that year with the Republic of Chile. The Army, which had ended the Civil War with those bright expectations which have never failed to deceive our military men after all our wars, found its budgets being cut down with a heartless regularity, until in the year 1878 they disappeared entirely with the failure of an appropriation bill, and the officers were compelled for a time to serve their country gratis. After that they resigned themselves to the arduous but minor glories of Indian fighting, and to the 'promotion hump'; and years afterward, when an infantry captain sprang forward to lead his company up the slope at El Caney, it was noted that his 'long, white beard' waved free in the wind. Our diplomatic service (once the really important questions of patronage had been satisfactorily adjusted) conducted its time-honored ritual with all the elegance and solemnity which it could muster, but the circumstance that we had almost no urgent interests abroad either to advance or to defend lent its activities an air of engaging unreality.

Throughout that contradictory and uncertain period the nation was conscious of its immense powers, but it lacked the background of a world stage against which to see them, and it was without unified psychological patterns through which they could be expressed. As a nation we were not sure of ourselves, of where we stood, or of what was happening to us. The national mind appears to have been uncomfortably divided between a glorious optimism and an inferiority complex; and those who look back upon those crowded years seem to do so without regret. It is a time which lies diffused across our history like a cloud, a time which was to find its greatest monument in the exhaustive perplexities of Mr. Henry Adams who (by a final appropriateness) quite failed to understand it. But his summary of its public life is comprehensive. 'The whole financial system,' he declared in pessimistic retrospect, 'was in chaos.... The whole Government from top to bottom was rotten with the senility of what was antiquated and the instability of what was improvised.' In the world of public men and affairs 'one might search the whole list of Congress, Judiciary, and Executive during the twenty-five years 1870 to 1895 and find little but damaged reputations. The period was poor in purpose and barren in results.'

But now at last it was over. By 1895, to begin with, the frontier was gone — and the change was fundamental. Mr. Adams himself had come out of the West in 1894 to report that there was no more West. 'Compared with the Rockies of 1871, the sense of wildness had vanished.' In Arizona and the Dakotas General Nelson Miles had put down the last Indian outbreaks, and with the battle of Wounded Knee, in 1890, the Indian wars which had lasted through three centuries had come to their long and bloody end. Men might still talk, as a matter of habit, of going 'beyond the hundredth meridian'; but the great romance had faded. The boundlessness which had once been measured, like the sea's, in degrees of latitude and longitude, was circumscribed by state lines across which the transcontinental railroads trundled tourists and drummers, while writers and artists were already hurrying to set down the West before it should be too late. In the spring of 1889, the crack of a starter's pistol had sent the white settlers across the line into Oklahoma Territory; at the turn of the decade, half a dozen new states were brought into the Union out of the heart of what had been the wilderness, and Utah, with a touching symbolism, formally renounced polygamy. The frontier had dissolved suddenly into the past, and we looked up to find nothing before our eyes save salt water and the nations of the earth which lay beyond it.

It was an inspiring moment, and a new national self-consciousness stirred in the hearts of the people — and of its politicians. It was found that the American fleet was rising from its decay; in

May of 1892, the U.S.S. New York was given her trials and 'the shame that for twenty-five years had rested on our Navy was wiped out' when even British naval writers were compelled to admit that she was one of the best war vessels of her class afloat. Oratory began to take on a deeper and more magnificent note; the Nicaraguan Canal project awoke abruptly from the lethargies of the past half-century, and keener minds — especially among those younger gentlemen who still had reputations to make — began to feel that there might be something in foreign affairs after all. Then in 1893 came the Columbian Exposition; through a long summer the nation trooped to Chicago, looked, and stood spellbound at the miracle of its own achievement. To the established confidence that we were as powerful as any nation in Europe there was added the dawning suspicion that we might even be almost as cultivated, and it was an inspiring thought. Mr. John Hay recorded the impression: 'We were all knocked silly. It beats the brag so far out of sight that even Chicago is dumb.' Or, as Henry Adams chose to put it: 'Chicago was the first expression of American thought as a unity.'

It was scarcely a coincidence that the year 1893 was to be remembered for other reasons than the graceful splendors on the shores of Lake Michigan. It was the panic year, when the financial world abruptly fell to pieces; the Democrats came into power at Washington only to struggle with the vanishing gold reserve; fortunes crumbled, and we were brought face to face with the economic issues that had been gathering since the Civil War had come to its end. The quarter-century which had demolished the frontier had also achieved the industrial revolution, and its pressing questions had to be answered.

How much the world had changed is now obvious. With a rising export of manufactures we were turning from an agrarian to an industrial system. The modern organization of business — an organization which was to prove the chief cornerstone of our success — had appeared in the unlovely form of the 'trusts,' and the public consciousness had been aroused to deal gropingly with it. In 1887, the Interstate Commerce Commission was created to control the railroads, and in 1890, Senator Sherman, already an elder statesman, had seen his famous anti-trust act written into the statutes, as the people's answer to monopoly. But at the same time Major McKinley, a younger representative of the same Ohio Republicanism, was making the first of his many successful applications of the ear to the ground, and was receiving the shrewd message that there were, or could be, two sides to every question. Mr. McKinley was a Congressman of some prominence, if of no very great distinction, and Mr. McKinley was more discerning than some others. Mr. McKinley became a protectionist.

American politics were still in the confusion of the period which was closing; political slogans and economic realities were out of that convenient adjustment which they generally maintain, and the new economic currents were still running strongly across the old party divisions. But the outlines of the future were already appearing dimly under the etching of events. Mr. McKinley sensed the need of the new economic powers for political expression; he also sensed the fact that the politics of power, if it were bold enough, could also be made popular. When Mr. McKinley became a protectionist he avoided the error of being an apologetic one. There was a new note in the statesman's ringing answer to the charge that tariffs would put an end to cheap goods:

I do not prize the word cheap. It is not a word of hope; it is not a word of comfort; it is not a word of cheer; it is not a word of inspiration! It is the badge of poverty; it is the signal of distress.... Cheap merchandise means cheap men and cheap men mean a cheap country.

And as the applause died away, the industrial age had found its voice in politics, and the tariff had been emblazoned in burning letters upon the banners of party. And when the McKinley tariff act — 'protective in every paragraph and American in every line and word,' as its author dramatically proclaimed it — became law in October of 1890, the foundations of the new age were adequately laid. The United States had become an industrial power, and its servants had read the signs.

But the immediate result of the McKinley tariff was of course disastrous. The Republicans were swept from control in the Congressional elections of the succeeding November, and an undiscerning Ohio electorate retired even Mr. McKinley himself. The apostle, however, was great even in defeat. 'Strengthen your organizations,' he wrote upon the night of the catastrophe, 'and be ready for the great battle in Ohio in 1891 and the still greater one in 1892. Home and country will triumph in the end.' But they were distressingly slow about it. In the 'still greater' battle of 1892 they omitted to triumph; the heavy form of Mr. Grover Cleveland came back unwillingly to the White House and for the second time since 1861 the nation witnessed a Democratic administration in the seats of power. There followed almost immediately the currency crisis and the terrible panic of 1893, and the wheels of industry slowed to an ominous stagnation. The spring of 1894 saw Coxey's Army in Washington, with the crowds hurrying down Pennsylvania Avenue to watch what looked almost like social revolution being suppressed through the simple expedient of arresting its leaders for walking on the grass. The crowds laughed; but it was less easy to laugh in the following autumn when Chicago (glorious only the year before with the Columbian Exposition) smelled smoke from the burning cars in the railroad yards and Mr. Cleveland ordered United States troops into the city to 'protect the mails' and put down the Pullman strike. His Attorney-General, Mr. Olney, made the first experiments in 'government by injunction,' while the vituperation of sudden terror was showered upon the mild figure of Mr. Eugene Debs, and an unpleasant tremor ran through the upper strata of established society as he was led off to judgment. The thoughtful perceived that an industrial revolution had its dangers.

Each of these many factors conspired to give the news of an insurrection in Cuba a peculiar interest for alert intelligences. The nation had completed its appointed task in the romantic West and found itself looking beyond the borders with a new energy, a new sense of union, a new self-consciousness. At the same time it was developing an industrial economy which gave it not only a fresh power and wealth, but a fresh interest, as a manufacturing competitor in the markets of the world, in its relations to other continents and countries. And there was a play of more particular and more personal motives. The politicians were finding the old issues breaking in their hands and were alert for new ones which would both catch the imagination of their constituencies and evade the politically dangerous problems which affairs were raising all about them. Editors who were perplexed by the intricacies of strikes, of the injunctive process, of free silver or of monopoly, could discover in foreign affairs a subject for their cogitations at once glamorous, conventional, and comparatively safe. While the mere fact that the Democrats happened to be in power lent a real, if accidental, sharpness to every motive, a heightened tension to every issue.

In vast numbers of American minds the presence of a Democrat in the White House and a Democratic administration in control of the Federal offices left the sense of an abrupt and unaccountable inversion of the natural order. Since the Civil War the country had been normally Republican; and where Mr. McKinley and his party had leaped nimbly to safety upon the rock of the new order, it was already evident that the Democracy was going to wreck upon it. Its principles were of that peculiarly useless character which prevented it from drifting with the tide, but did not permit it to resist; while changing conditions had produced so many discordant elements within it that it was rapidly being reduced to incompetence. The new leaders of the financial, industrial, and social worlds were more and more definitely identifying themselves with the Republican Party. Yet now — at a moment when the nation was suffering under industrial recession, when the specter of unrest and social maladjustment was suddenly active, and when the silver question, concealing within itself what was really a genuine class struggle, could barely be fended off — it was the Democrats who were in control of the nation. The partisan bitterness was of an intensity which has long since faded from the paler controversial styles of today, and the impulse to seize upon any issue which would at once enlist the public's enthusiasms and put the other party in the wrong was very powerful.

It was into this situation that the news of armed rebellion in the largest, the nearest, and to us the most important, of the adjacent West Indian islands was abruptly projected.

CHAPTER II
INSURRECTION IN CUBA

I

TO our innocent and altruistic publics the Cuban insurrection of 1895 seemed a simple case of an oppressed people rising spontaneously to free itself of an alien tyranny. Actually, however, it was a far more complex phenomenon than that; behind it there lay a long and sometimes rather dubious history, of which the American people remembered very little and understood even less. This was just as well, for it was a history in which we had ourselves played a commanding and not always creditable rôle, and we were not devoid of responsibility for the outbreak.

When the Spanish Empire in the Americas broke up in the years after 1808, Cuba — 'the Ever Faithful Isle' — had almost alone remained loyal to the old connection, and for a long time thereafter no real separatist sentiment was to develop among her people. But the idea of fomenting a rebellion from without went back at least to the days of Bolívar and the Panamá Congress of 1825; while as early as 1823 no less a statesman than Mr. Thomas Jefferson had advanced the thought that Cuba might with profit be annexed to the United States. Even then we played seriously with the idea of assisting Latin-American patriots to detach the island from 'the yoke of Spain'; thus early had the twin influences appeared which off and on through seventy years were to keep Cuban affairs in a turmoil. The plans of the Panamá Congress came to nothing, but they established a tradition which persisted. They left in their wake a number of obscure conspiracies, both within the island and without, while they bequeathed to every ambitious or disaffected leader who was to appear in Cuba during the next three quarters of a century the standing hope that the United States might be enlisted in the cause of 'Cuban freedom.'

Of such leaders there were to be many. Spanish colonial administration was no doubt both inefficient and corrupt. Spain herself during most of the nineteenth century was suffering under a succession of wars, revolutions, and dynastic overturns and had little time for Cuban affairs. Constitutions were made and remade at Madrid, but somehow it was never possible to give the island any real voice in its own governance. Spanish younger sons were sent out for the rewards of colonial jobbery, and it encouraged disaffection among the great creole families. The commercial restrictions imposed in the interests of the wheat-growers and manufacturers of the Peninsula were an obvious source of irritation, and among the influential classes a cleavage between the creoles and the Spanish official element gradually developed. But the mass of the population — made up of African slaves in the plantation areas or of a poor-white class in the mountainous districts — was of course permitted no part in politics; no real basis for rebellion existed, and, although innumerable insurrectionary attempts were to be launched for one reason or another, it was seldom that they achieved much support within the island.

There always remained, however, the safe shelter and the possible aid of the United States, and from an early date New York City became a chief center of Cuban patriotism. Indeed, the most celebrated of all these attempts was almost an American enterprise. Its leader, General Narciso Lopez, had spent a lifetime as a loyal officer in the Spanish Army, and had gone over to the creole party only after a grateful government had sent him out to a Cuban post as a reward for his services. In July of 1848, he arrived in New York; and he found that we were again, as we had been in the years around 1825, in one of our great moods of imperial enthusiasm. American infantry had stormed Chapultepec and unfurled the flag above the 'Halls of Montezuma'; Mr. William Walker was embarking upon his piratical career in Central America, and from the shores of California we were looking out upon the inviting sweep of the Pacific. Perry was soon to be at the gates of Japan, and a sudden interest in the Hawaiian Islands had stirred our statesmen. It was the great epoch of Manifest Destiny; and our destiny, curiously enough, had become manifest in precisely those regions in which it was to appear when a similar mood overtook us after 1890. Cuba had not been overlooked. It engaged the thoughts of our statesmen, while so great an enthusiasm for liberty burned in the breasts of our people that it was necessary to order the transports returning from Mexico to avoid touching at Cuban ports lest the volunteer regiments desert *en masse* to the cause of Cuban freedom.

General Lopez was acting in the interest of the great creole slave-owners, who wished to put themselves under the protection of our slave system. But in New York he found a public thirsting for almost any kind of military adventure, without much regard for its objects, while from the more popular and sensational newspapers he received, like his successors long afterwards, a powerful press support. Indeed, the five-barred flag with a single star, destined two generations later to float over the Republic of Cuba, was first given to the breezes, in the spring of 1850, from a staff above the offices of the New York *Sun*. It was curiously prophetic.

The plan was to launch a force of American volunteers (equipped from the sale of bonds and paid in promises of large bonuses and grants of land) as a rallying-point around which the Cuban people would rise. The first attempt was made in May of 1850; unfortunately, the Cuban people showed no inclination to rise, and it ended in a ludicrous fiasco. In the United States in the meanwhile the real bearing of the adventure as a scheme for bringing new slave states into the Union had become apparent, and in the North enthusiasm cooled. But in the South, Lopez found only a heightened ardor. He shifted his base to New Orleans, and in August, 1851, he tried it again with a liberating army of some four hundred American, German and Irish adventurers, and a few authentic Cubans. But somehow the islanders still failed to rally in the cause of their own liberty; the army was cut to pieces. Some of the survivors were shot at the Havana; the others were sent to the prison camps of Africa, and Lopez himself was garroted. There was a riot in New Orleans when the news was received and a crowd sacked the Spanish consulate; but President Fillmore, in his annual message of 1851, closed the incident upon a note of caustic disapproval.

Cuba relapsed into a comparative calm, but the Democratic politicians in the United States were for the next ten years to agitate Cuban annexation as a means of extending slave territory. In 1854 there was the astonishing Ostend Manifesto, when the American Ministers to Spain, France, and England gathered at the

Belgian watering-place to inform the State Department that we should offer Spain $120,000,000 flat for Cuba and fight her if she refused. The South would have seized the island had it dared, but it knew that the North would not permit it. Up to the very end, in the spring of 1860, the Democratic Party was writing the peaceful annexation of Cuba into its platforms. Then the slavery issue was extinguished in the deluge of our Civil War, and when that was over the world had changed.

The abolition of slavery in the United States had of course removed the motive for the Lopez attempts. Naturally, however, there was no lack of other grievances for ambitious patriots, and when next they sought to free Cuba they not only fought under Lopez's flag, but adopted many of his methods. And in the meanwhile the old economy of a feudal society living upon slave labor had begun to pass in Cuba as elsewhere; a growing artisan and small farmer class provided a basis for rebellion; Cuba was coming to life politically, and under the ineptitudes of the home government a genuine separatist sentiment was beginning to appear. Matters came to a head in 1868, when Spain was torn by another revolution at home and when a handful of creoles on a plantation in eastern Cuba 'launched the shout' (as the Spanish phrase went) which was actually to produce a real insurrection.

The Ten Years' War, initiated by the pronunciamento of Yara on the night of the 9th–10th of October, 1868, was not a great popular uprising. It rarely got beyond the stage of irregular guerilla fighting in the wild, unsettled regions at the eastern end of the island. It never penetrated the rich and populous west, where the real strength of the island was centered about the capital at Havana. Its principal support was a Cuban junta at New York — active in the established departments of propaganda, collections, and gun-running — and its chief leader in the field was General Máximo Gómez, a Santo Domingan. But it kept military revolt alive in Cuba for a decade and, like the Lopez expeditions before it, it awoke the immediate attention of the United States.

The Spanish authorities resorted to sternly repressive measures which aroused our indignant disapproval. American adventurers were attracted by the profits in gun-running, and there were some seizures and executions. Moreover, President Grant had a taste for West Indian empire; he got himself involved in a bizarre design upon Santo Domingo, and in June of 1869 he was casually asking Senator Sumner 'how it would do' to recognize the belligerency of the Cuban insurgents. But the temper of the times was very different from what it had been in the exciting atmospheres of 1848. Before adjourning in March, Congress had paused to slash our infantry establishment from forty-five to twenty-five regiments; fresh from the Civil War, the nation had no interest in foreign adventure, and by December President Grant had made up his mind that the United States should refrain from taking part 'in the quarrels between... governments and their subjects.' The Cuban war went on, but in the following summer, Grant was looking upon it without favor:

The condition of the insurgents has not improved and the insurrection itself, although not subdued, exhibits no signs of advance, but seems to be confined to an irregular system of hostilities carried on by small and illy armed bands of men, roaming without concentration through the woods and the sparsely populated regions of the island, attacking from ambush convoys and small bands of troops, burning plantations and the estates of those not sympathizing with their cause.

No doubt we should soon have forgotten all about it, and the insurrection itself have petered out into mere banditry, had there not suddenly intervened the famous case of the Virginius. This vessel, a kind of free-lance filibuster enjoying the protection of the American flag and papers of the most dubious authenticity, had been wandering about the Caribbean for some years, picking up a poor but dishonest living in the gun-running trade. In October of 1873, a Spanish gunboat managed to run her down and capture her, about twenty miles off the north coast of Jamaica and consequently upon the high seas. She was found to contain a cargo of arms and a large number of 'passengers,' most of them giving Anglo-Saxon names, but manifesting a strongly Cuban cast of countenance. The authorities at Santiago de Cuba, concluding not without reason that they were a filibustering expedition, began to march them out and shoot them in platoons on the convenient theory that they were pirates.

The Virginius was commanded by Captain Fry, an authentic

American citizen. Under this interpretation of international law he and fifty-two of the others perished before consular protests and the arrival of a British man-of-war halted the procedure. In the United States there was a cry of angry protest and a shower of headlines calling for war, and in the excitement the cause of Cuban freedom took a new lease of life. The Navy was ordered upon a war footing and the fleet assembled at Key West. Here, however, a difficulty appeared — practically speaking, there was no fleet. The Navy had been allowed to sink to its lowest point, and the real question arose of how, supposing that we should declare war, we should be able to fight it.

In the end we did not go to war. Secretary Fish pushed vigorous diplomatic protests; but as a matter of fact, although the summary methods of the Santiago authorities cannot be excused, the Virginius case was recognized to be a trifle disreputable. The American position was upheld with energy, but with dignity and forbearance; an adjustment was ultimately arrived at, and in the United States the interest died. Yet the insurrection dragged on. There were other incidents, and as the ministries shuttled helplessly in and out at Madrid, even Mr. Fish at last lost his patience. The Cuban war, which was obviously getting nowhere, was in fact a diplomatic nuisance, and in November, 1875, Mr. Fish despatched the warning that unless Spain could effect a reconciliation in the island 'the time is at hand when it may be the duty of other governments to intervene.'

But almost at the same moment Spain was herself undergoing one final revolution. In January, 1876, Alfonso XII entered Madrid to establish the dynasty which has since remained upon the Spanish throne, and as the new government demonstrated its strength and stability the idea of a Cuban intervention died. Mr. Caleb Cushing, our Minister in Madrid, declared that the barbarous methods of the Cuban patriots made his 'blood run cold'; the rebel leaders who were still active could expect little sympathy from the United States, and their cause was hopeless. Spain sent out her ablest military mind, General Martínez Campos, to pacify the island. He perceived that the outright extinction of the guerilla bands was next to impossible, but he realized also that independence had become a dead issue with them, and he finally induced them to lay down their arms by a promise of amnesty and of the concession to Cuba of the same governmental system as that enjoyed by Porto Rico. At nightfall on February 10, 1878, the 'Pact of Zanjón' was signed in a ruined farmhouse in Camaguey; the chieftains immediately departed to inform their scattered bands that they were to turn in their arms, an emissary was despatched to New York to notify the junta, and the Ten Years' War was over.

It developed later that when the Pact of Zanjón was signed neither side knew what the governmental system enjoyed by Porto Rico really was!

II

'I dread emigrant rebels,' Mr. Cushing had written in one of his outbursts against the patriots. The fear was prophetic. In the changing conditions of the next dozen years Cuba was to face many problems, while the Spanish administration continued to be both autocratic and inefficient. But it was not oppressive, and it seems reasonable to suppose that the island would have worked out its destiny in peace and within the framework of the Spanish connection had it not been for the exiled revolutionaries still comfortably established at New York and in other American cities. For the insurrection of 1895 was made in the United States, the work of *émigrés* who had no real stake in the island, who had dissociated themselves from its life, and many of whom had scarcely even set foot upon its soil during the whole period in which they were laboring to involve it again in civil war. It was these men — the unemployed generals of the Ten Years' War, the professional enthusiasts of liberty, and the agitators who had made a place for themselves in the emigrant colonies — who kept the passions of the earlier struggle alive, and abroad perfected the technique of insurrection until conditions made it possible for them to import it once more into Cuba.

In the meanwhile Cuba herself was being remade in her whole economic and social system. Slavery was finally abolished in 1886. The Negro population showed a relative decline, and a growing class of white agricultural laborers appeared. There was an influx of American and European capital into the great staple industry of sugar production; it introduced modern methods, but bore heavily upon many of the old-fashioned planter families. At the same time the industry as a whole was coming under an increasingly severe competition from other countries, and the long prosperity which it had enjoyed was drawing to an end. What the island needed was capital development and free trade; Spain was unable to supply the first, and Spanish finance ministers and monopolists were unwilling to grant the second. In Cuba, however, political life showed a growing realism and responsibility, and the Autonomist Party, commanding the overwhelming support of insular opinion, was founded to work for a solution of the island's difficulties by peaceable means and without separation from the Spanish flag. But among the Cuban societies in New York, in New Orleans, or in the great colonies of Cuban cigarworkers established in Florida, the idea of independence was sedulously maintained; annually upon the 10th of October (the anniversary of the Yara Pronunciamento) they would hold patriotic rallies with oratory and collections, while wandering generals came by from time to time to organize new descents upon the island from among the adventurous of 'the emigration.'

There were a number of actual attempts, but they were made by mere handfuls and came to nothing. Still, an observer in the Cuba of the eighties might have guessed that if ever another conflagration could be started, it would be very difficult to extinguish. The country was still wild and backward. Under the increasing economic pressure, bandits — some of them quite well known and even respected members of the community — were roaming freely through the countryside and up to the very outskirts of the capital itself. Not far from Cienfuegos there was a large sugar estate which was being developed by a Mr. E. F. Atkins. Mr. Atkins, a member of an old-established firm of Boston merchants, was one of the American capitalists who were making over the insular economy, and in 1887 a party of friends came out to visit him. One of them, a lady, left an impression of the visit:

We are met at the pier by the locomotive and car, and the armed guard drawn up looks quite like a traveling arsenal. Ned as soon as he steps on shore slings on a rifle and buckles on a pistol. Mr. Julius Brown of Georgia came up with us to spend the night. He evidently was prepared for the worst, as he had three pistols in his three pockets with twenty-five shots.

The ancient plantation house, they found, was built with the massive walls and small windows of a fortress, while before its entrance two armed men stood always on guard. But this was nothing unusual.

And on a larger stage significant events were taking place. Already the first currents of the new tide in our own history were making themselves felt — a tide which, precisely as in 1825 and in 1848, was to affect and be even more profoundly affected by the destiny of the Gem of the Antilles. Its deeper causes have already been indicated; and from the middle eighties onward their manifestations began to appear. In 1880, a young man with defective eyesight graduated from Harvard; at the time he entertained no idea of going into public life, but his name was Theodore Roosevelt. A little later there were strange stirrings amid the burial cloths enwrapping the Navy Department; there was suddenly a board of officers and a report in which optimistic admirals recommended the construction of a modern navy, to comprise forty-eight cruisers, five 'armored rams,' and no less than twenty battleships. Needless to say, the program was not adopted, but the exciting problems of national defense had become a topic of conversation.

This was a mere straw, but something more was soon to follow. It was in 1889 that an obscure clash of petty official dignities, naval pugnacity, and microscopic 'commercial interests' somewhere in the remote Pacific flared suddenly into the Samoan Affair. Our people discovered that an American squadron (of unhappily antique design) was facing German war vessels in the harbor of Apia, and the sensational possibility of a war with Germany actually fluttered for a time in the newspapers. There was no war, but there was a Congress of Berlin at which American diplomats not only appeared upon the full stage of European affairs, but even snubbed the Iron Chancellor himself. It was astonishing; and as American publics looked up their maps of the Pacific (to discover the exact nature and location of the Samoan Islands, of which most of them had never previously heard), they could not avoid being struck by that inviting sweep of blue water, by those romantically exotic place-names, and by the allurements of the great game of naval and commercial strategy.

Quite suddenly 'the desire for a vigorous foreign policy, though it jarred with tradition, had spread and become popular.' A whole series of warlike and stimulating incidents were to follow, rising in a steady crescendo. Indeed, the range and impartiality of our bellicosity during the next few years must seem surprising to any who retain a belief that the Americans are an unaggressive people. The Alaskan seal fisheries and boundary question were continually at hand to fan the martial ardors; naval appropriations took on added importance, and journalists and statesmen began to look into such novel matters as coaling stations, bases, and commercial outposts. In 1890 we authorized our first battleships.

Then in the fall of 1891 there was another exciting affair in the Pacific. A liberty party from the U.S.S. Baltimore was set upon by a mob in the streets of Valparaiso. Two of them were killed; others were covered with stab wounds, and the rest thrown into jail. The indignation evoked by this outrage against the American flag sounded a new and strangely ominous note, and so great a wave of belligerent enthusiasm swept the nation that for a time the fantastic prospect of a war between the United States and the Republic of Chile was measurably near to realization. Naval officers gravely explained that Chile was 'planning to control the Pacific'; our ships were fitted under rush orders for active service, and President Harrison is even said to have withheld a note in which Chile sought to apologize. In the end, however, she succeeded in doing so, and once more there was no war. But when Captain Winfield Scott Schley, the Baltimore's commander, came home across the continent, he found the trip 'in the nature of an ovation. Everywhere when the train stopped large crowds of our people had assembled to give expression of approval to the commander's action in protecting his crew and in standing for the rights and honor of the nation in far-off countries.' And upon Captain Robley D. Evans, the colleague who had relieved him at Valparaiso, a delighted public bestowed for some unexplained reason the sobriquet of 'Fighting Bob.'

The Chilean crisis died away; but a State Department which had so nearly tasted blood was not long to remain in inactivity. At the end of 1892 a proposal to buy the Danish West Indies as a naval base drifted momentarily through the despatches. After some indecision it was laid aside, owing to the fact that a sovereign people had just been unkind enough to elect Mr. Cleveland to the Presidency and thus number the days of the Republican administration. But then in January, 1893, a revolution broke out (under somewhat peculiar circumstances) in the Hawaiian Islands, and in spite of his loss of mandate President Harrison could hesitate no longer. It was an opportunity too good to lose.

The native Kingdom of Hawaii had off and on for many years been an object of solicitude to our statesmen; American settlers had been drifting steadily into the islands, and there was an obvious probability that some day they would be annexed to the United States. But Mr. Frederick L. Stevens, Harrison's Minister to the court of Queen Liliuokalani, was a diplomat alive to the new temper of his countrymen, and the idea of waiting patiently upon remote contingencies did not appeal to him. The American element, he reported, was already in effective economic control of the little kingdom, but 'unaided by outside support' was still 'too few in numbers to control in political affairs and to secure good government.' Mr. Stevens was naturally a devotee of good government, and he sent home an ardent brief for immediate annexation. This very debonair proposal received no official encouragement. But Mr. Stevens and the American-Hawaiians found a way. They organized a Committee of Safety.

In January of 1893, with an American cruiser conveniently in the harbor, the committee suddenly announced a *coup d'état*. The Marines were of course landed 'to preserve life and property'; in their presence Queen Liliuokalani was deposed, and Mr. Sanford B. Dole, one of her leading subjects and a justice of her supreme court, emerged as the head of a new government. The admirable device of preserving order before it had been endangered spared Mr. Dole the usual ardors of revolution — for the Queen could find no answer to the Marine Corps. Mr. Stevens instantly recognized Mr. Dole; a few days later he also proclaimed an American 'protectorate' and then gracefully informed his superiors in Washington that 'the Hawaiian pear is now fully ripe, and this is the golden hour for the United States to pluck it.'

Mr. Harrison had been repudiated at the polls, and his tenure was now practically at an end, but he could not disregard that inspiring appeal. The first act of the new Hawaiian Government was to charter a steamer and rush its plenipotentiaries to Washington with a treaty of annexation. They were immediately received by the Secretary of State, and within a bare three weeks after the news of the *coup* had first reached the State Department, the annexation treaty had been negotiated and signed, and Mr. Harrison had presented it to the Senate in the name, curiously enough, of 'the peace of the world.' But the 4th of March was too near; the treaty failed to pass while there was yet time and the Republican administration expired. The peace of the world remained unshattered.

But the tide by this time was beginning to run strongly. Although there was a good deal of denunciation in some quarters for these novel diplomatic methods, the people as a whole were acquiring a taste for the grand manner. Once more they were turning up their maps of the Pacific, or experiencing a pleasant glow at the thought of bringing new peoples into the happy orbit of our democratic institutions. Young Mr. Theodore Roosevelt contributed a vigorous article on foreign policy to the *Forum*, for which the admirals thanked him. And the editor of the Omaha *Bee* welcomed Mr. Cleveland to the White House in the belief that he could be counted on 'to promote as far as possible the "Manifest Destiny" doctrine which contemplates the ultimate extension of the United States over the entire North American continent and the absorption of whatever "outposts" it may be found expedient or desirable to possess.' These were significant words — but their author had mistaken Mr. Cleveland.

With the return of that obstinate conscience to the Presidency there came, in fact, an important pause. In the campaign which resulted in Mr. Cleveland's election, foreign affairs, though still a minor issue, had taken a new prominence. The two parties, which in 1888 had scarcely remembered the existence of a State Department, had both, in 1892, placed planks upon international relations at the head of their platforms. The Republicans, sensing the nation's growing preoccupation with the enticing subject, had been boldly nationalistic; and adopting the great phrase of fifty years before they had announced their belief 'in the achievement of the manifest destiny of the Republic in its broadest sense.' But the Democrats had found themselves divided, as has so frequently happened, between their principles and the popular current. Manifest Destiny, though it had once been their own doctrine, was hardly compatible with the 'liberalism' which they were professing, and the result was hopeful compromise. 'The Democratic Party,' they claimed, 'is the only party that has ever given the country a foreign policy, consistent and vigorous, compelling respect abroad and inspiring confidence at home,' but they went on to 'view with alarm the tendency to a policy of irritation and bluster' which they rightfully discerned in their opponents.

Mr. Cleveland had an old-fashioned habit of taking both principles and party pledges seriously, and it seemed to him that the rush-order annexation of a group of helpless Pacific islanders was a proceeding which squared neither with his platform nor with the national professions. Five days after taking the oath of office, he bluntly informed the Senate that he had withdrawn the Hawaiian treaty for 'the purpose of reëxamination.' He despatched a special commissioner into the wastes of the Pacific to find out what had really happened there; while the country, forgetting the matter, drifted into the long, disastrous summer of 1893.

It was the panic year, when prosperity ended, when angry and unhappy workmen tramped the streets or listened on empty stomachs to strange and impassioned oratory, when the silver issue became suddenly active, and when Mr. Henry Adams, concluding that the country 'had declared itself, once for all, in favor of the capitalistic system with all its necessary machinery,' quietly became a Republican. It was symptomatic.

III

The depression of 1893, though naturally attributed to the fact that the Democrats were in power, was of course world-wide; and upon the Island of Cuba it closed down with a crushing effect. The sugar industry, already depressed, became suddenly demoralized, and the whole economic structure of the country collapsed with it. Bandits infested the countryside. Governments at Madrid played with the idea of political reforms, but nothing was done, and it merely added to the unrest. Under such conditions the responsible leaders in Cuba were only the more anxious for peace and stability, and the Autonomist Party continued to work loyally for peaceful solutions. But the patriotic agitators of 'the emigration,' who had so long been living in memories and hopes, saw this as their great opportunity. The moment had arrived when it might at last be possible to revive insurrection in the island, and this time they were prepared to do so.

The innumerable earlier descents upon Cuba had been sporadic, badly organized, and undertaken with little relation to one another. But beginning in 1891, a remarkable New York Cuban, José Julián Martí, had been forging the Cuban colonies in the United States and the Caribbean countries into a single effective instrument for revolution. Like other die-hards of lost causes, Sr. Martí had taken no part in the previous fighting. He had been exiled to Spain at the age of sixteen, and though thus early a martyr to liberty, he had neglected to return to the island while the Ten Years' War was in progress. In fact, save for a brief moment when the amnesty was declared at the close of that war, he had never returned at all; but he had devoted his life to agitating the cause of Cuban freedom, and in the shelter of our flag he had created the organization which was at last to bring it to success. He was the founder and head of the Cuban Revolutionary Party, uniting the scattered members of 'the emigration' under a single autocratic discipline, providing a war chest by a regular levy upon the membership, enlisting the exiled chieftains of the Ten Years' War in a common effort, and even establishing within the island itself an organization to light the fires of revolt and to undermine the position of the moderates and autonomists.

So small a figure as Sr. Martí's of course passed unnoticed upon the crowded stage of our own great affairs. The American people knew nothing of his activities; but it is not improbable that Sr. Martí paid a close attention to the activities of the American people. For the trend by this time was appearing unmistakably. In December of 1893, Mr. Cleveland abruptly reintroduced the

Hawaiian question. His special commissioner, Mr. James H. Blount, had returned from the Pacific to reveal a most singular state of affairs; by what was in reality an act of war, Mr. Cleveland decided, 'the government of a feeble but friendly and confiding people has been overthrown. A substantial wrong has been done.' And confronted with such a situation, nothing better occurred to the President than that the wrong should be righted. The Senate arose in its wrath.

For the political situation was very different from what it had been in the previous year. The Republicans in the Senate (their talents now fortified by the shrewd mind of Mr. Henry Cabot Lodge, an intellectual and a student of foreign affairs) were in bitter opposition, while the silver men among the Democrats were either hostile to the President or lukewarm to his leadership. With the public already in a mood for expansionist adventure, the Hawaiian question presented an admirable opportunity for a political assault by both parties — none the less useful in that it distracted attention from the deeper, but more dangerous, economic and social questions which were in reality at the bottom of the fierce opposition.

The assault was immediate and violent. Mr. Cleveland was denounced for having exceeded his constitutional powers, for having withheld papers from the Senate, for having betrayed the confiding group of revolutionaries led by Mr. Dole. It was proposed to stop Mr. Blount's salary because he had ordered the American flag hauled down from the custom house at Honolulu. Senator Sherman, the elder statesman from Ohio, denied the President's right to utilize the military forces of the United States in restoring a despot Queen to power (from which our naval forces had just deposed her), and there was, of course, a Senate investigation. In the end Mr. Cleveland was compelled to give in — not because of Senatorial opposition, which had singularly little effect upon that obstinate rectitude, but because the attitude of Queen Liliuokalani herself made a restoration of the *status quo* impossible. Ultimately, Mr. Dole declared himself a republic; Mr. Cleveland, in common with other powers, was forced to recognize him as such, and the matter was thus left hanging in the air. But young Mr. Roosevelt wrote to his friend, Mr. Lodge:

Our foreign policy is to me of an importance which it is difficult to overestimate. I am surprised all the time to receive new proofs that every man, even every Southerner, who lives outside the country has gotten to have a perfect hatred and contempt for Cleveland's administration because of its base betrayal of our interests abroad. I do wish that our Republicans would go in avowedly to annex Hawaii.

Perhaps it was not such a bad idea. It was that spring that Coxey's Army was in Washington, and in July the Pullman strike was flaring ominously at Chicago. There were reasons enough why foreign adventure might be useful.

Yet the summer of 1894 passed (diversified by another martial incident, in which one of our admirals nearly declared war upon the revolution then current in Brazil), and none could have guessed how closely the Hawaiian affair was merely a rehearsal in miniature of a drama soon to be enacted upon a far grander scale. In August of that year, however, Mr. Cleveland permitted the famous Wilson tariff bill to become law without his signature; one of its provisions restored the duties on Cuban sugars, and the wreck of the island's economic life was completed as an accidental consequence of the exigencies of American party politics. Cuba's trade wilted, and as the island declined into the worst winter of all, Sr. Martí and his Cuban Revolutionary Party moved to action. Eight hundred rifles and 600,000 rounds of ammunition were purchased and shipped southward to Fernandina, Florida. Three fast steamers were chartered and assigned a rendezvous at the same port; arrangements were made for them to pick up the various generals of the Ten Years' War on their way to Cuba, and simultaneously to import the revolution, its arms, and its leaders into three different provinces of the island. The plan, it is true, ended in a disastrous *contretemps* when the United States authorities got wind of it, seized the steamers and confiscated the arms on the very eve of departure. But Martí's agents had already established an insurrectionary conspiracy within the island; the whole thing had gone too far to be halted; the leaders in New York summoned the devoted members of 'the emigration' to 'additional sacrifice,' and secret orders were despatched setting the night of February 24, 1895, as the date for the rising.

It coincided with a tense moment in our own history. The

terrible Pullman strike had held the attention throughout the preceding summer and fall. Then in November the Republicans had carried the Congressional elections; the sinking gold reserve revived the currency question in all its bitterness and danger; and it became apparent how deep and difficult were the issues which events were raising all about us. It was in February of 1895 that Mr. Cleveland, brought to the end of his resources over the silver problem, summoned to his aid the dread figure of Mr. J. Pierpont Morgan. There was the famous conference in the White House; the Morgan-Belmont contract for the sale of bonds to save the gold reserve was drawn up, and among the opponents of 'privilege' a cry of anger and dismay arose over the Judas in the Presidency who had, it seemed, sold the nation to the bankers. Mr. William Jennings Bryan, the rising young silverite from Nebraska, made a brilliant and moving address upon the floor of the House against this infamous contract with Satan. 'We cannot afford,' he cried, 'to put ourselves in the hands of the Rothschilds!' — and as the exclamation died from his lips one half the country felt that it had found a champion and the other half that it had discovered a brainless demagogue waving a firebrand in a powder magazine. But the gold in the New York sub-treasury was within forty-eight hours of exhaustion. On February 20, the bankers offered their bonds to public sale, and as they disposed of them at a handsome profit the torrents of abuse broke over the White House.

It was just four days after this, at a hamlet in eastern Cuba, that a little group of men gathered beneath a five-barred flag with a single star and 'launched the shout' which was the beginning of the Cuban insurrection.

IV

Could we fail to find it interesting? Only a month or so before, the editor of so stable a publication as the *Review of Reviews* had been observing that, while 'conquest is not desired by any group or party in the United States,' nevertheless 'the annexation of Hawaii, the undivided control of the Nicaragua Canal, the acquisition of a strong naval station in the West Indies, and the emphatic assertion of certain principles regarding European interference in the affairs of Central and South America would form a very moderate and reasonable American policy.' Observing the resolute, and unpopular, pacifism of President Cleveland, there were Republican statesmen who did not even seem to be sure of the undesirability of conquest. The March issue of the *Forum* had contained an article upon 'Our Blundering Foreign Policy' by that scholar in politics, Senator Henry Cabot Lodge:

We have a record of conquest, colonization and expansion unequalled by any people in the Nineteenth Century. We are not to be curbed now by the doctrines of the Manchester school, which... as an importation are even more absurdly out of place than in their native land.

It was not, he was willing to admit, 'the policy of the United States to enter, as England has done, upon the general acquisition of distant possessions in all parts of the world.' But it was to be remembered that 'there are outworks... which must neither be neglected nor abandoned.' Apparently there were — quite a few of them:

From the Rio Grande to the Arctic Ocean there should be but one flag and one country.... For the sake of our commercial supremacy in the Pacific we should control the Hawaiian Islands and maintain our influence in Samoa. England has studded the West Indies with strong places which are a standing menace to our Atlantic seaboard. We should have among those islands at least one strong naval station, and when the Nicaragua Canal is built the island of Cuba, still sparsely settled and of almost unbounded fertility, will become to us a necessity.

With visions such as these in the minds of our statesmen the actual appearance of separatist rebellion in Cuba was a matter of the most obvious possibilities. Yet in its opening movements the insurrection was not very impressive. Organized opinion within the island united to denounce it as an incitation to 'anarchy and barbarism'; Martí and the other real leaders did not set foot on Cuban soil until some time later; the Spanish authorities made a few quick moves, and the whole thing came very near to a fiasco. Perhaps Cuba would not, after all, offer an immediate field for a vigorous foreign policy.

But then almost immediately there intervened the fatal Spanish instinct for doing the wrong thing. On March 12, the American steamer Alliança of the Columbia Line arrived in New York from Colón. Her captain informed the reporters that on March 8,

while going through the Windward Passage and about six miles
off Cape Maysi, 'his vessel, flying the American flag, had been
fired upon and chased for twenty-five miles by a Spanish gunboat
on the high seas. It was,' said the news account, 'one of those out-
rages which Spain seems to think, from the long forbearance of this
Government, that she can commit with impunity.... The Alliança
is a vessel of nearly 3000 tons register, and could not, even by a
stupid Spanish commander, have been mistaken for a vessel bent
on a filibustering enterprise.' The sensation was immediate. The
Cuban insurrection hit every front page in the country, and with
a bang.

The Alliança had not been touched, and subsequent discussion
left some doubt both as to Captain Crossman's exact distance
from shore when fired upon and as to his wisdom in failing to heave
to when ordered. It did not matter. The flag had been outraged,
and our new martial ardor awoke in an outburst of fury which at
this length of time seems astonishing. The New York *Tribune*
(a leading opponent of what Mr. Roosevelt had called 'the brutal
stupidity and cowardice' of Mr. Cleveland's foreign policy) voiced
the remarkable opinion that 'the outrage would not have been
more flagrant if [the Spanish gunboat] had entered the harbor of
New-York and bombarded the City Hall.... Several American
cruisers ought to be sent to Cuban waters without delay.... The
revolutionary movement is evidently more serious than the
earliest dispatches indicated.'

The Spanish authorities mildly attempted to suggest that as yet
only one side had been heard. 'I am about tired,' Captain Crossman with dignity informed the reporters, 'of answering the absurd
rumors and suggestions set in motion by the Spanish Government
and Minister to Washington.' The newspapers were active.
Mr. Chauncey M. Depew deprecated the importance of the incident, but added his belief that the United States should own Cuba
and would do so one day. 'The United States,' he said, 'is too
conservative as far as the annexation of property is concerned.'
Mr. William C. Whitney, Secretary of the Navy in Mr. Cleveland's first cabinet, cabled from Naples that he did not recall 'so
wanton an outrage happening to any first-class power in fifty
years.' The New York *Sun* advised editorially that 'peremptory

orders' be given to our naval officers 'that the next shot fired by a Spanish warship on a vessel flying the Stars and Stripes shall be followed by a broadside from an American cruiser. The rule in such cases should be to strike first and explain afterwards.'

These were, of course, the expressions of unofficial opinion. But even members of the Foreign Relations Committee of the United States Senate did not seem to feel that their position imposed silence upon them. Senator John T. Morgan of Alabama declared that he would at once 'despatch a fleet of warships to Havana.' This, he was careful to add, should not be done in 'the spirit of jingoism and not in the way of a threat'; but the Senator realized that the fact that Cuban insurrections were fomented and carried on from within the United States was bound to cause 'irritation and resentment.' The solution for the difficulty, he said, 'is clear to my mind. Cuba should become an American colony.'

But if Senator Morgan's attitude seems curiously debonair, that of some of his colleagues was even more so. Senator Cullom expressed the piratical belief that 'it is time that some one woke up and realized the necessity of annexing some property. We want all this northern hemisphere, and when we begin to reach out to secure these advantages we will begin to have a nation and our lawmakers will rise above the grade of politicians and become true statesmen.' Senator Frye, also on the Foreign Relations Committee, showed his ability to rise to true statesmanship even more frankly. 'I had almost hoped,' he said a few days later, when the excitement was beginning to die, 'that Spain would assume such an arrogant and belligerent tone that it would be necessary for the United States to go over and take possession of Cuba. We certainly ought to have that island in order to round out our possessions as they should be, and if we cannot buy it, I for one should like to have an opportunity to acquire it by conquest.' Was it possible, as one editor asked in some alarm, that Americans were 'spoiling for war?'

It seemed very likely. But there was one penetrating brain which saw matters in a somewhat different light. Mr. E. L. Godkin, the editor of the *Evening Post*, paused to remind his readers of the Ostend Manifesto and the Democratic enthusiasm for 'annexing some property' in the years before the Civil War. The *Evening Post* continued:

This remarkable historical *volte face*, by which the Republicans take the place of the men whom they denounced as highwaymen forty years ago, has of course a political and psychological explanation. Republicans adopt the tactics of the slave party because they have got themselves into substantially the same position that the slave party occupied. They have tremendous and urgent domestic questions to confront and settle, but find the work dangerous politically and irksome....

But it is much easier to blink these matters,... get up a foreign war if possible, at any rate whoop loudly about our navy and our greatness as a nation, and try to distract attention in that way from the really pressing questions of public policy and national good repute.

But Mr. Godkin, of course, was a mere foreigner — as every one knew, he had been born in Ireland.

In the end Spain was permitted to apologize; the furor faded, and, besides, there were too many other inspiring topics of conversation. Senator Lodge, making a strong speech on Hawaii, had an immense map brought into the Senate Chamber upon which 'huge Maltese crosses indicated Great Britain's six powerful naval stations' along our Atlantic seaboard. With their aid he had given the august body a lesson in the fascinating subject of naval strategy:

I have no idea that England desires to go to war with this country. I do not think she does; but we may as well look facts in the face....

As for Hawaii, he said, 'in the one place where the hand of England has not yet reached out, to throw away those islands is madness.' Senator Lodge was a great admirer of England.

Then in the latter days of March there was a double crisis in Central America involving the Monroe Doctrine itself, and Cuba disappeared from the front pages. But it had been a most instructive episode; while its immediate result, of course, was greatly to strengthen the patriot cause. Spain, though still discounting the importance of the outbreak, prepared to throw a hundred thousand troops into the island, while it nominated Martínez Campos, the man who had brought the Ten Years' War to an end, as Captain-General. By the middle of April, General Campos had reached Santiago de Cuba on his way to Havana, and his first step was to issue a proclamation offering amnesty and promising political reforms as soon as possible. But by this time it was too late. The real leaders of the rebellion were at last actually upon the soil of Cuba.

v

José Martí, the 'soul of the Cuban revolution,' was killed in a Spanish ambush a few days after his landing. But his war went on, for his death left the undivided command in the competent hands of Máximo Gómez, the Santo Domingan who had led the patriots throughout the earlier struggle. The Santo Domingan — a thin, tough old man, austere, passionate, and resolutely devoted to success — was at once a thorough-going realist and a professional guerilla fighter of long experience. As lieutenants he had the other veteran leaders of the Ten Years' War — General Roloff, a Polish Jew naturalized as a citizen of the United States; Antonio Maceo, the dashing mulatto chieftain, and his brother José; Calixto García, who had been making a career for himself in Spain, and various others. Supported by an active junta at New York, financed by contributions from the cigar-makers of 'the emigration,' and operating from the wild eastern end of the island, they were soon able to fill the countryside with roaming bands of men, for the most part mounted, who harassed and evaded the Spanish columns in the immemorial fashion of irregular cavalry. Industrial depression and the Hispanic love of excitement combined to provide them with soldiers and an abundant natural food supply took care of the commissariat.

The detailed history of the Cuban insurrection — a war which was characterized, according to one who participated, by 'a larger amount of lying than any before or since' — is difficult to recover. But the broad tactics are easily understandable. General Gómez never had any idea of winning a military victory over the Spanish Army. What he actually proposed to do was to stop the economic life of the island by a system of irregular terrorism. By burning the cane fields (a safe and simple operation) he could destroy the sugar industry, thus depriving the Government of its tax revenues and adding to the prevailing want and unemployment. Under this and other forms of destruction the populace would be forced either into the insurgent ranks or into the garrisoned towns; but the towns in turn were to be starved by cutting off their food supplies from the surrounding country. Clearly, such a program involved the ruin of Cuba and misery for the Cubans, but Máximo Gómez was resolved this time to win his war. In one of his first general orders, on July 1, 1895, these measures were all prescribed, and they were thereafter followed.

American editors, however, failed to grasp the realistic basis of the insurgent strategy. Assisted by an unrivaled propaganda bureau in the United States, the insurgent 'armies' began to make an increasingly impressive appearance in the pages of our newspapers; while our publics, always hostile toward the effete autocracies of Europe and always ready to sympathize with patriots struggling to be free, began to picture the Cuban war in the dramatic (though wholly unwarranted) terms of formal military operations, sieges and pitched battles. The summer wore on, and Cuba (for summer months are notoriously dull) awoke more and more attention. The New York *Sun*, a traditionally pro-Cuban paper, was pained by President Cleveland's unenterprising coldness to the cause of liberty:

The good-will of the Cleveland administration is reserved for monarchists; it has no fellow feeling for republican revolutionists. But let not the Cubans lose heart on that account; let them fight a good fight and hold their own until next December! Then when the Fifty-Fourth Congress shall convene, the nation's sympathies will have an authentic expounder and enforcer, and if the President shall try to thwart them he will be roughly disciplined.

Oddly enough, another famous incident, which was to demonstrate the baselessness of such accusations, was even then in preparation. The British boundary issue in Venezuela, which had been dropping in and out of the news for the previous twenty years, was developing toward a crisis. Mr. Cleveland had been unable to encourage the new passion for 'annexing property' — especially the property of helpless Sandwich Islanders or the inoffensive Spaniards — but the popular resentment against the British policy in Venezuela was something which he could approve and support. The Venezuelan matter appealed to him as a genuine moral issue, and abruptly he went the limit. With the President's

Máximo Gómez

José Maceo

Calixto García

THREE CUBAN LEADERS

approval Mr. Richard Olney (just appointed to the State Department) prepared a celebrated despatch; and in the last days of July, Downing Street was lifting its astonished eyebrows over these words, in which an American Secretary of State announced the right to intervene in a boundary claim of the British Empire:

The United States is practically sovereign on this continent and its fiat is law upon the subjects to which it confines its interposition. Why? It is not because of the pure friendship or good-will felt for it. It is not simply by reason of its high character as a civilized state, nor because wisdom and equity are the invariable characteristics of the dealings of the United States. It is because in addition to all other grounds its infinite resources combined with its isolated position render it master of the situation and practically invulnerable against any and all other powers.

Comment halts before that arresting proof of how far the martial urge had brought even Mr. Cleveland's pacific mind. He called it 'Olney's twenty-inch gun,' and under the shock of its explosion Downing Street was stunned into six months of silence before replying.

As yet, however, this despatch had not been made public, and in the meantime the Cuban matter was producing new incidents. Sr. Dupuy de Lôme, the new Spanish Minister, had already opened what was to prove a long and painful correspondence with the State Department, reporting the filibustering expeditions joyously fitting out along our seaboard and imploring the American Government to stop them. But even when seizures were made this presented a difficulty. In August a ship laden with arms was held and her officers tried under our neutrality statutes. But they were acquitted; and it was plain 'from the spirit in which the case was conducted — the temper of the press and the public, the address of counsel, the wild hurrahs in the court and on the street with which the verdict was received — that an acquittal would equally have followed much stronger evidence.' There were to be many similar cases during the next three years. Ultimately a Supreme Court decision was secured which constrained the adventurous captains to some degree of caution, but amid the prevailing public opinion the export of arms and Cuban general officers continued to be a fairly safe occupation.

At the same time the opening of Gómez's campaign against the sugar estates brought an appeal for protection from three American citizens residing in the island. Their signatures were prophetic of another difficulty which was seriously to complicate the future. The question of affording diplomatic protection to such American citizens as Antonio M. Yznaga, José Rafael de los Reyes, or Eduardo Alvarez Cerice loomed ominously before a State Department which was already finding it hard enough to navigate a correct course through the Cuban intricacy. All three were connected with a prominent and wealthy Cuban family, and since they had been born in the island and had continued to live there, their acquisition of American citizenship appeared to have been largely a matter of local convenience. But it entitled them, and many others like them, to our protection. Unfortunately, the Spaniards never seemed able to appreciate the peculiar beauty of our naturalization laws.

That summer, also, the Populist agitation was running like wildfire through the West, while 1896 and the Presidential election were looming in the minds of the politicians. Might it develop, they asked themselves, into a battle over the dangerous issue of free silver, capable of tearing open the deep fissures concealed in our social and economic structure? Any diversion would be preferable to that. Whether or not such thoughts were in their minds, our eminent men developed a growing habit of announcing that 'Cuba must some day be ours.' A sentiment in favor of recognizing Cuban belligerency had appeared, and in September a newspaper poll of the members of the coming Congress showed that a large number supported such a step. While Senator Lodge, that cautious firebrand, undertook a vacation trip to Spain to look over the situation. In Madrid he had an interview with the Spanish Premier. 'To me,' he wrote home, 'Cánovas discoursed of Cuba and I replied guardedly. They are in a state of mind over it, and dreadfully afraid we shall intervene.' It was not, assuming that Sr. Cánovas had read the Senator's speeches, altogether surprising. Senator Lodge did not like Spain, but he formed a reassuring opinion of her military strength. 'They are beaten, broken and out of the race and are proud and know it. They depress and repel me like their landscape.'

During the rainy months of the summer Máximo Gómez had

confined his efforts chiefly to the eastern provinces. The time had been profitably filled in by erecting the façade of a 'civil government,' which would assist us in recognizing his belligerency, and in composing a constitution — 'for the only purpose,' as Dupuy de Lôme said, 'of printing it in the New York papers.' But it was in the west that the strength of the island lay; and Máximo Gómez knew that if he was to avoid a repetition of the long-drawn futility of the Ten Years' War he must carry insurrection up to the gates of Havana. On the night of October 29, accompanied by a small escort, he slipped across the military 'trocha' dividing Camaguey from Santa Clara Province, and advanced to ravage the western provinces and to raise them in arms. All plantations, he ordered, 'shall be totally destroyed'; all laborers who gave aid to the sugar factories were to be shot. A general manifesto was addressed to 'honorable men, victims of the torch': 'The war did not begin February 24; it is about to begin now.'

It was; and the insurgent 'invasion' passed westward carrying fire and desolation with it. Such methods, though realistic, were hardly elegant, and news of them threw a momentary shock into our enthusiasm for Cuban liberty. Some even began to wonder whether the whole insurrection might not be a 'gigantic brigandage,' while the bellicose fervor of our younger statesmen had produced a noticeable reaction in some quarters. The *Journal of Commerce* was almost alarmed:

What is the occasion for all this militant insanity we do not know. Some of it is probably due to the fact that a generation has elapsed since we have had a war, and its unspeakable horrors are largely forgotten.... Undoubtedly the reconstruction of the navy has done much in this direction.... There is no necessary connection between a reasonable naval policy and jingoism, but unquestionably naval officers are impatient to use their new fighting machines, and the people have... begun to catch the infection from the naval officers. The artificial patriotism being carefully worked up at the present time has contributed to the same end.

As an example of the latter, the editor cited 'this remarkable fashion of hanging the flag over every schoolhouse and of giving the boys military drill.' There were countless people in those years who believed that wars, especially American wars, were over forever — that the whole idea of war was a stupid and barbarous anachronism. But belief, it seems, is not enough.

In western Cuba by this time war had become decidedly real. In November the agent upon Mr. Atkins' sugar estate was reporting the district about Cienfuegos overrun with rebels and troops, and he was sitting up all night to watch the glow of cane fires upon the neighboring estates. The agent organized a small private army and the Spaniards sent up guards from Cienfuegos; at night-time there was the popping of rifles in the distance, sudden rides and hard work, but the fires continued, until one night the glow came nearer and they saw that it was American property which was going up in smoke.

The firing was done by a band of some eight Negroes who said they were acting under the orders of one Rego, their chief.... The insurgents were in force upon the neighboring hills and threatened to kill any of our employees who attempted to put out the fires.

In spite of this the assistant manager, a young Englishman, rode into the cane and managed to extinguish it, but not before ten thousand tons had been destroyed. They asked the local chieftain why it had been done. The answer was a copy of Gómez's orders, with the added and illuminating information that destruction of American property would lead to complications between the United States and Spain and might force us to recognize the insurgents as belligerents. The poor people of all parties suffered, of course, but the method was successful in one respect at least. Sr. Dupuy de Lôme, who for six months had been begging our Government to stop the filibusters, began to receive requests by return mail for action on his own part to protect American estates. But the fires, like the filibustering, continued.

Thus the conservatively minded were beginning to have their doubts about the Cuban revolution, and the attitude of the Administration remained one of coldness. But among the masses of our people enthusiasm for the heroic patriots ran only higher still; and by this time Congress — ominous fact — had reassembled. 'The nation's sympathies,' as the *Sun* had predicted, now had 'an authentic expounder and enforcer.'

VI

It was these same closing days of 1895 that witnessed two other events, each of which was to have its influence upon the final drama. That September a tall, horse-faced, rather unprepossessing youth (he had been expelled from Harvard only a few years before) arrived in New York equipped with an idea and $7,500,000. He concluded his business and went his way; but on the morning of November 6 the readers of the New York *Morning Journal* learned that their sedate newspaper had passed under the stimulating ownership of Mr. William Randolph Hearst. It was an event whose full significance they were only later to appreciate.

The other incident was of a far more dramatic character. Mr. Olney's 'twenty-inch gun' had exploded amid the silences of Downing Street toward the end of July. By October some echoes of its reverberations were beginning to leak out. In his annual message of December 2, Mr. Cleveland announced that the Olney despatch had been sent and gave the general purport of its contents. An answer had not yet been received, he said, but was expected shortly. Only a day or two later it arrived — couched in that tone of patient, reasonable endeavor to point out to other peoples the error of their ways which has never failed, throughout the centuries of British history, to make the other peoples rabid with indignation. Mr. Cleveland, it is recorded, was 'mad clear through.' On December 17, he sent in his special message, asking Congress for an American commission to decide for ourselves where the British-Venezuelan boundary lay, and concluding with the famous declaration:

It will in my opinion be the duty of the United States to resist by every means in its power as a willful aggression upon its rights and interests the appropriation by Great Britain of any lands or the exercise of governmental jurisdiction over any territory which after investigation we have determined of right belongs to Venezuela.

The sensation was profound. 'All the traditions of the Senate were cast to the winds when the message was read to that body, for the chamber rang with applause in which the Republicans seemed to take even a more hearty part than the Democrats. In the House the President's vigorous expressions were cheered to the echo.' Congress provided for the commission on the instant, and, as the stock exchanges staggered, the pulpits blanched, and the copy-paper sizzled under the patriotic pencils of the editorial-writers, the United States and Great Britain faced each other across the gulf of imminent war.

Mr. Chauncey Depew dined 'on Saturday night with a lot of financiers, among them Morgan, Lanier, and Sturgis, president of the Stock Exchange,' and they all foresaw disaster and a 'financial cataclysm.' But there were those in the country who were not bankers. Mr. Roosevelt dashed off a message to his friend, Senator Lodge:

I am very much pleased with the President's, or rather, with Olney's message.... I do hope there will not be any backdown among our people. Let the fight come if it must; I don't care whether our seacoast cities are bombarded or not; we would take Canada.

And a little later:

The antics of the bankers, brokers and anglo-maniacs generally are humiliating to a degree.... Personally I rather hope the fight will come soon. The clamor of the peace faction has convinced me that this country needs a war.

Mr. Roosevelt was by no means alone in this latter opinion. The situation, however, was materially complicated by the fact that if a war should come, it was after all a Democrat who would get the credit for it. This would never do. Senator Sherman, though avoiding any criticism of the President, discreetly suggested that the boundary commission bill be referred to the Foreign Relations Committee before action was taken. And Mr. John Hay sent off one of his sprightly little notes to his brother-in-law: 'It is incumbent on all sane men to be very careful how far they commit themselves to the support of one in so disturbed state of mind as the President at this moment.... A most unsafe guide to follow...'

But Mr. Godkin (who, as Mr. Roosevelt later said, was 'not a patriotic man') summed up the matter with greater seriousness:

The situation seems to me this: An immense democracy, mostly ignorant and completely secluded from foreign influences and without any knowledge of other states of society, with great contempt for history and experience, finds itself in possession of enormous power and is eager to use it in brutal fashion against any one who comes along *without knowing how to do it*, and is therefore constantly on the brink of some frightful catastrophe like that which overtook France in 1870.

Mr. Godkin possessed a sharp insight. There was only one factor which he overlooked; he failed to make allowance for that direct interposition of Providence which did so much to bear out our faith that we were acting under divine guidance. At almost the moment that Mr. Cleveland was appointing the boundary commission, the German Emperor despatched his famous Krueger telegram. As they read it the English awoke to the dangers nearer home, and it left them disinclined for any minor involvements with the United States. Once again there was no fighting. The Foreign Office unbent (a fearful and awe-inspiring process), and the matter was amicably compromised.

There was no fighting — not just then. But those flaming editorials, that passionate patriotism, that gorgeous thrill, were not lost upon a public now feeling its own strength and pride. Years afterward a discerning friend told Mr. Cleveland that he was 'the father of the spirit of imperialism which had grown up after the War with Spain.' It seemed to strike Mr. Cleveland with surprise. 'He himself,' the friend adds, 'had done so much to avert that foolish, unnecessary, and hurtful conflict that he could scarcely conceive that what he saw was only the logic of his own acts.' Yet in some degree it was the truth; and in the two and one half years that were to elapse before the crisis came, the inspiring echoes of Mr. Olney's 'twenty-inch gun' were to play their invisible part in the history of our War with Spain.

CHAPTER III
CUBAN LIBERTY AND AMERICAN POLITICS

I

IT was amid these sensational developments that the year 1896, splendid with a naïveté which cannot fail to elicit the admiration of a less confident posterity, was ushered in. Dr. Albert Shaw's *Review of Reviews* welcomed it upon a note of exuberant optimism. It was to witness many achievements (Dr. Shaw even expected that 'horseless carriages will begin to come into practical use during this interesting year'), but first of all it was 'to decide whether Spain must give up Cuba, the first gained and last retained of her American possessions.' The full program was nothing if not appetizing:

All sorts of political and social problems are pressing themselves upon the attention of the nations, and the outlook for improvement in the general condition of mankind is at least bright enough to encourage every earnest and hopeful effort.

But at the moment the general condition of mankind in the Island of Cuba was anything but promising. Throughout November and the early days of December, Máximo Gómez's bands had been moving steadily westward, and as the Christmas season approached, it became evident that Martínez Campos, the aged Captain-General, was unable to cope with the situation. His mobile columns were impotent to check the fluid forces of the insurrection; his policy of leniency and conciliation enlisted the support of no one. Máximo Gómez's own policy was softened by no humane considerations. 'I find myself obliged,' the chieftain declared in one of his propaganda documents, 'to dictate painful measures which, though they may torture my soul, will assure tomorrow the execution of my plans.' One of these measures was the wrecking of railroad trains. 'If innocent persons,' the patriot argued, 'have paid for their imprudence with their lives while traveling, it is not the fault of the revolution, as successive proclamations have ordered all persons not to travel.'

As the new year opened, the smoke of the burning countryside could be seen from Havana itself, and on January 6, Gómez was so near that a general order was issued giving the dispositions for the defense of the city. Martínez Campos realized that a stronger hand was needed, and cabled his resignation. It was accepted; and General Don Valeriano Weyler y Nicolau, an able officer whom Campos himself had recommended, was appointed to succeed him. In the meanwhile the 'invasion' swept onward. On January 22, Antonio Maceo, the mulatto leader, reached Mantua in Pinar del Rio; the insurrection had passed over the entire length of Cuba, leaving havoc in its wake.

But in the United States its popularity was undiminished. For a new and strangely powerful factor was coming into play. By this time many of the leading American dailies had established special correspondents under the pleasant skies, and within the pleasant bars, of Havana, and these gentlemen were finding their assignment remarkably productive of 'copy.' Whatever may have been their prowess in war, the Cuban patriots seem to have been the first of modern peoples fully to grasp the military value of propaganda. 'Without a·press,' General Gómez had written long before, 'we shall get nowhere.' Their armies may have been dubious, their government unreal, their fiscal system peculiar, and their war aims obscure, but they possessed a publicity service of the first order. One Havana correspondent (he had lived in the island and was one of the very few who did not sympathize with the insurrection) described the process:

The American public has been grossly deceived by many of the correspondents sent to Habana as representatives of our leading journals. Some have been imposed upon by the swarm of 'laborantes' who infest every corner of the large centers of Cuba. The correspondent... has to secure the services of an interpreter, and it is a well-known fact that nine tenths of the men available for such a post are naturalized Cuban-born American citizens, and their sympathies are actively engaged in furthering the extension of the insurgent propaganda.... Any other American who goes to Cuba to investigate for his own benefit is subject to the same influence, and is thrown in contact with the large number of insurgent sympathizers who are invariably naturalized American citizens and who haunt the hotel corridors, newspaper correspondents' offices and the American consulates....

Shortly after the news concerning some insignificant skirmish, some one starts the ball rolling by confiding to his neighbor that he has just heard from a very intimate friend employed in the palace that the Spaniards lost so many between killed and wounded. Of course this is supposed to be a strict secret; but in all such cases, before the 'laborantes' have finished spreading the tale, it invariably results that the whole Spanish column has been wiped out of existence and the commanding officer taken prisoner....

Filling his notebook with the stock stories of atrocities, battles, rapes, and other horrors attributed to the Spanish troops by interested parties, and which every street gamin in Habana is thoroughly posted in, he returns to the United States, and in due course of time drifts into Washington, there to offer his collection of 'fakes' as evidence before the committees.

The news collected in this interesting fashion now began to flow northward in an ever-widening and more incredible stream, to be spread prominently before our startled and avid publics. Battles of the most sanguinary character began to take place in all the American papers; Havana, despite the insurgents' total lack of artillery, fell three or four times over, while atrocities of the most appalling kind began to be perpetrated by the Spaniards upon nearly every American front page.

A lady correspondent heard (or thought she heard) rifle volleys in the morning from the direction of Cabañas fortress; her readers were assured that the Spaniards daily butchered their captives within those somber walls. The rather delicate question of whether the Republic of Cuba had progressed far enough to possess a capital city was solved by another journalist, who from his hotel in Havana discovered such a city — in a village several hundred miles away at the other end of the island — and in the Congressional debates now opening the largely imaginary 'capital' of Cubitas was to play a prominent rôle. The influence of Mr. William Randolph Hearst's invasion of the New York newspaper field now began to be felt. Sensation piled upon sensation was the essence of his original method, and his able representatives in Cuba devoted themselves to supplying the sensations. It was a correspondent of his revivified *Journal*, Mr. Frederick Lawrence, who single-handed captured the city of Pinar del Rio, utilizing for the purpose a non-existent battery of gatling guns manned by a crew of American volunteers who were wholly imaginary.

It was wild, self-contradictory, and impossible of credence, but American publics and statesmen believed it. The official Spanish denials were simply brushed aside by the propagandists, and the belief was early implanted in American newspaper readers that everything coming from Spanish sources was mere fabrication. The gentleman who had captured Pinar del Rio was subsequently expelled from the island. He immediately arrived in Washington to testify before the Foreign Relations Committee. He bore witness under oath that the Spanish communiqués were 'untrue.' The eager Senators pressed him about his own versions of the battles. He explained:

Personally I have no knowledge of it. I did not go outside the lines and did not count the dead and dying or anything of that kind; but the gentlemen who would bring me information — and I did not have to seek for it, they were only too willing to give it to me — were men of the very highest character....

Q.: Were these gentlemen on the side of the insurgents?

A.: Yes, sir.

Q.: So for that reason you were inclined to give their accounts greater credit than that of the censor?

A.: Yes, sir.

It was the same young gentleman who gravely submitted to Secretary Olney a statement 'embracing such of my observations of the condition of affairs in Cuba as it seems likely may be of interest to yourself and the State Department.' It was a document fairly dripping with blood, though blood of a regrettably anonymous character. But, then, names were nearly always lacking — or fictitious. However, nobody bothered about details of that sort. Rapidly the fearful and fascinating picture grew; and large sections of the American people were brought to look upon Cuba as a tortured land, where a decadent tyranny, unable to crush out the heroic aspirations of the populace, was endeavoring to drown them in torrents of blood. It shocked us profoundly — and it was extremely good reading.

II

On the day after Congress convened, Senator Call of Florida, impelled no doubt by the very large number of Cuban-Americans in his constituency, had introduced a resolution recognizing the belligerency of the insurgents. Normally this would not have mattered; for since he had entered the Senate eighteen years before, Mr. Call had been introducing resolutions 'at every session,' as he said, designed to relieve the island 'from the difficulties of government under which she has existed.' And always he had watched them accorded early and decent interment in the silences of the Foreign Relations Committee.

This time, however, everything was different; no longer was Senator Call alone in his desire to relieve Cuba from the governance of Spain. The even division of the parties, the bitter opposition to President Cleveland among Democrats as well as Republicans, and the imminence of the Presidential election had combined to create a deadlock upon all the things which really mattered, and to make it politically expedient for the statesmen to find things which did not matter to talk about. Fate, and the stimulating atrocities in the newspapers, readily provided them. The Call resolution was only the first of a flood which overwhelmed the desks of both houses, demanding recognition of belligerency, demanding Cuban independence, demanding the correspondence, or even in effect demanding war. They were confined to neither party and to no section. Like the earlier ones of Senator Call, they disappeared behind the portals of the Foreign Relations Committee. But this time every one knew that it was not for interment.

The Venezuelan crisis had interrupted their consideration, but by the first week of January the crisis had passed, leaving the honorable gentlemen only more alert than ever for new fields to conquer. The Foreign Relations Committee returned with energy to the Cuban problem. On January 11, Sr. Dupuy de Lôme ventured to transmit to it, through the State Department, an explanation of the Spanish view of affairs:

The insurgent chiefs have made a bold raid...., They know they cannot succeed, and their only hope is founded, directed by the Junta in New York, in what they most desire — in the possibility of bringing difficulties in the relations of Spain and the United States.

This was the official statement of a friendly power. But the eager members of the Foreign Relations Committee were in no mood to examine the evidence with impartiality. They excoriated the Spanish Minister for his impertinent interference in their business, and continued to base their deliberations upon the more vivid information supplied by the newspaper correspondents. Nor were other signs wanting of the Congressional state of mind. As invariably happens at such moments, both the people and the statesmen were swept by a mounting enthusiasm for the great doctrine of preparedness. The *Literary Digest* listed the bills:

Senator Chandler's bill calling for $100,000,000 to strengthen the military armament, Senator Hale's bill for six battleships at $4,000,000 each and twenty-five torpedo boats at $175,000 each, Senator Cullom's bill for revenue cutters on the Pacific Coast and the Great Lakes, Senator Squire's bill for $87,000,000 for coast armament, Senator Sherman's bills for reorganizing the army, Senator Hawley's bill for issuing Springfield rifles to the National Guard... and Representative Cummings' bill for the enrollment and further organization of the naval reserve, indicate that the question of national defenses is to occupy considerable attention at Washington this session. Senator Lodge has offered an amendment to the fortifications bill in the Senate proposing an issue of $100,000,000 in twenty-year coin bonds at popular subscription... the proceeds to be kept in the Treasury as a separate fund for coast defenses.

Perhaps these expenditures were proposed, as their authors said, for defensive purposes only. But the proceedings now going forward in Congress hardly sounded that way. On January 29, Senator Morgan of Alabama brought in a majority report offering a resolution which mildly requested Spain to accord belligerent rights to the Cubans. It was at once apparent that anything so gentle as this would not do at all; on February 5, the committee severely modified its resolution into a blunt declaration that we should grant belligerent rights to the insurgents 'in the ports and territory of the United States.'

Recognition of Cuban belligerency had been chosen for the issue mainly because it sounded less drastic than other measures. Its real importance lay in the psychological field; in strict legality such a recognition would have extended few benefits to the insurgents which they did not already enjoy and in some respects might actually have worked to their disadvantage. But it would tend to involve us in the Cuban struggle, while its moral effect would in any event be overwhelming. And by this time the situation in Cuba was sufficiently serious for the Spanish power. General Weyler arrived on February 10, to find the whole island in a state of chaos; Maceo was ravaging Pinar del Rio Province, the sugar industry was at a standstill, and the military helpless. Strong measures were called for, and General Weyler, with some energy and severity, set about applying them. At this distance of time his declaration of martial law and his announcement that summary procedure would be used against those guilty of dynamiting and incendiarism do not seem extraordinarily harsh. His first reward, however, was to have the nickname of 'The Butcher' pinned upon him in the American press, and 'Butcher Weyler' he thereafter remained, not only to our journalists and publics, but even to our statesmen.

The long debate began in the Senate on February 20. Senator Morgan, always splendid as an imperialist, recognized at the outset that 'great events may hinge upon our action here,' even war. The honorable gentlemen had no hesitation in using the word itself, and they proceeded to plunge into a discussion of the policies of the friendly Kingdom of Spain in language so inaccurate and so insulting as to bring the debate at times to the verge of simple blackguardism.

There was one notable exception. Senator Lodge, the scholar in politics, never departed from that loftier plane of pure statesmanship of which he was the master. Following a lifelong habit he was careful to grace his views with the elegances of quotation. 'Among all the Spanish-American colonies Cuba was the Abdiel, "among the faithless, faithful only he." Her reward was the title of "Faithful Cuba," and that was the only reward she ever received.' He was eloquent upon the oppression under which the island had subsequently labored; he also spoke of other considerations:

Our immediate pecuniary interests in the island are very great. They are being destroyed. Free Cuba would mean a great market for the United States; it would mean an opportunity for American capital invited there by signal exemptions; it would mean an opportunity for the development of that splendid island.... But we have also a broader political interest in the fate of Cuba.... She lies right athwart the line which leads to the Nicaraguan Canal.

'But, Mr. President,' said the Senator, turning his back as always upon the merely material, 'I am prepared to put our duty on a higher ground than either of those, and that is the broad ground of a common humanity.'

Senator Lodge announced his belief that the United States could put an end to conditions in Cuba 'peaceably.' From this time on it was to be the war party's strongest argument. The peaceable ejection of the Spaniards by the United States and the establishment of a free and independent Cuba was his object. It was dignified and effective; but to at least one mind it was also a trifle curious. Mr. Atkins, alarmed by the success of the insurgent propaganda and supported by other American property-owners in Cuba, had arrived in Washington determined to present the other side. He had called upon a number of the leading Senators and Representatives:

All listened attentively and acknowledged the danger of recognition of the insurgents as belligerents. I called upon Lodge in the evening at his house by invitation and went over the whole ground. He discussed the matter quite carefully and asked me this question: 'Mr. Atkins, do you think that if the Cubans obtain their independence they could establish a stable government?' I answered without hesitation that I did not believe the Cubans capable of maintaining a stable government. Whereupon he brought his hand down upon the table where we were sitting and said: 'I am glad to hear you say that, for it is exactly my opinion.' I naturally left him feeling encouraged; but within a few days he was supporting and advocating a bill for recognition of the belligerency of Cuba.

For many years thereafter Mr. Atkins avoided any interviews with the Senator from Massachusetts. Perhaps he forgot that less than a year before the Senator had been declaring his belief that Cuba would 'become to us a necessity'; while if Senator Lodge was a little less than frank, there were others who were frankness itself. Senator Vest of Missouri quite readily admitted that 'the ultimate and logical result of independence in Cuba would be that it would become a part of the United States.'

Senator Vest, however, thrust this aside as an 'ulterior ques-

tion.' Like Senator Lodge, he took a higher ground: 'Shall we...
declare that in our opinion the people of Cuba are able to maintain
their independence and have achieved it? Are we to wait until
that island is desolated by fire and sword?... Sir, if we do it, God
will curse us.' And thunderous applause from the gallery indicated that in this case the voice of God would also be the voice of
the people. The Senator, it is true, was asked whether in declaring
Cuban independence he proposed likewise to declare war on Spain,
but he evaded the question. The process of converting Spain into
the official aggressor, always so necessary at this stage of such
proceedings, was already well advanced. As one editor put it:
'Such is the infuriated condition of the Spanish mind that [forci-
ble] intervention would surely mean a stubborn though hopeless
war on Spain's part against the United States.' Yet it must not
be forgotten that throughout Spain was only an incidental object
of the oratory. 'I have sometimes been inclined to think,' as
Senator Hoar acidly observed, 'that when you saw uncommon
activity in our grave, reverend, and somewhat sleepy Committee
on Foreign Relations... it was circumstantial evidence, not that
there was any great trouble as to our foreign relations, but that a
Presidential election was at hand.'

As the measure, somewhat sharpened by amendment, came up
to the vote, Senator Sherman, the chairman of the Foreign Relations Committee and one of the most eminent figures in American
political life, declared his conviction that 'the condition of affairs
in Cuba is such that the intervention of the United States must
sooner or later be given to put an end to crimes that are almost
beyond description.' As an example of the evidence upon which
he had relied in forming this conviction — certainly a very serious
one in a man holding his office — Senator Sherman proceeded to
quote at length from a book by one Enrique Donderio. This book
(translated, as the Senator said, 'by one of the great journals of
the country, the New York *Journal*') was a description of incredible barbarities said to have been perpetrated by General
Weyler during the Ten Years' War. The fact that General
Weyler had not even been in the field during the period covered
by the work unfortunately seems to have escaped the Senator;
while even on internal evidence Sr. Donderio was hardly trust-

worthy — as when he based a charge that the Spaniards executed 43,500 Cubans during the war on the statement that they had taken 43,500 prisoners and that it was a well-known fact that the Spaniards invariably executed all prisoners. Nevertheless, Senator Sherman repeated the accusation.

But the Senate did not bother with the rules of evidence. On February 28, the resolution passed that body by the joyous vote of 64 to 6; and almost immediately riots of protest began to break out in the larger Spanish cities, while the Government had to close the universities. The Spanish Government itself kept its feelings under a rigid control, for the statesmen in Madrid were vividly aware of our immense superiority in wealth and power. They were early convinced of two things: that war with the United States was an imminent threat, and that the only result of such a war would be defeat for themselves and the loss of Cuba. But the American Congress felt itself under no such painful restrictions. The debate dragged on, now in the House and now in the Senate, and it is difficult to say in which body the oratory was more eloquent, more inflammatory, or more obviously misinformed. By this time somewhat more responsible journalistic evidence was available. William Shaw Bowen, a *World* correspondent in Havana, cabled that 'General Weyler has in my opinion been grossly traduced.... American newspapers publish charges that prisoners are ill-treated and killed by summary execution. Here again is an incorrect representation of facts.' But nobody paid any attention, except the few members of Congress who were still skeptical of the wisdom of freeing Cuba. Thus in the House Mr. Boutelle of Maine put a rather embarrassing question:

Somebody says, 'Oh, Spain don't amount to much anyhow. We can lick her easy.' How many lives do you want to sacrifice to do it?

But Mr. Skinner of North Carolina supplied the complete answer to such craven questionings:

I tell you, Mr. Speaker, the Cubans look upon [the American] flag today as the emblem of liberty, as we look upon the cross as the emblem of Christianity; and wherever you would advance the cross to establish the Christian religion, I take that flag as the counterpart of the cross, as the emblem of liberty. I would place it over Cuba.... I want to see it established in every land and on every sea, not only in America, but over every people on this continent who ask for the blessings of liberty.

Mr. Gillett of Massachusetts failed to share that inspiring vision. 'I do not especially object,' he said, 'to ambition for aggrandizement... but I think if the United States is going to be actuated by ambition she ought to say so, and not say she is actuated by philanthropy. I think hypocrisy is a vastly worse vice than ambition or greed of territory.' But who could be expected to agree with so revolutionary an opinion? It was all of no use. The moving tide of oratory flowed on, and the brilliance of the opposition had no effect upon either the size or the bloodthirstiness of the majority. Senator Turpie might deprecate the 'jingo jargon' of the extremists, or Senator Hale might declare his anxiety over 'the growth of what I may call the aggressive spirit as shown particularly within the last year,... the desire to incite trouble, the desire to make difficulties with foreign powers, the dealing with the discussion, the imagery, of war rather than of peace, the turning aside of the plowshare and the pruning hook and giving men's attention to the sword and the rifle.' Neither argument nor irony was of any avail. The final vote, after considerable amendment and conference, came in the House on April 6, 1896, when that body agreed to the final Senate resolution by 247 to 27. This was a 'concurrent' resolution not requiring the signature of the President; it declared that 'in the opinion of Congress a condition of public war' existed in Cuba. The United States should maintain a strict neutrality, but our friendly offices 'should be offered by the President to the Spanish Government for the recognition of the independence of Cuba.'

Thus spoke the 'authentic expounder and enforcer' of the nation's sympathies; thus did the House and Senate assert their sovereign control over foreign affairs and adroitly add to Mr. Cleveland's political difficulties. As partisan strategy against the coming election it was admirable; as a solemn declaration of American policy it was, perhaps, just a trifle silly. For it still left everything to the President and he, of course, paid no attention to the resolution. That, no doubt, was what the honorable gentlemen had been counting on.

III

The resolution had no immediate practical effect, and many of the statesmen would not have voted for it if it had been supposed for a moment that it could have. Nevertheless, those stirring speeches could be expunged neither from the record nor from the minds of men; their intangible consequences were beyond calculation. For two years more the fortunes of the insurrection were to wax or wane (principally the latter), for two years passions were to be fanned into a blaze or allowed to die in accordance with the requirements of the politicians and journalists. But it is not too much to argue that it was this debate which in fact determined the fate of Cuba. It confirmed us in an attitude which could not afterward be altered, and by so much bound the nation to the uncertain arbitrament of events.

In the meanwhile the diplomatic correspondence had been taking on a sharper tone. Mr. Olney had proved cold to the wrongs of Cuban patriotism, but an ever more bellicose public opinion compelled him to uphold the rights of American citizens in the island. The trouble lay in the peculiar character of so many of the citizens. The naturalization of Cubans was said to be 'a flourishing industry' in Tampa and Key West, and as Dupuy de Lôme pointed out, the number of patriots who adopted our nationality in order more safely to promote the Republic of Cuba was 'unfortunately very large.' It is impossible to go into the many cases which naturally resulted or to discuss the technical (and frequently very debatable) issues in international law which were raised. But these claims, coupled with the legitimate appeals of American capitalists in the island or the innumerable difficulties arising out of the filibustering expeditions, were a continuous irritation. And the Congressional oratory was a sufficient warning that the Cuban situation could not be prolonged indefinitely.

Two days before the final passage of the belligerency resolution, Mr. Olney, fully alive to the gravity of the matter, had made an effort on his own account. He addressed a carefully considered and friendly note to the Spanish Government, pointing out that the continuance of the general pillage and destruction in Cuba was a matter of serious concern to the United States. A final triumph of the insurgents, he said, could only be regarded 'with the gravest apprehension,' but he then frankly continued:

That the United States cannot contemplate with complacency another ten years of Cuban insurrection, with all its injurious and distressing incidents, may certainly be taken for granted. The object of the present communication, however, is not to discuss intervention, nor to propose intervention, nor to pave the way for intervention. The purpose is exactly the reverse — to suggest whether a solution of present troubles cannot be found which will prevent all thought of intervention by rendering it unnecessary. What the United States desires to do, if the way can be pointed out, is to coöperate with Spain in the immediate pacification of the island on such a plan as leaving Spain her rights of sovereignty, shall yet secure to the people of the island all such rights and powers of local self-government as they can reasonably ask....

Thus far Spain has faced the insurrection sword in hand and has made no sign to show that surrender and submission would be followed by anything but a return to the old order of things. Would it not be wise... to accompany the application of military force with an authentic declaration of the organic changes that are meditated in the administration of the island with a view to remove all just grounds of complaint?

It is for Spain to consider and determine what those changes would be. But should they be such that the United States could urge their adoption, as substantially removing well-founded grievances, its influence would be exerted for their acceptance, and it can hardly be doubted, would be most potential for the termination of hostilities and the restoration of peace and order to the island. One result of the course of proceeding outlined, if no other, would be sure to follow, namely, that the rebellion would lose largely, if not altogether, the moral countenance and support it now enjoys from the people of the United States.

This despatch, which was not made public, is of the utmost importance, for in it Mr. Olney stated a theory of the insurrection and of the best means for bringing it to an end that was to guide our policy from this time on. It was not a very realistic theory. The grant of political reforms could have had little effect upon the insurgent chieftains, for the simple reason that they did not want reforms; while the moderates to whom such measures might appeal had condemned the insurrection from the beginning, but had been powerless to stop it. Yet the Spanish Ministry must have weighed the note with care. It offered to place the influence of the United States behind a settlement (something very different from merely demanding, as Congress had been doing, that a settlement be reached), while anything that promised to detach the insurrection from the popular support it found in the United States must have been attractive, for this was in reality the key to the whole difficulty.

On the other hand, however, the military situation in the island appeared to be improving; General Weyler was making distinct progress and there seemed a chance that he might make good his promise to bring peace in two seasons. At the same time, even a friendly interposition by the United States would have its obvious dangers; once we took a hand in the matter, no one could predict what we would demand, while Mr. Olney was rather optimistic in suggesting that our people's enthusiasm for Cuban freedom could be damped by anything that Spain might do. Diplomatic relations, moreover, were being subjected to new strains. Our consul general at Havana resigned, and his place was filled by General Fitzhugh Lee, a Democratic politician from Virginia, a veteran of the Confederate Army and a portly gentleman resolved to stand no nonsense from Spanish captains-general. Our press cheerfully announced his appointment as one which would assist the Cuban cause; it hardly seems possible that this could have been President Cleveland's intention, but opportunity almost immediately arose to prove that it would probably be the result.

Toward the end of April, the Spanish Navy achieved its one success of the war when it captured the American filibustering schooner Competitor. The expeditionaries escaped with the arms, but her master, three of her crew, and a newspaper correspondent were taken. The latter was an undoubted American citizen and the others claimed to be, but only an accident of procedure saved them from summary execution as 'pirates,' like their predecessors of the Virginius. There was a hitch; before the case could be decided, the circumstances became known, and the new consul general, with great energy and asperity, at once invoked the treaty guarantees protecting American citizens. Thus the unhappy men were spared; but they remained in captivity, the subjects of a *cause célèbre* which, prosecuted for something like two years through all the sinuosities of Spanish judicial procedure by Mr. Lee, by the American press, by the House, the Senate, and the State Department, did a great deal to keep alive the passions which were to eventuate in war.

Such were the considerations which had to be weighed by Sr. Cánovas and his Conservative Ministry as they confronted Mr. Olney's offer. In the end they felt it better to fight things out on their own line. They did not doubt the friendly correctness of Mr. Cleveland's and Mr. Olney's attitude, but they knew that Mr. Cleveland would not survive the coming election. 'Could we feel the same confidence in the new President and his government?' It was, to say the least, most dubious; and in May a polite note conveyed their rejection of the proposal. The Spanish Government, it pointed out, was already pledged to execute all useful or necessary reforms, but only 'as soon as the submission of the insurgents be an accomplished fact.' To offer reforms while the rebels were still in arms would be worse than futile, as they would regard it only as a sign of weakness. If Mr. Olney really wished to coöperate in the pacification of the island his most effective means of doing so was to suppress the filibusters, put an end to the brazen activities of the New York junta (whose members, incidentally, were naturalized citizens), and refrain from adding to the difficulty of putting down the rebellion through protecting the Cuban-American insurgents when they were arrested.

This view was rather closer to the facts than was Mr. Olney's, but it, too, showed a lack of realism. The only hope of the insurrection lay in the encouragement which it received from the United States and in the safe base of operations which our territory offered. The American Government, however, could not take the suggested action without legislation by Congress, and that, of course, had become politically impossible. A realization of his own helplessness may have contributed to Mr. Olney's annoyance. He was not pleased, it seems, with the Spanish reply

IV

At all events, Sr. Cánovas and his Ministers had made their choice. At best it was a choice of evils. The American press by this time was freely discussing the probability of war and quite cheerfully predicting that it 'would probably be an extremely brief one, consisting of a naval engagement or two in the general vicinity of Cuba.' Spain now had to win in Cuba or lose everything — it was a race against time, along the narrow edge of two disasters. But in this first heat she won. June was safely reached, and with it, mercifully, came the rainy season in the island and in the United States the nominating conventions and the opening moves in a Presidential campaign which was to absorb our attention to the exclusion of all other issues.

At the beginning the crisis was not clearly seen. For months young Mr. Bryan had been traveling through the obscure places of the West, perfecting the strategy of his coming *coup*, and polishing every paragraph and phrase of that great extemporaneous effort which he was to produce at Chicago. Nearly a year before, Mr. Mark Hanna had announced his belief that the Republican Party should be committed to the single gold standard. The air was heavy with fate; but still it seemed that the issue, as happens so reassuringly often in American politics, might safely be sidestepped. The Republicans, to be sure, duly wrote the gold plank into their platform, but as they nominated Mr. McKinley, 'it looked as if the nomination were equivalent to election.' And Mr. McKinley himself was a genial and kindly man, devoted to the tariff; he was recommended not by his fighting power in the forefront of such a storm as the currency question implied, but by his ability to pour calming oil upon such disagreeable issues.

The Republicans had also been careful to seek other and less dangerous sentiments to make use of in their campaign. One of them, obviously, was the enthusiasm for an energetic foreign policy. Four years before the Republicans had detected the call of Manifest Destiny; it now appeared, under the special conditions of 1896, that in the intervening four years Destiny's manifestations had become wider, more concrete and much more exciting. Senator Lodge was active at the convention, and one seems to hear a familiar ring in its declaration upon foreign policy:

Our foreign policy should be at all times firm, vigorous and dignified, and all our interests in the western hemisphere should be carefully watched and guarded.

The Hawaiian Islands should be controlled by the United States and no foreign power should be permitted to interfere with them. The Nicaraguan Canal should be built, owned and operated by the United States. ... The massacres in Armenia have aroused the deepest sympathy and just indignation of the American people.... In Turkey, American residents have been exposed to gravest dangers and American property destroyed. There and everywhere American citizens and American property must be absolutely protected at all hazards and at any cost.

We reassert the Monroe Doctrine in its full extent.... We watch with deep and abiding interest the heroic battles of the Cuban patriots against cruelty and oppression.... We believe that the government of the United States should actively use its influence and good offices to restore peace and give independence to the island.

It was an inspiring note. All in all, the Republican delegates went home filled with confidence and the pleasant sense of duty well performed.

But the storm was rising. The Democratic Convention met at Chicago early in July. The platform committee began its labors; its interest in foreign affairs was of the slightest, and it dismissed the subject in two brief paragraphs:

The Monroe Doctrine, as originally declared, is a permanent part of the foreign policy of the United States, and must at all times be maintained.

We extend our sympathy to the people of Cuba in their heroic struggle for liberty and independence.

Almost the whole of the remainder of the document was devoted to the single problem of the currency. Tossing aside, for once in the history of American politics, all irrelevancies and all pretense at compromise, the platform offered an intransigeant assertion of the great heresy of free silver. The debate began, in a restless rising tide of suppressed emotion. The gold Democrats lodged their last protests in the accents of cold despair. And then, late one night, through the vast strained silences of the Chicago Coliseum a single voice was crying: 'You shall not press down upon the brow of labor this crown of thorns, you shall not crucify mankind...' And as the answering yell arose from twenty thousand throats the thing had come at last.

There was no time thereafter for paper issues or pictorial excitements. The Democratic Party fell into its fragments; and as they and the minor parties wrote their platforms in the days that followed, foreign relations, manifest destiny, the oppressed Cubans, the Armenians and the Turks were all tossed into the dustbin of things that did not matter. The startled ranks of the Republicans closed up to meet the enemy whom they thought to have been safely laid; and the leader whom they had chosen to win upon the comfortable simplicities of the tariff was abruptly switched (a maneuver not without its awkwardness) into the sterling standard-bearer of sound money.

For the Boy Orator of the Platte had abruptly transformed the easy workings of our party system into a terrifying combination of class struggle and sectional rebellion. Those who belonged to the upper classes and the ruling sections vividly responded, and the resulting violence of the campaign is even now astonishing. Mr. Roosevelt was publicly confident. 'I am,' he wrote, 'a good American, with a profound belief in my countrymen, and I have no idea that they will deliberately lower themselves to a level beneath that of a South American republic by voting for the preposterous farrago of sinister nonsense which the Populistic-Democratic politicians at Chicago chose to set up as embodying the principles of their party, and for the amiable and windy demagogue who stands upon that platform.' Mr. Walter Hines Page, then editing the *Atlantic Monthly*, took a somewhat gloomy comfort in the situation. Should Bryan be elected, as he wrote to a friend, 'the paralysis of industry would be something frightful, but the free coinage plan is so absurd that it could not even be tried. During the four months between Mr. Bryan's election and his inauguration the panic would produce such disastrous effects that the whole country would suffer a violent revulsion of opinion.' Mr. Whitelaw Reid, editor of the New York *Tribune*, spoke of the 'awful fact of the election' and even permitted himself a moment of doubt as to the wisdom of democratic government. Mr. John Hay saw the affair through the saving perspective of his own sprightly sense of humor and did not lose faith in the ultimate triumph of 'the Majah.' But visiting the city of Cleveland early in October, he found that 'most of my friends think Bryan will be elected and we shall all be hanged to the lampions of Euclid Avenue.'

Until the middle of October it was painfully uncertain. But Mark Hanna toured 'the high places of Wall Street,' levying the assessments with which he undertook his famous 'campaign of education' to teach the common man the mysteries of finance and why he should vote the Republican ticket. The terrible wave of Populism arose, crested — and shattered itself forever against the stocky figure of the business man from Cleveland. Sometime before election day Mr. Hanna perceived that barring accidents all was over. There were no accidents; and the deep issues which had been gathering ever since the Civil War had found their answer. Mr. Henry Adams went home, as he described it, 'with every one else to elect McKinley President and to start the world anew. For the old world of public men and measures since 1870 Adams wept no tears.'

Yet it had been a near thing; and the terror which it had inspired may be read in the *Tribune's* celebrated comment upon the morning after election day:

There are some movements so base, some causes so depraved, that neither victory can justify them nor defeat entitle them to commiseration.... The wicked, rattle-pated boy, posing in vapid vanity and mouthing resounding rottenness, was not the real leader of that league of hell. He was only a puppet in the blood-imbrued hands of Altgeld, the anarchist, and Debs, the revolutionist, and other desperadoes of that stripe. But he was a willing puppet, Bryan was — willing and eager. None of his masters was more apt than he at lies and forgeries and blasphemies and all the nameless iniquities of that campaign against the Ten Commandments.

The campaign had been defeated, and it was indeed a new world which had emerged. Yet the victory was of a regrettably negative character; after all, they had merely proved what three years earlier they had declared and thought to be proved already. What next? Mr. McKinley was quite content with the tariff — and so was Mr. Hanna. Nevertheless, there were some, especially among the younger Republicans, who seem to have felt that inaction might have its dangers, and that the gentle preoccupations of tariff revision were an inadequate answer to the dread vistas which had been opened by the election. Three weeks after the election Mr. Roosevelt was reminding his friend, Mr. Lodge, that 'Bryanism' was still a 'real and ugly danger, and our hold on the forces that won the victory for us by no means too well assured.' Besides, although 'Cabot and Teddy,' as Mr. Hay gracefully put it, had journeyed to Canton during the campaign 'to offer their heads to the axe and their tummies to the hara-kiri knife' for the good of the cause, they were not original McKinley men. On all accounts it behoved the astute to look about them.

They did so; and almost at once they discovered that the Island of Cuba was still there. During the rainy season Máximo Gómez had retired from Havana Province to the eastward to rest and recuperate, and the insurrection had temporarily died away. But by the latter part of October the rains were coming to an end and the military campaign was reviving; while General Weyler, following in Máximo Gómez's realistic footsteps, was initiating measures of another kind which were to supply an inexhaustible theme for American denunciation. One of the more serious was the Captain-General's effort to stop the sugar grinding on his own account. A principal financial source of the rebels was the black-mail 'tax' levied upon the sugar estates as the price of being spared destruction. As General Gómez had begun by burning the crops in order to cut off the Spanish revenues from the estates, General Weyler now sought to do the same for his opponent by making it plain to the estate-owners that there would be no harvest during the coming season. In so far as the order was effective, it tended to add to the general misery of the island and, of course, to the abuse showered upon General Weyler's head.

But the decree which was to prove most useful of all to the propagandists was that issued on October 21, ordering the 'recon-centration' of the populace of Pinar del Rio in the garrison towns and prohibiting the export of supplies from the towns to the countryside. Here again General Weyler was merely adopting a method applied long before by General Gómez. The latter had proposed to drive every one either into his own ranks or into the towns, and had decreed that no food should be introduced from the country into the towns. General Weyler now reversed this. The country people were no longer to be permitted to fight as rebels one day and appear as peaceable citizens the day after. Those not actively with the insurgents were to be gathered within the military lines; the countryside was then to be cleared of all supplies, and the starvation weapon turned against the insurgents. Though drastic, the plan was by no means so drastic as it sounded. In Pinar del Rio the general ruin and pillage had already brought great numbers of people into the towns, and the Spaniards could argue that reconcentration, rather than creating a new situation, merely permitted them to take advantage of the situation already produced by Antonio Maceo's insurgents. Perhaps this explains the fact that the unrivaled propaganda possibilities in the new decree at first escaped the alert minds of the patriots, and that it was not until later, when reconcentration had been extended to other provinces, that they proclaimed it as the cause of all the misery and want to which the island was reduced.

But in the meantime their invention was sufficiently fertile to make up for the oversight. They produced atrocities ranging all the way from the discovery that General Weyler was nightly removing prisoners from Cabañas fortress and feeding them to the sharks to such headlines as: 'Butchered 300 Cuban Women; Defenseless Prisoners Shot Down by Spanish Soldiers.' In such tales there was, of course, no truth whatever. A good many people undoubtedly met violent deaths in the three years which the war lasted and there appear to have been commanders (Cuban as well as Spanish) who committed acts of barbarity. The Spanish volunteer troops, recruited in the island, seem at times to have been guilty of excesses, but the regulars appear to have behaved very well throughout, and there is little evidence to support the current American belief that all Spanish military men were monuments of cruelty and lust. The higher commanders did nothing more, in fact they frequently did very much less, than has been done by the military authorities of every great colonial power, ourselves included, under similar circumstances. The American people were, however, led to think otherwise.

The insurgents' press campaign revived in full force as soon as the election news had disappeared from the front pages. But in spite of the victories which they were again winning daily in our newspapers, their military efforts were not doing so well. Maceo, the bravest and most energetic leader whom they possessed, had been shut up in Pinar del Rio by a military cordon and was being harried through the province; Gómez, to whom he appealed for aid, remained buried in the center of the island. This was serious. At a moment when our Congress was on the eve of reassembling, and when President Cleveland was preparing an annual message which could not fail to treat of the Cuban problem, it was above all essential that the patriots produce as dramatic successes as possible. Yet there were dissensions among the chieftains; Weyler was acting with energy against them; the Cuban insurrection was in fact slipping badly.

Congress met on December 7, and listened to Mr. Cleveland's message with an apathy broken only during the reading of the Cuban passages. Though cold, as ever, to the aspirations of Cuba Libre, Mr. Cleveland went further in the direction of intervention than he had ever gone before. The nation was in an expectant mood; the propagandists were redoubling their efforts, there was war talk in the air. But almost as the words were being read, a Spanish column in Havana Province was blundering into a party of mounted Cubans. There was a burst of rifle fire; and when the confusion was over, Antonio Maceo, the outstanding figure in the insurrection, was lying dead upon the ground. He had abandoned the remnant of his forces in Pinar del Rio, and, slipping out with a small escort, was making his own escape to the eastward when his party was accidentally intercepted.

For a moment it was enough to stagger even the propagandists themselves, and for the first day or two all they could do was to deny the news *in toto* as a Spanish fabrication. But then they recovered; they rose to the occasion and revealed the full measure of their ability. A Mr. J. A. Huau, of Jacksonville, Florida, a Cuban-American said to be of Chinese extraction, informed the reporters that he had just received a 'private letter' from Cuba. It 'confirmed' the news that Maceo was dead, but added, he said, that the general had been lured forth by a flag of truce and brutally assassinated by a Spanish soldiery too cowardly to meet him in fair fight. At once the northward-going wires were hot with this outrage. It created a sensation — but the sensation was favorable to the Cuban cause.

Three days before inspiration descended upon Mr. Huau, Senator Don Cameron of Pennsylvania had laid before his colleagues a resolution: 'That the independence of the Republic of Cuba be

and the same is hereby acknowledged by the United States of
America.'

V

The victorious Republicans had written the independence of
Cuba fairly into their platform, and in the days immediately following the election some of the most conservative of their newspapers had begun to work up a war scare. But then as suddenly
they had extinguished it. For the situation was complex. Mr.
McKinley was the 'advance agent of prosperity' and the nation
had duly placed its order. Unfortunately, in the stress of the
campaign the sales talk had been, perhaps, just a shade too
glowing and the contract might be difficult to fulfill. Even Mr.
Roosevelt had a moment of doubt; perhaps it had been an error to make 'all kinds of promises of immediate prosperity as a
result of Republican rule, instead of merely saying that we would
give conditions which would allow the chance of prosperity.'
That might have been better; and at all events the party could
scarcely afford the added risks of stirring up trouble abroad. Mr.
Whitelaw Reid was one of those who urged the longer view. 'Some
day,' he now wrote to the President-elect, 'we will have Cuba as
well as the Sandwich Islands. To that extent I believe in Manifest Destiny.' But the editor had concluded that under the circumstances Destiny might usefully be postponed. He advised
Mr. McKinley that should a crisis arise in our relations with
Spain it might well be tided over, and Mr. Reid's *Tribune* began
editorially to deprecate the belligerent attitude.

Mr. McKinley was a peaceable man, and he appeared to agree
with Mr. Reid. The curious result was that the Republicans, who
had led in the assault upon the 'brutal stupidity and cowardice'
of Mr. Cleveland's foreign policy, who had placed those stirring
planks on foreign relations in their platform, suddenly found the
official policy of their party converted into one of moderation,
caution, and extreme reserve when it came to warlike adventure in
Cuba. Yet in this there lurked an obvious danger. The South and
West — the strongholds of the free silver heresy — were less imperialistic than the Eastern jingoes, but much more deeply impressed with our Christian duty to right the wrongs of suffering

Cuba. Their representatives in Congress had manifested an even more lurid bellicosity than the Republicans. If the Republicans now showed themselves lukewarm toward their platform pledges, the Democrats might use the martial enthusiasms of the populace to unhorse Mr. McKinley precisely as the Republicans had used them to unhorse Mr. Cleveland. It was something of a dilemma; but Mr. Reid's was not the only advice which the President-elect was receiving.

On the last day of November the reporters observed the small and scholarly figure of Senator Henry Cabot Lodge descending from the train at Canton. He stayed only for lunch between trains, but it was time enough for an interesting conversation. Dear Cabot immediately imparted it to dear Theodore:

He very naturally does not want to be obliged to go to war as soon as he comes in, for of course his great ambition is to restore business and bring back good times and he dislikes the idea of such interruption. He would like the crisis to come this winter and be settled one way or the other before he takes up the reins.

It was an arresting thought. The patent advantages of an arrangement whereby Mr. Cleveland would get the nation into a foreign war while to Mr. McKinley would fall the happier task of getting it out again appealed at once to the practical and patriotic mind of Mr. Roosevelt. He replied without delay:

I am delighted at what you say about McKinley. I do hope he will take a strong stand about both Hawaii and Cuba. I do not think a war with Spain would be serious enough to cause much strain on the country or much interruption to the revival of prosperity; but I certainly wish the matter could be settled this winter.

And a little later:

I wish the Cuban question could be forced to an issue before Cleveland went out. What is the matter with Olney?

What steps, if any, Mr. McKinley took to further this ingenious policy is not recorded. But Senator Lodge finished his luncheon and hastened back to Washington; and it was just ten days later that Senator Cameron, his friend and colleague upon the Foreign Relations Committee, was laying his resolution before the Senate — a resolution which could have produced no result save war.

In his annual message Mr. Cleveland had publicly repeated both the warning and the offer which had been privately conveyed to the Spanish Government in the note of the previous April. But beyond this he lent no encouragement to the Senate war-hawks; he prudently refrained from telling them that the offer of good offices had already been rejected, while the correspondence was 'inadvertently' omitted from *Foreign Relations* for the year. Even so, the reception of the message was enough to demonstrate how illusory was Mr. Olney's hope that a grant of autonomy by Spain would destroy American sympathy for the rebellion. The Cuban junta instantly denounced any idea of autonomy as a futile palliative; while even Mr. Reid's *Tribune* felt that 'an offer to help Spain govern her own household must be classed among those diplomatic aberrations which Mr. Cleveland's best friends would most willingly forget.'

Congress, at any rate, was far beyond such paltering counsels as these, and the Cameron resolution was the Senate's answer to Mr. Cleveland. It was brought in on Wednesday; on the following Sunday Mr. Huau's inspired discovery reached the front pages. In dozens of cities there were mass meetings, enrollments of citizens to fight in the cause of Cuban liberty, and, of course, collections. Mr. Huau had chosen his day with the eye of an expert press-agent, and the perfidy of Spain must have been the topic in hundreds of Protestant pulpits that Sunday morning. 'It will be a disgrace to Christian civilization,' one pastor cried, 'if, with the morning light, the wires shall not flash messages from every part of our nation to our representatives at Washington demanding that this outrage shall be avenged at the point of the bayonet and the mouth of the cannon.' Christian civilization was not disgraced; the wires blazed as the reverend gentleman demanded; the Cameron resolution was rushed into committee, and for a moment, in the last hurried days before the Christmas recess, there seemed a very good chance that Mr. Cleveland might after all be brought to 'settle the matter' as Mr. Roosevelt had desired.

But there was still one major obstacle to this ingenious hope — and that was the sturdy conscience of Mr. Cleveland himself. Repudiated by his own party as well as by the nation, deluged with abuse and derision from every quarter, his influence at an end and his hopes betrayed, Mr. Cleveland was still, as he himself said, 'President of all the people, good, bad and indifferent.' One Sunday afternoon a group of Congressmen waited upon him:

They said: 'We have about decided to declare war against Spain.'... Mr. Cleveland drew himself up and said: 'There will be no war with Spain over Cuba while I am President.' One of the members flushed up and said angrily: 'Mr. President, you seem to forget that the Constitution of the United States gives Congress the right to declare war.'

He answered: 'Yes, but it also makes me Commander-in-Chief, and I will not mobilize the Army. I happen to know that we can buy the Island of Cuba from Spain for $100,000,000 and a war will cost vastly more than that.... It would be an outrage to declare war.'

War was not declared. The Senate, conscious of its dignity and its constitutional prerogatives, still seemed to thirst for blood, but in the House a distinctly cooler atmosphere prevailed. A year previously the honorable gentlemen had talked freely about war; it now seems to have occurred to them that if they went on talking about it a war might actually happen. Speaker T. B. Reed, who was always an opponent of jingoism, was quoted in the newspapers, while the attitude of others made it doubtful whether the Cameron resolution could pass the House. Yet the situation was confused and the Senate went ahead. On December 18 the Foreign Relations Committee agreed to report the resolution; in the West they were already organizing regiments for the war and there was a semi-panic on the New York Stock Exchange. And then Mr. Olney, that always original diplomat, adroitly interposed one of his most characteristic strokes.

On December 19, Mr. Olney astounded the Washington correspondents by supplying them unasked with a formal statement. 'I have no objection,' he calmly began, 'to stating my own views of the resolution respecting the independence of the so-called Republic of Cuba which, it is reported, is to be laid before the Senate on Monday.' He continued:

Indeed... it is perhaps my duty to point out that the resolution, if passed by the Senate, can probably be regarded only as an expression of opinion by the eminent gentlemen who vote for it in the Senate, and if passed by the House of Representatives can only be regarded as another expression of opinion by the eminent gentlemen who vote for it in the House.

The power to recognize the so-called Republic of Cuba as an independent state rests exclusively with the Executive. A resolution on the subject... is inoperative as legislation, and is important only as advice of great weight voluntarily tendered to the Executive regarding the manner in which he shall exercise his constitutional functions.... The resolution will be without effect and will leave unaltered the attitude of this Government toward the two contending parties in Cuba.

Every newspaper carried that remarkable pronouncement next morning; the Senate writhed under the lacerating affront to the dignity of the most august legislative body in the world, but what could the unhappy statesmen do? The House was plainly 'not in a belligerent mood,' and some one noted the curious fact that nearly all the Civil War veterans in its membership were opposed to the Cameron resolution. The resolution was reported out on the 21st, but the *Tribune* printed an editorial headed 'Steady Now!' and actually almost agreeing with Mr. Olney. The measure, as Senator Lodge recorded, 'slumbered on the calendar and was never called up'; and as Congress adjourned for the Christmas recess still another crisis had passed.

VI

Spain's troubles had in the meantime been increased by another revolution in the Philippine Islands; but the added burden was small, and in Cuba General Weyler was beginning to get results. After Maceo's death the situation in Pinar del Rio had been pretty well cleared up, and it became possible to withdraw most of the troops employed there. With them Weyler now undertook a thorough-going drive to the eastward, clearing the country as he went, destroying everything that could possibly aid the insurgents and sweeping up the cattle and other supplies to feed the 'reconcentrados.' Though Máximo Gómez had attempted another 'invasion,' in the face of this attack he was never to achieve it. The Madrid Government was emboldened to proclaim a measure of political reform — principally, no doubt, as a gesture toward the United States.

To offset these events the propagandists had, of course, redoubled their press campaign. They had by this time realized the full value of the reconcentration decrees, and tales of a starving peasantry huddled helplessly into garrison towns to die of disease, filth, and famine supplied new horrors for our avid people. They were repeated, moreover, from an unexpected quarter. In Spain the Liberal Opposition was becoming restive over the achievements of Sr. Cánovas' Conservative Government; for it is a cardinal rule in all countries that if the nation is to be saved it must certainly not be saved by one's political opponents. The Liberal press in the Peninsula was now launching an assault upon Weyler and his methods which often rivaled in intensity and exaggeration that which was under way in the United States, and which lent the greatest aid and comfort to the inventive 'workers' of the Cuban Republic.

Under the stimulus of their efforts bellicose oratory and dramatic resolutions were still being heard upon Capitol Hill. But the effect was not aways fortunate. There was, for example, the somewhat regrettable incident of the lady passengers in the American steamship Olivette. A despatch from Mr. Richard Harding Davis, Havana correspondent of Mr. Hearst's *Journal*, was published in that paper on February 12. 'Does Our Flag,' the headline shouted, 'Protect Women?' The story which followed announced that just as the Olivette was about to sail from Havana for the United States, some Spanish police officers had boarded her in order to search the persons of three young Cuban ladies, one of whom was supposed to be carrying insurgent despatches. It was illustrated with a drawing from the pencil of Mr. Frederic Remington, taking up one half of the newspaper page and showing the bestial Spanish soldiery prosecuting their search while the suspected young lady stood nude before them in the cabin.

So great, so titillating, an outrage upon womanhood, perpetrated beneath the very shadow of the American flag itself, could not pass without protest; the incident was indeed calculated, as the *Journal's* Washington correspondent telegraphed, to stir the statesmen 'from their lethargy.' Representative Amos Cummings instantly introduced into the House a resolution demanding that the Secretary of State furnish all information relevant to 'the stripping of three lady passengers on the United States mail steamer Olivette in the harbor at Habana.' War, exclaimed the *Journal*, 'is a dreadful thing, but there are things more dreadful than even war, and one of them is dishonor.'

But unhappily for Mr. Cummings he had overlooked the important fact that both Mr. Davis's story and Mr. Remington's picture had been exclusive to the *Journal*. It is generally conceded that a large part of the American newspaper ferocity toward Spain was due to the accidental circumstance that Mr. Hearst and Mr. Pulitzer were at the time locked in their famous struggle for supremacy in the field of sensational journalism in New York. It was a battle of gigantic proportions, in which the sufferings of Cuba merely chanced to furnish some of the most convenient ammunition. Whenever one side sprang a sensation the normal reply was of course for the other to spring a better one. But if this happened at the moment to be impracticable, it served almost as well to demonstrate that the opponent's sensation had been a 'fake.' So it occurred in this case. The *Journal* had barely got its latest outrage well under way, and was just beginning to work up the customary incidentals, when the *World* suddenly produced one of the young ladies in question herself. She gave her shocked and indignant denial that any such incident had ever taken place. The *World*, in fact, raised so great a scandal over this 'invention of a New York newspaper' that Mr. Davis had to explain in a letter to its editor that his despatch had never said that the ladies were searched by male police officers; that they were in fact examined (though he had omitted to make this clear) by a police matron in the privacy of a stateroom while the officers walked up and down on deck, and that the idea of their having stood disrobed before male examiners was wholly a product of the *Journal's* and of Mr. Remington's imagination. Mr. Cummings's resolution was never reported out by the Foreign Affairs Committee.

Accidents such as this, though no doubt unavoidable, did not improve Cuban prospects in the United States. And despite the sufferings of the reconcentrados, the Republican statesmen who were so soon to take over the responsibility of power were manifesting a growing caution. Such orators as Senator Turpie, a Democrat, might still publicly refer to General Weyler as 'this indescribably diminutive reptile,' but by the middle of February Sr. Dupuy de Lôme was cabling home that, 'in the opinion... of many who will have great influence in the new administration and even of McKinley himself,' the new Spanish reform project

AN IMAGINARY INCIDENT PICTURED BY FREDERIC REMINGTON IN
THE 'NEW YORK JOURNAL'

was 'as much as could be asked for.' There remained, of course, the outraged dignity of the Senate, which could hardly be expected to take lying down Mr. Olney's dismissal of its most solemn deliberations as a mere 'expression of opinion.' But the short session was almost at an end before the Senate got round again to Cuba, and when the issue did come up, its history, like that of the lady passengers in the Olivette, was not altogether happy.

The Foreign Relations Committee seems to have decided that this time it would take no chances with Mr. Olney's debonair legalism. It concentrated, not upon the wrongs of Cuban patriotism, but upon the more solid issue of American rights. It called for the correspondence. It called for a list of all American claims against the Spanish Government on file with the State Department. It called for a list of the American citizens (there turned out to be seventy-four of them) who had been arrested by the Spanish authorities in Cuba since the outbreak of the insurrection. It studied these cases with care, and finally selected one which it felt that it could go to the mat on. On February 24, Senator Morgan reported a Senate resolution: 'That the Government of the United States demands the immediate and unconditional release of Julio Sanguily.'

It is true that this citizen's name was regrettably Hispanic, but then, so were the names of nearly all the remaining seventy-three upon the list, and that consequently could not be helped. Otherwise Mr. Sanguily's case appeared to be a strong one. Mr. Sanguily had been arrested in Havana exactly two years before, at the outbreak of the insurrection, upon the suspicion (which was, incidentally, very well founded) of complicity in the rising. Since that time he had languished in jail, the subject of those awe-inspiring tortuosities which Spanish judicial procedure complicated by diplomatic intervention can alone produce. He was known to have served as a general officer on the patriots' side in the Ten Years' War, but his naturalization, unlike that of many others, was of long standing, since it dated from 1878. The resolution demanded not only 'unconditional' release, but just compensation for Mr. Sanguily's 'imprisonment and sufferings' as well.

The debate opened on February 25. There was a lively preface by Senator Allen of Nebraska, who pointed out that the Spanish authorities 'are gathering up the little girls in that island and selling them into a species of slavery, the worst conceivable in the human mind, selling them to lives of shame.' Mr. Allen (who apparently failed to read the *World*) could scarcely find language in which decently to refer to the Olivette outrage; while he believed it 'to be conclusively established that Spanish soldiers had in one or more instances taken little infants by the heels, held them up, and hacked them to pieces with the deadly machete in the presence of the mothers and fathers themselves.' With this picture before him, Senator Daniel of Virginia then swung into the serious business of the Sanguily resolution. His speech was long, it was eloquent, it was voluminously documented; the Senator read all the documents into the record and concluded in a fine peroration demanding that the nation should uphold the honor and rights of its citizens abroad.

Whereupon Senator Hoar arose and demonstrated that upon the statements contained in the very documents that had just been submitted, Mr. Sanguily's naturalization papers must have been fraudulent and that Mr. Sanguily was 'no more an American citizen than the Senator from Virginia is a citizen of Cuba.' This was a bombshell, and obviously called for strenuous measures. Senator Lodge himself hastily arose to snatch the standard from the wavering hand of Mr. Daniel. Senator Lodge plunged into an oration even more eloquent, and even less relevant to the point which had been raised, than that of the gentleman from Virginia.

Mr. President, the Committee on Foreign Relations did not think it was necessary to go behind the record of a court of record of the City of New York.... Does any one within the sound of my voice suppose that if a man bearing the naturalization certificate of the Queen of England had been treated as Julio Sanguily has been treated, England would have hesitated as to what she would do?

Senator Hoar interposed to insist that, according to the documents, Mr. Sanguily had been fighting in the Cuban insurrection until 1878, that his certificate was granted in 1878, and that he therefore could not have complied with the legal requirement of five years' prior residence in the United States when the naturalization was granted.

Mr. Lodge: Does my colleague think his statement overthrows the record of the court?

Mr. Hoar: I do. There were 60,000 fraudulent naturalization papers issued from the same New York superior court within three days in the year 1868.... These court records are of the slightest possible importance. ... It never was pretended that they are anything but *prima facie* evidence.... If we are going to plunge this country into a war, let us have something to stand on. Let us have some facts. Let us have an American citizen and not a man who has got a fraudulent naturalization to do it on.

This was bad, but much worse was to follow. While the Foreign Relations Committee had been choosing its American citizen, Mr. Olney had been indulging in a little strategy on his own account. The State Department had been negotiating to secure Mr. Sanguily's release on a pardon. On the very morning after the interchange above quoted, the honorable gentlemen learned from their newspapers that Mr. Sanguily had definitely been released upon this basis. In other words, not only was Mr. Sanguily's citizenship doubtful, but in accepting a pardon he had admitted, at the very moment that the Senate of the United States was moving heaven and earth in his behalf, that he had been guilty of the charges made against him! Mr. Olney had won again.

It was, really, too bad. Senator White remarked ironically that with Mr. Sanguily a broken reed in their hands they could scarcely retrieve their position even by substituting the name (it was another upon the list) of Mr. George Washington Aguirre; while Senator Hale wickedly inquired whether they might not move to substitute another island for Cuba. Senator Lodge observed icily that it was not a matter for 'sneers' and a number of the statesmen became visibly heated, but the Senate soon found it convenient to move on to other questions.

Yet in spite of the noticeable improvement in Spanish-American relations, the danger was still obviously real. The collapse of the Senate debate came on Friday, February 26. Less than a week remained of the old administration. Mr. Cleveland had done everything in his power to avert what he believed would have been a useless and disgraceful war, and he had himself passed beyond reach of either praise or blame. But that massive conscience would not let him rest. Mr. Cleveland must have doubted whether his successor either appreciated the full difficulties confronting him or had the resolution to cope with them. President Cleveland was determined that if he could prevent it there should be no war, and in the closing hours of his administration he made one final and extraordinary attempt.

On Sunday, the 28th, he summoned to the White House (for 'any hour between 8 P.M. and 2 A.M.') Mr. Frederic R. Coudert, an expert in international law. Mr. Coudert came, and discovered to his amazement that the President was asking him to undertake at once a secret mission to Madrid for the purpose of avoiding a war. It would come, Mr. Cleveland explained, as a result of the activities of the Americans in Cuba, and 'he mentioned the American consul general, General Fitzhugh Lee, as their ringleader.' If Mr. Coudert would accept, the President would set things right with Mr. McKinley; but even so, the lawyer felt it impossible to enter into this altruistic conspiracy. As soon as he had recovered from his astonishment, he refused. Four days later, the troubled history of the Cleveland administration was at an end, and its leader passed forever from political life.

But as he passed, a professor of history on the Princeton faculty paused to set an epitaph above that great career — an epitaph which might have served a quarter of a century later for the career of another Democratic President. 'Men have said,' wrote Professor Woodrow Wilson, 'that he was stubborn because he did not change and self-opinionated because he did not falter. He has made no overtures to fortune, has obtained and holds a great place in our affairs by a sort of inevitable mastery, by a law which no politician has ever quite understood or at all relished, by virtue of a preference which the people themselves have expressed without analyzing.'

CHAPTER IV
MR. McKINLEY'S POLICY OF PEACE

I

IT was the 4th of March, 1897; and as the bands, the uniforms, and the silk hats passed in triumph down Pennsylvania Avenue they were bearing with them, not merely a new administration, but a whole new rhythm in the life of the American people. Those dark omens of a few months before had been exorcised; those fears forgotten; those doubts set comfortably at rest. 'The Republican Party was coming back to power as the party of organization, of discipline, of unquestioning obedience to leadership'; and opportunity hovered brightly above that splendid and victorious unity. It was a unity so complete, in fact, that for a moment it seemed to embrace, not merely the party, but the nation as a whole. It is true that there were still unreconstructed Southern ladies upon the fringes of the crowd to emit, as the band played 'Marching Through Georgia,' 'suppressed, furtive hisses of implacable hatred,' but the music drowned them out. It was an era of good feeling. There was no important newspaper in any section adopting an aggressively hostile tone toward the incoming administration. The waiting majorities in House and Senate were overwhelming in their size; for the first time in twenty years a Republican President was facing a solidly Republican Congress. 'I think,' as Mr. Reid had already written to the victorious candidate, 'you have the greatest opportunity since Lincoln — as you have made the greatest campaign since his, and have had the greatest popular triumph.'

So the second Lincoln stood upon the steps of the Capitol, President of the United States, the unchallenged leader, facing the throng and the future for which he had made himself responsible. Of the many problems which confronted him, the Cuban problem was clearly one of the most serious. Only the night before, it is reported, he had declared himself emphatically upon it in a final conversation with Mr. Cleveland. 'Mr. President,' he had said, 'if I can only go out of office at the end of my term with the knowledge that I have done what lay in my power to avert this terrible calamity [a Spanish war] with the success that has crowned your patience and persistence, I shall be the happiest man in the world.' That Mr. McKinley, his reputation staked upon a revival of prosperity, detested the idea of war and earnestly desired peace, it is impossible to doubt. That the situation was in his hands, more completely than often happens in American life, is evident. And yet the war came. For when the martial processes have developed to the point which they had now reached, the avoidance of war itself is a thing that takes some doing. But this, apparently, Mr. McKinley failed to realize; he did not want a war, but he lacked Mr. Cleveland's resolute determination to prevent one.

Undoubtedly there came with the inauguration a further diminution of the official war fever. The aged Senator Sherman assumed the Secretaryship of State resolved to preserve the peace. On March 15, the President summoned an extra session to revise the tariff — thereby automatically hanging the Senate around the neck of his foreign policy — but the Senate for the time being was docile. Although Senator Morgan immediately brought in a Cuban resolution, it called for a mere recognition of belligerency, and nobody's heart was in it. Consul-General Lee was clamoring for battleships in connection with the latest newspaper atrocity, the alleged murder while in prison of the American citizen, Dr. Ricardo Ruiz. The despatch of battleships to Havana had long been a favorite proposal of the jingoes, but Mr. Lee did not get them. Instead, he got a special commissioner sent by the President to examine the facts.

The insurrection, in the meanwhile, was falling into ever-narrower straits. General Weyler held Máximo Gómez penned up far in the center of the island. There were still scattered bands of insurgents in the western provinces, and the country was in a terrible state, but the main insurgent effort was now confined to the 'eastern department' — the wilder territory in Puerto Principe and Santiago Provinces, where as yet the Spaniards had attempted little more than the defense of the ports and of a few inland garrison towns. Even in the 'eastern department' the insurgent forces, under the command of General Calixto García, did little more than wander aimlessly through the deserted countryside, until absolute want of stores compelled them to attack some isolated post.

To assist in such operations they had with them one or two light field-pieces, manned by a small group of American volunteers — practically the only native Americans who actually served with the patriot armies in spite of the many newspaper tales of American legions enlisted in the cause of liberty. After the death of Major Osgood, shot between the eyes while sighting his piece during the 'siege' of Guaimaro, the command of this diminutive artillery devolved upon an extremely youthful, though none the less adventurous, gentleman— 'a little fellow named Funston, a son of a Representative from Kansas,' who was later to become Major General Frederick Funston of the United States Army. General Funston left a picture of the state to which the eastern provinces, where the Spanish effort had been small, had been reduced:

The thousands of Cuban families living in the 'bush' off the lines of operations of the enemy's columns were eking out a miserable existence. All the able-bodied men being in the war, the women and children could barely raise enough vegetables to keep off starvation.... The insurgent forces... were always hungry. In the desolated and starving country the question of feeding the more than 4000 men about to be concentrated for the coming campaign was one that taxed the resources of our leaders to the utmost.... Pack trains [of the patriots] scoured the country, taking from the miserable people the last sweet potato, ear of corn or banana that could be found.

On the other hand, such sufferings merely provided the propagandists with a sharper weapon, and their terrible stories of famine in Cuba now began more and more to dominate the situation. To supply these stories invention was no longer necessary. Since the island had been in a depressed condition when the insurrection began, and since the insurgents had for two years been ravaging its crops and stopping its industrial life, people would probably have been starving to death even without the measures initiated by the Spaniards in the spring of 1897. Long before Weyler began to reconcentrate the populace and systematically to destroy the food supplies left in the countryside, famine had been foreseen as inevitable. The great ingenuity of the patriots lay in the success with which they now pinned the entire responsibility for the famine upon the Spaniards, and in particular upon the reconcentration decrees.

No doubt reconcentration did aggravate the suffering. Although it was theoretically a quite practicable measure in a country as fertile and as thinly populated as Cuba, and although Weyler was careful in every case to order the provision of housing, of rations, and of cultivated zones in which the refugees could grow their own food, Spanish administrative efficiency was never very high, and orders were easier to write than to see enforced. But even without reconcentration the misery would have been great; while the insurgents themselves, though protesting to high heaven over the barbarity of the Spaniards, often did everything they could to add to the suffering. Weyler cites a captured document ordering that the establishment of cultivated zones be prevented 'by every means possible'; while Mr. Atkins records a case near Cienfuegos in which the insurgents slipped through the wire one night and neatly destroyed every plant in a zone which the Spaniards had established for the support of the reconcentrated women and children.

The American press and public, however, made no attempt to distinguish the causes of the general wretchedness. Reconcentration was assumed to be responsible for it all; and where it was not set down to sadistic cruelty on the part of the Spaniards, it was held at least to demonstrate an incapacity so great as to have forfeited all right to further possession of the island. At the height of the excitement it was seriously believed that between 400,000 and half a million persons had actually died by starvation or associated disease, and our consul at Santiago at one time officially reported his belief that if a census of the island were taken it would show that two thirds of the population had disappeared.

Consequently, it was with some surprise that we later discovered, when a census was taken under American auspices in 1899, that the population in reality had decreased by only 58,895, or 3.6 per cent, since the last preceding census twelve years earlier. The census officials estimated that the total population in 1899 was about 200,000 less than it would have been had the normal rate of increase been maintained. But those twelve years had witnessed industrial depression, unemployment, four years of war and devastation, and the rigorous blockade which our own Navy imposed during the summer of 1898. They had also witnessed an emigration which is said to have been heavy. It is evident that the American people were being given an exaggerated idea of the catastrophe, based upon reports from a few localities where conditions were at their worst. In the spring and summer of 1897, however, there was no one to correct the impression, and as the weeks went by the reconcentration propaganda arose in an ever-darkening cloud over the heads of the Spanish statesmen.

II

Officially relations were improving, yet nothing was being done to check the tendencies through which war might at any time be precipitated. The war-hawks of the Foreign Relations Committee still listened attentively through the summer days as somewhat ambiguous witnesses testified to the dreadful facts of the Cuban situation; observant statesmen read the restless signs among the home constituencies; Mr. Hearst went happily on his way, booming Cuba and the *Journal's* prosperity; while Mr. Pulitzer, his rival, considered the question and decided, as he afterward confessed, 'that he had rather liked the idea of war — not a big one — but one that would arouse interest and give him a chance to gauge the reflex in his circulation figures.' And Mr. McKinley himself, pondering the policy which he should adopt in regard to Cuba, appears to have realized that too intransigeant a devotion to peace might have its dangers.

Perhaps after all it was not so simple as it had seemed that night before inauguration when he had given his generous assurance to Mr. Cleveland. There were the South and West, with their bellicose tendencies and their unhappy penchant for free silver. The South and West wanted to rescue the Cubans; well, there were doubtless many reasons to make such a step desirable. On the other hand, quite aside from the war danger, once we had the patriots squarely on the Constitution's doorstep, what would we do with them? As that acrid genius, Professor William Graham Sumner, had already pointed out, 'the prospect of adding to the present Senate a number of Cuban Senators, either native or carpet-bag, is one whose terrors it is not necessary to unfold.' Mr.

Reid had a solution even for that problem; the best plan, he thought, 'would be to give them a suitable measure of self-government, but to hold them as territories like Alaska — not threatening us with so large a half-breed citizenship and with a further deluge of new states and Senators.' Yet it seemed hardly probable that even 'a suitable measure of self-government' would satisfy the clamant spokesmen of the Republic of Cuba. President Mc-Kinley paused to wonder whether these were, after all, really representative of 'the best that Cuba has to offer in the way of citizens.'

It was all dreadfully difficult, yet history would not stand still. In April, Mr. McKinley resolved one of his lesser doubts; with the assent of Mr. T. C. Platt, who thought that 'Theodore' could 'probably do less harm to the organization as Assistant Secretary of the Navy than in any other office that can be named,' he appointed the belligerent Mr. Roosevelt to that very important post. Mr. McKinley had hesitated long over this appointment; and Mr. Roosevelt plunged at once into his new duties with a martial fervor indicating that the hesitation might have been justified. Then in the middle of May, while the Senate was debating, a trifle perfunctorily, the Morgan belligerency resolution, the President suddenly enlivened the scene by sending in a special message asking Congress for $50,000 wherewith to relieve American citizens in want in Cuba.

Two days later, the Madrid cables announced what seemed irrefutable proof from the Spaniards themselves of the truth of the starvation propaganda. Sr. Sagasta, the leader of the Liberal opposition, a statesman who for years had been alternating with Sr. Cánovas at the head of the Government, declared in a political meeting that 'after having sent out 200,000 men and poured out so great a quantity of blood, we are masters of no other territory in the island save that upon which our soldiers stand.... We have... ruin, desolation, and misery in four provinces of Cuba.' In our own Congress this political attack had an immediate repercussion. The $50,000 appropriation went quickly through both houses, while the Senate passed the Morgan resolution. But it was passed by only 41 to 14 (the vote a year before had been 64 to 6), and in the House it was never even considered. Speaker Reed gently buried it in the files of a Foreign Affairs Committee which had not yet been appointed.

In Cuba, General Weyler was continuing to make progress against the insurgents, though little against the famine. Mr. Sherman was led to prepare a diplomatic remonstrance over the cruelty of the reconcentration policy couched in a most ominous tone, at the very moment that he was lodging strenuous protest against the 'virtual' expropriation of an American-owned sugar estate in Matanzas Province. Since the 'expropriation' had consisted in adding the estate to one of the cultivated zones designed to preserve the people from the starvation against which we were protesting, this seemed to leave the Spaniards with singularly little alternative. Matanzas, moreover, was one of the points where the distress was at its worst, while the American owner of the estate had a Cuban name. It was too much even for the ironclad suavity of Dupuy de Lôme, and for once that perfect diplomat almost lost his temper. But June, and the rains, had once more been reached. In the island there was a breathing-space; in Washington Congress was at last adjourning (the Senate pausing only to vote down an arbitration treaty with England as a sign of its mettle) and the statesmen and the newspaper correspondents were retiring to the seashore. Another season had been safely passed; Mr. McKinley, weighing its lessons, was now free to perfect the policy which was to guide us in the future.

By the middle of July this policy had been definitely formulated. The President had already chosen General Stewart L. Woodford to represent him as American Minister at Madrid, and Mr. Woodford was now provided with a letter of instructions which he was to show to the Spanish Government. This letter was of an emphatic character. For, as has been intimated, when it came to the point, Mr. McKinley found himself divided between his desire for peace and the fact that a pacific policy would be unpopular and politically dangerous. It was a dilemma; and Mr. McKinley solved it by a subtle modification of the attitude which he had admired in his predecessor. Like Mr. Cleveland, Mr. McKinley urged that the Cuban war must be brought to an end. Like Mr. Cleveland, he suggested that Spain could do this by making 'proposals of settlement honorable to herself and just to her Cuban colony' — in other words, through granting some form of autonomy. But he failed to recognize, as Mr. Cleveland had done, our own responsibility in the matter. The Olney note had offered the coöperation of the United States Government in securing the acceptance of autonomy by the Cubans and (which was of primary importance) by public opinion in the United States. Mr. McKinley was careful not to repeat this 'aberration' of his predecessor. Instead, he replaced it with a clear threat that unless Spain reversed her policy, dropped the 'measures of unparalleled severity' which she was using in Cuba, offered some form of 'settlement' and thus brought the war to an end, we would intervene.

The extreme probability that no form of settlement, short of the evacuation of the island, would be accepted by the insurgents as long as they could count on our support was simply overlooked by Mr. McKinley. His policy came to this: We dictated the course to be followed, but we accepted no responsibility for its success. If Spain did not take our advice, we would fight her; if she did take our advice and it turned out badly, we still reserved our liberty of action, while we gave no promise (beyond a vague tender of 'good offices') that we would lift a hand to insure its turning out well. Though Mr. McKinley himself may not have realized the fact, at bottom his method of avoiding war was simply to insist that Spain yield to everything which we demanded. It was a method which protected him from the displeasure of his own martial countrymen. But it was a very poor way of avoiding war.

Nevertheless, whatever the President may have concluded as to the failure of General Weyler's campaign, the general himself was most optimistic. Backed up strongly by Sr. Cánovas and his Conservative Government, Weyler had pretty well stamped out the insurrection in the western half of the island and was preparing a final campaign in the eastern half for the coming season. He wrote home his belief that if only he were left unhampered he could extinguish the whole rebellion 'before the United States can precipitate hostilities.' It is possible that he might have done so, and thus automatically have solved the problem. But fate intervened. On August 8, Sr. Cánovas was assassinated by an Italian anarchist. Abruptly the whole effort upon which he and General Weyler had been engaged was brought to an end; and when our new Minister finally reached Madrid in September, it was to find Sr. Sagasta and the Liberals on the eve of taking over the Government. Mr. McKinley's demand for a new policy in Cuba was now to be considered by ministers who had themselves condemned the 'barbarity' and 'futility' of their predecessors' methods quite as violently as any one in the United States, and who were themselves committed to ending the Cuban war by conciliation and the grant of reforms. Sr. Sagasta telegraphically relieved General Weyler of his command, and then sat down to study the somewhat difficult position into which he had been precipitated.

Officially our policy was one of peace, and Mr. William R. Day, the Assistant Secretary of State (who was more and more taking over the active direction of affairs from the aged hands of Mr. Sherman), had announced that Mr. Woodford's mission was to be 'entirely pacific.' Yet at the same time Mr. Roosevelt at the Navy Department was pushing his own private plans for war with a zest which Mr. McKinley did not think it necessary to discourage. Mr. McKinley, in fact, was 'most kind.' He invited Mr. Roosevelt to dinner. The enthusiastic Assistant Secretary did not stop with a mere war against Spain; he was already laboring as well under that curious prepossession with the Yellow Peril which was to follow him throughout his career. A day or two later the President invited him on a drive in order to hear more, and as the two rolled on through the September air, it was to a torrent of exhilarating conversation:

I gave him a paper showing exactly where all our ships are, and I also sketched in outline what I thought ought to be done if things looked menacing about Spain, urging the necessity of taking an immediate and prompt initiative if we wished to avoid the chance of some serious trouble, and of the Japs chipping in.

Mr. Roosevelt had already evolved a comprehensive plan of campaign — one that would not only prevent the Japs from chipping in, but would end the war in 'six weeks.' It contained one item that may have come as a new thought to Mr. McKinley. Our Asiatic Squadron, Mr. Roosevelt believed, 'should blockade, and, if possible, take Manila.' This was an original and striking possibility, no less suggestive because of the fact that in the Philippines, as in Cuba, an insurrection was known to be active.

'However,' Mr. Roosevelt could still add, 'I haven't the slightest idea that there will be a war.'

President McKinley listened, in his pleasantly enigmatic way, and apparently said nothing. Perhaps it was true that even Mr. Roosevelt did not, really, believe that there would be a real war. To move the toy ships about upon the maps, to plan the toy strategy, and play with exciting possibilities, was a fascinating game. But was it more than a game? 'At that time,' as Admiral Dewey afterward remembered, 'not one man in ten in Washington thought that we should ever come to the actual crisis of a war with Spain.' The world had outgrown such barbarisms, and even military and naval men in those distant days 'had no clear idea or expectation that the United States would ever go to war again.' Yet in Havana at the moment a loyalist crowd was shouting vivas in the Plaza de Armas for General Weyler, 'the pacifier of Cuba,' and thereby suggesting to the earnest sympathizers with the patriot cause what was to prove a strangely useful idea. Suppose these crowds should begin to riot? Might they not, in their reactionary animosity, endanger American life and property? Would it not be an obvious aid to peace to forestall such an incident by sending American men-of-war to Havana after all? On the evening of October 8, the United States North Atlantic Squadron, steaming northward off the Virginia Capes, was intercepted by a destroyer with despatches. The U.S.S. Maine was detached from the fleet; she was put about, and directed to Port Royal, South Carolina. Her officers guessed that it was done so that we might have an effective naval vessel within reach of Havana against the possibility of 'anti-American disturbances.'

III

The public meanwhile was gasping over fresh sensations, for the attitude of the press in these rather delicate moments could scarcely be described as helpful. In fact, one of the most splendid sensations of all was now in progress. Some months before suitable material had been discovered in the person of an unfortunate young lady, Señorita Evangelina Cisneros, whose father had been condemned to a mild imprisonment in the Isle of Pines on charges of complicity with the insurgents. Miss Cisneros had voluntarily accompanied him into his exile, but eventually she had been arrested herself and returned as a prisoner to Havana. According to the propagandists and the American newspapers, her sole crime had been to resist an unprincipled Spanish officer in a design upon her virtue; and the virtue of young ladies was a matter to which American publics were seldom indifferent. It was reported that Miss Cisneros was to be sent to the penal colonies in Africa; at once the brilliant minds of Mr. Hearst's young men perceived an unparalleled opportunity. 'Enlist the women of America!' their chief is said to have exclaimed, and immediately the *Journal* plunged into a campaign which is still famous in American newspaper history.

The women were energetically enlisted. Mrs. Jefferson Davis, the widow of the Confederate President, was induced to sign an appeal to the Queen Regent of Spain, asking that she 'give Evangelina Cisneros to the women of America to save her from a fate worse than death.' Mrs. Julia Ward Howe was led to go Mrs. Davis one better — Mrs. Howe signed an appeal to Pope Leo XIII. The *Journal* then prepared a petition for general signature; the wrongs of Evangelina Cisneros were spread in screaming headlines, and the names of twenty thousand women were collected. Among them were to be found not only such prominent ladies as Frances Hodgson Burnett and Julia Dent Grant, but even Mrs. Mark Hanna, Mrs. Nancy McKinley, the mother of the President, and Mrs. John Sherman, the wife of the Secretary of State. Sr. Dupuy de Lôme, alarmed by the political eminence of these ladies, denied the truth of the *Journal's* version of the case, with the immediate result, of course, that the sensation became even more sensational. The *Journal* produced witnesses. The *Journal* spread the crusade abroad, and in England 'Mrs. Ormiston Chant, the great English temperance advocate, took up the work there, and soon petitions went from London with the signatures of officers of organizations representing 200,000 women.'

Doubtless General Weyler would have been glad enough to have released the young lady if only to save trouble, but naturally all this made such a course impossible, and it began to look as though the *Journal's* enthusiastic intervention had condemned her to perpetual imprisonment. One can hardly suppose that this would have worried Mr. Hearst very much, but to his extraordinary and fertile brain there now occurred another and even bolder idea. Mr. Karl Decker, one of the most redoubtable of his forces, was abruptly despatched to Havana under secret orders to rescue the Cuban Girl Martyr from her imprisonment 'at any hazard.' Mr. Decker reached Havana at the end of August. It took a month to perfect the plot, but finally, on October 10, the *Journal* announced in a paroxysm of typography that Evangelina Cisneros had been rescued and spirited from the island. 'An American Newspaper,' exclaimed the banner head, 'Accomplishes at a Single Stroke What the Best Efforts of Diplomacy Failed Utterly to Bring About in Many Months.' A quarter of the front page was consumed by two touching drawings: 'Miss Cisneros Before and After Fifteen Months of Incarceration.' There was another drawing: 'The Rescued Martyr in Her Prison Garb,' and a large part of the remaining space went to a beautiful facsimile of the *Journal's* petition to the Queen. There was still room, however, for a few paragraphs of the story. It began: 'Evangelina Cosio y Cisneros is at last at liberty, and the *Journal* can place to its credit the greatest journalistic coup of this age.'

The rescue itself had not proved very difficult; for when it came to the point, Mr. Decker merely climbed to the roof of a house abutting on the jail, broke the rotting bar of a window, and lifted Miss Cisneros out. She was hidden in a house in Havana for a few days and then smuggled aboard an American steamer. But the sensation was as much as even Mr. Hearst could have desired. At New York there was an immense reception in Madison Square Garden. A week later there was another in Washington. The Cuban Girl Martyr was even introduced to the President — by Mrs. John A. Logan, the widow of the Civil War general — and according to the *Journal* Mr. McKinley gave the exploit his 'unofficial' blessing. 'It was,' the *Journal* quoted him, 'a most heroic deed.'

Needless to say, it was anything but an aid to peace; while other stories of a dreadful character continued to flow in from Cuba. Our consul at Matanzas was officially reporting that unless 'prompt measures of relief' were afforded to the reconcentrados, 'sixty days hence the majority of them will be exterminated.' And amid these rising horrors and excitements Mr. Roosevelt at the Navy Department was not supine. Quite the contrary.

By an accident of service routine it happened that the command of our Asiatic Squadron was about to fall vacant. At this time the great mass of the American people was probably unaware of the existence of the Philippine Islands; but the American people — unlike Mr. Roosevelt and Senator Lodge — were not students of the great mysteries of foreign relations. Even Mr. Roosevelt, as a matter of fact, could have had only the vaguest knowledge of that archipelago; but he was already proposing, in the event of war, to take Manila. How such an action could be reconciled with an unaggressive intervention purely to rescue Cuba was not very clearly explained. However, the collection of Asiatic territory was the fashionable thing at the moment among all the very best diplomacies; the islands belonged to Spain, and they were said to be valuable. What more was necessary?

Fortunately, Spain also possessed an Asiatic Squadron, posted in the Philippines. Though it was difficult to get exact details as to its strength, enough was known to make its inoffensive character fairly apparent. To have left it alone altogether would hardly have endangered the success of any attempt to eject the Spaniards from Cuba; but the very existence of the squadron provided a satisfactory pretext for attacking it, and through it the territory which it was supposed to defend. Mr. Roosevelt threw himself into the project with a zestful secrecy; and he now selected his candidate for the Asiatic command with the express intention of getting a man who would fight the Spaniards at Manila. His choice fell upon Commodore George Dewey. But the Department officials, it seemed, did not approve of the selection. Mr. Roosevelt, however, had his own method for overcoming such difficulties. He summoned the Commodore. 'I want you to go,' he announced. 'You are the man who will be equal to the emergency if one arises. Do you know any Senators?'

The Commodore dutifully expressed his 'natural disinclination' to use such unorthodox means for securing promotion for himself, but admitted that he knew Senator Proctor of Vermont. Mr. Roosevelt overcame the Commodore's scruples by telling him that political influence had already been brought to bear by other candidates; the Commodore, realizing that in such case it was practically a patriotic duty for him to pull the wires on his own side, went at once to Senator Proctor. 'That very day' the latter 'called on President McKinley to receive the promise of the appointment before he left the White House.' Dewey's orders were issued on October 21, 1897; thus early were the Philippine Islands, had they only known it, being brought within the orbit of our beneficent institutions.

It is true that the Secretary of the Navy, Mr. John D. Long, who had old-fashioned ideas about promotion orders and who felt a certain annoyance at having Mr. Roosevelt run his department for him, manifested considerable displeasure with the Commodore. Called to account, the latter explained that he had pulled the wires only in self-defense. Mr. Long unexpectedly replied that no influence had been used by any one else; and Commodore Dewey was left in a rather embarrassing position until, a few hours later, the Secretary sent word that he had just found the letter in which another man's claims had been urged. Oddly enough, it turned out that this letter had arrived while Mr. Long was absent from the office and Mr. Roosevelt had been Acting Secretary; only now had it come to light.

Even so, Mr. Long could not quite forgive the Commodore. To that officer's chagrin he was ordered to hoist the pennant of his actual rank, instead of the flag of Acting Rear-Admiral, as had been the custom with all previous commanders on the Asiatic station. But perhaps one may excuse the Secretary's irritation, for even he, in the fall of 1897, does not seem to have appreciated the full importance of the issue. Aside from Mr. Roosevelt, Commodore Dewey, and a few of the Senate's more earnest students of foreign affairs, there were very few who did. The Commodore plunged at once into a study of 'all the charts and descriptions of the Philippine Islands that I could procure, and put aside many books about the Far East to read in the course of my journey across the continent and the Pacific.' He was shocked to discover that the Navy Department possessed no information about the Philippines of a date later than 1876, and he was still more shocked when he learned that the Asiatic Squadron was without even its

JOHN D. LONG

Secretary of the Navy

RUSSELL A. ALGER

Secretary of War

full peace-time ammunition allowance. And when he finally arrived at Nagasaki to assume his command, he found that it had never even occurred to his predecessor that intervention in Cuba might require a descent upon the ancient and helpless war-vessels at Manila. But Commodore Dewey (and Mr. Roosevelt) soon changed all that. Thus were we committed, by a lesser official at the Navy Department, to a course of action which was never contemplated by the American people and which was to have the most far-reaching and most dubious results.

But such moves as these were, of course, kept secret, and besides, they were purely 'precautionary.' In the diplomatic sphere the situation was if anything improving. Responsibility had served very greatly to modify Sr. Sagasta's views of the Cuban problem, but he was committed to autonomy and the conciliatory method and these were what Mr. McKinley was demanding. His note of October 23 (this was two days after Dewey's orders to the Far East) amounted to a complete acceptance of our position. It began by announcing a 'total change of immense scope' in the Spanish policy toward Cuba. It gave a solemn pledge that a measure of autonomy would at once be initiated, affording the Cubans full powers of self-government under the Spanish connection, and reserving only 'foreign relations, the army, the navy, and the administration of justice' as subjects involving the national interest. In support of such a régime the Government would endeavor to assemble 'all the prominent men [of Cuba] without distinction of origin or conduct, in order to oppose them to those professional agitators, by nature and habit, who subsist only by strife and have no other object than rapine, destruction, and disorder.' Against the latter, it is true, 'military severity' was still to be used, but it was to be meted out, not by the hated Weyler, but by his successor, a Liberal general who bore the disarming name of Blanco.

Sr. Sagasta, however, went on to remind the United States Government of its own responsibility:

It is very important that it should take all necessary measures, with determination and persistency proportionate to the vast means at its disposal, to prevent the territory of the Union from constituting the center in which the plots for the support of the Cuban insurrection are contrived. He who is not disposed to grant the means does not earnestly desire the end in view; and in this case the end, to wit, peace, will be attained by the United States exerting itself energetically.

Should the President lack authority in law for such action, Sr. Sagasta reminded him (a trifle tactlessly, perhaps) that the United States had itself declared that 'no nation may, under pretext of inadequate laws, fail in the fulfillment of its duties of sovereignty toward another sovereign nation.' It is difficult to deny the justice of this position, for it touched what was from the beginning the heart of the whole problem. Yet, even had the President wished to adopt the Spanish view of our obligations, he could not have done so; a much stronger man than Mr. McKinley would have found it politically impossible.

On the other hand, the patriots and the American press instantly devoted themselves to proving that the autonomy measures, which we had demanded, were perfectly useless. 'The insurgents,' Consul-General Lee reported, 'will not accept autonomy'; the Spanish property-owners would 'prefer annexation to the United States.' On October 31, Captain-General Blanco arrived in Cuba; on November 13, a decree was published designed to mitigate so far as was possible the worst features of the reconcentration system, and on November 25, the Queen Regent signed the decrees establishing an autonomist government in Cuba. It merely elicited our scorn. 'Nothing could be more futile,' the *Review of Reviews* declared, than 'the palliative of autonomy.' The Spanish cause 'is almost absolutely hopeless.' And as long as the American people thought so, no doubt it was. The chief result of the new policy was somewhat to facilitate the insurgents in their task of reducing the island to a state of affairs so atrocious as to bring about intervention. With the departure of Weyler, the Spanish military campaign had, of course, collapsed; while the food problem for Cuba's miserable and harassed population had by this time got entirely out of hand.

It was at once apparent that a mere revocation of the reconcentration decrees was totally inadequate to meeting this last trouble. To dispassionate observers it might have suggested that reconcentration was at most only one of the causes of the disaster, but from their reports it is impossible to feel that our consuls were dispassionate. Thus Mr. Brice at Matanzas had written in the middle of October that if the reconcentrados were allowed to go out into the country, 'in less than sixty days all will be well and starvation a thing of the past.' Now, just a month later, he reported that the order permitting this was useless. 'If they went, what can they do without money, food, or shelter? Only those who can obtain employment on sugar plantations can live. Insurgents say no one will be allowed to grind in province of Matanzas.' Whatever the Spaniards did they were still to blame; the insurgents' part in the matter was overlooked in the United States even when the consuls mentioned it. In some of the cities the death-rates were by this time mounting to appalling heights, and Mr. Sherman was demanding from Spain the 'instant abandonment of policy of depopulation and devastation that has so shocked the sense of this Government.' But the Spaniards, poor men, did the best they could; and in Madrid, at any rate, our Minister was assuring them that he would advise that the United States 'refrain from interference in Cuba for a reasonable time.'

Then, on December 6, the regular session of Congress opened, and Mr. McKinley in his annual message gave to the world his formal answer to Sr. Sagasta. But even so, Mr. McKinley's amiable intelligence was by no means the only one engaged in shaping destiny. As his message was being read, orders were going out from the Navy Department directing the U.S.S. Maine to proceed to Key West. The battleship was moved another step on the road to Havana, and fate moved with her.

IV

Responding to the currents of opinion now running so strongly in the United States, President McKinley's message discussed our 'duty toward Spain and the Cuban insurrection' in those accents of pained severity with which one generally does one's duty by errant neighbors. The reconcentration policy, he categorically declared, 'was not civilized warfare. It was extermination.' Of the possible courses of action now open to us, he frankly enumerated recognition of belligerency, recognition of Cuban independence, 'neutral' intervention to impose 'a rational compromise between the contestants,' and intervention avowedly in favor of one or the other parties. But one alternative he refused even to consider. 'I speak not of forcible annexation,' Mr. McKinley nobly declared, 'for that cannot be thought of. That by our code of morality would be criminal aggression.'

Recognition either of belligerency or of independence the President discussed at length and definitely rejected. 'Intervention upon humanitarian grounds,' he went on, 'has... not failed to receive my most anxious and earnest consideration.' But in face of the sweeping changes of policy effected by the Sagasta Government, the President rejected intervention likewise. Spain would be given 'a reasonable chance' to end the war — upon these new lines which we ourselves had urged. We stayed our hands.

But we did not do so without first publicly washing them of any responsibility for the 'new order of things' which we had done so much to bring about:

The near future will demonstrate whether the indispensable condition of a righteous peace, just alike to the Cubans and to Spain as well as equitable to all our interests... is likely to be attained. If not, the exigency of further and other action by the United States will remain to be taken.... If it shall hereafter appear to be a duty imposed by our obligations to ourselves, to civilization, and humanity to intervene with force, it shall be without fault on our part and only because the necessity for such action will be so clear as to command the support and approval of the civilized world.

Having called the tune, we not only refused to pay the piper, but formally dissociated ourselves from the consequences. President McKinley's intention, no doubt, was to keep his passionate Congressmen under control by making a show of brusqueness toward Spain. If so, it merely illustrates the difficulties inherent in the method which he had hit upon for avoiding war. For if our sense of obligation 'to ourselves, to civilization, and humanity' was not strong enough to compel us to withdraw our support from the rebels, it was extremely improbable that intervention could be avoided. President McKinley may have had the best of intentions. But he did not have the Cleveland touch.

In Cuba the possibility of a righteous peace by this time seemed pretty remote. Consul Hyatt reported from Santiago that the reconcentration system 'is now practically wiped out.... The insurgents and their sympathizers will unquestionably take advantage of the revocation to get from towns and cities what they need, and otherwise strengthen their cause.' Elsewhere the famine problem deepened; the Spanish authorities put forth strenuous efforts to meet it with appropriations and food distribution, but the consuls were soon scornfully reporting the inadequacy of such measures. 'The condition of these people,' Consul-General Lee tersely announced, 'is simply terrible.' The insurgents meanwhile were doing what they could to make it more so; while their generals pleasantly declared that any one even suggesting the acceptance of autonomy would be shot as a traitor to the Republic. General Blanco sent out emissaries to negotiate with them; and at least one of these, the unhappy Colonel Ruiz, learned that they meant what they had said. The Christmas season approached in a gloom which was hardly lightened even by our State Department's suggestion that Miss Clara Barton and her Red Cross be utilized for the relief of the starving. What was the use? On the night of December 20, Mr. Atkins's overseers watched 200,000 arrobas of their cane go up in smoke. A proclamation came with the fires: 'Fire, destruction!! Long live Free Cuba! Country and Liberty!'

In the face of almost universal apathy or opposition Captain-General Blanco pushed forward the organization of the autonomist government. Mr. Woodford at Madrid gave his assurance that we would maintain an attitude of 'benevolent expectancy,' but we made no move to help; while Mr. Lee at Havana was already far beyond either expectation or benevolence. On December 13, he made emphatic report: 'In my opinion there is no possibility of Spain terminating the war here.' That, at least, was definite enough, and seemed to spell the end. But now suddenly a new factor was at last to come into play.

Officially we had washed our hands of the matter. Yet, as President McKinley surveyed these disastrous consequences of his statesmanship, it seems to have dawned upon him that a practical situation had arisen which was intolerable. Despite the impeccable correctness of our diplomacy, the fact was that the population of the island was actually starving to death. It led him — under a genuinely humane impulse in strong contrast to the official nobility of his notes and messages — to sweep the whole solemn ritual of diplomacy aside with a move as unexpected as it was original. As an emergency measure President McKinley suddenly asked for and received the assent of the Spanish Government to official action by the Government of the United States in relief of the Cuban people. On December 24, the Secretary of State issued a formal proclamation announcing that contributions of food, money, and clothing might be sent to our consul-general at Havana, to be distributed, in coöperation with the local boards and authorities, through our consular service to the starving populace. The public response was immediate and generous, and as the relief began to flow in, the United States had at last assumed a direct share in the Cuban problem.

It was intervention, but it was a kindly one, quite irrelevant to the formal negotiations being conducted at Madrid. The sincerity of the emotion behind it is attested by the fact that Mr. McKinley's personal contribution of five thousand dollars to the relief fund was made anonymously and only came to light after his death. And it went far to supply the one element which was lacking to a real settlement of the Cuban question. Once we were associated in it, our attitude must have undergone a change. It is with difficulty that one retains one's enthusiasm for the objects of an expensive charity; and, indeed, the American people by this time were already giving signs of being just a trifle tired of the heroic Cubans. There was a nascent realization that the patriots were after all rather a mixed lot, and the shooting of Colonel Ruiz and the continued destruction of property were creating an unfavorable reaction. We could not have become involved in a large-scale relief undertaking without acquiring a more accurate idea of the real causes of Cuban misery, while the pouring of great quantities of supplies into the island would obviously have nullified Máximo Gómez's main strategic principle. In this generous act of Mr. McKinley's there was at last hope that the Cuban insurrection might be brought peaceably to an end. But accident, and Consul-General Lee, were to determine otherwise.

Mr. Lee, unfortunately, had once more become solicitous for the safety of American life and property. Early in December the Consul-General was reporting rumors of 'an extensive and dangerous' anti-American conspiracy in Matanzas, and urging that a strong naval force be concentrated off the Florida keys ready 'to move here at short notice.' The orders to the Maine had followed closely upon this recommendation, and on December 15 she had arrived at Key West, under confidential instructions to proceed at once to Havana in the event of local disturbances which might threaten American safety.

Recklessly enough, the decision as to when this hour might have arrived was left to our choleric Consul-General himself. Captain Sigsbee, the commander of the Maine, was in effect placed under Mr. Lee's orders, and though the conspiracy in Matanzas quite failed to materialize, Mr. Lee did not allow that to dull his 'prudence and foresight.' It was arranged, in the best tradition of such desperate enterprises, that upon the receipt of the code message 'Two dollars' Captain Sigsbee would prepare for instant departure, and would actually sail upon a second prearranged message. Thus, at a time when the whole policy of Mr. McKinley and his administration was still officially directed toward peace, a machine of the most incendiary character had been prepared, ready to be sprung at a touch of the finger by a minor diplomatic official who had given ample evidence of a bellicose temperament.

In the meantime Congress, like a gathering cloud, returned from the Christmas recess. The Democrats, since they were now in opposition, were of course eager to contribute to Mr. McKinley's embarrassments by proclaiming the wrongs of Cuba and the spinelessness of the official policy. But the Republicans were showing themselves increasingly reluctant to discuss the Cuban problem, and the situation was daily improving. And so it might have continued. The consular reports continued to make very dreadful reading, and Mr. Barker at Sagua la Grande was even proposing to solve the whole affair by the simple, if drastic, expedient of admitting the Cuban populace *en masse* to American citizenship. But General Blanco had managed to erect at least the framework of an autonomist government and Cuba was fading undeniably from the front pages. So it might have continued. But then, on January 12, that 'local disturbance' which Mr. Lee had so long been anticipating — or something, at any rate, that might be made to look like it — unhappily took place.

According to Mr. Atkins the fateful Havana riot was 'simply an attack on newspaper offices by some Spanish army officers in revenge for some articles reflecting upon the conduct of the army. Sparks, who witnessed the whole thing, said the rioters were unarmed.... It was over in an hour or so.' Our conservative papers gave it a few sticks only on their inside pages, and Mr. Atkins, who was in Havana the next day, found that there had been no demonstrations against Americans. To the prudent mind of Mr. Lee, however, it was a most alarming manifestation, and he announced it to the State Department in a brief and startling cable:

Mobs, led by Spanish officers, attacked today the offices of the four newspapers here advocating autonomy. Rioting at this hour, 1 P.M., continues.

Washington was left for some hours in an exciting suspense, which could hardly have been diminished when Mr. Lee, after strolling about the city without molestation, sent off a second despatch in the evening:

Much excitement, which may develop into serious disturbances.... No rioting at present, but rumors of it are abundant. Palace heavily guarded. Consulate also protected by armed men.

And Captain Sigsbee, sixty miles away, was reading another message. 'Two dollars,' it said; but there was no further word. Next morning the city was again quiet, and the Consul-General was observed going about his normal business. But his telegrams, though still a trifle vague as to precisely what had happened, continued upon an alarming note:

Heard once yesterday of a few rioters shouting a proposal to march to our consulate. Presence of ships may be necessary later, but not now.

And on the same day:

Uncertainty exists whether Blanco can control situation. If demonstrated he cannot maintain order, preserve life, and keep the peace, or if Americans and their interests are in danger, ships must be sent, and to that end should be prepared to move promptly. Excitement and uncertainty predominate everywhere.

This was singularly ambiguous. The Department anxiously

wired to be kept advised. On January 14, the Consul-General was forced to report 'all quiet' and he repeated this on succeeding days, but without any elaboration to counterbalance his first alarming despatches. Washington hesitated. In the United States the incident had abruptly reawakened attention; the sensational press had been running 'war extras' and Dupuy de Lôme gave way to foreboding. Badly informed as to the real state of affairs in Havana, the Administration seems to have fallen victim to conflicting emotions. To send the Maine would be provocative; yet if Americans should be attacked and the Maine were not there to protect them, a charge of negligence could be raised with deadly effect. It was not until ten days later that inspiration came — in the best style of Mr. McKinley's peculiar method. The Maine was finally ordered to Havana, but under the disarming fiction that it was as a friendly act of courtesy demonstrating, not that our citizens were in danger, but that any rumors of trouble were so completely unfounded that the ordinary visits of American naval vessels might now be resumed!

The orders were issued on January 24, and Mr. Lee was telegraphically advised to 'arrange for a friendly interchange of calls with authorities.' Mr. Lee appears now to have had some qualms, for a naval visit on these ingenuous terms was a large order. He immediately replied, urging that the visit be postponed for 'six or seven days to give last excitement more time to disappear.' The answer was that the Maine had already been ordered and that the Consul-General might expect her upon the following morning.

The Spaniards, perverse men, somehow failed to appreciate the disinterested friendship of the move. Sr. Dupuy de Lôme (if Senator Lodge can be believed) even reached the point of unofficially threatening war, but being informed 'quietly and decidedly by Mr. Day that the ship was going in any event, he quieted down.' When the American people decided to be friendly they were going to be friendly, and would stand no nonsense about it. The Spanish Foreign Minister writhed, but the best he could do was to announce that, since visits of courtesy had been resumed, the armored cruiser Vizcaya would shortly call at New York. The State Department gravely assured him that it appreciated the politeness. In the meanwhile, the Maine, at eleven o'clock on the morning of January 25, entered the harbor of Havana; and as she passed in under the batteries of the Morro, Mr. Lee tensely reported: 'No demonstration so far.'

The State Department may have been convinced of the correctness of its courtesy, but the Consul-General was evidently having a whole international crisis all by himself. Throughout the day he sent off almost hourly reports, describing Captain Sigsbee's progress through every step in the routine of official etiquette, and confirming in each message the absence of any demonstration. It was not until the final despatch that the truth appeared to sink home: there was to be no demonstration. 'Peace and quiet reign,' Mr. Lee finally cabled, and went to bed. Nor, throughout the remainder of the Maine's visit was anything to occur to ruffle the placidity of the situation. The Consul-General had underrated Spanish courtesy — or Spanish caution.

v

It is true that a section of the Havanese and of the army were less than cordial, but the Spanish officers were correctness itself, while Captain Sigsbee was nothing short of perfect. The Maine swung to her moorings, and though her commander, obeying instructions, was careful to post extra sentries at night and to take extraordinary precautions, peace and quiet continued to reign profoundly. Captain Sigsbee and his officers moved freely and without molestation ashore. They even brought themselves to attend a bull-fight, notwithstanding the immoral fact that 'the day of its celebration was Sunday'; while there was a note of distinct cordiality in their relations with the Acting Captain-General. He visited the Maine (General Blanco himself being absent at the time) and expressed his 'admiration for the splendid battleship.' He even sent a 'case of fine sherry' to the ship's officers; the gift was gracefully reciprocated by Captain Sigsbee with a copy of his work on 'Deep Sea Sounding and Dredging.' Nowhere, somehow, did either American life or property appear to be in the slightest danger.

Nevertheless, the Consul-General justified himself with the reflection that if another riot should occur, perhaps this time it might really be anti-American as well as anti-autonomist; and when the Secretary of the Navy, fearing tropical disease, seemed desirous of recalling the Maine early in February, Mr. Lee hastened to advise that 'ship or ships should be kept here all the time now. We should not relinquish position of peaceful control of situation.' Naturally, the fact that we had thus neatly contrived to secure it caused intense irritation to the Spaniards; and it was with a distinct and rather gloomy annoyance that Sr. Sagasta set himself to preparing still another note. But that was really only playing for time. The Spanish Ministry was privately fearful lest the Maine's presence at Havana might lead, 'through some accident or other, to a conflict'; barring that, however, if they were only given time they might pull through in the end. Mr. McKinley, they understood, did not really want a war, and conditions now were favorable enough.

How favorable they were may be guessed from the fact that the patriots, doubtless realizing how nearly their cause was lost, chose this moment to spring the most dramatic success of their long campaign of propaganda. For three years Enrique Dupuy de Lôme had stood, a delicate tower of strength, as the greatest single obstacle between the patriots and their goal. He was the most skillful, the most patient, and the most indefatigable of their enemies, and in spite of occasional mistakes he had been by far the most effective. He had served both Cánovas and Sagasta with an equal loyalty; under each he had been tireless in tracking down the filibusters, in neutralizing the patriot press bureaus, and in advancing through the treacherous atmospheres of official Washington the interests of his Queen and country. It was against him that the Cuban sympathizers now launched a deadly attack.

The blow fell on February 8, with an appalling suddenness. Dupuy de Lôme was informed that a personal letter of his own, written some months before to a friend in Cuba, had fallen into the hands of the junta and was about to be given to the newspapers. Apparently he could not recall exactly what he had written, but he remembered that he had spoken of Mr. McKinley and of Spanish-American relations in terms which made his continuance as Minister impossible. It was a catastrophe, but Dupuy de Lôme lost neither his presence of mind nor his loyalty to his sovereign. He sat down the same evening and cabled home his request to be relieved from his post.

On the following morning Mr. Hearst's *Journal* printed a facsimile of the Minister's letter, and every paper in the country ran the damning translation. Written in the preceding December, it had contained among other things Dupuy de Lôme's private estimate of the President's annual message:

Besides the ingrained and inevitable coarseness with which it repeated all that the Press and public opinion in Spain have said about Weyler, it once more shows what McKinley is, weak and a bidder for the admiration of the crowd, besides being a common politician who tries to leave a door open behind himself while keeping on good terms with the jingoes of his party.

The accuracy of this characterization could, of course, only deepen the crime of *lèse majesté* which it revealed; it was evident that no foreigner who could even think in such terms of an American President was entitled to a moment's consideration. Nor was this all. The Minister had allowed himself to speak of 'the newspaper rabble that swarms in your hotels,' and had concluded:

It would be very advantageous to take up, even if only for effect, the question of commercial relations, and to have a man of some prominence sent here in order that I may make use of him to carry on a propaganda among the Senators and others in opposition to the junta.

It is true that this was an entirely private letter, that it had been dishonestly abstracted from the Havana post-office by an insurgent spy, and that it had been deliberately held for use at a time when it would produce the greatest effect. Under the circumstances, Dupuy de Lôme's impiety toward our great and good President, though clearly ending his usefulness as a diplomat, could scarcely be made a charge against Spain. But the second passage seemed to indicate that the negotiations then in progress over a commercial treaty had been undertaken in bad faith; while the very thought of prosecuting a lobby among the Senators (an activity at which the junta had been tireless) was a blow directed at the very arcanum of the Constitution itself.

The sensation was instantaneous, and it was profound. The letter, as Senator Lodge said afterward, 'revealed the utter hollowness of all the Spanish professions.' Cuba and the perfidy of

Spain at once leapt back into the mind of every newspaper reader; the State Department really could scarcely believe its eyes, but that afternoon the original letter itself was placed in Mr. Sherman's hands. When Mr. Day laid the terrible evidence before the Spanish Minister, the latter at once admitted his authorship, for there was a certain greatness in Dupuy de Lôme's defeat. The State Department immediately cabled Mr. Woodford to demand his recall, and we eagerly prepared to force another public and bitter humiliation upon the harassed Government of Sr. Sagasta. But here the astuteness of the Minister's own telegram of the night before appeared. Sr. Dupuy de Lôme was able to inform Mr. Day that he had already cabled his resignation (to make sure he had cabled a second time on the morning of the 9th), and before our demand could be presented in Madrid by Mr. Woodford, the latter was informed that Dupuy de Lôme had been relieved of his mission and that the Washington Legation was already in the hands of a *chargé d'affaires.*

It took all the sting out. A disappointed State Department was balked of its prey, and one finds an obvious note of irritation in the subsequent correspondence, as we endeavored to fasten as much responsibility for the Minister's words as possible upon his Government and to exact the maximum of official apology. The war party shrieked for blood and the patriots did their best to cash in upon their triumph by forcing a major crisis. But the prompt resignation sufficed to keep the affair in the safe realms of correspondence, and it was evident in a day or two that the immediate danger had passed. Perhaps the triumph was Dupuy de Lôme's after all.

Indeed, the very fact that relations had managed to survive the strain served to improve rather than worsen the situation. The Navy, to be sure, did not lessen its secret preparations, and far away at Yokohama Commodore Dewey, having at last received his ammunition, was getting under way for Hong Kong — a long step on the road to Manila. This, however, was entirely upon the Commodore's own prophetic initiative, since he had received no 'hint whatsoever from the Department that hostilities might be expected.' For the tension was slackening. The insurgents, as they continued to demonstrate their right to liberty by burning American cane fields and dynamiting railroad trains, were making a less and less favorable impression. The 'de Lôme incident,' one editor declared, 'must not be permitted to drag us into war.' 'No peril,' another added, 'confronts our peace.... The incident is closed.' While a third justly remarked that 'if the insurgents were not entitled to recognition yesterday, an insult to the President of the United States, by whomsoever offered, does not entitle them to it today.' The Cuban problem was not solved, but Washington still seemed content to let matters rest.

By February 15, the situation was more or less back to normal. As Captain Sigsbee sat writing in his cabin that evening, it must have seemed to him that a war with Spain was an increasingly remote contingency. The Maine had lain for three weeks in the Cuban port; in obedience to his orders her captain was still taking every precaution, but nothing whatever had occurred even to suggest that precaution was necessary. The autonomist government — more or less what we had been insisting upon for so long — had at last been established and was functioning as well as the difficult circumstances would permit. The food crisis was shocking; Captain Sigsbee had himself heard the most frightful stories from both sides and had duly reported them, but American supplies were arriving in greater and greater abundance, and no one could doubt the sincerity and good intentions of the Spanish authorities. Nor could there be much doubt that if the food problem were met, the back of the insurrection would be broken. Captain Sigsbee had acquired an admiration for General Blanco 'as a man and as a patriot'; he had learned also that there was a good deal to be said for the Spaniards' side. Captain Sigsbee completed his report. It had nothing to do with international relations, but was an essay requested by Mr. Roosevelt on the advisability of fitting torpedo tubes in the new battleships.

It was an absolutely still evening, overcast, and excessively hot and sultry. A profound quiet reigned over the vessel, disturbed only by the gentle drone of the dynamo engines somewhere below. A couple of the officers were smoking in the deck space under the after turret. To escape the heat the Captain changed into an alpaca coat, seated himself at the table once more, and commenced a letter to his wife. In Madrid at the same instant the last talkers were drifting homeward from the cafés, and the worried servants of the Queen Regent and her boy King were going to their cool bedrooms. It is true that on the opposite side of the world Commodore Dewey was holding ominously southward through a bright morning in the China Sea; but in Washington the dinner-parties were well advanced and no one was in the mood for international politics. In New York the morning newspapers were preparing to lock up for their early runs; even Mr. Hearst's and Mr. Pulitzer's bright young men had nothing in particular on Cuba, and night editors were considering burying it in the inside pages. In the office of the *Tribune* the editorial page — that powerful voice of administration opinion — was doubtless on its way to the stereotypers. It carried a strongly pacific editorial on 'The Spanish Settlement.' 'Each day's news,' the *Tribune* would say next morning, 'brings fresh despair to those perfervent souls who think diplomacy between great nations is best to be conducted by vigorous "hollering" in town meeting....' On the Maine the first notes of Taps sounded from forward; the bugler was evidently doing his best, and Captain Sigsbee in the cabin laid down his pen to listen to the long, slow melody, sounding 'singularly beautiful in the oppressive stillness of the night.' The call came back perfectly upon the echo and died away; in the absolute peace of the moment it might have seemed to be announcing the end of all the alarms and wrangles of the past three years.

Captain Sigsbee turned back to his letter, and wrote on for perhaps another twenty minutes. He signed it, wrote his wife's name upon the envelope, and was in the act of sealing it...

CHAPTER V

THE DESTRUCTION OF THE MAINE

I

AT two o'clock on the following morning the Secretary of the Navy, Mr. John D. Long, was aroused at his home in Washington by a knock upon his door. He rubbed his eyes awake; a telegram was handed him — and in the cold, uncanny silences of early morning the Secretary suddenly found himself reading this astounding and incredible message:

Secretary of the Navy, Washington, D.C.:

Maine blown up in Havana Harbor at nine-forty tonight and destroyed. Many wounded and doubtless more killed or drowned. Wounded and others on board Spanish man-of-war and Ward Line steamer. Send lighthouse tenders from Key West for crew and the few pieces of equipment above water. No one has clothing other than that upon him. Public opinion should be suspended until further report. All officers believed to be saved. Jenkins and Merritt not yet accounted for. Many Spanish officers, including representatives of General Blanco, now with me to express sympathy.

SIGSBEE

One can picture Mr. Long's stunned astonishment as his mind took in the full import of those words. The Maine had been destroyed! It was difficult to credit his own eyes, but there was the message before him. After these years of waiting, of talk, of preparation, something, of the most momentous character possible, at last had happened. Mr. Long moved to action.

A few minutes later, a telephone bell was ringing in the stillnesses of the White House. The watchman on duty answered it and was told to awaken the President at once; it was the Secretary of the Navy. Mr. McKinley in his turn was aroused and brought to the instrument. Years afterward the watchman remembered the great man pacing the floor in the first shock of that unbelievable news, murmuring, as if he could not grasp it, 'The Maine blown up! The Maine blown up!'

At almost the same time Consul-General Lee's telegram had

THE MAINE PASSING MORRO CASTLE AS SHE ENTERED THE HARBOR OF HAVANA

reached the State Department. Already the first bulletins had dropped like bombs into the newspaper offices. Frantic wires had shocked the Washington correspondents into activity. Mr. Long had hardly taken in the first message before 'the bright representatives of the press,' as he called them, were besieging his house, and that of every other official in the city who might have news, guesses, or comment. Within the hour the press telegrams from Havana, from Washington, from Madrid, were pouring across the desks in hundreds of newspaper offices, while night editors tore the hearts out of their front pages and the triple-leaded type that was to electrify the nation shot sizzling from the linotypes. No one, of course, knew exactly what had happened or how; but the greatest of all the great sensations of the Cuban question had come, and it meant — it could only mean — war. In another hour the presses were turning; the newsboys were spreading the glaring headlines up and down the nation, and the American people were awakening in that cold February morning to the knowledge that the U.S.S. Maine had been blown up and destroyed in the harbor of Havana, whither she had been sent upon a mission of 'friendly courtesy.' 'It means war,' they told each other in hushed voices, 'war — war at last.'

No one knew how it had happened, nor has it ever been learned. Captain Sigsbee was in the act of sealing the letter to his wife when a dull roar and shock suddenly struck him; the lights vanished instantaneously; there was a confused darkness filled with the crash of falling fragments, screams of wounded men, and the rush of water underfoot, and the Captain knew at once that his ship had been blown up under him. He groped his way out of the cabin as rapidly as possible; in the passageway he ran into the Marine guard, dutifully coming to inform him that the ship had been wrecked. Together the two men reached the poop. Most of the officers and some of the crew were already collecting there, as it was the highest spot aft, and the ship was sinking fast. Forward they could make out only an enormous mass of tangled wreckage, the flames from burning woodwork already beginning to play over it, and some small-caliber ammunition which had been kept in the superstructure fitfully exploding. An officer was sent to put out the fire; he could, of course, do nothing amid the impassable ruin which he encountered, and he soon returned. It was already realized that the forward magazines must have gone up, and that most of the crew, whose quarters were forward and who had been turned in a half-hour before, had probably perished in their hammocks. However, there were people in the water; a quarter-boat was still hanging uninjured from the poop davits and Captain Sigsbee had it put overside, manned by some of the officers, to row about the wreck and pick up whoever could be found.

By this time boats from other vessels were already arriving. Those from the Spanish cruiser Alfonso XII, moored at the next buoy, were among the first on the scene, and assisted gallantly in the rescue in spite of the real danger from the exploding ammunition. Others from the Ward Line steamer City of Washington arrived at about the same time, and most of the survivors were picked up by these two vessels. Captain Sigsbee perceived that there was nothing more to be done and gave the order to abandon ship; the Maine settled gently to the harbor bottom, and as she came to rest with her poop deck just awash, the Captain, the last man remaining, stepped off into a boat. He was taken to the City of Washington.

Ashore, the whole of Havana had been shaken by the explosion. Consul-General Lee looked up with the sound, just in time to see 'a great column of fire go up into the air.' Mr. Lee, a portly man, got himself at once into a cab, and driving to the waterfront stopped at the Captain-General's palace on the way. In the reception room General Blanco 'came in directly by himself. He had just heard it and was crying; tears were coming out of his eyes. He seemed to regret it as much as anybody I saw in Havana.' Mr. Lee hurried on; and the Captain-General, left to his complex emotions, did what he could to meet this staggering calamity by despatching a high ranking officer as his personal representative.

The waterfront was, of course, crowded with excited people, but Mr. Lee thrust his way through them, secured a boat, and was taken off to the City of Washington. The dining-saloon was filled with wounded men laid out on mattresses, while on deck a group of strained and excited men — Spanish officers, members of the autonomist government, Cuban sympathizers, and a swarm of

American newspaper correspondents — was already collecting. In the privacy of the captain's cabin, Captain Sigsbee was composing his telegram to the Secretary of the Navy; and even as he wrote he was already finding it necessary 'to repress my own suspicions' that the disaster had been caused by foul play on the part of the Spaniards.

Captain Sigsbee was a painstaking and honorable officer and he had a vivid sense of the international importance of anything which he might do. Amid the shock and strain of these moments he remembered that, although he might repress his own suspicions, it was unlikely that his bellicose countrymen would repress theirs, and he was careful to insert his famous sentence: 'Public opinion should be suspended until further report.' The despatch was given to a newspaper correspondent to take ashore and it was not thought improper, in those golden days of reporting, when this gentleman, after sending the original to Washington, cabled a copy to his paper in New York. It appeared next morning, simultaneously with the first news of the disaster. Having got off this message, and another to Key West asking for lighthouse tenders and urging that no war-vessels be sent if ships of any other type were available, Captain Sigsbee finally lay down in the hope of getting some rest. It was about two in the morning, just as the news was reaching Washington. The fire had not yet burned out upon the wreck of the Maine.

Next day it was possible to check the full extent of the catastrophe. The Maine herself was beyond all hope of salvage. She had settled during the night into the mud of the harbor bottom, and nothing was now visible above water except the mainmast and the pile of tangled steelwork heaped above the bridge deck. Of the 350 men and officers on board at the moment of the explosion, 252 had been killed or drowned and eight others were mortally hurt. Jenkins and Merritt, unhappily, were no longer unaccounted for; they had been trapped below and drowned in the sinking hull. Owing to the fact of the explosion having taken place forward, the remaining officers were untouched, but of the crew it was found that only sixteen had escaped wholly without injury. During the night and morning the wounded, who had been taken to the Alfonso XII and City of Washington, were sent ashore, and all were finally collected in the two main hospitals of Havana. Their reception and treatment, Captain Sigsbee found, 'was most considerate and humane.' The Spaniards did for them 'all they habitually did for their own people and even more.'

The entire city dressed itself in a mourning which appeared to be as sincere as it was profound. On official and private buildings and on the shipping in the harbor the flags were half-masted; the theaters were closed and even the shops suspended business, while delegations from every kind of organization and authority tendered their expressions of official sorrow. By afternoon Captain Sigsbee had established himself at the Inglaterra Hotel, and there Captain-General Blanco waited upon him in person with offers of sympathy and assistance. In one of the hospitals Captain Sigsbee even found that a placard had been affixed by the door leading to the ward where the Maine wounded were lying, demanding that all who entered the room should remove their hats as a mark of respect.

On the 17th, the second day following the disaster, the military, civil, and ecclesiastical authorities of the city gave a great state funeral to the dead, conducted with every extraordinary mark of honor which could suggest itself, and with all those impressive splendors of which the Roman Catholic Church alone is capable. There was, it is true, a slight difficulty between Captain Sigsbee and the Bishop of Havana over the propriety of applying this ritual to Protestant dead. The Bishop, however, felt himself unable to yield, so the Captain read over the Episcopal burial service to himself in his hotel bedroom and in the carriage on the way to the cemetery, and hoped that it would be all right. Unfortunately, they were in a tropical climate and the matter did not admit of postponement.

So the long procession wound its way out to the beautiful Colón Cemetery; the last rites were performed; the coffins were lowered (into a plot of ground which the authorities had hastened to dedicate in perpetuity to the United States); the echoes of the volley died away; and the destruction of one of the prides of the new American Navy, with 260 of its men, was an accomplished fact. The thing had happened.

II

For with the destruction of the Maine the match had at last been applied. During the whole of the preceding three years the fateful powder-train had been laid — the grains, compounded of our new nationalistic pride, of our restlessness, of our self-confidence, our aggressiveness, and our celebrated humanitarianism, had been slowly heaped together. Whether consciously or unconsciously they had one by one been assembled, by the patriots and the politicians, by personal ambition and partisan rivalries, by the gentlemen who had talked war on Capitol Hill because it was politic and the gentlemen who had printed inflammatory sensations because they were lucrative, by Mr. Lodge who believed in statesmanship and by Mr. Roosevelt who believed in preparedness, and by Mr. McKinley who believed in peace, but who had no more courageous method for getting it than to threaten war. Many hands had assisted in one degree or another — the Democrats and Populists who wanted a silver standard, the gold Republicans who wanted a diversion, the idealists, the intriguers, the people who knew better and the people who ought to have. Perhaps none of them really desired a war, but between them all they had carefully prepared the train which could lead nowhere save to war. And now, as the flash suddenly leapt forth to run swiftly down the weeks into the explosion that by this time, perhaps, really was 'inevitable,' many of those who had done their part to make it so paused in a sudden and horrified astonishment.

On the evening of the 16th — it was the night after the disaster — Senator Fairbanks was summoned to the White House. He had 'never before seen the President in so serious a mood nor so careworn in appearance.' Mr. McKinley was already appalled at the probable consequences of a national bellicosity which his policy had omitted to discourage. Throughout the day the Administration had been laboring to mitigate the results of the catastrophe; at the Navy Department, Secretary Long, the Chief of Ordnance, and other high officers had been telling reporters that the explosion must have been purely accidental, and word had been sent out from the White House itself that there were no grounds for suspecting a plot of any kind. Fortunately, Congress for once decided that no action on its part was called for; while the New York *Tribune* prepared to dampen the war fever with the peculiarly futile argument that the horrors of battle would be even worse than the horror of the Maine. It was of no use. Mr. Hearst's inventive geniuses had not only discovered that the Spaniards had blown up the Maine; they were already preparing drawings showing exactly how the torpedo had been placed beneath the vessel and detonated from shore. 'The War Ship Maine Was Split in Two by an Enemy's Secret Infernal Machine' the *Journal* shrieked in a two-line, eight-column head; and its diagrams appeared so soon after the event that Captain Sigsbee took them as proof that there must have been a plot, since the *Journal* evidently had prior knowledge of it. The day passed in the wildest possible excitement, and the rumors mounted to such heights that by the evening of the 17th the Associated Press was finding it necessary to send out a blanket denial from its Washington bureau:

The cruiser New York has not been ordered to Havana; Consul-General Lee has not been assassinated; there is no conference of the Cabinet; Congress is not in session tonight, both Houses having adjourned at the usual hour until tomorrow; President McKinley did not go to the Capitol, and the situation is decidedly quiet.

It was all of no use. Mr. Pulitzer despatched a tug to Havana to learn the 'truth'; Mr. Hearst offered a $50,000 reward for evidence; the circulations of both leapt into the skies, and by the 18th the *Journal* had passed the million mark. The State Department attempted·rather feebly to stem the deluge by announcing that Spain had disavowed the de Lôme letter and that the incident was 'closed'; but a citizenry which had forgotten the de Lôme letter was already volunteering its services for war. The circumstance that there was no authority empowered to accept them did not lessen the ardor, and in New York a somewhat singular unit, described as 'five hundred sharpshooters made up of Westchester business men,' volunteered *en masse*. And then, at the very highest pitch of the excitement, the Spanish cruiser Vizcaya, which had been ordered to return the Maine's visit of courtesy, arrived at New York and came to anchor off Tompkinsville. With a righteous, but painfully pointed, ostentation she was immediately surrounded by a whole flotilla of guardships, adequate to protect her from every conceivable injury. A special guard was even mounted over Mr. Holland's 'submarine torpedo boat,' a curious device which had been undergoing trials in the harbor.

A naval court of inquiry had been immediately appointed and despatched to Havana. In the meanwhile official Washington continued to stress the accident theory, but the Navy early began to show reluctance to make what seemed tantamount to a confession of gross inefficiency. When the Spanish authorities on the 18th made the not unreasonable suggestion that the inquiry be jointly conducted by the two nations, Mr. Day sternly replied that it had already been initiated by our own officers, 'who will conduct this investigation independently.' Once more the Spaniards were forced to accede, while Mr. Long in Washington had reached the point where he was admitting that it 'might have been an accident or might have been by design.'

It was clear that Mr. McKinley's administration would not long remain impervious to the wave of belligerent enthusiasm which swept at once throughout the country and was echoed from Americans all over the world. A group of our countrymen meeting in the Methodist Church in Mexico City admitted their ignorance of the cause of the disaster, but resolved anyway that it was a 'sacred and significant sacrifice on the altar of humanity,' and offered themselves to the flag. President Dole of Hawaii did not fail to join with the other foreign governments in expressing his condolences. Our Minister to Lima was moved almost to poetry as he officially reported the sympathetic expressions of the Republic of Peru. The Spanish press on the whole made a gallant effort to turn the disaster to good account. The papers all expressed their sympathetic horror in as generous a vein as possible, and one editor even went so far as to hope that a common sorrow over the loss of the Maine's men would dissolve the political differences between the two powers. It was a hope in which the American newspapers failed to join. Our Government was by this time pushing forward its war preparations as rapidly as the highly pacific nature of our military system would permit; but our press was practically fighting the war already.

As to the exact grounds, there was still a considerable confusion. In a crisis like this it always takes a little time to construct a good, logical *casus belli* of sufficient moral impregnability, but the Administration papers were already beginning upon the task, while the Democratic editors were ready to leap at once over all such pure technicalities. As the New Orleans *Times-Democrat* put it:

Mr. McKinley may not have sufficient backbone even to resent an offense so gross as this, but war in this country is declared by Congress and no explanation of the Spanish Government, no offer to make reparation, could prevent a declaration of war, though it should develop that the Spanish authorities had nothing to do with the treacherous design, if treacherous design it were.

And very soon the New York *Tribune* was confessing editorially that the President was 'prudently' preparing for an 'emergency which the fault of Spain may possibly produce.'

The 'yellow press,' of course, joyously slipped every remaining shackle; it poured forth its 'war extras' in torrents, each extra achieving new heights of exclamatory typography and ingenious invention, which shocked the conservatives even as they unconsciously responded to it. Mr. Godkin was one who did not respond. Of the *World* and the *Journal* he wrote:

Nothing so disgraceful as the behaviour of these two newspapers in the past week has ever been known in the history of journalism. Gross misrepresentation of facts, deliberate invention of tales calculated to excite the public, and wanton recklessness in the construction of headlines which outdid even these inventions have combined to make the issues of the most widely circulated newspapers firebrands scattered broadcast throughout the community.

But Mr. Godkin had never grasped the basis of the new journalism. In one week the *World* sold 5,000,000 copies — 'the largest circulation of any newspaper printed in any language in any country' — and before the war was over it was to reach 1,300,000 in a single day. Both papers were original and indefatigable in their resource. The *World* tried to send its own divers down to examine the Maine wreckage; the *Journal*, remembering its triumphs in the Evangelina Cisneros episode, launched a monster subscription campaign among prominent people for a monument to the Maine's dead. Mr. Grover Cleveland responded in an acid telegram: 'I decline to allow my sorrow for those who died on the Maine to be perverted into an advertising scheme for the New York *Journal*'; but nobler minds were above such cynicism, and Mr. Henry White, our *chargé* in London, even cabled for confidential instructions as to whether he might properly preside at a fund-raising meeting which the *Journal* had engineered among Americans in England.

The naval court of inquiry, sitting in secret on the revenue cutter Mangrove in Havana Harbor, was prosecuting its researches. Pending the outcome, the official attitude was one of a righteous, a glacial suspense of judgment; all the more responsible of the Administration papers constituted themselves perfect monuments of self-restraint, and Uncle Sam appeared in dozens of cartoons balancing peace and war upon the scales of a strictly abstract justice. The court's methods were exhaustive; its sessions were in reality secret. Nevertheless, by the last week of February it began to be reported that the court would find for an external explosion, and the agitation in the United States took on a deeper tone. Senator Redfield Proctor of Vermont, a statesman of conservative reputation, arrived in Havana to make a personal investigation of the stories of suffering among the reconcentrados. It was a bad sign; and the Spanish *chargé* at Washington cabled home that matters had reached a point at which 'even the most conservative and influential men have lost their heads.'

'The slightest spark,' Secretary Long noted in his diary on February 24, 'is liable to result in war.' So great, indeed, had the strain become that the head of the Navy Department felt himself in need of a few hours' rest. Unfortunately, this would involve leaving the belligerent Mr. Roosevelt in charge; but Mr. Long decided that he could risk it for a single day, at least, and so withdrew on the afternoon of Friday, February 25, looking forward to a good night's sleep. Thus it happened that when Senator Lodge visited the Navy Department that afternoon, it was to find his friend, Mr. Roosevelt, Acting Secretary of the Navy. It was a golden opportunity.

Mr. Long slept well, but when he reached his office next morning, it was to discover an appalling state of affairs. 'I find that Roosevelt, in his precipitate way, has come very near causing more of an explosion than happened to the Maine.... He seems to be thoroughly loyal, but the very devil seemed to possess him yesterday afternoon.' Abetted by the Senator, Mr. Roosevelt had begun to 'launch peremptory orders,' distributing ships, ordering ammunition, summoning experts, providing guns for a still nonexistent auxiliary fleet, and even 'sending messages to Congress for immediate legislation authorizing the enlistment of an unlimited number of seamen.' It seems that Mr. Roosevelt had decided, as he later wrote, that 'it was vital' to be 'in readiness for immediate action'; and when Mr. Roosevelt made up his mind that something was 'vital,' he had little regard for loyalty toward his superiors. But Mr. Long's journal, in its published form at any rate, omits to mention the most fateful result of that splendid afternoon. The Philippine adventure was very close to the minds of both Mr. Roosevelt and Mr. Lodge; with this chance before them the two conspirators had concocted a subsequently famous telegram. It had been placed at once upon the wires:

Dewey, Hong Kong:

Secret and confidential. Order the squadron, except Monocacy, to Hong Kong. Keep full of coal. In the event of declaration of war Spain, your duty will be to see that the Spanish squadron does not leave the Asiatic coast, and then offensive operations in Philippine Islands. Keep Olympia until further orders.

ROOSEVELT

'And then offensive operations in the Philippine Islands.' Mr. Long indited a pathetic memorandum: 'Do not take any such step affecting the policy of the Administration without consulting the President or me. I am not away from town, and my intention was to have you look after the routine of the office while I got a quiet day off. I write to you because I am anxious to have no occasion for a sensation in the papers.' But Mr. Roosevelt seldom objected to sensations in the papers; and the thing was done by that time. Another and most important step had been taken in the development of the nation's destiny.

III

At about the time that Mr. Lodge and Mr. Roosevelt were putting their heads together in the Navy Department at Washington, Mr. Woodford in Madrid was being received informally by Sr. Gullón, the Foreign Minister, and Sr. Moret, Minister of the Colonies. On Saturday, the 26th, he transmitted the result of this interview directly to Mr. McKinley:

I think that I have now secured the practical adjustment of every important matter that has been committed to me up to date. Autonomy cannot go backward. It must go forward and its results must be worked out in Cuba.... They cannot go further in open concessions to us without being overthrown by their own people here in Spain.... They want peace if they can keep peace and save the dynasty. They prefer the chances of war, with the certain loss of Cuba, to the overthrow of the dynasty.

It seemed to place the decision absolutely in the hands of Mr. McKinley, who had dedicated himself to peace. The purely diplomatic questions had all been settled. In the matter of Cuba the Spanish Government had gone as far in compliance with our ideas as they thought it possible to go and still remain a government. The destruction of the Maine, according to the attitude which we had ourselves so nobly adopted, was not an issue, and could not be made one until some fault or negligence on the part of Spain had been proved.

The only possible ground upon which we could justify warlike action with any approach to decency was the continued suffering in Cuba. But even there, the autonomy which we had demanded as the solution was only now beginning to function; American supplies were just beginning to arrive in quantity in the island. Mr. Woodford, a prey to anxiety, frankly put the question to the President: 'Is the warning given in your message and repeated in the American note of December 20 sufficiently clear and definite as to justify effective action... which will be approved by the sober judgment of our people and the final judgment of history?' Was it? One cannot avoid the feeling that the moment had come, if it ever was to come, for a resolutely pacific stand. The mob was yelling at his heels, the Lodges and Roosevelts were plotting their international piracies, but Mr. McKinley would not have lacked a powerful support. Speaker Reed of the House — 'Czar' Reed, who was popularly supposed to hold that bellicose assembly in an iron grip — was ardently opposed to war, which he believed to be a barbarous anachronism unpredictable in its results. Senator Mark Hanna had no interest in imperialistic adventure. Such sturdy, old-time Republicans as Senator Hoar, Mr. Lodge's colleague from Massachusetts, were staunch until the end, and they were supported by the weight of opinion among the financial and industrial leaders of the East. Even among the political fire-eaters it seems likely that many did not really want a war. Though it would have been difficult and politically dangerous, it might not have been impossible for a courageous and strong-willed statesman to have asserted a policy which would have escaped the conflict. But President McKinley, in his successor's famous phrase, had 'no more backbone than a chocolate éclair.' President McKinley for a time did nothing.

In the meanwhile the international lawyers were hastening to rectify the serious weakness in our belligerence. Since it lacked any respectable grounds, it was necessary to invent them. No serious organ of opinion could argue that Spain was officially responsible for the destruction of the Maine, the suicidal nature of such an act being too immediately obvious. At most it was urged that some reckless junior officer with access to the mining defenses of the harbor might have blown up the ship; while the painfully evident fact that the insurgents would be the most direct beneficiaries of the disaster even led some to ask whether those ardent dynamiters might not have been its authors. The theory now being developed was sufficient to embrace any of these possibilities. A Chicago University Professor explained that Spain could be charged with 'culpable negligence' if one of her harbor mines had been used, no matter by whom; the New York *Times* held that Spain would be liable at least to the payment of an indemnity 'if the act were perpetrated by a private miscreant, were he loyal Spaniard or Cuban rebel,' while the New York *Press* put it even more effectively:

There is one ground upon which a *casus belli* can be deduced from the Maine. That is — in the event of the explosion having been proven to be designed — of the entire prevalence of anarchy in Cuba. In such event it might be, in the judgment of the administration, necessary for this country to... take possession — a task of which the difficulties we realize — of the port and harbor in the interest of humanity and civilization. If the

Spanish government is unequal to the restraint of dynamite atrocities in its principal provincial anchorage... then it is no government at all and the United States, as the conservator of social order on this hemisphere, must supply what government it can.

As these theories of international responsibility were developed, it became clear that Spain would only get off if the explosion were proved to have resulted from an accident on board the ship. And the American press already believed that a most unlikely hypothesis. 'No money,' a Populist editor cried, 'can pay for the blowing up of the Maine by the Spaniards. The only expiation will be the withdrawal of Spain from this side of the Atlantic.' A Democratic paper in Chicago thought the idea of accepting a mere money indemnity 'essentially Republican. It is cool, cringing, characteristically McKinleyish.' Yet even the most bloodthirsty in the political opposition appreciated the tenuous nature of the Maine issue, and never forgot for long that 'humanity' demanded that we should also go to war 'to put an end to Spanish butchery in Cuba.'

It was a tangled and exciting situation, and it all hung upon the harassed figure of Mr. McKinley. Mr. McKinley still hoped for peace; but his first move, when he did move, was in preparation for war. For the President could no longer conceal from himself the extreme probability that he would be unequal to the task of stemming the martial tide; he had got himself into the dilemma that to prepare for war would be to invite it, but not to prepare would be to invite military disaster when it came. The anxiety had brought haggard lines into his face when, on March 6, he finally chose the first as the lesser evil, and thus moved another step upon the road. That Sunday evening a hurried message informed Mr. Cannon, the chairman of the House Appropriations Committee, that his presence was urgently desired at the White House.

Mr. Cannon — endeared to his countrymen by the length of his cigars and the sobriquet of 'Uncle Joe' — was received in the library. The President did not even pause to sit down. 'Cannon,' he began, 'I must have money to get ready for war. I am doing everything possible to prevent war, but it must come and we are not prepared for war. Who knows where this war will lead us;

it may be more than a war with Spain. How can I get this money for these extraordinary expenditures?' As he spoke he 'paced the floor with quick, nervous strides'; the Congressman, who had known him for twenty years, had never seen him in a more agitated frame of mind.

But Mr. Cannon had foreseen this crisis. He had gone over the accounts of the Treasury and decided that it could stand an outright appropriation of $50,000,000 'without embarrassment and without having to provide for a bond issue or for new taxation.' He suggested that the President should at once draft a message asking it of Congress. But Mr. McKinley hesitated; he felt that he could not write such a message 'while he was still negotiating with Spain. It would be accepted by Europe as equivalent to a declaration of war and he would be accused of double-dealing.' To avoid so ignoble an accusation the President toyed with the idea of subterfuge — it might be possible to make the regular appropriations available ahead of time? In Mr. Cannon's opinion it was not possible. Finally the Congressman was asked whether his committee would not introduce a bill on its own motion.

I agreed to introduce a bill if he would prepare it.... The President walked over to the table and wrote on a telegraph blank a single sentence: 'For national defense, fifty million dollars.' It wasn't a bill nor a message nor an estimate, but it was the President's memorandum as to what he wanted done, and I put the slip of paper in my pocket.

Mr. Cannon retired at once to his hotel, where the bill was prepared the same evening. It seemed to him a case for urgent action; it even appealed to him, upon the theory of international relations which had been so popular throughout these months, as a peace measure. 'It might also impress Spain with the determination of this Government to induce her to give up Cuba, thus averting war.' On Monday afternoon the famous 'Fifty Million Bill' was reported in the House, amid scenes of 'more unanimity, more harmony, and more real enthusiasm' than Mr. Cannon had ever known or was ever to know again.

There was, however, just one discordant note. At the end of that thrilling and inspiring day, Mr. Cannon found himself walking toward the street-car from the Capitol in company with Speaker Reed.

'Joe,' said the Speaker sadly, 'why did you do it?'

'Because it was necessary,' was Mr. Cannon's firm reply.

The same day Mr. Long had wired the U.S.S. Brooklyn, then in Venezuelan waters: 'The situation is getting worse. Proceed without delay to Hampton Roads.' Undoubtedly it was. Mr. Whitelaw Reid, fresh from a transcontinental journey, was informing the President that he had never known 'a more profound readiness to trust the President and await his word,' but adding nevertheless that 'conservative public sentiment will sustain purchases of ammunition and even of warships.' That radical sentiment would do so there could be no doubt. Mr. Godkin had been reduced to helpless rage by the yellow journals and the 'baseness and corruption and satanism of their proprietors,' while the inexplicable fact that their circulations were as large as ever enabled him to conclude only that 'a better place in which to prepare a young man for eternal damnation than a yellow journal office does not exist.' The wilder Congressmen were already threatening to 'unhorse' the President if he did not give them blood, while Mr. Woodford in Madrid was frankly intimating to his Spanish friends that, in his personal opinion, there would be war unless Spain practically gave up Cuba.

On March 9 the Fifty Million Bill came up to the vote; the House after enduring no less than seventy-three separate speeches in its favor (most of them mercifully under the five-minute rule, however) passed it by 311 to 0. The Senate, eschewing the oratory, passed it with an equal unanimity (the vote was 76 to 0) and the bill was immediately signed. 'We do not need to say,' as one editor declared, 'that this is war'; it was now evident that 'a stupid, vindictive, and desperate public opinion' in Spain would certainly compel us to defend ourselves.

But from Madrid Mr. Woodford reported the reaction in different terms. 'It has not,' he wrote to Mr. McKinley, 'excited the Spaniards — it has stunned them.'

IV

'The time for debate,' as General R. A. Alger, our Secretary of War, justly put it, 'had passed — the time for action had come.' Unfortunately, General Alger, 'as kind and generous a heart as ever beat' and on the whole a rather harmless individual, seems to have made the serious mistake of supposing that the bill, which appropriated the $50,000,000 for national 'defense,' meant what it said. He apparently failed to appreciate the great principle that 'offense is the truest form of defense'; at any rate, he did not succeed in impressing it upon the President. Mr. McKinley allotted only $16,000,000 of the total fund to the Army, and the whole of this was gravely devoted to the seacoast fortifications — at a moment when the mobile army which we would have to use in Cuba was in the last stages of unpreparedness. Congress, after sagaciously rejecting a bill that would have reorganized our land forces on something resembling a war footing, did grant two new regiments of artillery. It was also possible to effect some departmental rearrangements without the expenditure of funds; beyond this General Alger felt himself unauthorized to go.

The Navy Department, on the other hand, labored under no such legalistic restrictions. Since the early part of January it had been doing everything possible toward a mobilization of the fleet, and had even overrun the legal limit on enlistments without authorization. It now secured $30,000,000, and plunged with a joyous ostentation into the task of equipping itself for the national 'defense.' Its preparations ranged all the way from the purchase of merchant shipping to form an auxiliary cruiser force to the refurbishing of the ancient Civil War monitors with their thirteen-inch smoothbore guns. An eager and dreadfully alert press reported each new step in detail, thus stoking fuel upon the flames of our bellicosity, and an admiring populace looked on in the breathless determination to defend itself to the last against the cruel and vindictive Spaniards.

The cruel and vindictive Spaniards, on their side, had not overlooked the wisdom of preparation, but unhappily they were without either $50,000,000 or such active military brains as that of Mr. Roosevelt. Obviously there was nothing much to be done for the army in Cuba, which had been upon a war footing there for three years, but the Spaniards still had hopes that they might accomplish something with their navy. In these hopes Rear Admiral Pascual Cervera y Topete, the commander of the principal Spanish squadron, did not share. Admiral Cervera, like the

Duke of Medina Sidonia three hundred years before him, had labored from the beginning under a conviction of failure. As early as January 30, he had recorded his forebodings:

> We may and must expect a disaster. But as it is necessary to go to the bitter end, and as it would be a crime to say that publicly today, I hold my tongue and go forth resignedly to face the trials which God may be pleased to send me.

The Admiral's resignation was not without reason. Even after the loss of the Maine the American Navy still possessed four first-class battleships and one second-class, two powerful armored cruisers, a large number of smaller cruisers and gunboats, and some torpedo craft, as well as our heavily armed coast defense monitors. Spain possessed one battleship, which was laid up and never saw service; one new and powerful armored cruiser which had not, however, received her main battery guns, and three other armored cruisers which had they been in good condition would have been fairly effective ships. She also had a flotilla of torpedo craft which caused much perturbation in the United States, but which was for the most part in such a poor state as to be useless. For the rest there was nothing save some new ships still uncompleted at the yards (and with no time or money with which to finish them) and a collection of marine antiquities in Cuban and Philippine waters which were with difficulty being kept out of the junkyards.

Even the four theoretically good vessels were in an appalling condition. The heavy guns for the Cristóbal Colón, in spite of endless and agonized correspondence with the Italian manufacturers, were never to arrive. The three other ships, the Admiral wrote, 'are apparently complete, but the 5.5-inch guns, the main power of these vessels, are practically useless on account of the bad system of their breech mechanism and the poor quality of their cartridge cases.... As for the supplies necessary for the fleet, we frequently lack even the most indispensable.... We have no charts of the American seas.' The Ministry of Marine endeavored to purchase two cruisers building in England for the Brazilian Navy, only to see them snapped up by the United States. At the naval base at Cartagena, Admiral Cervera, struggling without

funds to produce some sort of force, surrendered himself to the
composition of gloomy letters. On the day after the destruction
of the Maine he computed the ratio of Spanish naval power to
that of the United States as 1 to 3, and concluded that any war
would have to be 'a defensive or a disastrous one'; and by
March 7, when Mr. Cannon was whipping the Fifty Million Bill
into shape, Admiral Cervera was recording the melancholy fact
that he had been waiting for fifty-one days to get new boiler tubes
in a steam launch, and did not know when even that minor job
would be finished. The Minister of Marine attempted a cheery
optimism; the Admiral could only reiterate his readiness to accept
what God might send — and it became increasingly apparent
that he would get nothing from any other source.

About the Philippines they did nothing whatever. This singular
blindness, in Spain as in the United States, to the immense possibilities in the Philippine situation is one of the curiosities of
the whole curious episode. It had certainly not occurred to the
American people that a seizure of the Philippine Islands might
be a necessary step toward righting the wrongs of the Cubans.
And yet in the Far East the possibility had been taking form,
more or less vaguely, in a number of minds since the preceding
autumn; and the question of whether our duty toward humanity
could not be made as imperative in Spain's Asiatic possessions as
in her West Indian ones had undoubtedly arisen among the astute.

The outbreak of active insurrection in the Philippines in the
fall of 1896, offering so obvious a parallel to the insurrection in
Cuba, had early awakened attention in the western Pacific. The
Philippine insurgents had declared themselves a Republic, and,
following the useful example of the Cubans, had soon established
a 'foreign agent and high commissioner' upon the neutral and
friendly soil of Hong Kong. As early as November, 1897, this
gentleman, a Mr. F. Agoncilla, was calling upon our consul at
that port with the interesting and slightly startling proposal that
we should enter an 'alliance offensive and defensive' with the
Philippine Republic, to take effect whenever we should declare
war against Spain. Mr. Agoncilla, who seems to have been a
student of Cuban history, was not above offering practical as
well as humanitarian inducements; the Republic, he explained,

would like to buy 20,000 stand of arms from us and was 'not particular about the price — is willing that United States should make twenty-five or thirty per cent profit.' Our consul had duly submitted this proposal to the State Department; the latter hastily replied that 'you should not encourage any advances on the part of Mr. Agoncilla.'

It was the end of the matter for the time being; mails from the Far East were long in transit, and on the day before the answering despatch was written, the Philippine Republic had, as a matter of fact, ceased to exist. By the treaty of Biac-na-Bato, signed on December 14, 1897, in an obscure Filipino village, the insurgent leaders had agreed to lay down their arms and retire to Hong Kong — for a consideration of 800,000 pesos. Yet it was only three weeks later that Commodore Dewey, laden with all available information on the Philippines and fired with Mr. Roosevelt's strategic acumen, was taking over command at Nagasaki. Was it with disappointment that the Commodore learned from his predecessor that 'no information of any sort shows American interests to be affected' by the Philippine unrest? By February our new consul at Manila was reporting upon the situation in terms of the utmost gravity. 'Peace was proclaimed,' he wrote, 'but there is no peace and has been none for about two years. Conditions here and in Cuba are practically alike.'

In this state of affairs it was only natural that Consul Williams should keep in daily communication 'by cable and letter' with the Commodore. At that remote end of telegraph and mail services the Consul clearly felt the responsibilities of empire upon his shoulders — responsibilities which were not lessened when, after the destruction of the Maine, the Spanish residents began to adopt a threatening attitude. They even went so far, in the growing tension, as to offer to cut the throats of all Americans. The officials still treated him well, 'except one underling whose head I threatened to smash,' but the insurrectionary movements continued, and the Consul was soon able to report barbarities in its suppression exceeding, if possible, those alleged against the Spaniards in Cuba. Mr. Williams devoted himself to the compilation of atrocity reports and to his daily communications with the Commodore.

It is true that all this was buried in the secrecy of the State and Navy Department files. But in the great game of world politics which had now aroused the fascinated interest of our people, the East had been taking a new prominence. Publics which were tiring of the outworn counters of purely European diplomacy were turning with enthusiasm to a new set, bearing the romantic place-names of the Orient and scattered across a new chess-board of vaster distances and seemingly illimitable opportunities. The movement into the Pacific, precipitated by the Sino-Japanese War — that queer imitation of the more sophisticated wars of the West — ran in an undercurrent beneath the more immediate excitements of Cuba or Armenia or the Jameson Raid. Maps and articles on the East, and accounts of the diplomatic *démarches* being played there, couched in the picturesque and metaphoric language always used to hide the realities of international squabblings, were appearing in many of our periodicals; and it seems rather strange that so few realized how far a war with Spain, which was a Pacific power, might carry us.

Nor had American statesmanship itself been a passive witness of the trend. Commodore Dewey had barely reached his station before he was writing home that 'what we all want is Chinese trade, and we are gradually getting more and more of it.' The annexation of Hawaii, a station on the road to the East, had frequently been as lively a question as Cuba; and in the weeks just preceding the Maine explosion, Hawaii as a matter of fact, had been arousing much more attention than the Cuban problem. And now, with the country at a high pitch of martial enthusiasm and the board of inquiry still sitting in Havana Harbor, the Foreign Relations Committee of the Senate abruptly reintroduced the Hawaiian annexation into the general tension.

Hawaii and Cuba obviously tended to act and react upon each other as incitements to great things. The annexation of the Sandwich Islands would clearly open the way into the Pacific, into new commitments, into all those imperial splendors with which the European powers were dressing themselves as they played the spectacular rôles of late nineteenth century diplomacy. The urge into the Hawaiian venture was intimately bound up with the springs of our enthusiasm for a free Cuba, and it was an urge which might seem to have been irresistible. Unfortunately, however, it was resisted. Mr. McKinley had hurried an Hawaiian annexation treaty to the Senate during the extra session; but the humane argument, so useful where suffering Cuba was concerned, was absent in the case of Hawaii, and the statesmen of the new destiny had not yet converted everybody to their own vision. It had soon become apparent that the necessary two-thirds vote for the ratification of a treaty could not be obtained. Yet Germany was signing her lease of the Shantung Peninsula on March 9, and Russia was to carry off her share of Manchuria before the month was out. The Foreign Relations Committee rose to the occasion. On March 16 it brought in its report, recommending annexation, not by treaty, but by a joint resolution, for which a majority vote would suffice. It placed the matter, of course, upon the very highest grounds; annexation, said the report, was 'a duty that has its origin in the noblest sentiments that inspire the love of a father for his children... or our Great Republic to a younger sister that has established law, liberty, and justice in a beautiful land that a corrupt monarchy was defiling.... We have solemnly assumed these duties and cannot abandon them without discredit.' Resort to the joint resolution method, the committee also pointed out, merely placed the question 'within reach of the legislative power of Congress.' At that juncture anything brought within reach of Congress would most probably be taken.

The day after the Hawaiian report, Senator Proctor of Vermont, now returned from his expedition into Cuba, arose upon the floor of the Senate and delivered a report of his impressions which had a profound effect upon public sentiment. In spite of all the efforts of the jingo press and the propagandists, a certain skepticism concerning the Cuban atrocities had lingered among large sections of a public which has never been wholly devoid of common-sense. Senator Proctor, it will be remembered, was the statesman who had secured Commodore Dewey's appointment to the Far East, and according to Mr. Roosevelt he was 'very ardent for the war.' He was not, however, identified in the public mind with the jingoes; his opinions were respected and his honesty was not questioned. When he arose to describe what he had seen, he commanded the attention of the nation.

Senator Proctor's speech was, in comparison with others, temperate; but it was also terrible. He had himself gone to Cuba, he said, as a skeptic; he had returned convinced. He did not attack the Spaniards, but he gave an appalling picture of the existing state of affairs. The reconcentrados of the western provinces he numbered at about 400,000:

Torn from their homes, with foul earth, foul air, foul water and foul food or none, what wonder that one half have died and that one quarter of the living are so diseased that they cannot be saved?... To me, the strongest appeal is not the barbarity practiced by Weyler nor the loss of the Maine... but the spectacle of a million and a half of people, the entire native population of Cuba, struggling for freedom and deliverance from the worst misgovernment of which I ever had knowledge.

Where doubt had existed, there was doubt no longer. The most conservative papers now declared that intervention in Cuba was a necessity, while the religious press turned to proclaim a Holy War. Cuba must be saved. Nor, so violent had the popular demand become, was it only Cuba which had to be saved. Another motive was at work, to which the editor of the Chicago *Times-Herald* had the frankness to give expression:

Intervention in Cuba, peacefully if we can, forcibly if we must, is immediately inevitable. Our own internal political conditions will not permit its postponement.... Let President McKinley hesitate to rise to the just expectations of the American people, and who can doubt that 'war for Cuban liberty' will be the crown of thorns the free silver Democrats and Populists will adopt at the elections this fall?

And who can doubt that by that sign, held aloft and proclaimed by such magnetic orators as William J. Bryan, they will sweep the country like a cyclone?... The President would be powerless to stay any legislation, however ruinous to every sober, honest interest of the country.... No, the United States cannot afford to let the settlement of the Cuban question wait a single day after the court of inquiry has made its report to the President. The possibilities of further delay are too momentous to justify further consideration of the rights of Spain.

v

This was, in fact, the difficult and dangerous situation into which Mr. McKinley's policy had brought him. He was committed to peace; yet if he did not go to war the Democrats and the Populists would take the government away from him. To launch the nation upon this aggressive war would be to stultify all his own professions; but to attempt to curb this belligerence of the people involved a political risk which Mr. McKinley did not dare to face. Even for this problem, however, Mr. McKinley was adroit enough to find a solution; if he could not restrain his own people, he might be able to wring still further concessions from the Spaniards. Officially our position was that we were waiting for the Spaniards to bring the war in Cuba to an end. By insisting that they do this immediately, the President could still claim that he was working for 'peace.' To this disingenuous policy he now addressed himself.

There must be peace in Cuba. But on the 17th of March, Mr. Woodford at Madrid had definitely come to the conclusion that autonomy was a failure and that peace in Cuba could come only under the American flag. Mr. Woodford suggested that perhaps we could buy the island; the Spanish Colonial Minister 'grew very pale,' but our representative thought that he had found a way out and cabled for time. The reply was immediate — we could not withhold action for long. Mr. Woodford was told that the court of inquiry was going to find that there had been an external explosion, and that 'unless events otherwise indicate, the President, having exhausted diplomatic agencies to secure peace, will lay the whole question before Congress.' This would mean, of course, our active intervention; Washington was evidently holding the Maine report as a club with which to extort some dramatic action from Spain. But a day or two later, Mr. Woodford was informed by the Spanish Government that sale of the island was impossible and that 'the Queen would prefer to abdicate her regency and return to her Austrian home.' So that hope died.

Mr. Woodford then tried pressure, and the Spanish Ministers, seeing themselves being crowded ever closer to the wall, renewed their desperate efforts at escape. If only the Maine report could be withheld? The autonomist congress would be meeting in Havana on May 4, and the whole question of Cuban peace would be submitted to it. There was a lengthy memorandum. Spain would halt her forces in Cuba if the United States would guarantee the acceptance of the truce by the insurgents, and if the autonomist government could arrive at no settlement, then Spain and the United States would 'jointly compel both parties in Cuba to accept such settlement as the two governments should then jointly advise.'

It was an ingenious proposal, and had peace in Cuba been the real aim of our diplomacy, it might well have been accepted. But by this time it was no longer peace in Cuba which Mr. McKinley wanted; it was a victory over Spain sweeping enough to satisfy his own clamant public. His State Department was not to be trapped into any such obvious foreign entanglement as that suggested in the Spanish note, and we reserved our splendid irresponsibility inviolate. Mr. Day composed and sent off to Mr. Woodford a lofty statement of our position.

The President's desire is for peace.... It was represented to him in November that the Blanco Government would at once release the suffering and so modify the Weyler order as to permit those who were able to return to their homes and till the fields from which they had been driven. There has been no relief to the starving.... The reconcentration order has not been practically superseded. There is no hope of peace through Spanish arms.... We do not want the island.... [The President] wants an honorable peace. He has repeatedly urged the Government of Spain to secure such a peace. She still has the opportunity to do it, and the President appeals to her from every consideration of justice and humanity to do it. Will she? Peace is the desired end. For your own guidance the President suggests that if Spain will revoke the reconcentration order and maintain the people until they can support themselves and offer to the Cubans full self-government with reasonable indemnity, the President will gladly assist in its consummation. If Spain should invite the United States to mediate for peace and the insurgents would make like request, the President might undertake such office of friendship.

Another month was yet to elapse, filled with doubt and urgent telegrams, while the President worked for 'peace.' But a glance at this program is enough to show that Mr. McKinley's labors were based only upon the hope that he might force Spain into a complete admission of defeat without actual resort to arms. For, when Mr. Woodford cabled to be informed as to precisely what 'self-government with reasonable indemnity' would mean, the confidential reply was that it meant 'Cuban independence.'

Thus were we closing every possible avenue which the writhing ingenuity of the Spaniards could suggest, while President Mc-

Kinley, insisting upon the righteously pacific nature of our course, was asking his Secretary of War 'how soon can you put an army into Cuba?' And Mr. Alger's oversanguine reply was that he could put 'forty thousand men there in ten days.' By Sunday, March 27, it was decided that the report of the court of inquiry must go to Congress; the Maine disaster was already more than a month old, the report could not be held much longer, and it was no doubt thought that the sensation which it would produce might serve to extort surrender from the Spaniards. On Monday, the 28th, it was formally transmitted to Congress. The sensation was indeed profound.

The report itself had been completed a week before, after a month of study and deliberation in which the three distinguished naval officers composing the court had exhausted all the evidence which it had been possible to gather from examination of the wreck, of the survivors, and of eye-witnesses. Its findings read:

The court finds that the loss of the Maine... was not in any respect due to fault or negligence on the part of any of the officers or members of the crew of said vessel.

In the opinion of the court the Maine was destroyed by the explosion of a submarine mine, which caused the partial explosion of two or more of the forward magazines.

The court has been unable to obtain evidence fixing the responsibility for the destruction of the Maine upon any person or persons.

This was all; but it was quite enough. In the eyes of the American public Spain was convicted, if not of assassination, at least of gross negligence, and under the circumstances it did not make much difference.

Whether or not the findings were correct has never been established; for the destruction of the Maine remains to this day a mystery. Captain Sampson, Captain Chadwick, and Commander Potter, who composed the court, were of course under an immense pressure to find as they did; yet they were conscientious men and perhaps inclined to lean over backward in the effort to reach an unbiased verdict. Captain Chadwick declares that when the court was ordered he and one of the two other members 'thought the explosion internal. Both were convinced otherwise against their prepossessions.' A thorough examination into affairs on board the

Maine had revealed that all precautions had been taken and that all suggested theories of an internal explosion — such as overheating in the magazines, the introduction of a bomb into the ship by a visitor, a boiler explosion, and so on — were untenable. This left the alternatives of a spontaneous explosion from unexplained causes within the ship, or a cause external to the vessel.

The court then turned to the evidence of the wreckage. Great difficulty was experienced in the examination, since the enlisted divers were not trained naval constructors while the officers who understood the structure of the ship were not trained as divers. The water was muddy and the divers' reports not always intelligible. A great deal of the distortion had obviously resulted from the detonation of the magazines, but the court finally found certain other effects which they concluded could only have been produced 'by the explosion of a mine situated under the bottom of the ship at about frame 18 and somewhat on the port side of the ship.' On the basis of these facts they wrote their report. One cannot doubt their sincerity, and the findings appear to have been justified from the evidence available.

Yet in the thirty years which have elapsed since the catastrophe occurred, no shred of positive evidence has ever come to light to indicate that a mine existed. Successfully to have mined or torpedoed the ship would have required considerable and expensive equipment and a good many hands. No responsible officer of the Spanish services would have dreamed of doing it. Some rash subalterns might have conceived the idea of firing a mine previously planted for the defense of the harbor, but if there were such a mine it seems certain that its existence would sooner or later have become known. Insurgent sympathizers had every reason to plot the destruction of the ship, but one doubts both their technical ability to achieve it and the likelihood of their later being able to conceal all knowledge of the crime.

It also appeared, when the Maine was at last raised in 1911 and the wreckage could be directly examined, that the court of inquiry had been mistaken in its picture of the condition of affairs under water. A second court of inquiry held that the distortions about frame 18, which the court in 1898 had regarded as conclusive evidence of a mine and upon which it had mainly rested its opinion, were possible consequences of the magazine explosion and should be ascribed to that cause. The second court, however, discovered certain effects in the plating some fifty feet farther toward the stern, unknown to the investigators in 1898, which led it to conclude that 'a charge of a low form of explosive exterior to the ship' had been detonated at that point. But if the first court had been so badly mistaken, it seems quite possible that the second one may have been mistaken also. At all events, the hull was towed out to sea and sunk with military honors in water deep enough to render any further study of its evidence impossible. It is a matter of opinion; but the most probable explanation still seems to be that the U.S.S. Maine did in fact destroy herself, through the intervention of no outside agency save an act of God.

But to the American people the report of the court of inquiry was conclusive. Mr. McKinley, who was still trying to restrain Congressional belligerence in the hope that he might get off without an actual war, submitted it with a carefully neutral message. The only result was to start a revolt on Capitol Hill and to bring a delegation of both parties to the White House to warn the President that if his next message was not in a sterner tone Congress would start a war on its own account. The report of the Spanish court of inquiry, which naturally found for an internal explosion, was contemptuously swept aside — not without reason, it is true, since we had effectually denied it any opportunity for a real investigation of the wreck — while our Navy Department began to put its ships into their war paint and land the woodwork.

In the diplomatic sphere, in the meanwhile, Mr. Day had prepared and cabled what amounted practically to an ultimatum. Still, it was not an ultimatum; Mr. McKinley still hoped and Mr. Woodford (it was the 29th of March by this time) softened it as much as possible in the presentation. We did not, Mr. Woodford once more reiterated, desire Cuba; we did desire peace. And to this end the President wished two things:

He suggests an immediate armistice [in Cuba] lasting until October 1, negotiations in the meantime being had looking to peace between Spain and the insurgents, through the friendly offices of the President of the United States.

He wishes the immediate revocation of the reconcentration order, so as to permit the people to return to their farms and the needy to be relieved with provisions and supplies from the United States, the United States coöperating with the Spanish authorities, so as to afford full relief.

Then, 'with all possible kindness of manner and courtesy of language,' Mr. Woodford told them that he must have a reply within two days. They reluctantly agreed. It was the old difficulty. The United States would permit of nothing which did not involve acknowledged surrender to the insurgents and delivery of the whole problem from the hands of the Spanish Government into those of the United States. That it was tantamount to asking that Spain give up the island they no doubt realized; Mr. Woodford himself realized it, at any rate, and the Spanish Ministers must have seen that the end was closing in upon them. But still might not they evade, by some twist, that relentless fate? An armistice would be granted at once, Sr. Sagasta said, provided that the insurgents would ask for it; everything might be arranged if only America, 'which had waited so long,' would give them a little more time in the island, but he could not himself offer an armistice to the rebels without bringing the Spanish authority to an end. Mr. Woodford replied that 'the sober sense of the American people insisted upon immediate cessation of hostilities'; they bowed him out, and Mr. Woodford, returning to his legation, found a cable from Mr. Day telling him that the thing must be settled at once or a resolution for intervention would pass both Houses of Congress 'in spite of any effort that can be made.'

Mr. McKinley did not dare to wait six weeks. Speaker Reed, the 'Czar' of the lower House, had strained his influence 'to the breaking point,' to no avail. The Senate Foreign Relations Committee was suddenly reviving Senator Lodge's bill to buy the Danish West Indies as a naval base; the Legislature of the State of New York was appropriating $1,000,000 as a defense fund; the State of Iowa followed suit with a $500,000 fund, and other states were soon to imitate their example. A friend encountered Mr. Roosevelt one evening, coming away from the White House in a state of boiling indignation. 'Do you know what that white-livered cur up there has done? He has prepared *two* messages, one for war and one for peace, and doesn't know which one to send in!' And an anonymous group of financiers, calling upon the junta in New York with an offer to buy $10,000,000 worth of the bonds of the Cuban Republic for $2,000,000, were informed (after consultation) that the lowest which the junta could accept was forty cents on the dollar.

Would the Spaniards yield or would they fight? On Thursday, March 31, Mr. Woodford was once more received by the three Ministers to hear their reply to our demands. Spain, they told him, was ready to submit the loss of the Maine to arbitration. The reconcentration decrees had been finally and definitely revoked in the western provinces and a credit of three million pesetas made available for returning the people to the land. Peace in Cuba would be confided to the autonomist congress when it met on May 4. The Spanish Government would at once grant a truce should the insurgents ask for it. But there their statement ended. They would not grant an armistice of their own motion. It meant, Mr. Woodford commented, 'a continuation of this destructive, cruel, and now needless war,' for there was, of course, no possibility that the insurgents would ask for an armistice. But there was likewise no possibility that they would accept one even if it were offered. Putting the matter in another way, what the Spanish reply really signified was that Spain would not admit that she had lost the island. There was a point beyond which it was better to go down fighting than to yield. They bowed Mr. Woodford out, and waited upon Fate and Mr. McKinley.

VI

Fate, for the last time, was to prove unkind.

Mr. Woodford got the Spanish reply upon the cables by that Thursday evening. Yet, in spite of its definiteness, he still permitted himself to hope against hope. 'They know,' he telegraphed to the President, 'that Cuba is lost,' and he still believed that he might force them into admitting it without a war, if the President and Congress would give him time. Unhappily, the tangled and harassed week-end which was to follow was to bring the last of that remarkable series of accidents by which Spain was hurried almost indecently down the road to disaster. Perhaps it really was the hand of God. If so, the instrument this time was appropriately chosen — for the instrument was the Pope.

For a moment affairs had seemed to take a brighter turn. Mr. Atkins, hurrying up direct from Cuba, was in Washington on Saturday, engaged in a furious one-man lobby on the side of peace. 'All day yesterday,' he scribbled to his wife, 'I was busy with the President, Secretaries of State and Navy, and with many leading Senators. I talked as I never talked before, feeling that what I said might possibly turn the scales. Mr. Kotch, of the Cuban Relief Commission, was with me and made an excellent impression; he endorsed all I said.' Mr. Atkins thought he detected a gain in strength on the part of 'the better element in Congress.' Was it an illusion born only of hope? Senator Morgan in the Foreign Relations Committee was taking testimony from admirals on the pleasing probability that we would have to seize Porto Rico in the event of war, while the President was holding Congress in check only by promising that the issue would be placed in its hands as soon as a message could be prepared. Still, the message had not been prepared, and the Washington correspondents were detecting a relaxation in the jingo pressure. But just at this moment the Pope intervened; he offered his mediation.

In spite of the anti-Catholic agitation with which the A.P.A. had been disturbing the country, that in itself might have done no harm. It was Sr. Gullón, the Spanish Foreign Minister, who made the capital blunder. On Sunday evening, April 3, that official called upon Mr. Woodford and told him that 'the Pope, at the suggestion of the President of the United States, proposes to offer to Spain his mediation in order that the Spanish Government grant an immediate armistice to Cuba, which will facilitate and prepare an early and honorable peace.'

Mr. Woodford had heard nothing of this proposal and guessed at once that there was a mistake in attributing its origin to the President. But he also saw that Sr. Gullón was prepared to seize upon it at last as a way out. By making their surrender and granting the armistice at the Pope's request, the Ministry might avoid the disaster which they believed would engulf both themselves and the dynasty should they yield to the demands of the United States. Sr. Gullón asked only that the surrender be made easier by the withdrawal of the American fleet, which by this time had been mobilized at Key West, within sixty miles of Havana.

Mr. Woodford leapt at the suggestion, and at once (it was ten o'clock at night) placed his report of it upon the wires. 'He asks your immediate answer as to withdrawal of warships at once after proclamation of armistice. I still believe that when armistice is once proclaimed, hostilities will never be resumed and that permanent peace will be secured. If, under existing conditions at Washington, you can still do this, I hope that you will.' But unfortunately the Pope's offer had not been at the suggestion of the President. At two o'clock in the morning the reply came back: 'The President has made no suggestions to Spain except through you.'

It may have been that Mr. McKinley was exasperated by what must have seemed to him evidence of bad faith. It may have been that his astute political intelligence realized that to let the Spaniards off at last because of intervention by the Pope would have raised his Protestant countrymen to a pitch of disappointed rage and religious prejudice that would not only have wiped the Republican majority out of Congress in November, but might have wiped Mr. McKinley himself from the Presidency. Or it may have been that 'existing conditions at Washington' had indeed reached the point where Mr. McKinley dared to wait no longer. Mr. McKinley had desired peace and had labored for it, but at some moment between 10 P.M. on Sunday and 2 A.M. on Monday, the labors came abruptly to an end. There was going to be a war.

The remainder of the despatch was icy:

[The President] made no suggestions other than those which you were instructed to make for an armistice... and which Spain has already rejected. An armistice involves an agreement between Spain and insurgents which must be voluntary on the part of each, and if accepted by them would make for peace. The disposition of our fleet must be left to us. An armistice, to be effective, must be immediately proffered and accepted by insurgents. Would the peace you are so confident of securing mean the independence of Cuba? The President cannot hold his message longer than Tuesday.

With this cablegram it was clearly all over. The 'message' re-

ferred, of course, to the Presidential message which would place
the matter in the hands of Congress, and there was no doubt
at all as to what would happen once Mr. McKinley had allowed
the negotiations to pass from his control. The nation wanted a
war; it might as well have it.

The remainder of the negotiations were actually irrelevant,
although the laboring officials, who did not seem to realize the
fullness of Mr. McKinley's change of heart, still struggled to wring
the last surrender out of Spain. They struggled; and indeed, they
were to succeed, but already it was too late. Early on Monday
morning Archbishop Ireland, hastily despatched from St. Paul to
Washington on direct orders from Rome, conferred with the
President. He gained no comfort from the interview. The European powers at last were beginning to put their ponderous machinery of peace into operation, but what good could that do now?
Czar Reed smiled wryly as some one introduced Mr. Atkins to
him with the remark that the sugar man held the right views on
Cuba. 'Well,' said the omnipotent Speaker, 'what is the *use* of
being right when every one else is wrong?' On the same day
ships were despatched to Havana to bring away the American
citizens in the island, and the American flag was hauled down
from the naked monkey-gaff of the Maine, where it had been
flying continuously since the morning after the explosion. At
eleven o'clock that evening Mr. Day cabled Mr. Woodford that
the message would go in to Congress on the coming Wednesday;
and on the following day Mr. Roosevelt was dashing off a jubilant
letter to his friend, Mr. Elihu Root:

Thank Heaven, this morning it looks as if the Administration had
made up its mind to lead the movement instead of resisting it with the
effect of shattering the party and of humiliating the nation. Judge Day,
who, together with that idol of the mugwumps, Secretary Gage, has been
advocating peace under almost any conditions, has just told me that he
has given up and that the President seems to be making up his mind to
the same effect. Of course, from the military standpoint it is dreadful to
have delayed so long.

It was at this moment, when the decision had been taken and
the die cast, that Mr. Woodford suddenly thought he saw victory
within his grasp; as he had anticipated, the Spanish Ministers,

brought to the very ultimate brink of a war which they knew could end only in humiliating defeat, seemed ready to accept surrender as the lesser evil and to yield at last without condition to the imperious demands of the United States. At three o'clock on Tuesday afternoon, Mr. Woodford wired the President to know whether, if the Queen should at the request of the Pope proclaim 'immediate and unconditional suspension of hostilities in the Island of Cuba... for the space of six months,' Mr. McKinley would sustain the Queen and 'prevent hostile action by Congress.' Mr. Woodford, too, was aware that the possibility of 'shattering the party' was the great obstacle. 'I believe,' he added, 'that this means peace, which the sober judgment of our people will approve long before next November, and which must be approved at the bar of final history.... I believe that you will approve this last conscientious effort for peace.'

But Mr. McKinley did not approve. At midnight the reply was sent:

The President highly appreciates the Queen's desire for peace. He cannot assume to influence the action of the American Congress beyond a discharge of his constitutional duty in transmitting the whole matter to them with such recommendation as he deems necessary and expedient. ... If armistice is offered by the Government of Spain, the President will communicate that fact to Congress. The President's message will go to Congress tomorrow.

Spain was at last ready to meet every demand which we had made or could properly make without an outright seizure of the island, but her offer was rejected. Mr. Woodford might promise to get the party safely through the November elections, but Mr. McKinley was on the ground in Washington. The Administration managers in the Senate had reached the point where they were anxiously calculating whether they could 'muster strength enough to sustain a veto in case a war resolution should be prematurely passed.' One Senatorial belligerent even invaded the State Department to exclaim, with a menacing fist, 'Day, by God, don't your President know where the war-declaring power is lodged?' Is it surprising that Mr. Sherman regarded the Spanish proposals as 'obviously dilatory and intrinsically unacceptable'? The newspapers by this time were carrying columns on military prepara-

tions of a most exciting kind, interspersed with denunciations of
Papal meddling and shouts of 'no popery.' The fleet at Key West
was stripping for action; while the rumor that the Spanish destroyer flotilla was about to sail for the West Indies elicited from
Mr. Roosevelt the vigorous opinion that a squadron should at
once be sent to meet it without waiting for a declaration of war,
on the theory that the mere despatch of the Spanish vessels was
a *casus belli* in itself.

Tuesday passed amid these pleasurable tensions, and the fatal
Wednesday arrived. In Madrid Mr. Woodford transmitted the
President's reply, and the Spanish Ministers went into a cabinet
crisis over the issue of declaring the armistice anyway. Mr. Woodford waited; the Ministers came to no conclusion; the hours ticked
away. Finally, at six o'clock in the evening (1 P.M. by Washington
time), our representative regretfully informed the Ministers that
the Presidential message had been delivered to Congress and that
the matter was out of his hands.

And then there came a ridiculous hitch. It appeared that the
message had not gone to Congress after all. Mr. Woodford's note
had just been safely delivered to the Spanish Government when
a cablegram arrived to inform him that the message would be
postponed until the following Monday 'to give Consul-General
at Havana the time he urgently asks to insure safe departure of
Americans.' Still another exasperating delay was to take place.

At the very last moment the powers had moved; on Wednesday
morning the representatives of Great Britain, Germany, France,
Austria-Hungary, Russia, and Italy had presented at Washington
a 'pressing appeal to the feelings of humanity and moderation of
the President and of the American people' in favor of further
negotiation. But Mr. McKinley was prepared for them; mere
European monarchies could not be expected to teach us anything
about humanity, and the President answered immediately that
the Government of the United States, while appreciating the
disinterested character of the communication, was confident 'that
equal appreciation will be shown for its own earnest and unselfish endeavors to fulfill a duty to humanity by ending a situation
the indefinite prolongation of which has become insufferable.'
So far as humanity went, honors were even.

But this was the language of diplomacy. Certainly the press, if not the Government, of the United States was by no means convinced of the altruism of this attempt to restrain our righteous wrath. A cable from his home Government led Sir Julian Pauncefote, the British Ambassador, to perceive that in encouraging the joint appeal he had been a mere tool of the ulterior designs of Continental diplomacy. Sir Julian dexterously altered his course, and the powers' intervention collapsed. A few days later another attempt was made, but it came to nothing, and the 'whole proceeding,' as the *Review of Reviews* sternly observed, remained 'an excellent object lesson to the American people' in the dangers of having allowed these European intriguers 'to communicate with us at all in the collective sense.... We in this country can never consent to have the concert of Europe, as such, act diplomatically in any affair which concerns us.' So the concert of Europe, as an agency for peace, broke down.

If there were any hope at all, it now lay with the Spaniards. On Thursday morning Mr. Woodford hastened to retract his note of the evening before and place himself once more at the disposal of the Spanish Government; while Congress, now assured that the President's message would soon be transmitted, was content to adjourn for the rest of the week. On their side the Spaniards teetered upon the verge for three whole days, and then finally gave in. On Saturday Mr. Woodford was summoned by the Foreign Minister and told that the Queen's Government had decided to grant an immediate armistice in Cuba 'at the request of the Pope and in deference to the wishes and advice of the representatives of the six great European powers.' Once more, and for the last time, Mr. Woodford thought he saw the peace for which he had so ardently striven within his grasp. For Spain had now definitely yielded everything which we had asked and a cause for war no longer existed. Mr. Woodford placed the statement at once upon the cables and followed it, on Sunday morning, with a personal telegram to Mr. McKinley:

I hope that nothing will now be done to humiliate Spain, as I am satisfied that the present Government is going, and is loyally ready to go, as fast and as far as it can. With your power of action sufficiently free, you will win the fight on your own lines.

But unfortunately, they were no longer Mr. McKinley's lines; the Spaniards were just one week too late. The full proposals were delivered directly to the State Department by the Spanish Minister at Washington in the course of this same Sunday. The Captain-General of Cuba, it was stated, had been authorized to declare a suspension of hostilities, and had already published the decree. The United States was asked to indicate the nature and duration of this armistice, to be announced in a second decree. The reconcentration orders had been revoked. The future of Cuba would be left to the autonomist government in the island, which had been set up in accordance with our views. The questions of fact concerning the Maine would readily be submitted to arbitration. It covered everything — absolutely everything — upon which we had insisted.

Mr. McKinley's reply was that he must decline to offer any further suggestions than those already made, but that in submitting the issue to Congress on the morrow he would acquaint that body with this latest communication. At six o'clock on Sunday evening Mr. Woodford was advised of this reply, and that able Minister's services were over. It was, in fact, all over; sentence had been passed, and all that remained was to settle our own differences as to the manner in which it was to be executed.

On Monday, April 11, Mr. McKinley's message was transmitted to Congress. The fact that Spain had surrendered was imparted in two brief paragraphs, inserted at the end of nine closely printed pages written on the assumption that she had not.

VII

Mr. McKinley's message began with a terse review of the whole situation in Cuba. It listed the losses and cruelties of the civil war; it mentioned the reconcentration decrees as initiating a 'policy of devastation and concentration,' an 'inhuman phase happily unprecedented in the modern history of civilized Christian peoples'; it spoke of the damage suffered by American trade interests, and of the failure of the Spanish arms to remedy the situation. The President then reviewed his own efforts to ameliorate this state of affairs. He spoke of our relief work in Cuba, and traced the diplomatic negotiations down to our demand for an immediate armistice and the Spanish reply (of March 31) offering an armistice if the insurgents would ask for one. 'With this last overture in the direction of immediate peace, and its disappointing reception by Spain,' said Mr. McKinley, 'the Executive is brought to the end of his effort.'

The President then turned to the future. Once more he examined the possibility of recognizing the independence of the insurrectionary government; once more he rejected it, in terms which read a little curiously against our insistence that the Spaniards grant them the armistice which was tantamount to recognition. Recognition by the United States Mr. McKinley did not regard as either 'wise or prudent'; he felt that it was 'not necessary in order to enable the United States to intervene and pacify the island'; while 'to commit this country now to the recognition of any particular government in Cuba might subject us to embarrassing conditions of international obligation toward the organization so recognized.' With this very important reservation, Mr. McKinley then proceeded to the conclusion that 'the forcible intervention of the United States as a neutral to stop the war, according to the large dictates of humanity and following many historical precedents... is justifiable on rational grounds. It involves, however, hostile constraint upon both the parties.' That the Maine incident was a hollow pretext for war Mr. McKinley tacitly recognized; he mentioned it only as an illustration of the 'danger and disorder' involved in the Cuban situation. He repeated the Spanish offer to arbitrate the matter. 'To this,' he added simply, 'I have made no reply.'

Mr. McKinley then plunged into his peroration:

In the name of humanity, in the name of civilization, in behalf of endangered American interests which give us the right and the duty to speak and to act, the war in Cuba must stop. In view of these facts and of these considerations, I ask the Congress to authorize and empower the President to take measures to secure a full and final termination of hostilities between the government of Spain and the people of Cuba, and to secure in the island the establishment of a stable government,... and to use the military and naval forces of the United States as may be necessary for these purposes....

The issue is now with the Congress. It is a solemn responsibility. I have exhausted every effort to relieve the intolerable condition of affairs which is at our doors. Prepared to execute every obligation imposed upon me by the Constitution and the law, I await your action.

Then, and not till then, did Mr. McKinley mention the hardly insignificant fact of the Spanish capitulation.

Yesterday [he concluded, in a really remarkable anti-climax] and since the preparation of the foregoing message, official information was received by me that the latest decree of the Queen Regent of Spain directs General Blanco, in order to prepare and facilitate peace, to proclaim a suspension of hostilities, the duration and details of which have not yet been communicated to me.

This fact, with every other pertinent consideration, will, I am sure, have your just and careful attention in the solemn deliberations upon which you are about to enter. If this measure attains a successful result, then our aspirations as a Christian, peace-loving people will be realized. If it fails, it will be only another justification for our contemplated action.

The singular injustice of this final comment upon a measure which the Christian, peace-loving people had themselves extorted from their reluctant victims must be apparent. But the fact is, of course, that it had long ceased to be a matter of what the Spaniards did. Administration papers could still point to our feverish war preparations as efforts toward the preservation of peace, but they had by this time roused the whole nation to so intense an excitement that to have called off the war now would have been politically disastrous if not humanly impossible. Mr. Atkins could still delude himself with hope from the fact that the President had not specifically asked for war in so many words; but Congress turned at once to the exciting task of giving it to him.

In Spain there was an opposite reaction. The contemptuous treatment of their final sacrifice had at last convinced the Ministry that it was hopeless, and that from now on the best they could do was to go down fighting like men. An extraordinary council of ministers in Madrid ended with a defiant denunciation of the United States for intermeddling in the domestic affairs of Spain; while the crowds milled through the streets and the cafés outside, and the Spanish fleet (what there was of it) sailed from Cadiz for the Cape Verde Islands on its way to war. The common people were now fired with martial eagerness; the more intelligent and better informed were not beyond that philosophical outlook which reminds one that after all the Spanish is an old and experienced race. An American secret agent wrote home:

A Senator from the Kingdom told me yesterday that the thing that he dreaded most was the long period that the hostilities would last.... He said he could very well understand and appreciate the feelings and ambitions of a young and powerful nation like the United States for conquest. He could not help having a great deal of sympathy with an avowed proposition on our part to take the islands of Cuba and Porto Rico, the Canaries, the Balearics, the Philippines, and even to come to Madrid itself; but what he could not understand was, that while protesting a desire for peace, a decided disinclination to the annexation of any territory, the people of the United States had done everything in their power to foment the rebellion in Cuba and to make it impossible for Spain to overcome it, either by peaceable or forcible means.

It was, indeed, very difficult to understand; so difficult, that the American people seem scarcely to have understood it themselves. While their representatives in Congress assembled, brought at last to the point which our aggressiveness and our altruism had jointly prepared, were now to find themselves bogged for nearly a week longer in the intricacies of a peculiar difficulty, springing directly from that confusion of motive.

It was the difficulty which had been hinted at in Mr. McKinley's message — what was to be done with the insurgent 'government'? Behind all our enthusiasm for the Cuban patriots that trouble had lurked; even the most altruistic could not entirely blind themselves to the slightly disreputable character of the Republic, while the aggressive were by no means anxious to invade Cuba for the sole benefit of the rather ambiguous propagandists in the smoke-filled offices of the New York junta. Yet if we calmly steam-rollered those patriots, where were our lofty protestations?

Two exciting days were to elapse before the Foreign Affairs Committee of the House and the Foreign Relations Committee of the Senate were able to bring in their solutions for the problem. Both reported on Wednesday, April 13. The House committee took the more statesmanlike course; its resolution simply authorised the President to 'intervene' in Cuba, secure peace, and establish 'a stable and independent government' there. As to the existing 'government' nothing was said. The resolution passed the House on the same day by 324 to 19.

The Senate machinery worked less smoothly. The committee submitted a long and bellicose report. The resolution it recommended began with the impressive, if slightly unintelligible, declaration that 'the people of the Island of Cuba are, and of right ought to be, free and independent.' It continued to demand that Spain relinquish her authority in the island, and to direct the President 'to use the entire land and naval forces of the United States... to such extent as may be necessary to carry these resolutions into effect.' This might have been all right. But a minority of four Senators added that they favored 'immediate recognition of the Republic of Cuba as organized in that island.'

A few tangled days followed. So intense was the feeling among the honorable gentlemen of the House that it produced a 'riot' on the floor in which one Representative even went to the length of hurling 'a big bound volume' at a colleague. Mr. Roosevelt dashed off another of his illuminating missives to Senator Lodge:

I have just had word that the Administration is very anxious for the House resolution, because under it they will not have to take immediate action. They regard that resolution as requiring immediate intervention, by which they understand diplomacy to be included, but as not requiring them to use the Army and Navy at once. I earnestly hope that it will not be passed by the Senate and that you will stick to your own resolution; otherwise we shall have more delay and more shilly-shallying.

But the Senate was to do much worse than adopt the House resolution. It had no desire for shilly-shallying — 'a spirit of wild jingoism,' the President's secretary noted, 'seems to have taken possession of this usually conservative body' — but on Saturday, the 16th, it adopted its own minority report, thus not only directing the use of military force, but also recognizing the existing Republic. This, the worst possible combination, was effected by the votes of the Democrats and Populists against the conservative Republicans. Mr. Cortelyou, the President's secretary, jotted in his diary that 'a rude awakening is in store for these self-constituted apostles of freedom and humanity.... The President does not look at all well. He is bearing up under the great strain, but his haggard face and anxious inquiry for any news which has in it a token of peace tell of the sense of tremendous responsibility.' But Mr. Roosevelt's diary of the same date bore a very different entry: 'The President still feebly is painfully trying for peace. His weakness and vacillation are even more ludicrous than painful.'

Just before the vote was taken, Senator Teller, one of the 'self-constituted apostles of freedom,' sought to make assurance doubly sure by offering another amendment:

> That the United States hereby disclaims any disposition or intention to exercise sovereignty, jurisdiction, or control over said island, except for the pacification thereof, and asserts its determination when that is accomplished to leave the government and control of the island to its people.

This, the famous and fateful Teller amendment, was adopted without a vote in the excitement. Yet it was ultimately to be the instrument whereby, although the junta was put aside, our honor was preserved and annexation was prevented.

With affairs in this position the Sunday holiday intervened. Early on Monday the House received the Senate resolution and, so excellent was its discipline, struck out the clause recognizing the Republic. All that day the resolutions passed from House to conference room, to Senate and back again, while the great crowds of excited spectators who were filling the Capitol trooped with them from one gallery to another. Amid these feverish (and eminently democratic) surroundings the statesmen labored on into the night, while a nation hung upon their decision. 'The scene upon the floor of the House resembled a political convention,' and in the middle of the evening there came a strange moment as the statesmen were waiting for a conference report:

> A half hundred of the Representatives gathered in the lobby in the rear of the hall and awoke the echoes with patriotic songs. 'The Battle Hymn of the Republic' was sung by General Henderson of Iowa, 'Dixie' and other songs were sung, led by some of the ex-Confederates, and then in tremendous volume the corridors rang with an improvisation: 'Hang General Weyler to a Sour Apple Tree as We Go Marching On.'... Soldiers bivouacking about the camp-fires in the enemy's front could not have been more enthusiastic.

At last, toward three o'clock on Tuesday morning, agreement was reached. With the Teller amendment preserved, the Senate consented to the striking out of the recognition clause, and so

passed the war resolution by the rather narrow vote of 42 to 35.
The House concurred by 310 to 6, and the morning papers of
Tuesday were able to announce a result which under the circum-
stances meant that war had practically begun.

Only the formalities remained. It was not until Wednesday
morning, April 20, that the President actually signed the resolution. Immediately thereafter Mr. Woodford was instructed by
cable to demand that 'the Government of Spain at once relinquish
its authority and government in the Island of Cuba and withdraw
its land and naval forces from Cuba and Cuban waters.' There
was a queer, despairing little maneuver by the Spaniards to avoid
receipt of this last indignity and the appearance of having begun
the war by a refusal of our demands. The President's signature
had hardly dried upon the resolution before the Spanish Minister at Washington was asking for his passports; while before
Mr. Woodford could carry out his instructions at Madrid, he was
informed that, the resolution being 'equivalent to an evident
declaration of war,' all diplomatic relations had been broken off.
The ultimatum was never delivered. Mr. Woodford had no option
save to ask for his passports; and on Thursday, April 21, the two
diplomats were rolling northward, one through the Pennsylvania
hills on his way to Canada, the other over the bare, hot plains of
Castile on his way to France.

'In the opinion of nearly all writers on international law,' as
an American student of the subject later found, 'the particular
form of intervention in 1898 was unfortunate, irregular, precipitate, and unjust to Spain. The same ends — peace in Cuba and
justice to all people concerned — in themselves good, could have
been achieved by peaceful means safer for the wider interests of
humanity.' But one may question whether the American people
by this time were in fact interested either in peace or in humanity.
Certainly amid the splendid excitement of that Thursday afternoon the officials and bureaucrats, upon whom the responsibility
of action had now devolved, entertained no doubts. With their
offices and corridors 'thronged with Congressmen and citizens-at-
large,' assailed by perspiring and patriotic gentlemen offering their
services, offering their advice, demanding favors and claiming
contracts, with the air filled with the intoxication of war plans and

war preparations and war possibilities, with the crowds milling before the bulletin boards in the streets and with the 'eager representatives of the press' in every corner, how could they have paused before that deep, bloody, and irresistible fascination of impending battle? Whether we were really at war or not nobody seemed to know. But now nobody cared.

Mr. McKinley, it is true, seems up to the very last to have toyed with the idea that he could still conduct an armed intervention without beginning a war. When on this same afternoon the President at last gave the word, it was a word devised in that peculiar ambiguity which was so striking a characteristic of his statesmanship. Mr. McKinley ordered a 'blockade.' But a definite order had finally been given; Mr. Long despatched it by telegraph to Admiral Sampson, and the fleet which had been swinging so long to its anchors in the harbor at Key West was at last unleashed.

At 4.30 next morning, April 22, the American squadron was outside the reef and under way, and at about three o'clock in the afternoon the officers — and the newspaper correspondents — on the flying bridge of the flagship saw the low hills of western Cuba and the dark, mediæval parapets of Morro Castle emerging from the sea. A press boat was hurried back to Key West with the news. The blockade of Havana had been established. Hostilities had begun. It was the real thing at last.

CHAPTER VI

THE CRUSADE IS LAUNCHED

I

HOSTILITIES had indeed begun. It is true that several rather confusing days were yet to elapse before the two governments could convince themselves that war, likewise, had commenced — a circumstance which makes it a trifle hard to fix the precise date at which the latter event took place. So difficult was it to believe that the peace-loving American people could actually start a war, so skillfully had our diplomatic justifications been elaborated, that even now we seemed hardly to grasp what had happened. In ordering the blockade of the north coast of Cuba, Mr. McKinley could not have supposed that he was beginning a war, for war can be declared by Congress alone. Yet when Congress finally did declare it, four days later, it was with the statement that war had existed from the day upon which Mr. McKinley had ordered the blockade. This not only bequeathed to future international lawyers a subtle and engaging problem; it also gave to our entry into war the appearance less of a conscious decision by responsible statesmen than of an inevitable natural phenomenon, unascribable to any human agency. The war, in other words, just happened. Perhaps it was for the best. At some point between April 21 and April 25 (the date of the declaration), it seems to have become evident even to Mr. McKinley that it really was a war which he was fighting, but this important transition appeared to flow simply from the logic of great events, and nobody could exactly be held responsible for it.

Apparently it had for some time been decided, by a kind of general consensus, that a blockade would in any event be the first step. This singular method of opening a campaign primarily designed to relieve the starving Cubans becomes no less extraordinary when one notes that in his war message, delivered a bare ten days before he signed the blockade proclamation, Mr. McKinley had recommended that the distribution of food and supplies be continued in the island and had even requested a Government appropriation for the purpose. But the Navy and the public at the time were in the full glow of their pride over the strategic genius of our own Captain Mahan; and under the great principles of sea power which that brilliant theoretician had laid down, a blockade was clearly the proper thing. It was impossible to have a correct naval war without blockading somebody, and since the Cubans were the only people available, it was necessary to blockade them. As early as March 23 there had been a memorandum, based upon suggestions from the famous captain himself, outlining this procedure; the President's request for a relief appropriation was not even noticed, and the blockade was duly adopted as the first move.

It was even thought quite generally that it might also be the last; and a 'member of the cabinet' appeared to sum up the official attitude when, a few days before the rupture, he explained the matter to the press:

> If Spain refuses to evacuate Cuba prompt measures will be adopted.... A blockade of Cuba will, so far as it is at present understood, be begun at once. There are an adequate number of war-vessels in the vicinity to make this effective. I think such supplies as the Spaniards now control will not last them more than a month. Then steps will be taken with a view of increasing the equipment of Gomez's soldiers and furnishing them with sufficient hardtack and food, which will enable them to harass the Spaniards from the rear, which will materially assist in bringing them to terms.
>
> My own individual idea is that it will probably take two months to bring about the results which will compel the Spaniards to evacuate and enable the island to be occupied by the United States without molestation.

Such a program had obvious advantages. It would not only leave the actual fighting to the Cubans, while reserving to American troops the more impressive, but less bloody, ardors of 'occupation'; it might also avoid a technical war, since a blockade was at most only a quasi-belligerent step. Thus it was decided; and the first result of our humane intervention was the withdrawal of all American relief agencies from the island and the initiation of a starvation campaign the immediate effects of which could fall only upon the reconcentrados.

But here the approved plans came to a sudden end. Perhaps it was unfortunate. If Mr. McKinley had supposed that his excited fellow countrymen and their eager servants in the War and Navy Departments would sit down quietly in these tremendous days to await the outcome of a blockade of Cuba, he was quickly disabused. The nation was aflame with the martial spirit; Washington was filled with eminent gentlemen outdoing each other in the effort to lay themselves upon the altars of patriotism; Mr. Roosevelt was planning to resign from the Navy Department in order to raise a force of volunteer cavalry; ministers in their pulpits were proclaiming the war for Christian (or at any rate Protestant) civilization; and the high-priced war correspondents in Sampson's ships off the Cuban coast were clamoring for blood with which to justify their telegrams. How was it possible to check so vast a tide? And, besides, there was always the possibility that the Spaniards, after all, might not obligingly evacuate.

On April 22, Congress empowered the President to summon volunteers from the various states to increase the Army 'in time of war,' and on April 23, the President issued his first call for 125,000 men. This also appeared to be a logical step under the circumstances; this also was not in itself directly belligerent. But it fed the already roaring flames; and to them the strategic geniuses in the Navy Department now added fresh fuel.

The Navy Department had not forgotten that in addition to Admiral Sampson's force engaged in eliminating the Spaniards from Cuba, another squadron was waiting upon the opposite side of the world with the very different mission of eliminating the Spaniards from the Philippine Islands. On the day that Sampson was ordered to Havana the Navy Department, according to Secretary Long, had come to the 'unanimous opinion' that we should also 'strike at once at the Spanish fleet in the Philippines' — an opinion, as Mr. Long need scarcely have added, concurred in by his forceful assistant secretary. But a difficulty arose. Mr. McKinley 'thought it not quite time'; he was evidently not yet prepared to endorse anything at once so definitely belligerent and so obscurely connected with the wrongs of Cuba as this. The Department was forced to curb its impatience for strategic conquest; and after ordering Sampson to the blockade, it cabled

Dewey: 'War has not yet been declared. War may be declared at any moment. I will inform you. Await orders.'

He was not to wait for long. Under the pressure of the next three days the War President's ideas appear rapidly to have advanced. On Saturday, when he was issuing his call for volunteers, he was already deciding to ask Congress for a formal declaration, and early on Sunday morning he summoned the Secretary of the Navy to the White House. Mr. Long has described the scene:

So vivid is the picture he presented on that memorable occasion that it has remained in my memory with the distinctness of a first impression. It was a lovely, sunny spring day, a bright contrast to the grim business in hand. We sat on a sofa, he thoughtful, his face showing a deep sense of the responsibility of the hour.... The President gave me that morning the desired authority, and the despatch... was put in cipher and cabled.

It read:

Dewey, Hong Kong:
War has commenced between the United States and Spain. Proceed at once to Philippine Islands. Commence operations at once, particularly against the Spanish fleet. You must capture vessels or destroy. Use utmost endeavors.

LONG

The process by which Mr. McKinley had arrived at the discovery that war had commenced is not recorded. But its results were to be profound, and the President may well have looked thoughtful. For it was upon that sunny spring forenoon, amid all the hurry and excitement of a nation lumbering into battle, that the design which had so long been prepared by Mr. Roosevelt, Mr. Lodge, and the ambitious strategists in the Navy Department was definitely slipped into the national policy. It was on that beautiful Sunday morning that Mr. McKinley upon his sofa not only began the war which Congress had authorized to free oppressed Cuba, but began as well another war, which Congress had not even thought of, which had a very different aim, which was to produce very different results, and which was to set in motion a long train of unanticipated consequences the ultimate end of which is even now beyond prediction. Whether Mr. McKinley, as he granted the 'desired authority' for the onslaught upon the Philippines, quite appreciated what he was doing one can only guess.[1]

But he appreciated, at any rate, that after this there could no longer be any question of a mere 'armed intervention.' In the course of the same day Spain issued a declaration recognizing the existence of a state of war; and on Monday, the 25th, Mr. McKinley sent in his message requesting of Congress a 'joint resolution declaring that a state of war exists.' Congress immediately acquiesced. Doubt no longer remained. We had the war. How were we to fight it?

II

Though the Navy Department had early developed its ideas on the subject, it now appeared that not only the Army but even the editors had omitted almost entirely to go into this aspect of the problem. Nor was it altogether a simple one. The declared object was to secure the Spanish withdrawal from Cuba. In anticipation of its part of the task, the Navy had assembled its heaviest squadron under Sampson at Key West. Spain had no useful naval force with which to oppose these vessels. Two of her modern cruisers had been in Cuban waters, but as the crisis approached they were prudently called home to join Admiral Cervera, beyond the immediate reach of our mobilized fleet. Admiral Cervera had started for the West Indies, but had got only as far as St. Vincent in the Cape Verde Islands, where he remained. As a protection for our coast against any raids which he might attempt, we had stationed Commodore Schley — the dashing hero of the Chilean episode — at Hampton Roads with a powerful 'flying squadron'; while at the last minute a reassuring, if quite useless, 'patrol force,' consisting largely of armed merchantmen, had been organized to allay the nascent fears of the New England seaboard. Except for Cervera's four armored cruisers, Spain had nothing available. Sampson moved out unhindered to the blockade, and until the

---

[1] It should be noted that the phrasing of Mr. Long's telegram was such as to make operative Mr. Roosevelt's telegram of February 25 (p. 112) ordering 'offensive operations in Philippine Islands.' Dewey interpreted it in this sense and took the two together as his orders; Mr. Roosevelt's foresight had thus relieved the Department of the necessity for sending explicit instructions of which Mr. McKinley, in April, might not have approved.

Spaniards should make some move there was nothing else for the Navy to do.

There remained, however, the Spanish land forces in Cuba. At first these had not been seriously considered, and up to the very eve of hostilities it was still reported to be 'the general belief in the Army and Navy that Spain is not going to offer any physical resistance whatever to the freedom of Cuba, but will surrender in presence of superior force.' Three years of Cuban propaganda had created a profound contempt for the Spanish troops in the minds of the American public and of the authorities. On his return from Cuba, Consul-General Lee, who had been a military man himself thirty years before and consequently spoke with all the weight of expert knowledge, had solemnly assured the Foreign Relations Committee that the Spanish army was 'not drilled, not organized,' and 'not officered well'; and that an American army of occupation could be put into the island 'with safety' both as regarded the climate and 'everything else.' The thought that the expulsion of the Spanish forces might constitute a really difficult task seems to have occurred to hardly any one in the country; while the immensely superior power and wealth of the United States in comparison with Spain's had been taken for granted in both nations for years. The Navy rested in its confidence that a 'rigid blockade' with, perhaps, a little light bombardment now and then would be all that would really be required.

But even the Navy appreciated that some kind of expeditionary force would be necessary 'to occupy any captured stronghold,' as Mr. Long put it, 'or to protect from riot and arson.' Clearly, if we were going to take over Cuba, something of the sort was an essential. But when we at last began to look about for one (this was along toward the middle of April, after Mr. McKinley's war message had actually gone to Congress and the crisis was at hand), we found, oddly enough, that there wasn't any. That superior force, in the presence of which the Spaniards were to surrender, unhappily did not exist. The full implications of this discovery, it is true, were to dawn only gradually; but it was quite early appreciated — all of a week, in fact, before the actual outbreak of hostilities — that even to prevent riot and arson a certain minimum of military preparation might be almost indispensable. It was on April 13 that a Washington correspondent explained the trouble:

One of the generals at the War Department remarked today that no difficulty would be found in landing 50,000 men in Cuba next week, but it was exceedingly doubtful of what use they would be in so short a time. From this it appears that no actual invasion is contemplated inside of two or three weeks, and within that time conditions may change altogether, rendering invasion for intervention superfluous, although making it absolutely essential [in order] promptly to establish stability of government.

This was putting it mildly. There were understood to be about 80,000 Spanish effectives in the island. The entire Regular Army of the United States amounted to only 28,183 officers and men. Many of these were required to man the coast defenses which Mr. Alger had been hurrying to completion; the remainder were scattered all over the country, garrisoning the innumerable political army posts in detachments of single battalions or even companies. Individually, the regulars were at a fair standard of efficiency as a result of the long Indian wars, but they were without experience in anything save the most minor type of maneuver. There was no plan of mobilization, no higher organization, no training in combined operations, no provision for the assembling or transportation of an overseas expedition, or for the handling of any large body of troops whatever. The disconcerting discovery was made that there had been no brigade formation of troops in the United States for thirty years — except for the ageing veterans of the Civil War, there were no officers in the Army who had ever even seen a force larger than a regiment together in one place, and there were few who had even seen that much. Field maneuvers even by regiments were almost unknown; and it might be added that the amount of improvisation which was to be required — in staff work, supply, communications, evacuation and hospitalization — was as yet unsuspected by the regular officers themselves.

In addition to the Regular Army there were the National Guard organizations of the various states, numbering in all about 100,000 men. In this martial force there reigned an almost total want of everything except a certain familiarity with close-order infantry drill. The National Guard was lamentably weak in artillery, cavalry, or the necessary technical branches; its infantry units were in all stages of inefficiency, and it was endowed in addition with a unique, a truly American, concept of military discipline. It was armed with rifles firing a black-powder cartridge which were regarded as useless in warfare; it lacked equipment, shoes, blankets, tentage, and anything approaching genuine field service experience, while its officers, as in the opening stages of the Civil War, were chosen by popular vote of their men. And above all this it enjoyed a peculiarity of organization of an obviously embarrassing kind.

The National Guard was under the control, not of the President or the Federal Government, but of the respective Governors of the sovereign states. As it stood it presented the pleasantly baffling picture of some forty or more separate armies, all intensely jealous of their rights, devoid of any form of coördinating organization and directed by an equal number of civilian executives none of whom ever overlooked those political considerations which so greatly complicate public affairs within the United States. In a nation which quite naturally assumed that the war, like every other governmental activity, would of course be conducted as a preliminary to the next election, this situation was likely to make the National Guard a force of limited effectiveness.

Some two or three weeks before the rupture came, it had occurred to General Nelson A. Miles, the General Commanding the Army, that something ought to be done. Confronting this splendid anarchy in our forces, General Miles was unable to share the optimistic views which were prevalent; for after all there were those 80,000 Spanish troops in the island, veterans of from one to three years' active service under the special conditions of Cuban campaigning. To assume that they would immediately yield to superior force might be a trifle unwise, especially as it was so difficult to perceive where the superior force was to come from. General Miles had begun to recommend very strongly that a mobilization, at least of the regulars, would be useful as a precautionary measure; and by April 9 he was urging that the entire Regular Army be got together at Chickamauga Park, near Chattanooga, where it might be 'fully equipped, drilled, disciplined, and instructed in brigades and divisions, and prepared for war service.'

It was not, however, until April 15, when the war resolutions were actually going through Congress and war itself was less than a week away, that the War Department at last awakened to the virtues of preparedness. But by this time the nation, no less than General Miles, was clamoring for action and Secretary Alger (who had been a general officer in the Civil War, but who had spent most of the intervening thirty years in Michigan politics) was not content with any plan so purely precautionary. The cavalry and artillery were ordered to Chickamauga, but the twenty-five regiments of infantry were to be distributed between New Orleans, Mobile, and Tampa, where they would be ready for an immediate descent upon Cuba — and where, incidentally, they would be beyond any possibility of that combined training with the two other arms which they so much needed.

This was the first plan. It was, however, soon modified, and some of the infantry regiments were diverted to Chickamauga after all. The more the problem was examined, the more difficult did an immediate descent upon Cuba appear. A principal complication was the fact that the rainy season, which was also the yellow fever season, would set in with the early summer. It was generally believed that it would be impossible for unacclimated troops to operate in the island from May until October. Under the circumstances the theory that the Cubans should be allowed to do the actual fighting undoubtedly had its attractions. On April 18, General Miles again submitted his views:

> In my opinion it is extremely hazardous, and I think it would be injudicious, to put an army on that island at this season of the year, as it would undoubtedly be decimated by the deadly disease, to say nothing of having to cope with some 80,000 troops.... By mobilizing our force and putting it in healthful camps and using such force as might be necessary to harass the enemy and doing them the greatest injury with the least possible loss to ourselves, if our Navy is superior to theirs, in my judgment we can compel the surrender of the army on the Island of Cuba with very little loss of life and possibly avoid the spread of yellow fever over our own country.

And it seems to have been this policy which was accepted for the time being by the War Department, in so far as that harassed organization possessed any policy at all. The Regulars were set in motion for 'healthful camps.' Even so, however, there were only 28,000 Regulars. Some provision for reënforcing them had become imperative. The War Department turned to survey the National Guard; and it surveyed with misgivings.

The simplest method, of course, would have been to dispense with the existing Guard units at once and to enlist the individual Guardsmen in a new volunteer army, to be built from the ground up in the Federal service. Unfortunately, however, the National Guard was endowed with a pride in its own organizations; it was likewise endowed with the vote, and throughout the war the political consequences were a major element in all our problems of generalship. The National Guard had already manifested a lively antipathy to any independent volunteer army in which the identity of its units would be lost. It was a social as well as a military organization; there was a pleasant *camaraderie* within its armories, and it could depose as well as elect its own officers. In Brooklyn a 'well-known Guardsman who belongs to an excellent family' expressed to a reporter his righteous indignation at the prospect of being asked to surrender these mitigations of the natural horrors of war:

> One of the reasons that we would not go willingly into the Regular Army is that we would have to serve under West-Pointers. For a self-respecting American of good family to serve as a private, corporal, or sergeant under a West Point lieutenant or captain is entirely out of the question. West-Pointers have seen fit to introduce a class feeling — no, I will go farther and say a caste feeling — between themselves and non-commissioned officers and privates that is unpleasant in the extreme....
> To fight for my country as a volunteer in the regiment that I love would be a glorious pleasure, but to serve in the Regular Army and do chores for some West-Pointer — well, I would rather be excused.

Nor were such sterling democratic sentiments as these the only ones to be considered. The Guardsmen had the vote; but the Governors of the states, who were their commanders-in-chief, were important leaders in the great political machines whereby votes were controlled. They were unlikely cheerfully to surrender the magnificent opportunities for patronage opened by their ability to appoint officers to this popular war; while the Congressmen, who were members and creatures of these same machines, could hardly be expected to force them to do so. The War Department, in 'many conferences,' wrestled with the problem of devising some method whereby the Guard could safely be incorporated in the Federal service as it stood.

But the memories of the disasters produced by the state militia system in the Civil War were too vivid, and the Department was compelled to decide against the employment of the state troops as such. It hurriedly drafted a bill providing for the creation of an independent Federal force, all the officers to be commissioned directly by the President. An effort was made to meet the objections of the Governors by pointing out that, since these troops were for service beyond the borders of any state, the President should properly retain the appointing power, and to satisfy the Guardsmen by providing that the army, although to be composed of volunteers, should not be called a volunteer army. Unfortunately, these efforts proved inadequate; and the 'militia interests' were powerful. Before the bill was even submitted to Congress, the War Department was obliged to concede that any National Guard regiments which were at full strength would be taken bodily into the new army, and that no West-Pointers would be appointed to it. Having thus assured the prospective volunteers that they would be deprived in battle of the only trained leadership which was available in the country, the Department hoped that perhaps the bill might get through. It was turned over to the House Military Affairs Committee just as the war resolutions were being voted; and a newspaper report of the fact paused to note that 'Army and Navy experts are beginning to take a less hopeful view of an easy and quick campaign than they entertained a short time ago. Months are now mentioned instead of weeks as the probable length of hostilities.'

The bill was offered with a companion measure providing for the reorganization of the regular establishment and its expansion 'in time of war' to about 61,000 men, by the addition of a third battalion to each of the existing regiments. In the patriotic hastes of the week following the war resolution, both measures passed rapidly through Congress, though not without opposition. Mr. Oscar Underwood, the youthful Representative from Alabama who was later to play so distinguished a rôle in the nation's history, thought that the bill increasing the Regulars was merely an ulterior attempt to foist a large and permanent 'standing army' upon the people:

Your constituents and my constituents do not want the standing army of the United States to fight this war. There is hardly a man on this floor who has not received letters from his constituents stating that they would be glad to volunteer, glad to fight for their country, if they can be officered by their home men. They want to know their officers and be officered by men who have been raised and who have lived among them.

There must be no standing armies created simply 'because we have gone to war'; there must be, the legislators insisted, no 'West Point martinets.' Perhaps it made little difference, since the West Point martinets were as scarce as they were later to prove valuable. But the volunteer bill did not pass until modifications had justified practically all the War Department's fears. It had to be made clear that the National Guard units would be received bodily into the Federal service if their Governors desired, while the bill itself, though stating that 'all the regimental company officers shall be appointed by the President,' explicitly added that he was to do so only 'upon the recommendation of the Governors of the states.' The act became law on April 22, and on the following day, as has been said, President McKinley issued his call for 125,000 men under its terms. Practically nothing had been gained except that the reënforcement of the Army had been made possible, and that the reënforcements, when they came, would at least be under Federal control. The Guard retained its organizations and the Governors their appointive powers, and there would be no martinets.

But even with these safeguards some among the state forces were not reassured. With the whole country, as it seemed, flocking into the recruiting stations; with men of wealth falling over each other in the anterooms at Washington in their haste to offer their means and energies to the nation; with the less fortunate besieging the flag counters at the 'dry-goods stores' from morning to night in their patriotic desire to do their bit; and with the war-cry 'Remember the Maine, to Hell with Spain!' echoing through every class, there was still considerable doubt as to whether the National Guard could so far compromise with its principles as to fight under a Federal autocracy. In Brooklyn, Colonel William L. Watson, commander of the Thirteenth Regiment, issued a formal statement to the effect that the whole treatment of the state troops was 'merely part of a scheme to crush the National Guard so that there will appear to be a necessity for a greater Regular Army'; and the command made so many difficulties about volunteering that it ultimately had to be disbanded. The Populist Governor of Kansas would not permit his National Guard regiments to enter the Federal service at all, but organized new units in order that the existing commissioned personnel might be replaced with assured friends of the people; while, when the Navy Department endeavored to recover a monitor which it had lent to the Naval Militia of North Carolina, the commander of the battalion 'peremptorily declined to surrender the monitor, hoisted the state flag over her, and defied any one to haul it down.' He was as good as his word, and in order to secure its vessel the Navy Department had to request the state adjutant-general to order the commander to release her.

On April 26, the day after the official declaration of war, the armories of the New York State troops presented a curious spectacle as the men were solemnly assembled, in uniform and by orders of their adjutant-general, to poll the question of whether they would consent to join the war on the terms offered by the Federal Government. It was a singular illustration of our devotion to the democratic principle — an illustration, it might be added, which later military authorities have taken care shall not recur. Though the reporters waited eagerly for the decision, the outcome was never really in doubt. Overwhelming majorities in nearly all the organizations offered to volunteer. But at one armory there was a different result. In the famous Seventh Regiment — the best-known National Guard unit in the country, an organization celebrated alike for its efficiency, its traditions, the splendor of its uniform, and the fact that it numbered in its ranks the sons of many wealthy and socially prominent New York families — it had been reported that the men, though they would be glad to 'march away with the regiment,' would probably 'be slow to join a company with Tom, Dick, and Harry and be commanded by an officer other than the one under whom they are now serving.' That evening their colonel gave out a brief announcement to the effect that while the Seventh was always ready to serve the nation if called upon as such, it would not volunteer to enlist in a Federal army. Thus it was that the crack regiment of the National Guard and the pride of New York State maintained its dignity — and remained at home when it came to fighting. Months afterward, when the war was won, the Seventh United States Artillery was hissed in the streets of New York by a crowd which, seeing the numeral on its haversacks, mistook its identity.

But at all events, provision had at last been made for a second line reserve which might be expected to be ready some day. How soon that day would arrive was by this time a matter of considerable doubt. As the full magnitude of the project slowly dawned, the outgivings began to postpone the occupation until October at the very earliest; while the Surgeon-General of the Army, a recognized expert on tropical disease, issued the disconcerting opinion that an invasion undertaken any sooner would result in a mortality from yellow fever of from thirty-five to fifty per cent. And though the men had now been provided, as yet there was nothing else whatever.

Concentration camps had not been decided upon, there were no modern rifles for the volunteers, there were no tropical uniforms and no provision for them, there was a want of horses, mules, and every kind of transportation, and there was an overpowering, all-embracing want of staff organization, or officer material out of which it could be created. And above all, there was no time. The regulars were already at their mobilization points or were being poured into them every hour by the southern-going railway lines. The volunteers, already gathering at their state camps, were clamoring for immediate attention and priority of employment. Innumerable gentlemen wielding a political influence which it was impossible to disregard were demanding offices, demanding commissions, demanding the right to raise independent troops, batteries, and regiments. Quite aside from anything which the Spaniards might do, the purely administrative problems of the mobilization had descended in an avalanche of the most pressing urgency; while an impatient and martial public was already beginning to cry out for blood, action, and an instant assault upon Havana. A desperately overworked and understaffed War Department, suddenly confronted by the strange necessity of actually waging a war, found itself signing contracts, issuing orders, and trying to prepare its plans in an appalling and developing confusion. While above the whole of this incomparable chaos there reigned a mild-mannered, inoffensive gentleman who was permitted by the exigencies of our democratic institutions to give to it anything but his undivided attention. Incredible as it may seem, we have it upon Secretary Alger's own statement:

The life of the Secretary of War [he wrote with feeling] was not a happy one in those days of active military operations.... It seemed as if there was hardly a family in the United States that did not have a friend or relative in the service, and that for one reason or another some member from each of these found it necessary to write to, or personally visit, the War Office. Members of Congress, departmental and state officials cannot, as a rule, be denied audience. The office of the Secretary was daily visited by not less than one hundred persons whose business or position entitled them to a personal hearing. So urgent was the pressure that almost the entire day was given up to them. Therefore it became necessary to devote the greater part of the night and Sundays to the consideration of the administrative features of department work.

In this atmosphere the plans were made; and in this way the nation swung cheerfully into a war which it was to allow its War Secretary to conduct only in his spare time.

III

It was a war entered without misgivings and in the noblest frame of mind. Seldom can history have recorded a plainer case of military aggression; yet seldom has a war been started in so profound a conviction of its righteousness. If there was, indeed, a lingering perplexity in some minds as to what it was really all about, this failed to dampen the grandeur of our altruism. Even so sturdy a liberal as Mr. Carl Schurz could conclude, as he debated the problem, that it must be 'a case of self-sacrifice.' Mr. Schurz was unable to see anything which we might gain from the war commensurate with the costs of fighting it; it led him to a triumphant demonstration that 'all our real compensation for our sacrifices and risks... will consist in our moral consciousness of having delivered Cuba of Spanish misrule.' There could be no clearer case, he thought, of untainted altruism.

Of course there were a few recalcitrant minds unable to follow this reasoning. Somewhere in the shadows Mr. Cleveland was taking up a sorrowful pen to supply Mr. Olney with gloomy, if accurate, prophecy:

> With all allowances I can make [he wrote on the day after the declaration of war]... I cannot avoid a feeling of shame and humiliation. It seems to me to be the same old story of good intentions and motives sacrificed to false considerations of complaisance and party harmony. McKinley is not a victim of ignorance, but of amiable weakness not unmixed with political ambition. He knew, or ought to have known, the cussedness of the Senate and he was abundantly warned against Lee, and yet he has surrendered to the former and given his confidence to the latter. The Senate would not hesitate to leave him in the lurch and Lee will strut and swagger, I suppose, as a major-general and the idol of the populace. Roosevelt, too, will have his share of strut and sensation, and Miles will be commissioned General of the Army....
>
> My only relief from the sick feeling which these thoughts induce consists in the reflection that it affects no one but myself, and in the hope, almost amounting to expectation, that we shall find Spain so weak and inefficient that the war will be short and that the result may not be much worse than a depreciation of national standing before the world abroad, and, at home, demoralization of our people's character, much demagogy and humbug, great additions to our public burdens and the exposure of scandalous operations.

It was the bitterness of an age that was dying; the last words of an old-fashioned idealism, of old-fashioned standards, of an old-fashioned integrity perishing before the new epoch which it could not understand. The virtues of nineteenth-century America died upon Mr. Cleveland's lips, while outside the window the livelier concepts of the new era were being ushered in by the cheering crowds, the crashing brass bands and the long tramp of the volunteers. Mr. Cleveland was forgotten; and in Kansas City a shoemaker who had hung crape upon his shop door with the notice, 'Closed in memory of a Christian nation that descends to the barbarity of war,' was very properly mobbed by a right-thinking populace.

It is true that alien minds were even yet incapable of appreciating the loftiness of our motives. On the morning of April 23, the newspapers of Germany, of every shade of opinion, condemned the United States 'with singular unanimity'; out of fifty-two papers appearing that morning in Paris, only three (*L'Intran*, and the journals of those two radicals, M. Jaurès and M. Clemenceau) could be counted in our favor; and even in England, where the official attitude was one of almost sentimental friendliness, such papers as the *Saturday Review* were 'teeming with insults.' But at home there were no qualms. Innumerable editors, ministers of the Gospel, political and even business and financial leaders were fearlessly 'standing behind the President.' A thumping war revenue bill was already on its way through Congress — and though it was to get badly mired for a time in the sloughs of the free silver controversy, there was no opposition to providing the money. In every city the enthusiastic crowds were standing day-long in the spring weather before the newspaper bulletin boards, across which rumor, sensation, and denial pursued each other in an endless and feverish procession.

The music of 'Dixie' blended with 'The Star-Spangled Banner' as the files went down the streets; and Mr. McKinley, commissioning as major-generals in the new army both Mr. Lee and 'Fighting Joe' Wheeler (who had likewise served as a general officer of the Confederacy), seemed to cement forever the bonds of sectional reunion and to bury the bitterness which had been festering for thirty years. The Civil War faded at last in the great crusade to free Cuba from the Spaniard, and it was as a united nation that we faced the enemy. Miss Helen M. Gould offered $100,000 out of her private fortune as a free-will gift to the Navy. The Governor of Texas patriotically placed his entire force of Rangers upon the border to repel any possible invasion from Mexico by 'Spanish sympathizers.' At the Knickerbocker Theater in New York, where 'The Bride Elect' was running, the chorus 'Unchain the Dogs of War' nightly brought down the house. The Governor of Georgia announced that he would personally lead the militia of his state to battle. The manufacturers of American flags were unable to satisfy the demands of patriotism; even the supplies of bunting began to run short and the looms could not replace them in time. A complete regiment was organized among the Wall Street brokers and their clerks. Mr.

William Astor Chanler offered a regiment to the Government; his cousin, Mr. John Jacob Astor, supplied a complete battery of artillery, the guns and ammunition having been imported from abroad at his own expense. And Mr. Roosevelt, who for weeks had been filling his office at the Navy Department with cavalry equipment and younger military men, prepared to abandon the ardors of the Naval Strategy Board for more spectacular service upon the field of battle.

The war extras followed one another through the streets in a torrential outpouring; and the war correspondents, flocking into every camp, every naval station and every possible or impossible theater of action, loaded down the wires with detailed accounts of every move made or contemplated. Any feeble opposition put up by the browbeaten authorities on the score of secrecy was imperiously brushed aside. After all, if it was not the newspapers' war, whose war was it? When the Navy fitted out a vessel as a hospital ship, she was immediately stormed by whole battalions of reporters, who calculated that, as she would have to hurry from the scene of battle to land the wounded, she would be the first to reach the telegraph wires. Mr. Long managed to keep them off; not, however, because they might reveal military secrets, but because he believed news to be 'contraband of war' and thought that their presence might destroy the ship's neutrality. It made no difference. The *World*, the *Journal*, and the press associations chartered their own squadrons; and Mr. Hearst, sailing as admiral of his own navy, was to take personal command of his forces in the presence of the enemy. Already, by April 26, Mr. Pulitzer was selling 1,300,000 copies of the *World* a day; and as the editorial-writers of the country settled to the serious business of conducting operations, a triumphant journalism was definitely in command. Even the sedate *Atlantic Monthly* stunned its readers by appearing, actually, with an American flag upon the cover, and after that it seemed that patriotism could indeed go no farther.

It is true that patriotism also had its more regrettable manifestations. Secretary Long's diary for these days contains a sorrowful entry:

This morning Congressman Brumm calls with a delegation of Pennsylvanians to urge the use of anthracite, instead of bituminous, coal on board ships. It is interesting to note how every section of the country, although all are patriotic, has an eye on the main chance.

The Navy Department, with its usual foresight, had early arranged with various coastwise transportation companies for the conveyance of its coal when the crisis should arrive, but when the war did come every firm except one declined to adhere to its offer on the ground that war risks were too high. When the Department, caught in this serious situation, turned to buy a collier fleet of its own, it was pained to find that the owners of the suitable vessels 'knew well the necessities of the Government and generally demanded exorbitant prices.' The emergency was critical, and the Navy had to pay. Later on it was able to buy its colliers at more reasonable prices from the British, and so break the market among the patriotic ship-owners at home.

It is said that upon other occasions vessels which had been rejected as useless by the naval boards of survey were nevertheless purchased by the Government — after the exercise of a little political pressure. The Army, compelled to buy mules in large quantities, discovered that animals which had been selling at $70 to $90 a head had jumped overnight to $130 or $150. Nor were other similar instances lacking. But after all, when the politicians and the editors were making such a good thing out of the war, one can scarcely blame the business men if they saw no reason why they should not do likewise. Besides, it would be unjust to cite such isolated instances alone. There was the case, for example, of Mr. John P. Holland, whose remarkable 'submarine torpedo boat' had been arousing so much interest and speculation at New York. Mr. Holland offered the boat to the Navy for $175,000, but, in spite of the strongly favorable recommendations of Mr. Roosevelt, a naval board reported adversely. According to the report, Mr. Holland then rushed in person to Washington and informed the Department that he would, with his own crew, enter the harbor of Havana and throw a dynamite bomb into Morro Castle, provided the Navy would guarantee to purchase the vessel upon the completion of the exploit. The Department was forced to reject this slightly piratical proposal, but it indicated the spirit.

Amid such events as these the mere preparations for war were sufficiently exhilarating. But within a week the tone had already begun to deepen; the sound of actual gun-fire was heard off the north coast of Cuba. On April 24, an optimistic Spanish battery had taken three pot-shots at the destroyer Foote (she was lying far out of range) and her astonished commander reported that he had actually been fired upon. Then on April 27, Admiral Sampson took his flagship, the cruiser New York, down the coast to Matanzas to put a stop to what looked to be the construction of some earthworks. She opened fire at four thousand yards, and our first shots of the war flung the yellow dust into the air and the newspapers into a paroxysm of headlines. The blockade was, of course, very fully reported, and Mr. Richard Harding Davis himself was at the time one of the feature writers in the New York's complement. Judging by Mr. Davis's account the fire discipline in the Navy was a little peculiar:

Captain Chadwick ran down the ladder from the forward bridge, and shouted at Ensign Boone, 'Aim for 4000 yards, at that bank of earth on the point.' Then he ran up to the bridge again, where Admiral Sampson was pacing up and down.... The ship seemed to work and to fight by herself; you heard no human voice of command, only the grieved tones of Lieutenant Mulligan, rising from his smoke-choked deck below, where he could not see to aim his six-inch gun, and from where he begged Lieutenant Marble again and again to 'take your damned smoke out of my way.' Lieutenant Marble was vaulting in and out of his forward turret like a squirrel in a cage. One instant you would see him far out on the deck,... and the next pushing the turret with his shoulder as though he meant to shove it overboard; and then he would wave his hand to his crew inside and there would be a racking roar.

But posterity must remember the influence of Mr. Kipling on the prose style of the period. To the excited publics at home it was, at last, real war; and the popular demand for action arose in a crescendo which Mr. McKinley could not possibly disregard. Originally, it will be remembered, several of the regular infantry regiments had been ordered to Tampa, Florida; General Miles had not succeeded in getting them withdrawn for his projected general mobilization at Chickamauga, but some of the cavalry and artillery units had been sent on from Chickamauga to Tampa. Tampa already appeared to be gravitating into the position of our principal jumping-off place, presumably because it was nearer to Cuba than either Mobile or New Orleans. Experience was to demonstrate that as a base for an expeditionary force it was lacking in almost every other qualification; at this stage, however, the importance of such details was as yet unappreciated. Brigadier-General William R. Shafter — an extremely corpulent warrior, but one who enjoyed the very important advantage of being without political ambitions — had been selected for promotion and the Tampa command. By the 28th he had arrived in Washington for his orders. It became necessary to determine what orders should be given him.

General Miles was still impressed by the unwisdom of sending raw troops on a tropical campaign in the rainy season, and was still urging the desirability of training and of deferring the attack until autumn. The nation, on the other hand, was demanding blood, and the nation possessed more votes than General Miles. The War President in this difficulty took a resolute attitude; he informed General Shafter that 'no matter what clamor the newspapers made he would not order the volunteers who had been called out into Cuba during the sickly season. He would wait until later in the autumn.' But the Regulars remained, and although there were not enough of them to risk in a genuine attack upon the Spanish army, General Shafter was told that he was to take a small force into the island as a 'reconnaissance' and for the purpose of conveying arms and ammunition to the insurgents. General Miles did manage to get the force increased from the four or five thousand men originally contemplated to about ten thousand, but it was the best he could do. General Shafter departed at once for Tampa; the necessary reënforcements were ordered after him, and as the newspapers spread the full plan across their front pages it seemed that the first hurdle, at any rate, had been safely taken.

To a later generation it may not appear to have been exactly war even yet, but undoubtedly it was becoming so. Mr. Roosevelt had at last reached his great decision; the Navy, he concluded, needed him no longer now that his great work there had been achieved, and it was announced that he had received his appointment as lieutenant-colonel in the volunteer cavalry. Mr. Roosevelt did not immediately resign as Assistant Secretary, but his projected regiment of cowboys and college men already began to take space upon the front pages under the pleasant title of 'Teddy's Terrors.' As yet, of course, it did not exist except upon paper, but it was confidently reported that the organization would be completed and in Cuba within three weeks, there to engage upon a 'roving campaign,' apparently all of its own, against the Spaniard.

And then a despatch suddenly arrived from the other side of the world, announcing that Commodore Dewey's squadron had sailed, at 2 P.M. on April 27, from Mirs Bay, near Hong Kong. Its destination was the Philippine Islands; and the general public learned for the first time (and to its considerable astonishment) that the war to liberate Cuba was expected by the authorities to begin in an Asiatic archipelago ten thousand miles away of which most of them had scarcely even heard. It was a dramatic surprise in the midst of days already tense with excitement; and as uncounted thousands dragged forth their atlases to look up this unanticipated theater of battle, the lineaments of Destiny herself — slowly, splendidly, intoxicatingly — became manifest at last, standing in majestic fascination above the farthermost rim of the Pacific.

But even as Dewey disappeared into the silences of the China Sea, and hurried editors raked every possible source of information in order to fill their columns with something about the Philippine Islands, a worried Cabinet Minister in Madrid was lifting a telegram from his desk.

'Am going North,' it read; and it was signed by Admiral Cervera.

IV

For three weeks the cables between St. Vincent, in the Cape Verde Islands, and Madrid had been the messengers of an extraordinary correspondence. Admiral Cervera had arrived at St. Vincent on the 14th of April, and by the 19th had assembled there his full squadron, the only Spanish squadron which could even be called effective. It consisted of four armored cruisers — the Infanta Maria Teresa, Almirante Oquendo, Vizcaya, and Cristóbal Colón — and six torpedo-boat destroyers. Of the latter, three were quite useless and the remaining three very nearly so.

The Colón, the newest, fastest, and best of the armored ships, was still without her main battery, which alone could make her a formidable unit. The Vizcaya's bottom was fouled to an extent that seriously reduced her speed. The crews were without adequate training in gunnery; ammunition was lacking; supplies were lacking; everything was lacking. And even though they had been in perfect condition, the four cruisers together could not throw a broadside equal in weight to that of the battleship Oregon alone. The squadron had been despatched thus far on its way to Cuba with nothing more definite in mind, apparently, than a vague idea that it would defend the island. Admiral Cervera was without exact information of American naval movements; he was without positive orders, and his best efforts had been unavailing to extract anything like a plan of campaign from his helpless Ministry of Marine.

The Admiral's own pessimism had not lightened. To attack the American fleet off Cuba seemed obvious suicide. The Ministry talked of sending him to the defense at least of Porto Rico, but that was hardly better. Convinced of the futility of any move which he might make, the Admiral had summoned a council of his captains as soon as his squadron had assembled. They expressed their belief in the 'immense superiority' of the American Navy, and urged the advisability of returning to the Canaries or the Peninsula, where they might be of some service, at any rate, in protecting the home waters. On April 21 (the day that war began), Admiral Cervera cabled his own views: 'The more I think about it, the more I am convinced that to continue voyage to Puerto Rico will be disastrous.'

But in Madrid, no less than in Washington, purely military considerations were never uninfluenced by the political. The Captain-General of Cuba was cabling that unless the fleet came out 'disappointment will be great and an unpleasant reaction is possible,' while the Government was under pressure from the home public which it feared to resist. On April 22, the Admiral was told that 'it is absolutely necessary to go out as soon as possible.' Admiral Cervera bowed his head, 'disclaiming all responsibility for the consequences,' and asked for precise instructions. The Minister of Marine could not furnish them. The Admiral bombarded him with cablegrams: 'I beg Your Excellency to permit me to insist that the result of our voyage to America must be disastrous for the future of the country.' 'I need precise instructions.' 'I do not know location of hostile ships.' Even to the distracted office-holders at Madrid the despatch of the squadron under such protests must have seemed less than wisdom. The Minister could not shoulder the responsibility, and cabled that he would summon a council of war. It met immediately, and in an extraordinary proceeding, characterized chiefly by an absence of anything approaching military realism and a general desire to escape responsibility, twenty high officers of the Spanish Navy gave their views. The consensus seemed to be that the honor of Spain (or at least the reputations of the authorities) demanded that the squadron should leave at once for the West Indies. What it was to do when it got there was left to the unhappy Admiral.

It was necessary that there should be at least some fighting in order to save the face of the Government, but beyond that the Spanish strategists do not seem to have gone. The idea that they could win the war, or even inflict any serious damage upon the United States, does not appear to have occurred to them, and their only thought seems to have been to get through with it with the minimum of discredit to themselves. From the civilian heads of the Government down to the subordinate military and naval commanders there reigned a paralyzing defeatism. Crippled though they were by lack of means, the Spaniards, had they acted with courage and energy, might have given us a punishment severe enough to have mitigated the terms of their defeat. But the spirit of resistance was dead in them at the start; and the war was over before it had begun — except for the unfortunate soldiers and seamen who were to be sacrificed to the exigencies of statesmanship, and politics.

Admiral Cervera received his definite orders on the 24th, and replied that he would sail as soon as he had finished coaling, which he hoped would be upon the following day. This turned out to be impossible, and the code message 'Am going North' which had been agreed upon to announce his departure for the West Indies did not arrive. The squadron was still in a deplorable state. 'I am in despair,' the harassed commander cabled, not once, but again and again. They had found that they could not make the after turret of the Oquendo train, and after two weeks had not yet discovered what was wrong. They lacked proper equipment for coaling and the work progressed 'very slowly.' A swell arose and increased the difficulty. The Admiral had scarcely enough money in his ships to pay the crews, to say nothing of supplying them while away from home. It was evident that three of the destroyers were in such bad shape that they would have to be left behind. Whether the other three would stand the trip they did not know. But they managed to get through somehow. The Oquendo's turret was repaired. On the 28th, the Admiral cabled that he would certainly leave next day, and on the 29th, at last, the ships weighed anchor. 'Am going North,' the Admiral cabled; the squadron sailed.

The code message was a useless precaution. The American press was at least impartial, for it had devoted itself to reporting the Spanish movements as thoroughly as our own. Its representatives not only watched the squadron sail; they even followed it far enough to sea to make sure of its course, and as Cervera's ships disappeared over the western horizon, the correspondents returned to put upon the wires the news that the Admiral was on his way to America. On the morning of April 30, the American public learned that it might expect him off our coasts within a fortnight. His coming was awaited with an excitement not unmixed with a dawning trepidation.

Even so it was still, to the eager crowds standing for hours before the newspaper bulletin boards, a glorious, comic-opera adventure, a kind of magnified baseball game with the war bulletins for box scores, a sort of continuous election night with all the candidates winning. To the officers in the Spanish vessels it must have seemed, as they pounded steadily westward through the immense loneliness of the sea, a business of a different kind. Villaamil, the commander of the destroyer division, left his thoughts on record in a letter to the Prime Minister himself:

I deem it expedient that you should know... that, while as seamen we are all ready to die with honor in the fulfillment of our duty, I think it undoubted that the sacrifice of these naval forces will be as certain as it will be fruitless and useless for the termination of the war.

The Admiral endorsed that view. Their orders, they believed, were their death warrants; Villaamil himself was one of the many for whom they were to prove so.

v

So April ran out; May Day fell upon a Sunday, with a Sunday morning pause. The Army was getting on with its plans for the 'reconnaissance' in Cuba, and in the headlines Mr. Roosevelt's cavalry regiment had progressed from 'Teddy's Terrors' to the more dignified but no less alliterative 'Rocky Mountain Rustlers.' The battleship Oregon, making her famous run from the Pacific Coast by way of Cape Horn, was reported from Rio, where she had safely arrived the evening before. But it seemed that the day would be enlivened by nothing more exciting than the oratory, of a patriotic and bellicose kind, which poured from every pulpit; and as the congregations went home to their Sunday dinners they had to content themselves with a glowing sense of the holiness of the crusade. It was not until late in the afternoon that the first despatches began to trickle in to the officials at Washington; it was not until well on into the evening that the rumor ran and the crowds flocked out to storm the bulletin boards and learn that there had been, at last, a great naval battle in the Far East and that Manila Bay was enshrined forever in the military history of the nation.

For a moment there was doubt as to what had happened. The news all came by way of Madrid, and the earlier reports were confusing. Evidently there had been a battle, but who had won? Mr. McKinley, 'in company with his advisers,' anxiously hung over the press bulletins in the library of the White House during the earlier part of the evening, but finally adjourned to his office where he continued 'to peruse every despatch with the deepest interest.' The first cables spoke of the Spanish flagship being on fire and reported one of her consorts blown up, but the American fleet was said to have 'retired' behind some merchantmen in the harbor. These bulletins were received in Washington like the early returns of a close election; there was the same suspense, the same atmosphere of repressed excitement. Then, as the evening deepened and admission after admission came over the cables from Madrid, the pent-up feelings burst out; the crowd became 'uproarious'; every 'scintilla of news was received with enthusiastic cheers'; and by ten o'clock the crowds and officials had convinced themselves that it was all over but the shouting. Evidently it had been a landslide, and Commodore Dewey, of course, was already being named as the next President.

With the morning papers of Monday the entire country had the news and passed into a paroxysm of rejoicing. Brass bands joined the crowds before the newspaper offices and led the populace in patriotic song. That evening fireworks and red fire glowed throughout the nation; at the offices of the junta at New York there were roof-raising celebrations; undergraduates built bonfires on a hundred campuses, while a witticism of that peculiar fatuousness which marks great emotion swept through the throngs and everywhere ordinarily sane people were heard repeating: 'Philippine. We get Manila.' On the same day the National Guard regiments of New York marched off to their encampments, the bands playing 'The Girl I Left Behind Me' and the streets jammed with enthusiastic patriots, wildly cheering, and waving the Stars and Stripes. The security markets had rebounded with a rush on the Manila news, and the problem of what disposition we should make of the 'captured islands' was already appearing in popular discussion. But as yet there had been no word from Dewey.

There had been no word of any kind, in fact, except what came through Spanish sources. The only communication between the Philippine Islands and the outside world was through a single cable running to Hong Kong, and the Manila end of it was, of course, in the hands of the Spaniards. By midnight of May 1, Madrid had learned of the loss or destruction of every one of the principal Spanish ships, and nothing had been reported as to losses in the American squadron. One despatch spoke fleetingly of the Americans having landed; but there had been that other announcing a 'retirement.' As to what had happened to Dewey, what casualties or damage he had sustained, whether he had even approached the city of Manila or what the nature of the landing had been, absolutely nothing was known.

At this juncture Hong Kong reported that the Manila cable had ceased to work at about five o'clock Monday morning, New York time. It had been cut or broken near the Manila end.

CHAPTER VII
MANILA BAY

I

IN the moment of what seemed to have been a victory Dewey had been cut off from the world. But as yet this gave rise to no anxiety; it did not enter the heads of our ebullient people that it might not have been a victory; and that Dewey had made himself master of Manila and ended the Spanish rule in the Philippines was everywhere assumed as the merest matter of course. The dazzling prospect of Asiatic empire arose almost spontaneously in thousands of minds, and its startling incongruity with the altruism of our declared war aims was hardly even noticed. How could it have been at such a moment? 'I speak not of forcible annexation,' Mr. McKinley had solemnly declared five months before, 'for that cannot be thought of. That, by our code of morality, would be criminal aggression.' But now? Once more Mr. McKinley applied his ear to the ground.

On the afternoon of May 2, there was a council of war in the White House. Throughout the nation the cheers, the brass bands, the fireworks and 'aërial bombs' were still announcing our joy over the glorious victory. Within, the War President was in consultation with his Secretaries of the Navy and of War, with General Miles and Admiral Sicard. General Wesley Merritt, one of the ablest officers in the Army, had been summoned from New York and arrived by an afternoon train. Mr. McKinley faced his advisers in a mood for action; and for the dramatic decisions which followed one must assume that he was chiefly responsible.

As to Cuba there was considerable discussion; but the President must already have perceived that the plan of permitting the Cubans to do the fighting — however admirable from a military point of view — had by this time become a political impossibility. General Miles's technical misgivings were overridden before that superior necessity, and it was 'finally agreed that a force of 40,000 or 50,000 men... should be at once prepared and embarked' to make a landing at Mariel and thence advance to a direct assault upon Havana. It was decided to cancel Shafter's 'reconnaissance in force' because of the approach of Cervera's squadron, and his troops were to make up the advance échelon of the new movement. The remainder, however, would have to come largely from the volunteers. Only a week before, Mr. McKinley had declared that no amount of newspaper clamor would induce him to risk raw troops in the rainy season. The National Guardsmen were not yet mustered into the Federal service, to say nothing of being trained or equipped for action; the terrors of the rainy season were no less than they had been a week before and the Spanish forces in the islands were undiminished. It made no difference; the cry of 'On to Havana!' had been raised, and Mr. McKinley, perhaps, had underestimated the force of newspaper clamor. With that fine disregard for the time element which throughout characterized our dispositions, it was determined that the first Havana expedition should sail in about a fortnight, providing Cervera had been located by that date.

But with the sensational news from the Far East, Cuba had already sunk, in the minds of the more astute, to a secondary importance. After all, there was the Teller amendment to make annexation of that island impossible — and in the dizzy rush of events a prospect had opened far more inviting than the mere relief of Cuban wrongs. Mr. McKinley had placed his ear to the ground; the result was to appear with a striking promptitude. Mr. Alger states that the decision 'to send an army of occupation to the Philippines was reached before Dewey's victory occurred'; in this he may have misremembered, but at all events the President must have given his assent to the project not later than this conference on May 2 or immediately thereafter. It was on May 4 that he directed in writing that the troops should be assembled in accordance with 'verbal instructions heretofore given.' The occupation of the Philippine Islands was thus determined before there had been any reliable news whatever that Dewey had even succeeded in carrying out his mission of destroying the Spanish squadron. It is difficult to conclude that our annexation of the Philippines was a wholly accidental proceeding.

The decision is one which excites the curiosity. So important in

its consequences, its origins remain obscure, while it was itself
of that usefully ambiguous nature which characterized so many
of the important decisions of the war period. We have seen the
President agreeing, in a Sunday morning conference, to unleash
Dewey; how much he expected to flow from that action it is impossible to know. Ostensibly, the assault on the Manila squadron
had no other purpose than to prevent its attacking our commerce
in the Pacific or threatening our west coast. This, of course, was a
military objective of unimpeachable legitimacy. It is also obvious
that once Dewey had destroyed the Spanish fleet, he would have
to establish a base for himself at Manila or else return the whole
long distance to the United States, since the neutrality laws barred
every other harbor to him. And yet? The utter inability of the
Spanish fleet to cross the Pacific or even to raid the scanty shipping
which we possessed in that ocean was well understood by the Navy
Department. Months before, Mr. Roosevelt had been hinting that
we might attack 'and if possible, take' Manila. Mr. McKinley
was himself interested in promoting our Chinese trade. And now,
before any authentic news of the battle had been received or anything was known of Dewey's needs, an expeditionary force was
being organized to travel seven thousand miles across the Pacific
and occupy the archipelago. For a nation which had disavowed
even the thought of annexation we seemed to move with an almost
indecent haste; and one finds a rather curious contrast between the
deliberation with which we prepared our plans for the descent
upon Cuba (which we were pledged not to annex) and the light-
ning-like speed with which, in the space of twenty-four hours, we
determined to set out for the Philippines, where our hands were
not tied. On May 4, Mr. McKinley approved the orders. 'But
beyond this,' his biographer notes, 'he entertained no scheme of
aggression.' Perhaps he did not. The War President, however,
had heard the cheering crowds; while somewhere amid his papers
there survived a memorandum of about this date in his own hand-
writing: 'While we are conducting war and until its conclusion we
must keep all we get; when the war is over we must keep what we
want.'

The decision to occupy not merely Manila but the whole of the
islands was at once made known in Washington and published to

the nation; and everywhere the amateur diplomatists were already arguing the question of whether we should sell the archipelago to Germany or Japan or keep it for ourselves. For now, as the long, inviting pathway of imperial splendor opened before the delighted statesmen who had labored so long and so skillfully to set our feet upon it, anything had become possible. There seemed to be no limits; and Senator Burrows of Michigan, emerging from the White House, stopped to tell the reporters: 'Everything is moving along smoothly and well. What we want now is Porto Rico. We ought to have that tomorrow.'

'Will it be as soon as that, Senator?' some one asked.

'Yes, probably in a day or two.'

By this time holidays were being proclaimed throughout the nation in celebration of the victory. On May 4, in New York, 'several of the hotels had patriotic little references in their menus ... aside from liberal decoration with flags and bunting. Ices à la Dewey were served, moulded like battleships, with appropriate favors.' The city was 'ablaze with flags' and the price of bunting was up three hundred per cent above a few weeks before. St. Patrick's Cathedral appeared with 'what is said to be the largest flag ever seen in this city,' forty by thirty-five feet, suspended between the tall spires on Fifth Avenue; while the crowds that milled beneath it were showing all kinds of patriotic emblems. Lapel buttons (again it was the election note) were being sold by the thousand; a particularly popular one bore the legend: 'We didn't Dew-ey ting to 'em!' The ladies, with greater opportunity, rose to even greater heights, and one appeared in 'a blue gown with a buff stripe down each side of the skirt, like the stripe on a cavalryman's trousers; a zouave jacket caught with gold frogs which, thrown open, revealed a red, white, and blue striped waist beneath. She wore a campaign hat with crossed sabers.'

But all this was, of course, mere froth and enthusiasm. It remained for the seal of a more authoritative respectability, a more evidently altruistic motive, to be placed upon the enticing possibilities in the Pacific. As early as May 5, Mr. Whitelaw Reid's *Tribune* arose to the occasion, and in an impressive leader revealed the moral obligation which might compel us to acquire territory on the opposite side of the world. The *Tribune* wished the ultimate fate of the islands to be left until the end of the war, and disparaged premature discussion. But it pointed out:

It is to be observed that the United States Government has, so far as its own utterances are concerned, an entirely free hand in the matter. It has neither proclaimed nor disclaimed any intentions concerning these islands.... Yet in one respect the United States has not a free hand in the Philippines. A grave and imperative obligation has been already imposed upon us. We have stricken down Spanish sovereignty and set up our own. All that hereafter remains of Spanish rule in the islands will be under sufferance of the United States. That is a momentous fact. We cannot turn Spain out and leave the islands to their own devices. We cannot abolish the only government the islands have and leave them without any. That would be barbarous. This country will be bound, in honor and in morals, either itself to assume the administration of the islands or to empower some other competent authority to do so.

The *Tribune* believed that in any event we should permanently retain the most suitable harbor in the islands as a 'fortified coaling station,' and went on to argue the advantages of keeping the entire group as opposed to selling it or leaving it in the hands of a native government. The *Tribune* had already arrived at the confident opinion (which was not shared, incidentally, by many who were much nearer to the Philippines than the *Tribune* had ever been) that 'the islands are, so far as now appears, about as little fit for self-government as any land on the surface of the globe.'

And all, it must be remembered, before Dewey had even been heard from.

But there were still other possibilities. If our moral obligation to annex the Philippines was still open to argument, the military necessity for annexing the Hawaiian Islands (now that all Spanish opposition in the Pacific had been destroyed) was clearly evident. President Dole was once more offering up his country, upon the altar, this time, of our military needs, and Mr. McKinley was being urged to accept. What had been so difficult to arrange while it was merely a question of opening a perpetual free entry for Hawaiian sugar had become simplicity itself under the imperative demands of war. 'Czar' Reed, it is true, remained obdurate, for to him 'it appeared no more necessary to annex Hawaii in order to conquer Spain or to promote the purposes for which we went to war than it was to annex the moon.' But in these matters the

Speaker's power had long since evaporated. The Hawaiian annexation resolution, which had slumbered since the middle of March, at once revived in House and Senate. On May 5 it was discussed in the House Foreign Affairs Committee, and the Republican committeemen were understood to be a unit for favorable action. The Democrats, who may have been awakening at last to the consequences toward which their war for Cuban freedom was so rapidly trending, were more inclined to the Speaker's view; but sentiment was strong, and among the House membership many who had been opposed three months before were observed to be 'as strongly in favor of it now.' And an enthusiastic, if slightly bewildered, public looked on with approval.

Still, however, there was no news from the Far East, and as the days passed there was a gathering anxiety. Could there have been, after all, some mistake? From Manila to Hong Kong was not much more than two days' steaming, and in a war in which such careful attention was given to the publicity, the idea that Dewey might not immediately make report had occurred to no one. Yet two, three, four days elapsed, with nothing more authoritative than the first fragmentary despatches *via* Madrid. In official Washington the tension became severe; twenty-four-hour watches were set up in the Navy and State Departments to receive the earliest advices, and by Friday evening the anxiety began to leak into the newspapers. It was possible, the reporters were told, that Dewey might have encountered some unexpected difficulty 'in the capture of the city.' What had been happening in that remote corner of the world, behind that veil of impenetrable silence? Was it conceivable that there had not really been a victory? The country waited in a deepening tensity of apprehension.

It was not until the early dawn of Saturday, May 7, that Mr. Cridler, the Assistant Secretary on watch at the State Department, was awakened by a telegram. At about the same time a Hong Kong cable arrived upon the telegraph desk of the *World* in New York. The presses were stopped while it was shot feverishly into what remained to be printed of the final edition. The victory had been complete. Not a man nor a ship had been injured. It was all true!

II

Unfortunately, however, it was not quite the whole truth; for the actual situation in the Far East lacked something of that beautiful simplicity which it appeared to have from the first news despatches. The fact was that our moral obligation to assume Pacific empire had already been complicated by one or two circumstances of which our patriots were as yet in ignorance; while the fact that all our statesmen and editors were ten thousand miles away from the scene of operations was to give rise to some regrettable misunderstandings later on. The Battle of Manila Bay was preceded by a brief, but rather curious, history.

Commodore Dewey, it will be remembered, had taken over his command at Nagasaki on January 3, fresh from the stimulating influence of Mr. Roosevelt and thoroughly indoctrinated with that statesman's forward-looking policy. The Commodore appeared to be ready for anything — 'our ships,' he wrote home a few days after his arrival, 'are all, with the exception of the flagship, in the Chinese or Corean waters, looking out for a right to protect American interests, of which there are many more than is generally known.' The technique of looking out for a right to protect unsuspected national interests had already been highly developed by the acquisitive diplomacies of the period, but China, of course, was merely something with which to pass the time. Commodore Dewey's great objective was the Philippines.

And here an important element soon entered into his calculations. The Philippines were — more or less — in a state of insurrection. They thus offered a parallel with Cuban conditions no less useful on the military side than on the political; and when Dewey, after the destruction of the Maine, moved his squadron to Hong Kong, he was brought within easy touch of the Filipino patriots who had emigrated thither under the terms of the 'treaty' of Biac-na-Bato, to prepare themselves for another assault upon the Spanish rule. He was also, as has been said, brought into daily communication with Mr. Williams, our consul at Manila. Mr. Williams, though with 'no instructions,' was devoting himself to reporting both the atrocities of the Spaniards and their utter helplessness against the patriots. It was all in the best Cuban tradition, save for one difference — the Filipino patriots, unhappily for themselves, were without a press bureau in the United States. No intensive propaganda campaigns had educated the American public as to their right to freedom or their ability to govern themselves; their wrongs had not been proclaimed widely enough to compel us subsequently to respect them, and there was no public opinion to insist upon a Teller amendment in their behalf. This was important, and even Mr. Williams did not fail to guard his statements.

As long before as the preceding December the State Department had warned its representative at Hong Kong not to 'encourage any advances on the part of Mr. Agoncilla,' the Filipino foreign agent. Commodore Dewey, however, engrossed in the military problem and under Mr. Roosevelt's orders concerning 'offensive operations' in the islands, did not seem to appreciate the full delicacy of the situation. From Hong Kong he wrote home to his sister:

I believe we will make short work of the Spanish reign in the Philippines. The insurgents are ready to rise at our first gun, and long before this reaches you we may be masters of Manila and Philippine cities.

But only, one notes, with the aid of the insurgents. Nor was Commodore Dewey's the only intelligence at work in the Far East. Fourteen hundred miles away at Singapore there was an American consul, Mr. E. Spencer Pratt, who had been impressed by the greatness of our destiny in the western Pacific. He had also been impressed by the altruism of our declared policy; indeed, the rather involved correspondence leading up to our rupture with Spain seems to have spread throughout much of the Far East a kind of vague, general notion that the United States was embarking upon a great mission to free almost any oppressed people almost anywhere that we might find them. Amid the glowing literature that drifted out to them even our consuls do not seem to have understood that Cuba was distinctly a local — and special — problem; and there was an unfortunate tendency to be a trifle uncritical of the exact basis and extent of the commitments made in our name.

It was on the evening of April 23, in the very height of the diplomatic crisis and while the nation still seemed to be hanging somewhere between armed intervention and actual warfare, that Mr. Pratt learned of the arrival in Singapore of General Emilio Aguinaldo, the titular head of the Philippine insurrection. It was the moment in which Americans everywhere were standing behind the President, anxious to demonstrate their initiative, their patriotism, and their title to subsequent reward by a grateful people. Mr. Pratt at once sent for General Aguinaldo, and a secret conference took place on the morning of Sunday, the 24th — at just about the time that Mr. McKinley in the White House was endorsing the orders to Commodore Dewey. General Aguinaldo turned out to be a small, sharp-eyed, and astute Filipino gentleman of intelligence and force. 'An hour's interview convinced me,' Mr. Pratt later declared, 'that he was the man for the occasion.'

Accordingly, Mr. Pratt pointed out to the Filipino leader the folly of continuing his insurrection on his own hook, and 'the expediency of coöperating with our fleet, then at Hong Kong.' The Consul did explain that he had no authority to speak for his Government, but the General was convinced, and on the same day Mr. Pratt cabled to Dewey:

Aguinaldo, insurgent leader, here. Will come Hong Kong arrange with Commodore for general coöperation insurgents Manila if desired. Telegraph.

This was, perhaps, a trifle ambiguous. But the reply was immediate and unequivocal:

Tell Aguinaldo come soon as possible.

DEWEY

The Consul at once arranged for the despatch of the patriot. General Aguinaldo left on April 26, under an assumed name, for Hong Kong. Just before his departure he had another conference with Mr. Pratt. Toward the end:

The General further stated that he hoped the United States would assume protection of the Philippines for at least long enough to allow the inhabitants to establish a government of their own, in the organization of which he would desire American advice and assistance.

These questions I told him I had no authority to discuss.

Was it possible that General Aguinaldo's suspicions had been aroused? It was just about this time that another American representative in the East, Mr. John Barrett, our Minister to Siam, was giving a press interview at Bangkok in a different tone:

> It is of the greatest importance that the United States should take the Philippine Islands. Their value is not realized at home. They are richer and far larger than Cuba, and in the hands of a strong power would be the key to the Far East.

General Aguinaldo may not have known of this interview, but he was evidently determined to take no chances. The conferences with Mr. Pratt had been conducted with the utmost secrecy, but just before his departure the Filipino patriot was careful to visit the offices of the English-owned Singapore *Free Press* and tell the whole story to that journal, which a few days later placed it upon public record. According to the *Free Press*, Aguinaldo had explicitly declared to Mr. Pratt his (Aguinaldo's) 'ability to establish a proper and responsible government on liberal principles' and his willingness 'to accept the same terms for the country as the United States intend giving to Cuba.' Mr. Pratt forwarded this account to the State Department without denying that such a statement had been made. He forwarded, also, the *Free Press's* comment that 'General Aguinaldo's policy embraces the independence of the Philippines.' Nowhere did he say that he had disabused the General of such hopes.

On the contrary, it was after General Aguinaldo had placed these views upon record that he was allowed to accept our own invitation and depart under our auspices for Hong Kong. Mr. Pratt had no authority to discuss such questions. It was most unfortunate.

Our consular and naval representatives at Hong Kong labored under a similar disability. It was even worse. When the British authorities ordered Dewey to leave the port by April 25 (in order not to violate their neutrality), it was of course evident that General Aguinaldo himself could not arrive in time to sail with the squadron. But the Filipino leaders at Hong Kong had grasped the idea, and they issued a proclamation to their countrymen:

> Compatriots! Divine Providence is about to place independence within our reach, and in a way the most free and independent nation could hardly wish for. The Americans, not from mercenary motives, but

EMILIO AGUINALDO

for the sake of humanity and the lamentations of so many persecuted people, have considered it opportune to extend their protecting mantle to our beloved country.

And neither Commodore Dewey nor Mr. Wildman, our consul at Hong Kong, thought it necessary to destroy so inspiring a faith, and one so useful, under the circumstances, to our projects.

On the morning of the 25th, the Commodore left Hong Kong in accordance with the British demand. He did not wish to set out for the islands, however, until Mr. Williams could arrive from Manila with whatever information he might have concerning the Spanish dispositions; he anchored, therefore, in Mirs Bay, on Chinese territory opposite to Hong Kong. China was incapable of enforcing neutrality laws.

Mr. Williams reached Hong Kong on the 27th, and was present when Mr. Wildman received a delegation of the Filipino patriots. In the absence of Aguinaldo the consuls agreed to allow two of these Hong Kong leaders to accompany the fleet to Manila, after the patriots had bound themselves 'to obey all laws of civilized warfare and to place themselves absolutely under the orders of Admiral Dewey.' Mr. Wildman at once took a tugboat, loaded himself, Consul Williams, and the two Filipinos aboard her, and set out for Mirs Bay.

The picture holds the attention. One sees a small vessel, laboring to the long swells of the China Sea, the lofty bluffs of Hong Kong fading astern, and the outlines of the China coast growing up ahead, until, dim against the background in their dark warpaint, the hulls of Dewey's men-of-war slowly become visible. The four passengers must have watched them as, perhaps, a dash of spray spattered over the tugboat's bows, and the outlines of a great adventure, dim as Dewey's ships, formed in their four minds. But the outlines were not the same. If they spoke to each other, it is not recorded. Curiously enough, the tug's name was the Fame.

III

Commodore Dewey, in the meanwhile, had been 'not only impatient but incensed at the delay in the arrival of Consul Williams from Manila.' The Commodore seems to have been under no misapprehension as to the difficulty of the task before him; he did not make the mistake of overrating his enemies. 'I believe I am not overconfident,' he wrote in these days, 'in saying that, with the force under my command, I could enter the Bay of Manila, capture or destroy the Spanish squadron, and reduce the defenses in one day.' A very similar opinion (though our cheering publics were later to forget the fact) was held in most informed quarters and had been published in our own press. Commodore Dewey had with him four 'protected cruisers' (his flagship, the Olympia, was considered the best of the type in the Navy), two gunboats, and a revenue cutter. To oppose him Admiral Montojo had two small protected cruisers, and five unprotected cruisers and gunboats of miscellaneous types and sizes. One was a wooden hulk, used as a receiving ship and incapable of movement. Another was without two of her heavier guns. The whole five were reported abroad to be 'worthless.' But counting everything available, even the immobile Castilla, the Spaniards were still heavily outclassed in gun power. Commodore Dewey's squadron mounted ten eight-inch rifles, twenty-three six-inch and twenty five-inch. The heaviest guns in Montojo's ships were his 6.3's, of which there were only seven, and four ancient 5.9's in the Castilla. He also had twenty 4.7's and eleven of lesser calibers.

The land batteries defending Manila Bay were reported to be armed with 'old smooth-bores.' The Commodore learned that there were also a few modern rifles of medium calibers, some of which had been taken from the ships, but in the main the guns were old-fashioned muzzle-loaders of small value, or ancient bronze pieces dating from a distant past, admirable for gracing a military museum, but of no other use whatever. Years after the battle the courtyard of the Maestranza at Manila was still covered with the neatly cut, square fragments of flint which had been used in their firelocks.

The Spaniards' only remaining hope was in the mine defenses. On April 19 the Ministry of Marine had ordered Montojo by cable to close the ports of the archipelago with mines. The order to close the ports with mines, as the Admiral afterward wrote, 'when we possessed only fourteen and these without fuses or cables, surprised me exceedingly — so much so that I responded on the 21st of April: "Your Excellency knows that we have no mines. I will do what I can." ' He did make a desperate effort to improvise something out of the torpedoes in the ships, but it was more or less futile. The Governor-General, Augustín, fell back upon a traditional Spanish method in emergencies and issued a thumping manifesto. Dewey heard later that it had been composed by the Archbishop:

> The North American people, composed of all the social excrescences, have exhausted our patience and provoked war with their perfidious machinations, with their acts of treachery, with their outrages against the law of nations and international conventions....
> Vain designs! Ridiculous boastings! Your indomitable bravery will suffice to frustrate the attempt to carry them into realization.... The aggressors shall not profane the tombs of your fathers, they shall not gratify their lustful passions at the cost of your wives' and daughters' honor, or appropriate the property your industry has accumulated as a provision for your old age.... Filipinos, prepare for the struggle!

There was little else they could do.

In the meanwhile Consul Wildman and his three charges were nearing Mirs Bay, and at about noon (April 27) they were alongside the flagship. A council of captains was called immediately; Mr. Williams was brought in and quickly pumped of what information he possessed. The Consul seems to have been a trifle alarmist, and he erroneously supposed that Montojo had just received a consignment of mines from Madrid. But the Commodore dismissed the danger as a 'negligible quantity,' for he did not believe that mining was practicable in so deep an entrance. Mr. Williams had added little; he was soon ordered into one of the other cruisers, and at two in the afternoon the squadron — including seven men-of-war, 1743 officers and men, and three newspaper correspondents — weighed anchor and stood out into the China Sea. 'With a smooth sea and favoring sky we set our course for the entrance to Manila Bay, six hundred miles away.'

There is always something profoundly impressive in the thought of men-of-war steaming toward battle. The officers on the bridge, the men about the decks or in the engine and boiler rooms, find themselves still amid the established security of their normal world and their familiar routine, but knowing at the same time that every beat of the engines is bringing them nearer to a tremendous adventure, perhaps to a catastrophe. Throughout the 28th and the 29th the squadron held steadily to the southward, alone upon the immense surface of a placid sea, ringed by the ominous circle of the concealing horizon. Their commander may have been confident, but the Hong Kong papers for weeks had been predicting their destruction and even the friendly English in the clubs would not take a bet upon their safe return.

Dewey kept them busy with drills and in clearing ship for action. Outwardly 'everybody seemed to take the matter lightly,' hardly wishing to admit even now that it was real war and that there would be, probably, real fighting. Early on the morning of Saturday, the 30th, they made out the shape of Cape Bolinao in the darkness — it was their landfall — and held on southward along the tropical coast. With daylight Commodore Dewey sent forward two of his ships to reconnoiter Subig Bay, a deep indentation thirty miles north of the entrance to Manila. It was known that the Spaniards had begun a naval station there, and the Commodore was afraid that Montojo would choose it for his position. In the heat of the afternoon the squadron came up with the two scouts; they reported that the place was empty. 'Now we have them!' the Commodore exclaimed. The squadron was stopped to wait for darkness, and the captains were once more called aboard the flagship. 'We shall enter Manila Bay tonight,' Dewey informed them, 'and you will follow the motions and movements of the flagship, which will lead.' There was 'no discussion and no written order and no further particulars as to preparation,' he afterward recalled. 'For every preparation... had been made.'

With the coming of darkness the squadron was again put in motion. As Admiral Fiske, then a lieutenant in the Petrel, remembered it:

The night was clear and calm and the hours from eight to twelve rather dragged. There was nothing to do, for all preparations had been made; there was nothing to see except the dim outlines of a few ships and the vague outline of the coast two or three miles distant; and there was nothing to hear except the sound of the engine and the swish of the water along the sides.

The Commodore himself was not impervious to the tense beauty of the moment, and as he stood upon the navigating bridge of the Olympia in the pregnant darkness, the small, familiar ship noises about him, and his men waiting at their guns on the decks below, his mind was carried backward into memories:

By degrees the high land on either side loomed up out of the darkness, while the flagship headed for Boca Grande, which was the wider but comparatively little used channel. A light shower passed over about eleven o'clock and the heavy, cumulus clouds drifting across the sky from time to time obscured the new moon. The landmarks and islands were, however, fairly visible, while compass bearings for regulating our course could readily be observed.

It was thirty-six years since, as executive officer of the Mississippi, I was first under fire, in the passage of Forts Jackson and St. Philip under Farragut.

Presently they saw lights flashing on the shore and judged that they had been discovered, but nothing happened. A little later and they were fairly in the entrance, between Corregidor Island and the rock of El Fraile. Both had been fortified with batteries, they knew, but there was no sound or movement from either. Just before midnight the flagship changed course for the northeast; she had passed the entrance, and so far there had been no opposition.

The revenue cutter McCulloch was the last ship in the column. In her engine room the temperature stood at 170 degrees; and her chief engineer, 'a very stout man who took little or no exercise,' collapsed with heat prostration as they came up abreast of El Fraile. It was just at this moment, too, that the McCulloch suddenly threw out a flame from her smokestack. It was followed almost immediately by a rocket mounting into the air from Corregidor. They had been discovered? Still nothing happened; minutes passed away, and the squadron was well through the entrance when, at a quarter past twelve, there came an abrupt 'screech and boom' from El Fraile. The batteries had at last opened fire. But the fleet was safe by that time; the rear ships replied, there was a twinkle of gun-flashes, sudden reverberations in the profound placidity of the night, a moment of anxiety, and it all died away once more. El Fraile fired only three shots altogether; Corregidor never opened at all. The squadron stood onward into the bay; the silence and the heat fell once more like a blanket, and the McCulloch's engineer, giving up the struggle in the stifling darkness, died. In the Petrel, Lieutenant Fiske was left to listen again to the water swishing along the sides. 'The night was so beautiful and the stars so bright and the sea so calm that the scene was soothing and peaceful.' The lieutenant was sent below for some sleep, and the last thing he remembered as he dropped off in his bunk, with the steel deck-plating close overhead, was 'how very flat I would be squashed out against that deck if a torpedo exploded under the ship. This idea was very vivid.' But there were no torpedoes; or, if there were, they did not explode.

It is twenty-two miles from El Fraile to Manila, and Dewey reduced speed so as to arrive off the city, where he expected to find Montojo's ships, with the daylight. They came up just at dawn; through the early mist of that Sunday morning they saw the ponderous masonry of the ancient city walls and the romantically anachronistic bulwarks of Fort Santiago above the Pasig River, with the mouths of its eighteenth-century bronze cannon looking through their embrasures. Palms waved their fronds from the shore; there were native boats below the hoary sea-wall, and the American officers upon their bridges gazed upon the strange romance of the East, which they had come to conquer. But Montojo was not there. The Spaniards took some futile pot-shots at them from the more modern batteries which had been erected before the city, but Dewey paid no attention. Six miles away to the southwest, where the coast curved around to the peninsula upon which the navy yard of Cavite was located, he made out the hulls of the Spanish squadron. The helm was put over, and the Commodore steamed into action.

A typical tropical day, scarcely a breath of air and a haze that resembled that which one observes arising from a hot steel plate; a fireman coming on deck for a breath of air described it perfectly when he remarked to a seaman: 'We people don't have to worry, for Hell ain't no hotter than this.'

Admiral Montojo had elected to accept battle at anchor under the batteries of Cavite. To have taken station before the city itself would have afforded him a much stronger artillery support from the shore, but it would have exposed the city to the fire of the American squadron. The inevitable council of war had been summoned and it had 'unanimously decided' to retire to the navy yard and there take position 'in the least water possible' and await destruction. As usual, the idea that there could be any other outcome seems never to have occurred to the Admiral or his captains. With a striking fatalism Admiral Montojo, it is said, spent his last evening at a party in Manila. But he was on board his flagship in ample time for the ordeal, and at four in the morning signaled to prepare for action. Three quarters of an hour later he made out, through the rising mists of the tropic sunrise, the gray hull of the Olympia bearing down upon him, followed in grim and silent procession by the five [1] remaining vessels of the American squadron. Admiral Montojo and his crews stoically awaited their fate. At five o'clock the shore battery on the point to his left opened fire; ten or fifteen minutes later, the Admiral himself gave the signal.

Commodore Dewey held his reply until he had closed to an effective range. It was not until about half-past five that the Olympia, coming up on the eastern end of the Spanish line, opened with her eight-inch guns. A little later, and the action had become general. The American squadron passed westward along the front of the Spanish line, turned, and came back again. The firing was incessant and, for that day, rapid. Some of the Spanish vessels slipped their cables and were seen to be moving about in a rather aimless fashion, getting in one another's way. As time passed, however, the great clouds of smoke from the old-fashioned black powder which both fleets were using began to obscure everything and it was difficult to see what was happening.

The action wore on. The Spanish shells were falling both short and over, and one light-caliber projectile struck below the spot on the Olympia's bridge where the Commodore was standing. But the flagship did not appear to be taking any damage. The column turned once more, closing the range as the leadsmen found that they were getting more water than was marked upon the charts. Montojo's flagship started forward in what appeared to be an attempt to ram the Olympia, but was driven back. Still the Spanish fire did not materially slacken. Time was advancing;

[1] The McCulloch, of small military value, was detached and took no part in the action.

nothing, it seemed, was being accomplished. On the bridge of the Olympia there was a deepening atmosphere of gloom, and the Commodore was manifesting an increasingly unfavorable opinion of his squadron's marksmanship. Two hours after the opening of the battle, when the American column was just completing its fifth passage along the Spanish front, the report was made that the Olympia had but fifteen rounds of five-inch ammunition remaining per gun.

It was a disaster of the most serious kind. Commodore Dewey was seven thousand miles from his nearest sure base of supplies, and once his ammunition was gone, he would be in a most embarrassing predicament. He had already been hammering away for two hours with no apparent result; and the possibility that he might actually fire away all his ammunition without disabling a vastly inferior opponent left him confronting a fiasco which would not only be grave in itself, but extremely humiliating. The powder-smoke by this time had practically concealed the hostile squadron; the Commodore abruptly decided to break off, allow the smoke to clear, and take stock of his situation. Instead of returning along the Spanish line, he led his column away to the northward.

Almost immediately his apprehensions vanished. Looking back they could now see that they had done far more damage than they had supposed. Some of the enemy ships were on fire; the flagship was being abandoned by her crew; the other vessels were retreating behind the point. At the same time it was discovered that the report about the ammunition supply had been a mistake; it should have been, not that they had only fifteen rounds per gun remaining, but that they had fired only fifteen rounds. The Olympia herself had escaped, miraculously it seemed, with no real damage of any kind. The Commodore signaled for his captains to come aboard and at the same time took the opportunity to have breakfast served out to the crews. The captains arrived to make report, and to discover to their astonishment that what each had supposed to be the extraordinary good luck of his own ship had in fact been shared by all the others. A shell had struck and exploded a box of three-pounder ammunition in the Baltimore wounding two officers and six men 'very slightly.' Otherwise, although there had been

COMMODORE DEWEY (LEFT) WITH CAPTAINS GRIDLEY AND LAMBERTON
ON THE QUARTERDECK OF THE OLYMPIA, MAY 1, 1898

WRECK OF MONTOJO'S FLAGSHIP, THE REINA CRISTINA, IN
MANILA BAY

a number of hits, there had been no structural damage and not a man had been injured. The only death in the American squadron at Manila Bay was that of the chief engineer of the McCulloch, who had died of heat stroke. It was unbelievable.

For the American crews it had been a pleasant battle, and their cheers were still resounding as they went to breakfast. But in the Spanish ships a different and terrible situation reigned. In the flagship, according to Admiral Montojo, 'there came upon us numberless projectiles.'

A short time after the action commenced one shell exploded in the forecastle and put out of action all those who served the four rapid-fire cannon, making splinters of the foremast, which wounded the helmsman on the bridge.... At seven-thirty one shell completely destroyed the steering gear. I ordered to steer by hand.... In the meantime another shell exploded on the poop and put out of action nine men. Another destroyed the mizzen-mast head, bringing down the flag and my ensign, which were replaced immediately. A fresh shell exploded in the officers' cabin, covering the hospital with blood and destroying the wounded who were being treated there. Another exploded in the ammunition room astern, filling the quarters with smoke and preventing the working of the hand steering gear. As it was impossible to control the fire, I had to flood the magazine when the cartridges were beginning to explode....
One of the large ones penetrated the fire room, putting out of action one master gunner and twelve men serving the guns. Another rendered useless the starboard bow gun. While the fire astern increased, fire was started forward by another shell, which went through the hull and exploded on the deck.

As the action wore on, he found it impossible to serve even the undamaged guns, 'as the guns' crews had been frequently called upon to substitute for those charged with steering, all of whom were out of action.' Montojo himself was hit in the leg. The ship, 'confused with the cries of the wounded,' was on fire fore and aft, and in a sinking condition; half her crew was disabled; her decks were in the condition of a butcher-shop. The Admiral ordered her to be sunk and abandoned 'before the magazines should explode.' Montojo transferred his flag in safety to the Isla de Cuba, but the flagship's captain was killed as he was directing the rescue of her personnel.

The experience of other ships in the little squadron was similar, if less terrible. The Ulloa was sunk by a shell. The ancient Castilla, the wooden hulk which could not move, caught fire and had to be abandoned after a loss of twenty-three killed and eighty wounded. The lighter vessels seem to have suffered much less severely, as the American gun captains instinctively tended to concentrate their fire upon the large ships, but to continue fighting was obviously useless. Out of a complement of about 1200 men, the Spanish squadron had already lost 381 men killed and wounded in this curious and peculiarly senseless butchery. As the American vessels drew off, Admiral Montojo 'ordered the ships that remained to us to take position in the bottom of the roads at Bacoor, and there to resist until the last moment, and that they should be sunk before they surrendered.'

Bacoor Bay is the wide and shallow indentation within the peninsula upon which Cavite stands. Our people saw them go. The flagship and the Castilla, left behind, were burning fiercely; and presently, when the fire reached the former's magazines and she blew up, the American crews cheered again. Spanish naval resistance, they realized, was at an end. Lieutenant Fiske, coming into the Petrel's wardroom for breakfast, paused as usual to wash his hands. A brother officer stopped him: 'No, don't wash your hands; no one is allowed to wash his hands. We don't go into battle every day, and we are not going to wipe off any of the smoke and dirt.' It was all very glorious.

About eleven o'clock Dewey once more got under way to put in the finishing touches. Coming up on the outside of the point the Baltimore silenced the shore batteries, and presently a white flag fluttered from the shears at the dockyard. The Petrel, the only one of our ships which could get into the shoal water behind Cavite, was ordered in to destroy the remaining ships. In spite of Montojo's orders to resist to the last, they were found abandoned. An officer was sent away to set them alight.

While this was being done a curious little incident occurred. Lieutenant Fiske volunteered to go in to the arsenal in a small boat and bring out a number of tugs and launches they saw lying there. He was thus the first American ashore.

I got up on the stone dock and looked about me. I had scarcely done so when I saw advancing toward me a large number of Spanish officers. I should say from recollection at least twenty-five. Behind them, farther up the dock, was what looked to me like a small army of soldiers drawn up in regular formation under arms, and a crowd of some hundred sailors. ... I advanced toward the officers and they advanced toward me and we exchanged most punctilious salutes. We tried to talk in English and Spanish, but they could not talk English well enough and I could not talk Spanish well enough; but I managed to get along fairly well with one of the officers in French.

The Spaniards were anxious to find out, it appeared, whether there was to be any more fighting. Lieutenant Fiske assured them that the American vessels would honor their white flag. 'Americanos siempre caballeros!' they cried. There was some more conversation, in which both sides seemed desirous of being mutually helpful, and when Mr. Fiske's boat crew had difficulty in clearing the mooring lines of the tugs, and he ordered some of the armed Spanish sailors who were 'congregated about, looking on with languid interest,' to assist, they did so with the best will in the world. The Petrel finally steamed away with her string of prizes towing astern and the Spanish gunboats blazing behind her.

The events just narrated [as Mr. Fiske later put it] seemed at the time perfectly natural and to be expected. When the battle was over we did not feel that we had done anything wonderful; and I do not believe that anybody in the fleet appreciated the fact that the Battle of Manila was one of the most important battles that had ever been fought in any country or in any age.

But they were soon to make the discovery.

Dewey had in the meanwhile sent the McCulloch back to Manila bearing the consul, Mr. Williams, with a note to the Governor-General of the islands. In spite of the excited assumptions of his compatriots in the United States, the Commodore had abandoned any intention of capturing or annexing the archipelago himself, or even of occupying Manila. He had no troops with him, and the entire personnel of his fleet numbered less than two thousand men. His plan was to leave the land fighting to the insurgents, and to go no farther himself until an Army contingent could be sent to make good the conquest. He therefore demanded merely that the Manila batteries should not fire upon him (under penalty of an immediate bombardment of the city) and asked for the use of port facilities and of the Hong Kong cable. In the course of the afternoon Mr. Williams was put on board a British merchant ship lying in the harbor; he requested her master to send the note ashore for transmission through the British Consul.

About midnight a reply was sent out to the Commodore: it was agreed that there would be no firing, but the other demands were refused. The Commodore immediately ordered that the cable be dredged up and cut; he then retired with his fleet to Cavite, and after taking possession of the arsenal and dockyard and destroying its fortifications, he settled himself to blockade the port and await developments. Such was the position of affairs at a moment when the home publics were confidently assuming that Manila was ours and were already discovering our moral duty to establish our own governance over the archipelago, since we had 'stricken down Spanish sovereignty.' Actually Spanish sovereignty, save within the confines of the Cavite dockyard, had not even been impaired.

Certainly the Commodore showed no haste in getting home the reports which would have corrected the error. As the nervous tension increased in Washington, the placid tropic days drifted across the shimmering water of Manila Bay, while the details of the action were mopped up, while the Commodore wrote out two brief despatches, and while Mr. Williams devoted himself to the composition of a report to the State Department in a prose style worthy of what Mr. Williams, if not the naval men, already felt to be the grandeur of the occasion.

'With magnificent coolness and order, but with greatest promptness,' Mr. Williams wrote in the sweltering heat, 'our fleet, in battle array, headed by the flagship, answered the Spanish attack....' The superlatives tumbled out. 'The method of our operations could not have shown greater system... our officers and crews greater bravery....' The Consul worked up to a climax: 'History has only contrasts. There is no couplet to form a comparison.'

It was not until Thursday afternoon that the McCulloch finally cleared for Hong Kong, bearing Commodore Dewey's flag-lieutenant, the despatches, and the three newspaper correspondents. Mr. J. L. Stickney belonged to the New York *Herald*; Mr. Edwin Harden, a Treasury agent who had been traveling in the Far East when the war began, had been retained by the *World*; while his friend, Mr. John T. McCutcheon, had been secured by the Chicago *Tribune*. The Navy undertook to see fair play, and the flag-lieutenant exacted a promise from the three journalists that they would not attempt to file anything until the official despatches had gone. He would then give them the word 'go' and leave it to their ingenuity. They arrived at Hong Kong on the afternoon (Hong Kong time) of May 7; the three respected their pledges, but the astute Mr. Harden filed a brief despatch at full rates. The others sent their accounts at press rates, and so lost a couple of hours in transmission. Thus it was that the *World* scored the great news beat of the war — a dazzling triumph, but a hollow one. Saturday afternoon in Hong Kong is Saturday morning in New York; the terse paragraphs got into only 'a few copies of a late morning edition, but all the New York evening papers fattened their circulation figures that day on the *World's* news.'

CHAPTER VIII
SPLENDID IMPROVISATION

I

THE enormous relief with which the direct news of Manila Bay was received indicated how intense had been the anxiety. It was at half-past four on Saturday morning that Mr. Cridler, sleeping on his cot in the State Department, had been awakened by the preliminary message announcing the arrival of the McCulloch at Hong Kong. Almost immediately, in the gray hour of dawn, official Washington was in a turmoil. Messengers were despatched at once to arouse the Secretary of the Navy and the principal officials; the news that Dewey was about to be heard from was telephoned to the White House and the rumor was already at large in the city.

Before eight o'clock it had run like wildfire through the town, creating the most intense and excited curiosity. When the Department building [the State, War and Navy Building] opened for business at nine o'clock, a great crowd of newspaper men had gathered at the Navy and War Departments.... Half an hour passed without result. Secretaries Long and Alger, the latter much more nervous and anxious than his colleague, sat together in the Navy Department.... About nine thirty Mr. Marcan, manager of the Western Union Telegraph Company, appeared at the Department bringing with him a sheet comprising four lines of the mysterious jargon which makes up the naval cipher.... Senators, Representatives, officials from all the departments added to the throng in Secretary Long's reception room, until that apartment and all the corridors leading to it were uncomfortably crowded with an eagerly speculative and intensely patriotic crowd. No less than fifty newspaper men stood just outside the Secretary's inner office.

Impressed by the solemn importance of the moment, Mr. Long had announced that he would in person give out the despatch from his inner office when it was ready. But Mr. Long (as had happened before) had failed to reckon with his irrepressible Assistant Secretary and that officer's genius for the front page. At about ten o'clock Mr. Roosevelt (whose service at the Navy

Department was practically over, and who had received his Army commission the day before) came pushing through the throng on his way from the room in which the despatch was being decoded. A gathering of fifty newspapermen all in one place was an opportunity which Mr. Roosevelt could not resist; and with the dramatic preface that it was probably the last good news he would have to give them from the Navy, he announced the full gist of Dewey's message. There was a wild rush for the telephones and the messenger boys. A little later Secretary Long appeared with a copy of the translated message in his hand. 'He had already telephoned its contents to the President, who had directed him to make it public without delay.' But the effect was spoiled.

By this time the cheers were resounding throughout the building, and the passageways and corridors were jammed in a scene 'of indescribable confusion and enthusiasm.' At about eleven a second despatch arrived by a Postal messenger; this time the Secretary took no chances, but carried it to the White House himself, and only gave it out to the press later through a clerk at the Department. Neither message contained more than a brief announcement of the main facts, but they confirmed what had already been reported, and that was all that was wanted. The news was soon all over Washington, and that ordinarily indifferent capital was thrilling 'with an excitement it had not known since the morning President Garfield was shot.' The nation, of course, blazed at once. Letters and telegrams of congratulation poured forth on their way to the Commodore. Mr. McKinley appointed him an Acting Rear Admiral on the spot; while a bill adding another rear admiral to the permanent establishment was rushed through Congress on Monday, and Dewey appointed to the vacancy thus created and confirmed.

Dewey's report indicated the falsity of the assumption that he had ended Spanish sovereignty in the islands or taken the city. But who noticed that small detail? 'I control bay completely,' the despatch read, 'and can take city at any time, but I have not sufficient men to hold.' The thing was as good as done already; this only made it more imperative than before to hurry out the troops. At a great celebration at the Manhattan Club in New

York, Mr. James B. Eustis, a former Senator and member of the
Foreign Relations Committee, cried out:

From the foundation of our government it has been a question debated
by the ablest of statesmen whether the acquisition of territory would be
beneficial to this country. But Dewey has settled the question.... He has
conquered foreign territory, and I am afraid that he has given Uncle Sam
a damn big appetite for that particular article of food.

And the 'laughter and cheers' rang out. About the appetite
there could be no mistake. There were a few doubtful voices —
the Boston *Herald* thought that to take the islands as a colony
would 'rend the Monroe Doctrine from top to bottom' and the
Washington *Star* felt that 'we belong in the western hemisphere.'
But even for these there was Porto Rico, which was in the western
hemisphere; while in other quarters there were no restraints. The
idea that we could justify a seizure of the Philippines on the
ground that they were a war indemnity was quick to formulate.
The Philadelphia *Record* discerned that the retention at least of
a naval base in the Philippines would be 'inevitable.' The Philadelphia *Press* observed that the 'United States is forced to step
upon the world's stage and deal with the world's problems.' While
the Providence *News*, with a magnificent readiness to take a
chance, pointed out that 'we do not know much about our new
possessions in the far Pacific, but what little we do know indicates
that they are of great value.... They are certainly well worth
keeping.' Western papers were hardly less confident and enthusiastic. The Milwaukee *Sentinel* found that we were under no
obligation 'formal or implied' to abandon the Philippines. While
the *Rocky Mountain News* printed a cartoon showing Uncle Sam
holding the world between his knees and sticking small American
flags into the various Spanish islands scattered over its surface.
'By gum,' Uncle Sam was saying, 'I rather like your looks.' And
— as we scanned our atlases, observed those splendid expanses of
blue water and read those strange, romantic place-names — so
did we.

It is true that Mr. Godkin had not ceased to rage against the
'new journalism,' and it was in these same days that the *Nation*
printed its famous editorial, directed at the youthful Mr. Hearst,
and excoriating 'a régime in which a blackguard boy with several

millions of dollars at his disposal has more influence on the use a
great nation may make of its credit, of its army and navy, of its
name and traditions, than all the statesmen and philosophers and
professors in the country.' But there were other intellectuals more
alert to the temper of the times. Mr. Walter Hines Page, in a
letter to his friend James Bryce, took scholarly account of the
larger aspects:

> We see already the beginnings of an 'Imperial' party here. Indeed, I do
> not see, nor do I know anybody who sees, how we are going to get rid of
> these islands, even if it were certain that we shall wish to get rid of them.
> The possession of the Philippines and the Hawaiian Islands will bring an
> overwhelming reason for as close an alliance as possible with Great
> Britain.... There can be little doubt but a wider-looking policy has come
> into our political life to remain.

Or as Dr. Shaw's *Review of Reviews* put it: 'We Americans adapt
ourselves to new conditions very readily,' even though 'the
average man is somewhat mystified by the Philippine campaign.'

It was impossible, of course, that these inspiring events and
glorious emotions should not have their repercussion upon official
Washington. If there had ever been any doubt as to the popularity of war — real war (especially when the Spanish ability to
inflict casualties seemed so negligible) — it had vanished. 'The
President,' a correspondent was telegraphing on the day after the
receipt of the Philippine news, 'has determined that the fighting
shall be vigorously forced.... The bugbear of the yellow fever
scourge is to be ignored, and the Spaniards are to be ejected from
Cuba before mid-summer if American soldiers can drive them
out.' That same Sunday, May 8, the President directed General
Miles 'to take an army of 70,000 men and capture Havana.' As
yet the volunteers were not ready — nothing was ready — but
the detail was immaterial. Early on Monday morning General
Shafter at Tampa was receiving telegraphic orders to 'move his
command under protection of Navy and seize and hold Mariel or
most important port on north coast of Cuba and where territory
is ample to land and deploy army.' Thirty-six hours later these
orders were cancelled — the fact that there was as yet no army
to deploy may have turned out to be a bugbear which could not
be 'ignored' — but the movement was postponed only until the

following week, May 16. In the meanwhile the Philippine expedition was being pushed as rapidly as possible, and it was hoped to get the first twelve hundred men off from San Francisco on the same date. General Merritt was designated for the Philippine command, and it was planned to give him in all 'two and possibly three divisions.'

Then there was sudden news from the Cuban blockade, and the war began to seem almost warlike. On May 11, the torpedo boat Winslow was sent into the harbor of Cardeñas (as a result, apparently, of too profound a confidence in the inaccuracy of Spanish gun-practice) and immediately drew an overwhelming fire from a gunboat lying at a wharf and from some light batteries on shore. There was a lively five minutes; the Winslow's commander was wounded, the paper-thin hull was riddled, the steering gear put out of action, and one of the main engines disabled. An armed tug came in to bring her away, but as the hawser was being passed a shell exploded on the Winslow's deck, killing one officer, Ensign Worth Bagley, and five men. A shocked nation realized suddenly that in war, even this war, men could be killed; and in the angry pain of the discovery there was a mutter of criticism against the Navy for the 'needless sacrifice.'

But a day or two later the news arrived of another sacrifice, made at almost the same hour on the opposite side of Cuba. On the morning of May 11, the gunboats Nashville and Marblehead, lying on blockade off the entrance to Cienfuegos, sent in their boats to cut the cable lines which came ashore there, and over which the island was in communication with the outside world. The low, deserted point on the east side of the entrance was a picturesque place, but an uninviting one for a boat action.

The cable house, a small, square stone building, was on Colorado Point, a short distance east of the lighthouse; the neighboring land was low, ending at the sea with the vertical, weather-worn coral so common along the Cuban coast, the brown and ragged character of which gives an uncanny appearance to the shore. Back of the edge was close chaparral; rifle pits were known to exist close by. Still further back there was a slight, densely wooded ridge parallel to the shore, with low growth, the whole forming dense cover for the movement of men.

Upon this forbidding shore the two sailing launches and two

steam cutters cheerfully advanced, with the intention of dredging up the heavy armored cables and cutting through them. As tools for this operation they were provided with nothing beyond cold-chisels, axes, hack-saws, and wire-cutting pliers, and the whole thing had to be executed within a hundred feet or so of the rifle pits.

With the ships firing over their heads and with riflemen in the steam launches to keep down interference from the shore, the two pulling boats got in, fished up a cable, and hacked and sawed their way through it. The Spaniards kept up a slow fire, but for the first hour or so our faith in their marksmanship was justified, and the boat crews worked on. Another cable was found and cut, and a third had just been fished up when the chaparral suddenly blazed forth with small-arm, machine-gun, and even light-caliber artillery fire. The bullets were dropping in the water all around; men were falling in the boats, and one of the sailing launches was being holed so rapidly that she began to fill. They managed to get away without being annihilated, which was remarkable considering the range, but two men had been mortally wounded and five others injured. This sacrifice was more justifiable, from a military standpoint, than that at Cardeñas, but it failed in its object. Unfortunately, there were more cables at Cienfuegos than had been supposed, and it was later discovered that communication between Havana and Madrid had not been interrupted.

II

These casualties of May 11 were the first of the war upon the American side; and they fell with a slight chill upon our blood-thirsty populace. A sudden note of reality ran through the pageant; while now, in a hidden undercurrent, a new anxiety began to gather and make headway. The possibility that war might have its serious side came home with an unpleasant abruptness as our eastern public turned its eyes from the Pacific to the less romantic, but far more important, coasts of Long Island.

Where was Admiral Cervera? The problem had for some days been bringing furrows even to the ordinarily placid brows of Mr. McKinley, while less responsible strategists were in a state of considerable excitement. Admiral Cervera had left the Cape Verde

Islands on the 29th of April, to vanish into the silent emptiness of the Atlantic. It was assumed that his destination was the West Indies, and we had been calmly waiting for him to turn up there some time about May 8 and deliver himself into the hands of the overwhelming American naval force in those waters. But now the calculated date had passed; Admiral Cervera had not appeared.

It had early occurred to the Navy Department that his destination might not be the West Indies, which even Spanish strategy might have preferred to avoid, but the rich, accessible, and comparatively undefended reaches of our own North Atlantic coast. It was an idea which soon began to spread to the coast cities. In the very midst of the enthusiasms over Dewey's victory a sudden nervousness appeared. A telegraph operator in Newfoundland thought he heard gun-fire at sea, and the report was flashed up and down the Atlantic coast. Incoming sea captains began to report strange shapes, undoubtedly torpedo boats, off Fire Island, and the whole North Atlantic was abruptly filled with Spanish cruiser squadrons of the most formidable character and the most dubious authenticity. Inoffensive gentlemen who happened to have dark complexions began to be picked up along our beaches on suspicion of having signaled to hostile warships on the horizon, and the nation which had just been hotly demanding an onslaught upon the effete and incompetent Spaniard surrendered itself, for a moment, to something strangely like a panic. The whole coast all at once perceived that danger was urgently impending, and its response was both quick and characteristic. It wired its Congressmen.

The flood descended upon a Washington already sufficiently distracted. Nervous people with seaside properties frantically pulled the familiar wires; mayors, governors, and important contributors to party campaign funds bombarded the capital with their demands for protection. The crisis had already begun to develop before Mr. Roosevelt left the Navy Department, and he described it in a moving passage:

Members of Congress who had actively opposed building any navy came clamorously around to ask each for a ship for some special purpose of protection connected with his district.... Not only these Congressmen but the Chambers of Commerce and Boards of Trade of different coast cities all lost their heads... and brought every species of pressure to bear on the administration to get it to adopt the one most fatal course — that is, to distribute the Navy.

One Congressman demanded that a ship be stationed off Jekyll Island, the wealthy winter resort and game preserve in Georgia. An influential lady insisted upon having a man-of-war anchored off 'a huge seaside hotel' because she 'had a house in the neighborhood.' The safe-deposit vaults in Worcester were unable to receive all the securities which Boston business men attempted to transfer there, and in Mr. Roosevelt's own section of Long Island 'clauses were gravely put into leases to the effect that if the property were destroyed by the Spaniards the lease should lapse.' Even the fire-eaters had their sudden qualms. 'Senator Frye,' Mr. Long noted in his diary, 'who has been a blazing jingo, shouting for war, comes in with an appeal that a vessel be sent down to protect points along the coast which he represents.' Senator Chandler, another jingo, did the same. The sacred principles of Mahan themselves could not save the Navy from the seaports clamoring for battleships; a number of vessels had to be detached to calm the storm, and the axiom of the 'fleet in being' was considerably impaired. While if this was the Navy's experience, in the War Department the unhappy Alger was simply overwhelmed:

The calls made upon the Department about this time for immediate rescue from the advancing Spanish fleet were pathetic in their urgency. Telegrams, letters, and statesmen representing the imperilled localities poured into the War Department. They wanted guns everywhere; mines in all the rivers and harbors on the map; and their demands, joined with the tempestuous importunings of the applicants for appointments, lent to that period of the Secretary's life an affliction which it is difficult to find appropriate words to describe.

To this state of undignified apprehension we had been abruptly reduced by four badly found armored cruisers and three torpedo boats at large somewhere between the North and South Atlantic oceans.

In its plans to combat the menace the Navy in the main clung to its original dispositions. Commodore Schley, with as much of his Flying Squadron as they had been able to save from the Congressmen, was still held at Hampton Roads as the chief reliance in case of a direct raid upon the coast. The St. Louis and

Harvard — two large but comparatively fast trans-Atlantic liners which had been taken over from the American Line and armed as auxiliary cruisers — had been stationed to the eastward of Martinique to report the enemy if he should come through the Leeward Isles. The remaining possibility was that Cervera might be making for San Juan, Porto Rico, a fortified base and the nearest to the Peninsula of all Spain's West Indian harbors. This seemed the most likely chance; and in the hope that Cervera might be found and destroyed there, Admiral Sampson, with the bulk of our heavy ships, was now making a painful progress eastward along the north coast of Cuba.

This cruise to Porto Rico was not an altogether happy experience. As the squadron set out, towing two of the ponderous coast defense monitors (they could not carry enough coal to make the journey unaided) and accompanied 'naturally and almost unavoidably' by a 'number of steamers belonging to the press,' it must have presented an appearance rather like a cross between a regatta and a salvage operation. The dignity of the occasion was scarcely enhanced when the flagship wasted part of the first afternoon 'in chasing a strange steamer, which proved to be a Brazilian chartered by a press association'; while the profound secrecy in which the enterprise was undertaken was rather damaged by the fact that its departure and probable destination were promptly published throughout the United States. The progress toward Porto Rico was desperately slow. There was endless trouble as the monitors parted their tow lines, or the squadron had to be stopped, in periods of calm, in order to coal them. The Terror's steering gear failed, and there was more delay. The Indiana, one of the four first-line battleships which were the pride as well as the backbone of our fleet, could only make seven knots because of her badly leaking boilers; while the despatches which were brought from time to time by the torpedo boats or the ubiquitous press lent a distressing uncertainty to the whole operation as they fixed the Spanish squadron almost everywhere from Cadiz to Cape Haitien.

The Navy was not entirely, perhaps, that model of efficiency which Mr. Roosevelt and his admiring countrymen believed that he had made it. It took them eight hot and exasperating days to make the 960 miles from Havana to San Juan; but at dusk on

May 11 they found themselves at last approaching the Porto
Rican capital. At four next morning they called all hands and
stood in for San Juan, 'the lights of the town being plainly visible.'
There was a heavy ground swell running and a gray dawn breaking, through which they slowly made out the 'lofty precipices'
upon which the town stood, crowned by the picturesque and moss-
grown masonry of its ancient fortifications — impressive symbols
of the majesty of mediæval Spain. It was a queer and mystic
moment, instinct with romance, tense with the apprehension for
what might lie ahead.

Over the misty, heaving sea a deep stillness brooded which seemed only
accentuated by the distant boom of the surges against the low coral shore
west of the harbor entrance; the whole, with the deeply rolling ships, and
with the lofty battlements of the Morro Castle showing gigantic in the
dim light, forming a picture not soon to be forgotten.

There was a nervous half-hour or so until in the growing light
they made out, about five o'clock, that the harbor was empty.
Cervera was not there. It almost seemed as though no one was
there. The town was asleep or dead; no flags had yet been hoisted;
in the mysterious light a few people could be seen hurrying along
the ancient battlements with what looked like rammers and
sponges in their hands, but there were few other signs of life. The
American squadron went to quarters at five o'clock.

Cervera was not there; the object of the cruise had been defeated, and nothing was to be gained by waiting. It occurred to
Admiral Sampson, however, that he might as well afford his crews
some battle practice and 'develop' the batteries — the risk now
seemed small — and at quarter-past five the fleet opened fire. It
was not until eight minutes later that the forts replied. Sampson,
like Dewey, steamed slowly back and forth over an elliptical
course before the town, but the results were less satisfactory than
they had been against the ships in Manila Bay. The monitors'
shooting was 'very bad' owing to their gift for rolling in a swell,
and in the after turret of the Amphitrite a man died of heat prostration. It was impossible properly to ventilate these floating
batteries on tropical service. Before long the black powder employed in the secondary batteries had shrouded the squadron in so
deep a pall of smoke that it was necessary to discontinue their use.

At a quarter to eight, Sampson signaled to cease firing altogether, and hauled off to the northwest. One shell had landed in the superstructure of the New York, killing one man and wounding four others, and three men had been wounded in the Iowa, but beyond these there were no casualties. The only real damage the ships had sustained had been from the blast of their own guns. It was not impressive; but they had seen the dirt leaping from the fortifications as their own shells struck, and the action was reported as a brilliant success in which the enemy must have suffered severe losses. Later reports from Madrid indicated that this was an error, and even implied that what little loss of life there had been had occurred mainly among the civil population. But of course nobody believed such obvious enemy propaganda as that.

With the breaking off of the action, Admiral Sampson set his course once more for Havana. If Cervera were not in San Juan he might be almost anywhere; the gunboats and other light craft which had been left on the Cuban blockade were weak and open to attack, and Sampson with the heavy supports was now nearly a thousand miles away from them. Filled with anxiety lest the Spanish squadron had slipped past him, the Admiral pushed westward over the course he had come, with all the speed possible to a squadron which had averaged about six knots on the trip out.

The operation had not served to allay the anxiety upon the eastern seaboard. On May 10 there had been a reassuring rumor that the Cape Verde fleet had actually turned up in the harbor of Cadiz; and Washington believed it just long enough to revise all the Army plans once more and order everybody direct to the Gulf coast for an immediate descent upon Cuba. The orders were hardly dry, however, before they had to be torn up again; the rumor, it appeared had been a mistake. Then there was a new fear. The battleship Oregon was now nearing the end of her long journey from Seattle, and the idea occurred to our strategists that Cervera might be headed for the South American coast to intercept and destroy her. Then a day or two later somebody heard that somebody else had positive information that Cervera was off the New England coast, and there was another violent flurry on the telegraph wires.

General Miles frantically ordered the New York headquarters

to 'report at once any information you have about Spanish war boats on our coast. Give full information.' The Seventy-First New York was already in transports at Bedloe's Island, ready to sail for Florida, but the regiment was immediately disembarked and sent on by rail. There was agitation at Portsmouth, New Hampshire, where the commandant of the navy yard had retailed the rumor, and the Mayor of the city and the Governor of the state wired for permission to retain the New Hampshire volunteers for the defense of their native soil. 'The alarm,' Mr. Alger found to his exasperated dismay, 'quickly spread to every coast town on the Atlantic,' but even as this was happening the cause for the alarm was already past. The newspapers on the morning of May 13 announced that Admiral Cervera in the flesh had at last appeared — off the Island of Martinique in the Lesser Antilles.

We had not, after all, done the Spanish strategists an injustice. The Cape Verde fleet was deliberately placing its head in the lion's mouth, and all danger of a raid upon the Atlantic coast had passed. If, indeed, there had ever been any.

III

During all this period the Army plans had been attaining a state of increasingly splendid confusion, through which it is not easy to trace the main thread of events. Disregarding, however, the minor motifs in the majestic theme, the general development of our Cuban strategy may be recapitulated. At the end of April the War President had directed General Shafter to make a hasty 'reconnaissance in force' *via* the south coast of the island. He was to take only about ten thousand men, all of them regulars; he was to stay only a day or two, and was to confine himself principally to supplying arms to Gómez in order that the latter might do the necessary fighting.

Next day, however, it had been remembered that the Navy was too busy looking for Cervera to supply a convoy, and the movement was postponed.

On May 2, after the first news of Manila, this project was torn up; the President forgot his solicitude for the volunteers, and the plan to send 40,000 or 50,000 men direct to the assault upon Havana was adopted, Shafter's troops to be the advance guard.

With the arrival of definite news from Dewey, the War President's ideas still further expanded, and on May 8, General Miles was ordered to collect 70,000 men for the Havana project; while General Shafter on the 9th received positive orders to advance and seize Mariel, some twenty miles west of Havana, as a bridgehead.

By the evening of the 10th, however, it began to look as though this might be a trifle precipitate; Shafter was informed that the invasion could not be undertaken until the 16th. In the meanwhile he was directed to move his command to Key West, preparatory to taking the final departure from the coral reef of Dry Tortugas.

But it was, of course, dreadfully hard to think of everything; and what between the politicians, the coast cities, and the myriad problems of the mobilizing volunteers, who can blame the War Department for having overlooked the fact that it would have been difficult to find standing room for ten or twelve thousand men on the islet of Key West, to say nothing of finding anything else for them? On the evening of the 11th there arrived a despairing, and unsigned, telegram from Tampa:

Water for large body of troops at Key West is serious question. Absolutely no water there.... It is imperative that water be placed in Key West before troops begin to arrive.... Dry Tortugas reported to have brackish water in cisterns. Am now trying to ascertain quantity and quality.

Washington, it appears, had forgotten about water. So that plan had to be abandoned.

Amid such developing annoyances, difficulties, and changes of policy the actual accomplishment was already beginning to look rather small. But there still remained that original project of sending arms to the Cubans, and though nothing of the sort could now be attempted on a large scale, it seemed an appropriate moment for getting off some kind of expedition, if only to prove to an impatient press that the Army was not behindhand in its services to the nation. The Navy, it had to be admitted, had been getting a disproportionate share of the publicity.

Thus it was determined to land a shipment of arms near Mariel; and two companies of the First Infantry, under the command of Captain J. H. Dorst, a cavalry officer, were designated to act as guard. Something, it appeared, was at last about to happen; and as far as the publicity went, nothing more could be desired, for the attention of a continent was at once fastened joyously upon the proposed undertaking. But even here the Army, one must confess, was inexpert. The vessel selected for the transport was an ancient side-wheeled river steamboat with a walking-beam engine — ample, no doubt, in her carrying capacity, but of an unfortunately non-military appearance. And however suitable she may have been in other respects, she labored under one overwhelming disadvantage which ought to have been conclusive. She was named the Gussie. Apparently it never even occurred to our unsophisticated commanders to alter that dreadful appellation, and thus it was, by an inadvertence of the Army itself, that its first important military operation was doomed to go down in history as 'the Gussie Expedition.' It was a major error.

What made it far worse was the fact that the whole operation was trumpeted in detail throughout the length and breadth of the country. The troops were loaded on board in the secrecy of night, but the Gussie did not sail until noon next day (May 10) and 'every one in Florida went to see her off.' In addition to the regular troops and some Cuban insurgents, she also carried a distinguished group of newspapermen, including 'Mr. Akers of the London *Times*, Poultney Bigelow and R. F. Zogbaum, the artist.' Mr. Stephen Bonsal was another, and Mr. James F. J. Archibald of the San Francisco *Post*. Mr. Frederic Remington, from the shore, had sketched the embarkation. All this was not enough, however. When the U.S.S. Wasp, one of the blockade squadron, encountered her off the Cuban coast two days later, she was 'accompanied by the newspaper tugs Triton and Dewey.... The party was proceeding westward along the beach, about three quarters of a mile from shore.'

The 'party' appeared to be in a rather aimless state. They had tried to land at Mariel, but the Cubans on board had refused. The fact was already dawning that the publicity had not been confined to the United States. If every one in Florida had seen them off, it began to look as though every one in Cuba had come down to receive them ashore. They drifted slowly along to the westward. A command of cavalry — some hundred men — appeared upon the beach and for nearly an hour pursued them, but were finally left behind. Off the harbor of Cabañas it seemed that a landing might be safely attempted. They anchored about a hundred yards off Arbolitos Point, at the west side of the entrance, and sent away some forty men in two boats. A heavy tropical downpour had broken, to dampen the brilliance of the afternoon, but to make up for it they had collected an admiring audience of American naval vessels, which, attracted by the curiosity of the proceedings, had gathered about in a semi-circle behind them and now afforded their moral support.

The boats pulled in through the rain, filled with an excited eagerness as the first landing of American troops upon Cuban soil seemed about to take place. But at the height of the tension (a skiff containing three Cuban guides had just upset in the surf and the patriots were seen to be swimming for it), the two newspaper tugs came hurrying in 'with their whistles blowing and their crews wildly gesticulating, thus leaving no room to doubt that they had information of the most vital importance to impart.'

Throughout the operations in Cuban waters the newspaper despatch boats were frequently a principal reliance for military communications. For this reason, if for no other, it was not possible to disregard them, and the leading boat lay upon its oars waiting to hear what the trouble was.

It was an exciting moment. The rain had died away again into a drizzle; the wind had veered around to the north, and was blowing up quite a sea on shore. The breakers went to pieces with a tremendous roar upon the coral reefs. It was with difficulty that we at last made out, above the roar of the surf and the rising winds, what the Samaritans and Scribes were singing out through their speaking trumpets.

'What's the name of that man in the bow of the first boat?'
The soldier answered timidly, 'Metzler, of E Company,' and so it was written down in history that Metzler was the first soldier of the United States Army to land upon Cuban soil. But he was not, for Captain O'Connell's boat, which had cleared first from the transport, got into difficulties in crossing the reef and was finally upset, while the second boat went ahead and landed first.

Once ashore they found themselves in a jungle. Volley-firing came out of the bushes; the Americans replied, going ahead in skirmish order, and the opposition presently dissolved. The gunboats obligingly did a little shelling of the bush — a kind of primitive barrage fire — and presently they swam off the horses of the three Cuban guides. The latter mounted and rode away in safety to find the insurgent forces, but it was evident that there were no insurgents in that neighborhood and that the supplies could not be landed. The troops were withdrawn from the beach. We had suffered but a single casualty, when one man was grazed in the arm. It was Mr. Archibald, the correspondent of the San Francisco *Post*.

The Gussie continued to wander up and down the coast for a day or two longer, to the admiration and surprise of all who saw her, but never managed to find any Cubans. On the 16th she was back again at Tampa, her supplies still aboard and the reputation of the Army scarcely enhanced. Captain Dorst remarked severely that the failure was due to the newspaper publicity. This really seems hardly fair; but at any rate, he found that he had been made a lieutenant-colonel in his absence.

The day that the Gussie returned was that which had been set for the formal advance upon Havana. But in the meanwhile this plan, too, had gone bodily into the discard. On May 13, with the news that Cervera had arrived in the West Indies, the Navy put an abrupt end to the matter. It had become necessary, Mr. Long curtly informed his colleague at the War Department, to protect the light ships on the blockade and to track down the Spanish Admiral. 'For these reasons,' he announced, 'it is considered by the Department to be inexpedient to expose the Army or any part of it on the waters in the vicinity of Cuba.... In consequence of this new state of affairs the orders which were lately issued for the Navy to convoy the army expeditionary corps for Cuba have been countermanded.' Considering the state of the Army on that date, it was just as well.

IV

On the 15th of May, Mr. Cortelyou, the President's secretary, made a gloomy entry in his diary:

> The President is again looking care-worn, the color having faded from his cheeks and the rings being once more noticeable about his eyes.... Uncertainty as to the whereabouts of the Cape Verde fleet, the growing

unrest and threatening character of the European situation — these, coupled with the many difficulties constantly arising as a result of the short-sighted policy which for so long a time has been pursued by Congress, leaving the country poorly prepared for hostilities, make the burden upon the Executive shoulders a heavy one. Added to these things is the struggle for place among the ambitious gentlemen who desire to serve their country in high-salaried and high-titled positions. And then, too, the present conditions are attended by the usual differences and bickerings among the officers of the Army and Navy, which in certain high quarters are altogether too apparent.

The situation, undoubtedly, was developing its serious aspects. A fortnight or so had elapsed since the volunteer commands had marched out of their armories, everywhere amid scenes of the most heartfelt and unbounded patriotism, to take up the sword in the defense of the national honor. But the volunteers were already assuming the proportions of a calamity. Even the task of mustering them into the Federal service, performed at their various state camps, had taken time; and it was not until May 12, two and a half weeks after the President's call, that the Seventy-First New York, one of the first regiments actually got under way, left its camp at Hempstead, Long Island, to join the national army. The enthusiasm was undiminished; the arrangements, it was noted, were poor.

The hour of the departure had been set for early afternoon; but though 'thousands of the regiment's admirers stood around the grounds just outside the strictly maintained guard line' and 'mothers, sisters, and sweethearts were quietly weeping,' it was not until a quarter to five that they actually swung out of the camp. Even then there was a long and irritating wait upon the railroad siding. One patriotic father took advantage of it:

Charles Eiseman, father of Private Eiseman of Company F, has promised to give $1,000 to any member of the company who captures a Spanish flag. If young Eiseman thus distinguishes himself, he will receive the $1,000 and a half share of his father's business, a liquor store at Sixth Avenue and Thirty-Sixth Street.

It was past six o'clock before the train started. In the meanwhile a vast crowd had collected at the station in Brooklyn, to cheer them upon their march to the ferries. The crowd waited with patience, but the regiment did not arrive; late in the evening the throng set out upon a hunt for them through the wildernesses of Queens County, and at last, about ten o'clock, discovered them marooned in the railroad yards at Long Island City. And there, although the ferries had all the time been in readiness to carry them to their transport at Bedloe's Island, the Seventy-First New York had to spend the night. It was evident that the staff-work was imperfect. But it turned out to be an accurate foretaste of the staff-work which they were to encounter throughout.

The larger part of the Regular Army had by this time been concentrated at Tampa, where it was comparatively well off. But the gathering host of volunteers was being poured, as rapidly as rail transportation could be provided, into Camp Thomas, the concentration point which had been chosen by General Miles in the Chickamauga National Park, near Chattanooga. Sometimes five or six regiments were arriving there in the course of a single day, and over 44,000 men were dumped into the camp in the last two weeks of May. Fortunately the regulars had been there before them and had organized the place to some extent; but it mitigated only slightly the appalling condition of the militia army which revealed itself to the shocked eyes of the inspectors. Their visit in the latter part of the month developed the fact that none of the regiments was ready for service 'either as to equipment or instruction.' In the First Missouri 'many men appeared in ranks without shoes or stockings'; while the lack of underclothing throughout all the regiments became, 'in view of the limited bathing facilities,' a 'very important deficiency.' In the kitchens there were few cooks 'able to handle the rations as issued,' and because the National Guardsmen had brought no bakers with them they were compelled to live on hardtack.

They were everywhere short of medicines and hospital supplies, while as for arms 'it seemed as if the states had unloaded on the regiments entering the service of the United States all the old arms, with the idea that they would be replaced by the Government.' Washington had been confident that in military equipment, at any rate — cartridge belts, haversacks, and so on — there would be no deficiency, since great quantities of these things had been issued to the Guard during the peace years. Washington was quickly disabused. The Guard brought its equipment, but it was found that the stuff was no longer 'in fit condition for field service' and it had to be replaced. The Ordnance Department established a special factory for the purpose; and by the time the war was over, it was just beginning to catch up.

The National Guard officers were incompetent. They had little idea of how to care for the health or comfort of their men, while their ignorance upon the conduct of troops in the field was all-embracing. When the Governor of Kansas insisted on replacing all his old officers with men who should not suffer under the taint of militarism, he was not doing so great a disservice to his troops as might be supposed. The Twentieth Kansas, in fact, was peculiarly fortunate; the Governor chose for its colonel Mr. Frederick Funston, the adventurous youth who had been in command of García's rudimentary artillery the year before. Mr. Funston knew nothing whatever of the orthodox military art, and modestly supposed that a few months of irregular skirmishing in the Cuban jungles hardly fitted him for the command of a regiment of United States infantry. But his soldiers were lucky compared to most of the others.

Such were the troops which from the middle of May onward descended in an ever-increasing avalanche upon a War Department designed to conduct the peace-time affairs of an army of 25,000 men. When the President issued his call there were only fifty-seven officers in the entire Quartermaster Department. They had enough clothing and material on hand for the existing establishment and perhaps 10,000 men in addition. At the last moment they got about $1,500,000 from the 'Fifty Million Bill,' but there was no legislative authority and no money for making really adequate preparation; and up to the day upon which the President's call was issued, the Quartermaster-General had been unable to find out how large a volunteer force was to be summoned. And yet within the single month from April 25 to May 25 they found themselves called upon to uniform, supply, and equip an army of 275,000 men.

It was indeed a 'massive undertaking.' They bought 200,000 yards of canvas tenting — all they could find in the country which seemed of even fair quality — only to discover that much of it was 'short-lived.' The uniform cloth they secured was prepared with dyes of an unfortunate impermanence; it lent to the Army a startlingly variegated appearance, and in the camps in Florida 'there would be a purple and a green and a blue coat' seen in brilliant juxtaposition. They had a large stock of mess pans left over from the Civil War, so that was all right; the wagon transportation, on the other hand, had to be built entire after the outbreak of hostilities. Then the clothing question was complicated by the unexpected necessity for sending troops on tropical service. They improvised a uniform of cotton duck and let quantity contracts for its manufacture. Deliveries began to be made just as the Army was returning from the tropics and the cool weather of fall had set in.

The Ordnance Department had only 67,000 rifles and carbines of modern pattern on hand at the outbreak of war; 27,000 more were delivered before the close of hostilities, but there were never enough to arm the volunteers with them. The National Guardsmen had to use the old-fashioned black-powder Springfields. Efforts were made to supply a smokeless powder ammunition for them, but as 'the capacity for making such powder in this country' was found to be 'limited,' the few volunteers who were to do any actual fighting had to face the enemy under the murderous handicap of the smoke-producing variety. The Rough Riders, an exception, had modern weapons and ammunition, but the Rough Riders also had the politically influential Mr. Roosevelt as their lieutenant-colonel. The Seventy-First New York was less fortunate.

The want of means was paralleled by the total want of organization to handle the stuff when it was provided. Nor was this all. Left to itself, the War Department might have been able to stagger through its stupendous assignment without serious failure. But there was no general plan; the various troop concentrations were ordered, cancelled, ordered again, enlarged, postponed, from week to week, and no one ever, at any given moment, knew where he was or what he was supposed to be doing. 'There were,' as the Quartermaster-General later pathetically testified, 'so many changes.'

There were also so many politicians. At almost every point outside importunities or influence intervened to tear up plans or alter dispositions. Against Capitol Hill Mr. Alger appears to have been without defenses. Senators got their friends appointed to (or even preserved from) active service; Congressmen dictated what regiments were to be sent or where. The Governors, of course, were giving endless trouble, the effects of which were felt from the top to the bottom of the machine. When the Second Wisconsin arrived at Chickamauga, one of its privates was found to be a West Point graduate who, after resigning from the Army, had served for a time as a captain in the regiment. When he had appeared to rejoin for the war, he had learned that despite his qualifications no commission was open to him; and he had consequently enlisted in the ranks. At Chickamauga he was discovered by two brother officers of the regulars, now serving in an Ohio volunteer regiment. They applied at once to have this invaluable man transferred to their own organization, intending to secure a commission for him and thus mitigate the terrible dearth of trained officer personnel against which they were struggling. They got the order for the transfer, only to find that the Wisconsin colonel would not give him up. The colonel explained that the private (whom he addressed as 'Charlie') was needed to instruct the regimental officers in their duties, and it required a special order from the White House itself to pry loose the former West-Pointer.

This was finally accomplished, however, and the demotion of two incompetents in the Ohio regiment conveniently left room for the trained man. But the Governor of Ohio refused to issue the commission; it appeared that he had promised the first vacancy to a political friend. It was regularly found thereafter that whenever a commission fell vacant the Governor still had a personal or political candidate upon his waiting list, and throughout a war in which the lack of trained officers did perhaps more damage than any other factor, this graduate of West Point continued to serve as a first sergeant.

In face of the impossible task so abruptly assigned to it, one cannot help feeling that the War Department on the whole did a surprisingly good job. But in this opinion Mr. Roosevelt (who of all the Department's difficulties was to prove one of the most difficult) failed to share. On the day after he had been sworn in as lieutenant-colonel of volunteer cavalry, he was already jotting into his diary his sweeping verdict upon the organization which he proposed to ornament:

The delays and stupidity of Flagler and the Ordnance Department surpass belief. The Quartermaster Department is better, but bad. The Commissary Department is good. There is no head, no management whatever in the War Department. Against a good nation we should be helpless.

Perhaps it was true; but it was distinctly unkind. Mr. Roosevelt, who had been devoting himself for a year to running the Navy, addressed himself almost from the beginning to the performance of a similar task for the Army; and the very important detail that, while he had been Assistant Secretary in the former organization, he was merely a junior officer in the latter somehow appears to have escaped his attention. Mr. Roosevelt was to prove a very peculiar lieutenant-colonel.

His regiment was likewise a peculiar organization. Its precise origins were always a little obscure, but it is difficult to suppose that it was called into being for purely military reasons. The War Department might have got on without it; but the idea of riding into battle at the head of a command of cowboy cavalry had long been a dream of Mr. Roosevelt's own more martial mind. Twelve years before, while spending a summer upon his ranch in the Dakotas, he had scented a pleasing possibility of 'trouble with Mexico' and had at once offered to 'raise some companies of horse riflemen' from among the 'harum-scarum rough riders of the West.' That was in 1886, and there was no trouble. But when trouble happily came at last in 1898, the bill for increasing the Regular Army contained an inconspicuous provision which made possible the gratification of Mr. Roosevelt's dream.

This provision authorized the special enlistment of three thousand volunteers directly by the Federal Government, and distinct from the state quotas and organizations; and the authorization was used to organize three regiments of 'United States Volunteer Cavalry.' The honor of raising and commanding them was eagerly sought after by many influential civilians (there seems to have been no thought of assigning the task to experienced regular cavalry officers); but oddly enough, the first of them went to none other than Mr. Roosevelt. No doubt there was a general belief that Cuban warfare was especially suited to the use of irregular horse; but neither the War Department nor any one else ever took the slightest interest in the other two after that, and, though one of them reached Florida, they were not destined to figure in the history of the war. Mr. Roosevelt's command, however, was destined to figure so very largely that at times it almost seemed to be the war, and one might have supposed that the whole scheme had been primarily designed to display Mr. Roosevelt's remarkable qualities before an admiring nation. Perhaps it was.

For this purpose, at any rate, the regiment was from the very beginning a conspicuous success. It was soon taking up that strategic position upon the front pages from which it was never afterward to be dislodged. Even before it had come into existence, the newspapers had begun to give it picturesquely alliterative nicknames, and these soon settled into 'Roosevelt's Rough Riders' — the euphonious combination which Mr. Roosevelt had himself used twelve years before, and under which they were to go down to history. With a becoming modesty — and a certain caution — Mr. Roosevelt bestowed the colonelcy upon Dr. Leonard Wood rather than upon himself. It was a popular move. Dr. Wood was a young Army surgeon whose friends had just got him the Congressional Medal of Honor for his part in an Indian skirmish a decade before; he was also of that able but rather colorless type which was unlikely to dim very seriously the martial glory to be won by his second in command. At all events Dr. Wood very soon departed for the mobilization point at San Antonio to devote himself to the serious business of raising and training the men. Mr. Roosevelt lingered in the more brilliant publicity of Washington.

Even before he had left the Navy Department he was busy recruiting the picturesque contingent of college athletes and sons of wealthy men who were to add so much to the dramatic value of the undertaking; he was busy also pulling every wire which he or his friend Senator Lodge could lay their hands upon in order to secure for the Rough Riders the modern arms, smokeless powder, tropical uniforms, and preferential treatment which were unavailable to the less fortunate volunteers. Mr. Roosevelt early made

OFFICERS' MESS OF THE ROUGH RIDERS AT SAN ANTONIO, TEXAS
Colonel Leonard Wood and Lieutenant-Colonel Roosevelt at the head of the table

up his mind that his part of the war, at least, was going to be run upon the great principle of individualism, and an eager press readily abetted him. He finally extracted a promise (or so the reporters understood) that the Rough Riders would be among the first upon the firing line, and at last managed to tear himself away from the Navy and from Washington. Mr. Roosevelt arrived in San Antonio on May 16 to join his regiment. 'He was busy all day,' said the newspaper report of this event, 'receiving callers.'

It may help to explain why the military authorities twenty years later were to look with alarm upon his proposal to raise, not a regiment, but a whole division. And even in 1898 the political possibilities in this splendid adventure were overlooked by no one. Among the gathering originals whom he found awaiting him in Texas there was a common characteristic. As one of them later put it:

We rendezvoused at San Antonio. Twelve hundred as separate, varied, mixed, distinct, grotesque, and peculiar types of men as perhaps were ever assembled in one bunch in all the history of man... and one — possibly two — Democrats. (All except the possible two were straight Republicans.)

It was an important advantage. In Nebraska another ambitious young politician was to awake to the situation and offer himself patriotically upon the altar of his country; but he was not to enjoy the same facilities. Mr. William Jennings Bryan was an opponent of imperialism; his party, however, had been even more eloquent in its support of Cuban liberty than the Republicans, and Mr. Bryan was quite consistent in attempting to cash in upon the glories of what he had proclaimed as a holy war. But the Bryanite Democrats, who had been so enthusiastic in pushing on the war, were now to discover that the war, having come, had been dexterously and basely appropriated by their opponents. Mr. Bryan was rather late in starting his own regiment; and when he did he was to find that the way was beset with difficulties. The idea of permitting the man who had so nearly led 'that league of Hell' to victory two years before to distinguish himself upon the battlefield — the Republican battlefield, as it had become — was one from which the Republican authorities recoiled. Colonel Bryan's Third Nebraska was not promised a first place upon the firing line; indeed, it was with difficulty that it even achieved a place in Republican newspapers.

The War Department does appear to have strained a point to be fair to Colonel Bryan. Anything else would hardly have looked well in a war which was to put an end (under Republican auspices) to all party strife and to bind up the wounds of sectional difference. Southerners and non-political Democrats were, within reason, admitted to appointment and promotion. Bands of Northern regiments arriving at Southern camps were careful to play 'Dixie' to the cheering crowds. The Sixth Massachusetts on its way South was marched through Baltimore, where thirty-seven years before, going South upon a different errand, it had been mobbed by the populace and had suffered some of the first casualties of the Civil War. Once more it was mobbed — by a crowd bearing a 'floral tribute' with the inscription: 'Massachusetts and Maryland: Flowers not Bullets,' done in violets and rosebuds. It was an atmosphere in which one had to be fair, at least, to Colonel Bryan. Ultimately the Third Nebraska was accepted for Federal service and sent on to Florida; but it did no harm there, since it never got to Cuba, and, anyway, Mr. Roosevelt had collected all the glory by that time.

v

Such were the triumphs and tribulations with which the volunteer army, during the last fortnight in May, was being mobilized. In the more exciting department of actual battle news there was something of a lull. Since May 10 the striking force assembled at Tampa (consisting of some fifteen thousand regulars and about an equal number of the best among the volunteers) had received no further orders and was endeavoring to restrain its impatience amid the depressing scenery and climate which at that time characterized the west coast of Florida. Somewhere in the Caribbean the Navy was understood to be hunting for Admiral Cervera. But the Navy, aided by geography and its own complete ignorance of Cervera's whereabouts, had at last established a fairly effective censorship, and there was no news from that theater. Terse despatches from the Far East informed the nation that Admiral Dewey was still maintaining a close blockade of Manila, but the high cable tolls from those vast distances, together with the Admiral's convenient detachment from the cable terminus at Hong Kong, shrouded the whole of that situation in considerable obscurity.

It was an obscurity which did not, however, make the situation any the less interesting. The debate over how we should dispose of our 'captured' possessions was already lively. Senator Morgan of the Foreign Relations Committee was even preparing an article for the June *North American* in which he was disposing not only of the Philippines but the Caroline Islands as well; while the fear was already beginning to creep into the comment that unless we made haste Spain might bring the war to a close before we had captured all that we wanted. A new uncertainty, moreover, had been discovered in the attitude of the European powers. Late nineteenth-century diplomacy was conducted in a generally felonious atmosphere, and it seemed possible that Germany might intervene to acquire some of the loot for herself. The feeling between the United States and Germany had long been bad; the German press maintained an ominous reticence, and editors elsewhere quite freely discussed the probabilities of a 'clash.' It lent our policy toward the Philippines an added interest and the public turned eagerly to Washington to learn what our policy was to be.

What they saw was indefinite — but it was undoubtedly interesting. It had originally been hoped to get off some twelve hundred men from San Francisco by May 16, as the advance detachment of a force of about five thousand, the whole to be composed of west coast militiamen. Such an expedition would scarcely have been a formidable one, and might have been construed in different ways. On the 15th, a cable had arrived from Admiral Dewey:

I can take Manila at any moment. To retain possession and thus control Philippine Islands would require, in my best judgment, well equipped force of 5000 men.

But Washington's ideas had already gone far beyond this, and a much larger expedition was being contemplated. It was evident by this time that not even twelve hundred men could be got off on the 16th; it was equally evident that no force composed wholly of volunteers could be regarded as 'well equipped.' General Merritt, who had been appointed to supreme command, was asking the President for 14,400 men in all, with a large proportion of regulars; while the commander of the advance contingent was being instructed to occupy, not merely Manila, but 'such part of the islands as you may be able to do... until the arrival of other troops.' Dewey's cable effected no modification of these larger plans, and in the third week of May they were being pushed forward as rapidly as the general disorganization would permit.

As to just what the expedition was supposed to do there was still considerable uncertainty, even among those who were to be in command of it. On the 15th, General Merritt was writing to Mr. McKinley:

I do not yet know whether it is your desire to subdue and hold all of the Spanish territory in the islands, or merely to seize and hold the capital. It seems more than probable that we will have the so-called insurgents to fight as well as the Spaniards.

Apparently Mr. McKinley did not know either. As late as the 18th, General Miles was still laboring under the impression that 'the force ordered at this time is not expected to carry on a war to conquer an extensive territory,' but simply to establish a garrison which would 'command the harbor of Manila and relieve the United States fleet under Admiral Dewey with the least possible delay.'

On the 19th, the War President spoke at last — not for publication, but in the orders which could no longer be withheld from General Merritt. But upon the great question of our intentions toward the islands he managed to preserve, even here, that oracular ambiguity which was so striking a feature of his statesmanship. Dewey's actions in Manila Bay, as the President put it, 'have rendered it necessary in the further prosecution of the measures adopted by this Government for the purpose of bringing about an honorable and durable peace with Spain to send an army of occupation to the Philippines for the twofold purpose of completing the reduction of the Spanish power in that quarter and of giving order and security to the islands while in the possession of the United States.'

The President went on to point out, however, that 'the first effect of the military occupation of the enemy's territory is the severance of the former political relations of the inhabitants and the establishment of a new political power.' This appeared to dispose of the Spaniards. Did it dispose of the Philippine insurgents as well? It was a delicate question. Mr. McKinley asserted that 'the powers of the military occupant are absolute and supreme,' but was careful to add that he desired the General to impress upon the populace that we were coming 'not to make war upon the people of the Philippines nor upon any party or faction among them.' It would seem, as one recalls Mr. Pratt's conversations with General Aguinaldo at Singapore, to have been rather a difficult order; but Mr. McKinley closed the paragraph upon a lofty note: 'Our occupation should be as free from severity as possible.' By an ironic coincidence, it was early on that very morning that William Ewart Gladstone had died at Hawarden, and another pillar of the old-fashioned moralities had crumbled into the dust of time.

How equivocal a position we were preparing for ourselves was only slowly to become apparent. General Aguinaldo had not reached Hong Kong until May 2, and it was not until May 16 that Consul Wildman got him aboard the McCulloch and on the way to Manila. During the interval the Consul had had time for reflection, and it had already occurred to him that the insurgents might prove to be a 'necessary evil.' This was a new note. But he decided that 'if Aguinaldo were placed in command... Admiral Dewey or General Merritt would have some one whom they could hold responsible for any excesses which might be otherwise perpetrated upon the Spaniards by the Filipino army.' The leader, with seventeen of his officers, was therefore despatched. Mr. Wildman was careful to make no promises. If Aguinaldo was laboring under a misapprehension, on the other hand, he was not undeceived.

It is evident that a question of the first importance was being left unanswered. Where was the Philippine insurrection to fit into the final scheme of our expansion in the Far East? Its leaders were fighting for the declared aim of Philippine independence and a republic; knowing this, we had invited their aid, we were bringing them to the islands, and we were to rely heavily upon their and their people's efforts during the next two months. At the moment that General Aguinaldo, upon the deck of an American man-of-war in the China Sea, was watching for the outlines of the land to which we were bringing him as a liberator, General Merritt at Governor's Island was writing that 'the work to be done consists of conquering a territory... inhabited by 14,000,000 people, the majority of whom will regard us with the intense hatred born of race and religion.'

The incongruity is apparent. Hong Kong correspondents were already making the helpful discovery that 'the rebels are useless as allies of Admiral Dewey. They are utterly disunited, quite half of them being in favor of Spain'; but the Admiral himself was soon receiving Aguinaldo with cordiality at Cavite, supplying him with arms and ammunition and looking on with approval as he organized his army and began an advance upon Manila — unaided by American forces. In actual fact it was the insurgents, not Dewey, who were capturing the Philippines. But the State Department was indicating that General Merritt's status, when he arrived, would be that of a governor-general; while the Navy Department was announcing that the U.S.S. Monterey, a monitor which was the only heavy-gun ship left for the defense of the Pacific Coast, would be despatched to Manila. It is patent that the eastern operations, ostensibly begun for the protection of that coast, had been subtly transformed into operations for the defense of our new 'possessions' in the Far East.

It was the cause, in some quarters at any rate, for profound satisfaction. A sprightly note came out of San Antonio:

Give my best love to Nannie and do not make peace until we get Porto Rico while Cuba is made independent and the Philippines at any rate taken from the Spaniards.

And from Senator Lodge's office at the Capitol there went back a joyous reply:

DEAR THEODORE:
It is a great delight to get your letter.... The one point where haste is needed is the Philippines, and I think I can say to you, in confidence but in absolute certainty, that the administration is grasping the whole policy at last.... The Monterey, which I have been breaking my heart to send, is

now coaling for the trip, and will be off inside of a week. We are not going to lug that monitor across the Pacific for the fun of lugging her back again. They mean to send not less than twenty thousand men to the Philippines. As to Cuba I am in no sort of hurry. Our troops are fresh and raw.... Porto Rico is not forgotten and we mean to have it. Unless I am utterly and profoundly mistaken the administration is now fully committed to the large policy that we both desire. We have had some dark days since you left, and my very humdrum and unexciting part in the struggle has been one of constant work and anxiety. I think now, however, from the information I get that the cloud has lifted.

So it had, and to this statesman, at least, the possible claims of Filipino patriotism seem to have offered no difficulty. It is true that Washington's rapidly developing Philippine policy was thrown into some anxiety by a despatch from Dewey, received on the 24th, which mentioned that Aguinaldo had arrived and was 'organizing forces near Cavite and may render assistance that will be valuable.' But what were a few insurgents after all? No one thought very seriously of them; though Mr. Long, to be on the safe side, wired back:

It is desirable, as far as possible, and consistent for your success and safety, not to have political alliances with the insurgents or any faction in the islands that would incur liability to maintain their cause in the future.

It was all, of course, with the best of intention and in the loftiest of motives, but General Emilio Aguinaldo, one regrets to report, had been neatly double-crossed.

The day before the cable went, the first contingent of American troops had passed out through the Golden Gate, bound for the other side of the world, the first Army expeditionary force which had left the continental United States since the war with Mexico half a century before, and the first which had ever left for a destination beyond the western hemisphere. For a week or so their commander at San Francisco, struggling with volunteer units, none of which was properly equipped and all of which lacked 'articles of ordnance, tentage, and light clothing,' had been 'at a loss to understand that it is the intention of the authorities that I, with staff and not to exceed an infantry regiment of untrained troops, proceed to the Philippines and occupy such parts of the islands as I may be able.' But it was. They gave him five companies of regulars and some more volunteers, and the expedition was sent away:

Every street leading from the Presidio to the Pacific Mail dock, a distance of about five miles, was lined with people.... At Vanness Avenue the entire police force of San Francisco was waiting and fell in ahead of the soldiers.... There was one continuous roar of cheers, flags were waved frantically.... Nothing like the sight on Market Street was ever seen here before. Many weeping women followed along after the soldiers. As the marching men neared the waterfront bombs were fired, steam whistles blown, and every device imaginable for making noise was put into full operation.

The transports did not immediately sail, and all day the crowd hung about the high dock gates, hoping to catch a glimpse of the soldiers. It was not until two days later, at four o'clock in the afternoon of May 25, that the three ships at last swung out from their docks and headed for the open sea. The watchers followed them as they passed out through the Golden Gate at about five o'clock, and dipping silently to the heavy swells of the Pacific, set their long course for Manila, seven thousand miles away. So they vanished upon their mission of conquest, in the long sunshine of late afternoon, just as spring was deepening into summer. The sun set, and those three tiny worlds, crowded with their excited men upon the lonely ocean, held onward.

VI

But if we were after all setting out to conquer the Philippines, what about Porto Rico, which was so much more easily available? And if the Filipino insurgents were to be gently steam-rollered, might not even the Cubans, in spite of all our hopes, turn out to be unprepared for self-government? On May 25, the Washington correspondents observed an 'extraordinary activity' in the War and Navy Departments and there were 'rumors too definite to be ignored' that the War President had decided without further delay to 'seize San Juan de Puerto Rico and establish a permanent colonial government in the island similar to that which General Merritt is charged with creating in the Philippines.'

No one would deny it; while 'many Senators' having 'influential relations with those carrying on the war' said that it was true. Does one, perhaps, detect the style of that influential member of the Foreign Relations Committee who the day before had sent off his happy letter to the lieutenant-colonel of the Rough Riders? The anonymous Senators had developed, at any rate, a viewpoint in startling contrast to that which had guided Mr. McKinley's pen when he had denounced 'aggression.' They explained that 'the United States Government has awakened to the necessity of actually possessing Porto Rico before the end came. That island and the Philippines had come to be looked on as an essential recompense to the United States for its expensive intervention,' while unless we secured these territories 'before Cuba fell, embarrassing complications, leading possibly to grave international complications with European powers, might not be avoided.'

The demonstration was simple — so simple that the mind almost naturally turned to the possibilities that might be latent in the Cuban situation. A special despatch to the New York *Tribune* of May 23 showed that Washington had been making interesting discoveries:

> For nearly two years positive assertions had been numerous that the Cubans, with merely the moral encouragement of the United States through a recognition of belligerency, could quickly encompass their own independence. Within the last month the falsity of these assertions has been demonstrated to the complete satisfaction of the authorities here, and... it is now definitely known that little or no assistance from the vaunted 'armies of liberation' need be expected.

It was a discovery which might have thrown rather a queer light upon our earlier position toward Spain; had anybody now been interested in that. Far more arresting was the illumination which it seemed to cast upon the future — for if the Cubans couldn't give themselves self-government, might not a moral obligation lie for us to supply the government for them? There was, of course, the Teller amendment, but the Teller amendment had included no time limit. And then President McKinley issued a call for another 75,000 volunteers. As we already had nearly 200,000 men under call — and were finding it extremely difficult to train or equip even that number for immediate service — the inference as to our ultimate aims seemed obvious.

Thus May ran out; the mild spring days gave way to summer — to heat and dust and perspiration in the camps; to the dropping rains in Cuba, to straw hats, to marvelous balloon sleeves and white dresses in the crowds that still jammed before the newspaper bulletin boards in the cities. The Philippines had been 'conquered,' Porto Rico (it was understood to enjoy a healthy climate in the worst of the rainy months) would soon be likewise, and Cuba — well, Cuba, whose miseries we had of course set out to end, could wait until the fall. The volunteer army might be ready by that time, the fever season would be over, and when we got around to it we could have a splendid full-dress siege of Havana with plenty of glory, no doubt, for all.

And then there was news from the Navy.

CHAPTER IX

THE ADVANCE ON SANTIAGO

I

THROUGHOUT the middle and latter part of May, the Navy had been engaged upon an earnest pursuit of Rear Admiral Cervera and his armored squadron. On the morning of May 12, it will be remembered, Admiral Sampson had arrived off the harbor of San Juan, Porto Rico, and found it empty. But at the very moment that his gunners were watching their shells burst upon its ancient fortifications, a lieutenant of Marines had been standing upon the hillside behind the harbor of Fort de France, Martinique, some five hundred miles away to the southeast. Lieutenant Kane belonged to the U.S.S. Harvard, one of the two converted liners which had been stationed off Martinique to intercept and keep track of Cervera should he indeed be coming to the Caribbean. Putting into the neighboring port of St. Pierre the day before, the Harvard had heard of a strange destroyer at Fort de France. Lieutenant Kane was despatched thither (it involved an all-night journey in a rowboat) to investigate. When he arrived, the destroyer was gone, but he made out upon the horizon, hull down in the early morning sunlight, the authentic outlines of Cervera's ships. The Cape Verde squadron had been discovered, and before Sampson had hauled off from the inoffensive batteries of San Juan, the naval campaign of the Caribbean had begun.

Admiral Cervera, having thus appeared, almost immediately faded out again into the west, whither the Harvard was prevented, both by neutrality laws and an understandable prudence, from following him as had been intended. Her report, however, definitely placed the hostile fleet in the Caribbean area; it ended the fears of the North Atlantic coast, released the vessels which had been held for its defense, and set the full machinery of the Navy Department in motion to seek out and entrap the enemy. Despatch boats were at once sent forth to meet Sampson on his return voyage from San Juan and hurry him on to the defense of the Havana blockade, while a telegram to the gallant Schley, who had been waiting so long with his Flying Squadron at Hampton Roads, started him on his way south as a striking force with which to encompass Cervera's destruction.

The nation watched as Schley passed out into the Atlantic, and eagerly awaited news of the exciting operations which this seemed to portend. Here, however, the nation was doomed to disappointment. The Navy was able to conduct the Caribbean campaign under the veil of a censorship which, if quite inadequate to conceal its movements from the Spaniards, was at least sufficient to conceal its errors from the home population. In this (which is perhaps the most important) function of censorship the Navy was throughout to prove remarkably successful — a circumstance which was to contribute greatly to the high esteem which the Navy enjoyed by comparison with the Army. The disparity between the actual achievements of the two services hardly seems as great as the public of the time believed; but the Navy had its war correspondents more or less where it wanted them. Thus it was that during the next two weeks the Navy all but disappeared from the front pages, and the public remained in ignorance of its moves in pursuit of Cervera. It was just as well.

Two days after Admiral Cervera had passed westward from Martinique,[1] he reappeared once more off Curaçao, the Dutch island upon the coast of Venezuela. Our consul there reported his arrival on the 14th and his departure again on the 15th, after he had sent in two of his armored cruisers to coal. From Curaçao a wide range of action seemed open to him. He might head back for Porto Rico; he might make for Cienfuegos, on the south coast of Cuba opposite to and in direct rail communication with Havana; he might try to slip around Cape Maysi and reach Havana from the east or around Cape San Antonio to reach it from the west; he might run direct for Santiago de Cuba, his nearest fortified harbor; or he might even refuel from the colliers which were known to have been sent out to him and return to Spain. A Navy Department which was on its mettle endeavored to provide for all contingencies. Fast scouts were ordered to Venezuelan waters to

---

[1] One of his three destroyers, rendered unserviceable by the Atlantic passage, had to be left behind. Eventually she reached San Juan, Porto Rico.

find and keep touch. Others were stationed in the Mona and Windward Passages, on either side of Haiti. Sampson was hurrying back to cover Havana and Schley was rushing southward to Key West. The Navy Department awaited developments.

But there were no developments. Cervera simply melted into space. Early on May 18, Schley was at Key West; and in the afternoon of the same day Sampson, pushing on ahead of his slow-moving squadron, arrived there likewise. Three days had passed since the last news of the enemy, and with every hour the radius of the circle within which he might be found was widening. The Navy Department was worked up to a high pitch of apprehension; 'telegrams came and went with painful frequency,' while the Admiral and the Commodore conferred in the former's cabin. The Admiral was already inclining strongly to the view that Cervera had gone to Santiago; but the Navy Department had what it believed to be authentic information that he had been ordered to Cienfuegos, and was urging that a strong force be sent there by way of Cape San Antonio. Admiral Sampson complied with these wishes; he also yielded the command of the force to his junior, Commodore Schley. Sampson retained one armored cruiser, one battleship, and the monitors to cover Key West and Havana; Schley was given one armored cruiser, three battleships, and some light vessels. At eight o'clock on the morning of the 19th, the Commodore sailed from Key West, his orders directing 'that you should establish a blockade at Cienfuegos with the least possible delay, and that it should be maintained as close as possible.' Hardly was he well on his way when, toward the end of the afternoon, a secret report arrived to the effect that Admiral Cervera had entered the harbor of Santiago.

There was a day of hurried telegraphing between Washington and Key West before Admiral Sampson could be convinced of the authenticity of this report. At last, on the evening of May 20, it was confirmed directly by a secret message over the cable from Havana, and early on the 21st, Admiral Sampson despatched an order to Commodore Schley at Cienfuegos:

Spanish squadron probably at Santiago de Cuba.... If you are satisfied that they are not at Cienfuegos proceed with all despatch, but cautiously, to Santiago de Cuba, and, if the enemy is there, blockade him in port.

As the day wore on, the more probable did it seem to the Admiral that Santiago was the spot, and further messages were sent off designed to hasten Commodore Schley to the eastward. The Admiral himself prepared to take station two hundred miles east of Havana at the narrowest part of the Bahama Channel, in case Cervera, emerging from Santiago, should come around by Cape Maysi. He was delayed in his departure, but finally got away on the 23d — with a collection of ships in such a general state of disrepair that it was known as the 'Bargain Counter Squadron.' Its guns were sufficient, however, to demolish Cervera should he approach; and with Schley (as the Admiral supposed) on his way to Santiago by the south side of the island, it seemed that the Spanish force had been entrapped.

But Commodore Schley, unfortunately, was not on his way to Santiago. The Commodore was naturally unaware of the continuing reports, which by this time had removed all doubt at Washington, that Cervera was at Santiago. Nor does he seem to have been as much impressed as Washington had by this time become with the urgency of his mission definitely to locate the Spaniards. He had arrived off Cienfuegos on May 22 under orders to blockade that port, and he was blockading it. On the morning of the 23d, Sampson's message directing him to proceed onward to Santiago if he was 'satisfied' that Cervera was not at Cienfuegos arrived. But it was worded with a vagueness which, while ample to protect the Admiral, left the Commodore in considerable uncertainty. He was not satisfied that the harbor was empty. The Admiral seems to have believed that one could look over the low hills by the entrance into the anchorage; the Commodore was under the impression that it was possible for the Spaniards to anchor in a portion of the harbor that was invisible to him. The Commodore continued to blockade. Whether or not he might have been more energetic in ascertaining the actual state of affairs — through landing scouts or communicating with the insurgents — was afterwards to become a matter of bitter dispute; but at all events, the Commodore remained upon blockade until late on the evening of the 24th. By that time another light vessel had arrived whose commander knew the code signals arranged for communicating with the insurgents, and it had been established

ADMIRAL WILLIAM T. SAMPSON   ADMIRAL WINFIELD SCOTT SCHLEY

definitely from them that the Spanish fleet was not at Cienfuegos. At 7.30 in the evening Commodore Schley got under way for Santiago.

Even so, however, the order had directed him to proceed 'with all despatch, but cautiously.' Caution seemed to be taking the upper hand in the Commodore's mind. The speed of his squadron was greatly reduced in order not to outdistance a small converted yacht which was laboring heavily in the rising sea. She was of no military value, and had the Commodore been aware of the frantic impatience which by this time had possessed the Navy Department he would doubtless have left her behind. But he did not appreciate Washington's state of mind. Already he had begun to be troubled by thoughts of his coal supply. He had a collier with him, but he had found it difficult to take fuel from her in the open sea before Cienfuegos and as the wind rose the fear of being left at sea with empty bunkers rose likewise. With Sampson and the Navy Department at an agonized pitch of expectancy, Commodore Schley held slowly onward at a speed of about seven knots; and it was not until the afternoon of May 26 that he finally arrived at a point some twenty miles south of the entrance to Santiago Harbor. There he found three of our fast scouts which, he learned, had been standing off and on in the neighborhood for several days past. They had seen nothing.

The Commodore pondered the situation. 'The air was very clear, and the high mountains back of Santiago could be seen, but nothing else.' The Commodore might have gone in closer than twenty miles, but he understood from the scouts that nothing was visible, and he knew that the peculiar conformation of the harbor made it quite impossible to look into it from the sea. The entrance is a mere gut between two high bluffs, while a point of land immediately within cuts off the view even through this opening. Commodore Schley did not believe in the Santiago theory; he had various reasons for thinking that the enemy's real destination was Cienfuegos or Havana, and he was worried about his coal supply. For four hours he allowed his ships to drift where they were until he finally made up his mind. Toward eight o'clock his astonished captains read the flagship's signal: 'Destination Key West *via* south side of Cuba and Yucatan Channel.' Shortly after nine they got under way, solemnly retracing their course to the westward, with Cervera's whereabouts still an unsolved mystery.

The Flying Squadron belied its name on the return voyage even more notably than it had done on the voyage out. The collier broke a valve-stem and the rest of the night was spent in efforts to repair or tow her, while the fleet drifted aimlessly. They had made little headway by the middle of the following morning, when a scout arrived with despatches. Both Admiral Sampson (by this time returning toward Key West from his cruise into the Bahama Channel) and the Navy Department were necessarily somewhat behind the course of events on the south side of Cuba, but both were becoming alarmed at what appeared to be a strange procrastination in the Flying Squadron. In the despatch from Washington there was an impatient note:

All Department's information indicates Spanish division is still at Santiago de Cuba. The Department looks to you to ascertain the facts, and that the enemy, if therein, does not leave without a decisive action.

It was impatient — but there was that recurrent vagueness. Again the Commodore deliberated. The sea was still 'boisterous' and there was the coal difficulty. By afternoon he had once more come to his decision, and written out his despatch. It began in a chapter of accidents and fears for the coal supply and continued:

Cannot remain off Santiago present state squadron on account of coal. ... Much to be regretted, cannot obey orders of Department. Have striven earnestly; forced to proceed for coal to Key West by way of Yucatan Passage. Cannot ascertain anything positive respecting enemy.

Having sent off this message, Commodore Schley resumed his halting progress westward.

The despatch was at Washington and Key West late on the following day (May 28) and galvanized both into a violent activity. Admiral Sampson gathered up all the serviceable ships he had available and prepared to set out directly for Santiago by way of Cape Maysi, in order himself to clear up the mystifying conduct of the Flying Squadron. Mr. Long was with President McKinley, reviewing the volunteers at the great camp that had been established near Washington, when Schley's message was handed to him. 'It was incomprehensible,' he felt, 'the first flinching of the campaign. It was the darkest day of the war.... Undoubtedly it is a fair criticism of the Department that Schley was not relieved at once and an inquiry ordered.' Instead, the Secretary contented himself with a scorching telegram, to be delivered to the Commodore 'as soon as possible; utmost urgency.'

Unless it is unsafe for your squadron Department wishes you to remain off Santiago.... You must not leave the vicinity of Santiago de Cuba unless it is unsafe your squadron or unless Spanish division is not there.

Fortunately for Commodore Schley, however, before the telegram could be delivered, there had ceased to be any need for it. The Commodore had reconsidered.

After starting westward on the afternoon of the 27th, the Flying Squadron had again been stopped. The sea appeared to be moderating. The Commodore found by experiment that it was not, after all, entirely impossible to take coal from the collier. They knocked about indecisively that night and most of next day. Possibly the Commodore reflected upon the gravity of announcing to one's superiors that one cannot obey orders. On the afternoon of the 28th, the Flying Squadron was again headed eastward, and at about eight o'clock that night was off the entrance to the harbor of Santiago.

They steamed up and down before it during the darkness. With the first clear daylight of May 29, Commodore Schley turned actually to look at the harbor to which he had been ordered six days previously with the duty of finding the Spanish fleet. The first thing he saw was the unmistakable outline of the Cristóbal Colón, the newest of Cervera's four cruisers, not even attempting concealment within the harbor, but anchored stem and stern across the entrance, in plain view and with her awnings spread. One of her consorts was less clearly visible behind her. Unhappily for the later reputation of Commodore Schley, Admiral Cervera had been at Santiago all the time; while the Cristóbal Colón, it was subsequently learned, had been anchored in the entrance ever since the 25th of May — the day before the first approach of the Flying Squadron — and might have been observed at any time by an even mildly courageous reconnaissance. Indeed, the reason why our scout cruisers had not seen her remains somewhat obscure, unless it is that they had been too busy making 'frequent chases of strange steamers, which turned out to be press boats.'

The fact was that Cervera's movements had not been dictated by any strategic acumen. Upon his arrival off Martinique he had found his problem in one sense simplicity itself — he did what he did because nothing else was possible. He was under orders to defend Porto Rico; but the state of his coal supply was 'extremely critical,' no coal was to be had at Martinique, and he was informed that there was none at San Juan. He departed for Curaçao because he believed that one of his chartered colliers had been sent there. In this he was disappointed. He was able to get a small amount of coal at the port, but the Dutch authorities made trouble on the score of neutrality, and he was in momentary fear that the American scouts would discover him. He hoped that there might be coal at Santiago; at any rate, his supply did not permit him to attempt any more distant adventure; he understood that Sampson was covering Porto Rico; Cienfuegos was a poor refuge since it was practically undefended, and Santiago was all that remained. With its tortuous entrance and its batteries he might at least be safe there. On the evening of the 15th, he dropped Curaçao astern, taking up the direct course for Santiago. The steaming qualities of his ships were poor, but the sea was calm, and though they had a bad moment off Jamaica on the night of the 18th, when a strange ship passed at a distance, they continued on their way unmolested. At eight o'clock on the morning of May 19, the exact moment at which Commodore Schley was sailing from Key West in their pursuit, they ran in through the lofty entrance to Santiago Harbor. With poor vessels, wretched equipment, and the least possible assistance from his home government, Admiral Cervera had crossed the Atlantic Ocean, sailed straight into the center of operations of our overwhelmingly superior Navy, and had made port — without once having sighted or been sighted by an American vessel. Not without reason did the Governments at Madrid and Havana cable him their enthusiastic congratulations.

From our point of view the incident, once more, had not been an unqualified success.

II

Although President McKinley had been 'essentially a civilian,' as his biographer points out, since the close of his Civil War service thirty years before, he was now to assume in earnest his constitutional duty as commander-in-chief of our forces.

Daily conferences were held in the White House.... Mr. McKinley kept his finger upon every detail. He rarely left his office until one or two o'clock in the morning and frequently was there until a later hour. From the war room, adjoining his office, he kept in telegraphic touch with the front. War maps covered the walls of this room and tiny flags used as pins showed the positions of the armies and of the ships of the Navy.... The stream of callers increased enormously.

Such a conference took place on May 26, and for three hours the War President listened to the views of his official advisers. Though three or four days were yet to elapse before the Navy could definitely report Cervera's presence at Santiago, the reports had been so persistent and authoritative that little doubt was now entertained as to the true situation. Thus the naval problem appeared to have solved itself. The question of what should be done with the Army remained.

General Miles — reënforced by a cablegram from Europe in which no less a strategist than Mr. Andrew Carnegie, 'that patriotic philanthropist,' had advised him to 'take Porto Rico first, for its effect on Europe,' and to eschew Havana — was deeply impressed by the Porto Rican possibilities. He had prepared a memorandum, suggesting that the Army should move on Porto Rico, capture that island (for military reasons which were not very clearly stated), and then commence 'a movement to the west.' This was to be done by landing a large force of cavalry and light artillery upon the eastern end of Cuba and organizing the insurgents to assist them in a guerilla advance through the length of the island — thus safely and profitably employing the rainy months until the volunteers could be trained and landed for a frontal assault upon Havana.

To this broad plan General Miles, in spite of numerous discouragements, was to cling through thick and thin; and it had the merit, at least, that it was a plan, which may have been why the other directing minds upon the President's strategy board regarded it with suspicion. But the General had prefaced it with an interesting suggestion. If Cervera had in fact gone to earth at Santiago, why should not the Army stop off on its way to Porto Rico and assist the Navy either in driving him out or in forcing its way in after him? Here was something obvious, immediate, and definite. It looked easy; it would commit us to nothing, and it would satisfy the clamant publics thirsting for blood. Up to this moment Santiago had never entered our thoughts. But by taking refuge there Admiral Cervera had now relieved our strategists from what had been, from the beginning, their greatest difficulty. He had provided them with an objective.

Mr. McKinley gave his approval. On the following day Mr. Long informed his colleague, Mr. Alger, that as soon as they had positive information of Cervera's whereabouts 'the movement to Santiago should be made without a moment's delay, day or night.' Mr. Alger himself was no less eager; General Shafter at Tampa was notified to hold himself in readiness, and May 29, with the arrival of Schley's despatch announcing that the Spaniards had at last been sighted, he was telegraphically instructed:

Place on your transports your most effective force of regulars and volunteers, 500 rounds ammunition per man, with a strong force of artillery, siege guns, howitzers and mortars with two months' supplies, small number of animals and transportation, two squadrons of cavalry.... Telegraph when you will be ready to sail with naval convoy.

Definite orders were wired next day informing him that he was to take this force to Santiago de Cuba and there aid the Navy in the capture or destruction of the Spanish fleet. The War Department, mindful of its responsibilities to Mr. Roosevelt's career, brought the cowboy regiment on from San Antonio and hurried reënforcements from other points. On the 30th — Memorial Day — the fact that something was in the wind was allowed to leak out, and though the objective was kept secret, the nation thrilled to learn that the striking force at Tampa was at last about to make a movement. So important did these developments seem that General Miles himself determined to 'take the field in person,' and he left Washington for Tampa at eleven o'clock that evening. There was an inspiring scene in the Sixth Street Station as he departed; Secretary and Mrs. Alger and scores of friends were there to cheer him, and the General Commanding the Army rolled away to the front in a special train, accompanied — one is pleased, if a little surprised, to note — by 'Mrs. Miles, Miss Miles, and Sherman Miles,' as well as by the twelve officers of his staff. It was a civilized war.

The tempo was again quickening. The Navy had by this time relaxed its censorship, and a delighted public was permitted to learn that Cervera had been found and bottled up by the 'most clever maneuvering' of Commodore Schley, who had 'allowed the Spaniards to think he had left in disgust' so that the latter 'took the bait and ran into the harbor.' In this form the news only endeared the gallant Commodore to his countrymen, and the Navy Department kept its own opinion to itself. It was a course which was to pave the way for subsequent embarrassment; but it served to conceal from the public how completely the Navy had failed in its mission of destroying Cervera.

There was, indeed, to be still another failure. The Cristóbal Colón continued to lie in plain view and fairly easy gunshot within the entrance, inviting destruction. She was defended by the harbor fortifications, but they were not powerful, and experience had already indicated the comparative harmlessness of Spanish artillerists, while Commodore Schley had a strong squadron under his command. He considered the problem for two whole days before he decided to risk it; finally on the 31st he steamed in with three of his vessels, and running rapidly back and forth past the entrance permitted each ship to fire through it at the Colón as they went by. The action was brief. No American ships were hit; neither was the Colón. She remained quietly lying in full view until next morning, when she got her anchors and disappeared within the harbor. The opportunity was lost.

But that same day (June 1) Admiral Sampson, hurrying from Key West by way of Cape Maysi, arrived off the entrance and took command of the blockade. So that was all right.

Indeed, for all practical purposes the war was over. With Spanish naval power immobilized, it was obvious that Spain could neither attack the United States nor supply or reënforce the Cuban garrison, and Mr. McKinley might have stopped where he was to await the surrender which had now become inevitable. The one danger — that the hurricane season was approaching and that a storm might scatter the blockaders long enough to permit Cervera to escape — Admiral Sampson immediately set himself to eliminate. Just within the entrance, the ship channel narrowed to a width of only about a hundred yards. The Admiral determined to send in a block-ship, run her bow aground upon one side, allow her to swing with the tide and her own momentum until her stern grounded upon the other, and thus effectually close all possibility of exit.

It was to give rise to a famous incident. The task of organizing the undertaking and preparing the old collier Merrimac for the sacrifice was entrusted to a young naval constructor, Mr. Richmond Pearson Hobson. The attempt was risky, because the blockship would be exposed to fire from the shore batteries and from infantry on the beaches, but it did not seem impracticable. Mr. Hobson, providing himself with a volunteer crew of seven men and a life-raft upon which to make his escape, steamed into the entrance before daylight on June 3. The watching ships saw and heard a lively attack being opened upon him. There were some anxious minutes; then the artillery and small-arm fire died away; it was impossible to tell what had happened. At daylight a steam cutter which had been sent in behind the Merrimac to pick up survivors returned. She had seen no one come out. The Merrimac herself was visible by this time, evidently sunk, but not exactly in the intended spot. Admiral Sampson feared that the entire crew had perished in this gallant attempt; but in the afternoon a flag of truce was seen approaching from the harbor mouth. It was Cervera's chief of staff, coming out to inform them, with an admirable courtesy, that Hobson and all his men had been found unwounded in the water, clinging to their life-raft, and had been made honorable prisoners of war. The Spanish officer extolled 'the bravery of the crew in an unusual manner,' while Admiral Sampson could not 'too earnestly express' his appreciation of the courage of the undertaking.

The news was flashed throughout the United States. A press which had been finding it rather a long time between battles, and a public which so far had been forced to content itself with the somewhat coldly official heroism of Admiral Dewey, took Assistant

Naval Constructor Hobson to their arms instantly, enthusiastically, and with all of that thoroughness which the high organization of American journalism alone makes possible. Here was a real war hero at last; and in the wave of sentimental adulation which broke over Mr. Hobson's defenseless head, the fact that his enterprise had been a total failure was overlooked. But so it proved. It appeared afterward that the Merrimac's tiller-ropes had been shot away and that she had become unmanageable. Instead of anchoring herself 'almost automatically' in the desired spot, as had been hoped, she actually ran far up the harbor before Mr. Hobson could succeed in sinking her — in deep water and with ample room to pass. Cervera was not blocked. But everything was to turn out for the best in the end. The Navy was soon to realize that Cervera was not merely an incident in the war. He was likely to prove all the war that there would be; and the Navy did not repeat the blocking attempt.

The task in which the Navy had failed was now to be accorded to the Army — a proceeding which, if it was to be far more costly in human life, was at least to provide that spectacular element without which no home population could regard any war as a success. The final orders telegraphed to General Shafter on the evening of May 30 had ended with the terse query: 'When will you sail?' It was an easy question for the impatient strategists at Washington to ask. But its answer was a different matter.

III

For six weeks the Regular Army had been assembled at Tampa, enjoying a scene rather curiously combining aspects of a professional men's reunion, a county fair, and, as the volunteer regiments began to arrive to augment the force, a major disaster. Tampa, 'a city chiefly composed of derelict wooden houses drifting in an ocean of sand,' stood at the end of a railway line which had been built by Mr. Morton F. Plant largely as a real estate speculation. From the midst of this desert there arose, in vast and more than Oriental magnificence, the striking outlines of the hotel which Mr. Plant's optimism had caused him to erect there. It was 'a giant affair of ornamental brick and silver minarets'; its spacious central hall embellished with the statuary, the potted palms, the columns, and circular stuffed sofas of the late-Victorian age; its miles of piazza presenting the gingerbread decoration and the ranked rocking-chairs of the summer-hotel architecture of the times. This edifice was all there was in Tampa; it was the only place to go and the only place to stay. Automatically it became the headquarters of the Army, as well as of the war correspondents, the sight-seers, the anxious parents, the influential gentlemen, and (when presently they began to arrive) the ladies. 'For a month the life of the Army was the life of an hotel.... One of the cavalry generals said: "Only God knows why Plant built an hotel here, but thank God he did!"' The Army sank comfortably into the rocking-chairs upon the piazza, and the ensuing weeks were aptly named by Mr. Richard Harding Davis the 'rocking-chair period' of the war.

At first it was, if unheroic, by no means unpleasant. The Regular Army was miraculously finding itself together in one place for the first time in thirty years. Officers who had been classmates at West Point or associates in the Far West renewed the acquaintances of the past. So slow, indeed, had promotion been that the memories ran even farther back. 'Many of the captains were Civil War veterans,' and in the Tenth Infantry the youngest company commander had just been promoted captain after serving as a lieutenant in that organization for no less than twenty-two years. 'So they talked and argued and rocked and drank gallons of iced tea and the hot days wore into weeks.' The military attachés of foreign powers, 'in strange, grand uniforms,' contrasting sharply with the even stranger, though far less grand, costumes variously adopted by our own officers, at times lent an almost military touch to a scene which otherwise was hardly warlike. Mr. Ira Sankey 'busied about in the heat, preaching and singing to the soldiers'; the famous Clara Barton was present with her Red Cross organization, at that time something of a novelty; while the vast bulk of Major-General Shafter, weighing three hundred pounds and suffering already under the heat, the unwonted responsibility, and the war correspondents, physically if not spiritually dominated the variegated scene.

The staff-work had early shown signs of serious weakness and the inadequate railroad communications were an obvious danger, but at the beginning things were not bad. There were moments when a dreadful fear assailed them lest the war should end before they had a chance to fight; and there was one terrible day when, through an oversight in promotion orders, the camp discovered that it had three co-equal Major-Generals on its hands, each one under the impression that he was in command and would lead the Army on Cuba. The three walked the hotel veranda all day, each surrounded by his own coterie of staff and personal adherents, and hostilities seemed about to break out until Washington managed to rectify its inadvertence. Aside from such incidents, however, things were tranquil enough at the hotel, while the troops made themselves as comfortable as possible in camp-sites where the sand was ankle-deep, the water supply deficient, transport in confusion, and all forms of *matériel* lacking.

But with the continued arrival of the volunteer units the confusion had begun alarmingly to grow. The volunteers, of course, were badly supplied; while the stores now being rapidly forwarded were shipped without system, order, or even adequate markings, and were received by a supply organization which was almost non-existent. Congestion grew slowly toward chaos. 'It always seemed to us,' as one caustic observer wrote, 'that if Mr. Plant had been one-half as energetic in doing the railway work of mobilizing the Army as he was in running excursion trains to Tampa from every point and quarter of the United States... not only would the excursionists have enjoyed a finer spectacle, but Mr. Plant would have proved himself a better patriot.' To increase the already formidable difficulties there was the unfortunate circumstance that the camp at Tampa was actually some nine miles away from the embarkation point at Port Tampa, with a single railway track as the only connection. At the port there was again only one long pier from which men and stores could be transferred to the transports when the time came. Though the task of loading the army was clearly going to be a complicated one, and though the force had been waiting since the beginning of May in daily expectation of orders to advance, nothing seems to have been prepared and no real embarkation plans drawn up. It was a grave deficit in staff-work, but in justice to General Shafter one must add that the War Department had omitted to provide him with anything which by modern standards could possibly be called a staff.

Upon this situation the peremptory orders of May 30 fell like something of a bombshell. General Shafter ordered the regiments to hold themselves in readiness, and addressed himself to the preliminary task of finding, forwarding to Port Tampa, and loading the necessary stores. It was to prove a task of Herculean proportions. The stores could not be found. The box-cars containing them were scattered, it seemed, all over the State of Florida, unmarked, in no order, with no way of telling what was where. Invoices were lacking, and while an impatient high command at Washington was hourly expecting word that Shafter had sailed, his officers were still breaking open cars or unloading whole trains in order to find the harness that went with the artillery carriages or the small-arm ammunition that should have been loaded with the food. When the stuff was finally got to the pier, it arrived without system; but orders were imperative, there was no time to sort or arrange it, and things had to be thrust into the first hold available as they came to hand. In the meanwhile the waiting regiments continued to wait. So did Washington.

The whole of May 31 passed in perspiring confusion. Major-General Miles arrived on June 1 — thus adding a divided command to the other difficulties — and cheerfully reported that 'men are working night and day.' But he committed himself no farther. An already exasperated War Department wired curtly for 'an early report of progress made.' General Shafter replied that progress was 'rapid,' but that he could not start before Saturday morning, June 4.

This was bad; it was soon to become worse. More volunteer regiments arrived to intensify the breakdown of the railroad system. On June 3 there was still a further distraction as the Rough Riders and their ebullient lieutenant-colonel appeared upon the scene. Mr. Roosevelt came in a characteristic mood. 'Railway system,' he noted in his diary, 'in wildest confusion; it took us twelve hours to get into camp with our baggage.' Then a sudden doubt assailed General Shafter's mind as to whether Cervera's whole squadron really was safely bottled up in Santiago Harbor. He was reassured. Though the evidence was still a little slim, no question, apparently, had occurred to the Navy Department. Mr. Long, indeed, had been sending helpful little suggestions to Mr. Alger as to how the Army should manage the business — suggestions which, as the delays continued, took on an increasingly caustic tone.

Early on June 4 it was evident that the expectation of starting on that date had been unduly optimistic. There was a brief and pathetic telegram from Shafter:

It is not possible to complete embarkation before Monday night. Regiments ordered from Chattanooga and Mobile not yet all in. The difficulties in loading cannot be appreciated.

The same day General Miles supplied more complete details:

Several of the volunteer regiments came here without uniforms; several came without arms, and some without blankets, tents or camp equipage. The 32d Michigan, which is among the best, came without arms. General Guy V. Henry reports that five regiments under his command are not fit to go into the field. There are over 300 cars loaded with war material along the roads about Tampa.... Every effort is being made to bring order out of confusion.... To illustrate the embarrassment caused by present conditions, fifteen cars loaded with uniforms were side-tracked twenty-five miles away from Tampa, and remained there for weeks while the troops were suffering for clothing. Five thousand rifles, which were discovered yesterday, were needed by several regiments. Also the different parts of the siege train and ammunition for same, which will be required immediately on landing, are scattered through hundreds of cars on the side-tracks of the railroads. Notwithstanding these difficulties, this expedition will soon be ready to sail.

An unfeeling War Department responded only: 'When will you leave? Answer at once'; while even Mr. McKinley had by this time become anxious and added his personal inquiry. Sunday wore away. 'No word can paint the confusion,' Mr. Roosevelt angrily confided to his diary. 'No head; a breakdown of both the railroad and military system of the country.' At Washington the impatience grew and festered. The Navy was pointing out, with a chill formality, that its vessels were ready and waiting. Censorship sufficed to keep the worst from the nation, but there was a growing public restlessness. On Monday, the 6th, Mr. Alger was almost querulous:

> Twenty thousand men ought to unload any number of cars and assort contents. There is much criticism about delay of expedition. Better leave a fast ship to bring balance material needed than delay longer.

This somewhat dangerous expedient was not, however, to prove necessary. Late on Monday night General Miles was at last able to telegraph that the troops were being marched on board.

Yet there were still more delays; the telegram was a trifle premature. The orders had indeed been given, but owing to the appalling congestion on the single-track line to the port, it was not until the early hours of Tuesday that the first troops actually arrived upon the pier. Day broke, the morning hours dragged along, while upon the pier men, mules, railway trains, stores, and general officers were slowly aggregating in a vast and mounting disorder. In Washington there was a cable despatch from Admiral Sampson: 'If 10,000 men were here, city and fleet would be ours within forty-eight hours. Every consideration demands immediate Army movement.' But the afternoon ticked away and the expected despatch from Tampa announcing that the movement had begun did not arrive. Urgent telegrams were sent off: 'You will sail immediately.' 'Time is the essence of the situation.' 'Early departure of first importance.' But without result. At last, at 8.50 in the evening, higher authority was enlisted and it spoke with emphasis:

> Since telegraphing you an hour since the President directs you to sail at once with what force you have ready.

This left no option to the exhausted commanders upon the spot, and they had recourse to a desperate and extraordinary expedient. The word was simply passed to the regiments still waiting at Tampa that the expedition was going to sail at daybreak on the following morning. Whether or not they would go with it was left to their own discretion — and ingenuity.

A memorable night ensued; but it is a testimonial to General Shafter's understanding of his men that orders which in almost any other army in the world would have spelled a disaster worked with a brilliant success. There seems to have been one wild rush for the means of transport. The Ninth Infantry stole a wagon train from the Sixth and set forth, leaving the latter organization to get along later as well as it could. The Seventy-First New York sent out an advance party to scout for transportation; at about 11.30 they heard a railway train coming along. It was said to belong to the Thirteenth Infantry, but the party captured it, loaded it, and held it at the point of the bayonet until the rest of the regiment came up. It was not until eight o'clock next morning that the Thirteenth Infantry finally made good the loss. They managed to discover an empty train and some cattle-cars; a reconnaissance produced an ancient wood-burning locomotive, while an engineer was found asleep in bed, promptly hauled out from between the covers, and put to work. At 10.30 in the morning they steamed triumphantly up to the pier, wildly cheering as they discovered that, late though they were, they still had beaten the Twenty-First and Twenty-Fourth Infantry.

It was a situation, of course, almost ideally designed for the peculiar talents of the lieutenant-colonel of the Rough Riders:

We were ordered [Mr. Roosevelt afterward remembered] to be at a certain track with all our baggage at midnight.... At the appointed time we turned up, but the train did not.... Wood and I and various other officers wandered about in search of information which no one could give.... Some regiments got aboard the trains and some did not, but as none of the trains started this made little difference. At three o'clock we received orders to march over to an entirely different track, and away we went. No train appeared on this track either, but at six o'clock some coal cars came by and these we seized.

They arrived upon the pier (by this time it was Wednesday, June 8) to find it jammed with regiments and trains, most of the transports still out in the stream, a wild confusion reigning, and Colonel Humphrey, the chief quartermaster, undiscoverable. But Mr. Roosevelt was determined that whoever got to Santiago he would be one:

At last, however, after an hour's industrious and rapid search through this ant-heap of humanity, Wood and I, who had separated, found Colonel Humphrey at nearly the same time and were allotted a transport — the Yucatan. She was out in midstream, so Wood seized a stray launch and boarded her. At the same time I happened to find out that she had been allotted to two other regiments, the 2d Regular Infantry and the 71st New York Volunteers.... Accordingly, I ran at full speed to our train; and leaving a strong guard with the baggage I double-quicked the rest of the regiment up to the boat just in time to board her as she came into the quay and then to hold her against the 2d Regulars and the 71st, who had arrived a little too late.... There was a good deal of expostulation, but we had possession.

When they found they could make room, they consented to take four companies of the Second Infantry aboard, but the Seventy-First New York was driven to other expedients. Their colonel, surveying the anchored transports, picked out the largest and best-looking. Having already captured a railroad train, it was a mere nothing to hire a small boat and despatch a naval expedition (consisting of his lieutenant-colonel and twelve men) to seize her and bring her up to the pier.

The trouble was primarily due to the railroad, which, having only one track, had soon become completely clogged with the trains which were all attempting to go in one direction. But service was restored by Wednesday morning, and throughout the day the embarkation went rapidly forward. At last, after all the agonizing delay, after the whole terrible week devoted to the task of loading, after withstanding alike the heat and chaos of Florida and the hot impetuosity of Washington, General Shafter saw that the worst was over. Though some regiments were still waiting to embark, the main task had been accomplished. The Army was practically ready to sail; at about two in the afternoon the worn-out commander went aboard his headquarters ship, and as she passed into the stream he lay down to snatch some rest for his enormous frame.

General Shafter's head had scarcely touched the pillow when his adjutant was at his side, shaking him back into consciousness. 'Here, General, this is important.' The tired officer forced himself to look at the paper:

Major-General Shafter, Tampa, Florida:

Wait until you get further orders before you sail. Answer quick.
R. A. ALGER, *Secretary of War.*

'He sat up, rubbed his eyes, read the telegram and replied, "God, I should say so!"' For they were not to sail after all.

IV

Throughout another week the Army, embarked in such desperate haste, was to swing at anchor in the sweltering harbor of Port Tampa while the troops decorated the air with profanity. Mr. Roosevelt was reduced to the last extreme of angry exasperation by this example of bureaucratic mismanagement. But strangely enough, the onus for this celebrated anti-climax lay not upon the badgered heads of the despised War Department, but upon Mr. Roosevelt's own Navy, which once again had omitted to perform an essential duty. While Mr. Long had been caustically commenting upon the Army's delays, and while Admiral Sampson was cabling for haste in capturing Santiago and the Spanish fleet, they had neglected to ascertain definitely that the whole of the Spanish fleet was in Santiago.

On Tuesday night the converted yacht Eagle, cruising in St. Nicholas Channel, thought she saw a Spanish armored cruiser and torpedo-boat destroyer. Since the Navy Department did not know positively that all of Cervera's ships were in the blockaded harbor, it had to investigate the Eagle's report before it could permit the Army transports to go to sea. The naval vessels composing the convoy were sent into St. Nicholas Channel to find the strangers, while Admiral Sampson despatched one of his officers, Lieutenant Victor Blue, to look into Santiago Harbor and tell him finally whether all of the Spanish fleet was present or not. There were of course no hostile ships in St. Nicholas Channel, and the truth was soon established. But it was not until June 14 that the Navy could reassemble and coal its convoy, that the transports could in turn be watered and provisioned, and that the last of Shafter's argosy had got down the difficult channel from Port Tampa and disappeared at sea. The interval, though enlivened by a curious telegram in which General Miles offered to unload the army, supply the transports with 'guns, revolving cannon, and mortars,' and despatch them to assist the Navy in solving its problems, improved no one's temper.

Meanwhile the war in its broader and less immediately practical aspects had been advancing with a steady splendor. While the generals were suffering through that dreadful fortnight at Tampa, the statesmen and the editors alike had been entertaining only wider vistas. The Chicago *Inter-Ocean* announced a wonderful discovery: 'People at home and abroad seem to believe that the war will help the country rather than injure it.' It was a fact. The conflict which Mr. McKinley had so much feared for its adverse effect upon the program of prosperity was actually proving to be a stimulus. Business was reviving; maleficent Democrats, who had sought to start a war as an embarrassment, were confounded in their scheming — the 'advance agent of prosperity' had merely gathered in the credit for conducting a popular crusade while delivering the promised article as well. Providence was indeed upon the side both of the nation and the Republicans.

In the June *Atlantic Monthly*, Mr. Walter Hines Page was putting the inspiring question: 'Shall we be content with peaceful industry, or does there yet lurk in us the adventurous spirit of our Anglo-Saxon forefathers?' The editorial continued upon a plane of statesmanlike philosophy:

The decline in the character of our public life has been the natural result of the lack of large constructive opportunities.... It has been a time of social reforms, of the 'emancipation' of women, of national organizations of children, of societies for the prevention of minor vices and for the encouragement of minor virtues, of the study of genealogy, of the rise of morbid fiction, of journals for 'ladies,' of literature for babes, of melodrama on the stage because we have had melodrama in life also, of criticism and reform rather than of thought and action. These things all denote a lack of adventurous opportunities, an indoor life, such as we have never before had a chance to enjoy; and there are many indications that a life of quiet may have become irksome.... Is it true that, a thousand years of adventure behind us, we are unable to endure a life of occupations that do not feed the imagination?

At any rate, it seemed highly probable. Senator Lodge, that earnest worker in the vineyard, was 'in no hurry to see the war jammed through.' By May 31 he had put the last doubt behind him, and was bestowing his scholarly approbation upon Mr. McKinley. 'The Administration,' he wrote, 'I believe to be doing very well.' There was still Speaker Reed and the recalcitrant minority who could not appreciate the 'large policy' which the Senator envisioned. Those small-minded men were thorns in the statesman's side, and their persistence in holding up the Hawaiian annexation — 'this important military measure' — impressed

him as 'in the highest degree discreditable.' The Senator was so
shocked, indeed, by their unpatriotic conduct that he even hoped
that Mr. McKinley might simply annex Hawaii on his own responsibility. The War President's method was not of that debonair character; he could afford to wait — Mr. McKinley could
always afford to wait — but the full revelation was at last opening before him. 'We need Hawaii,' he told his secretary in the
early days of June, 'just as much and a good deal more than we did
California. It is Manifest Destiny.'

And that, of course, was enough to settle it. As for Porto Rico,
there was a modest little memorandum from the 'Executive Mansion' on June 4, signed 'W. McK.,' inquiring of General Miles the
'earliest moment' at which a Porto Rican expedition could be got
ready; and the General, from the very height of the excitement
at Tampa, replied that it could be prepared as soon as transports
were provided. Even the microscopic island of Guam, lying conveniently in mid-Pacific upon the route of the Philippine expedition, was not overlooked, and the advance detachment sailed
under orders to collect it on the way.

But of all the 'large constructive opportunities' which had thus
dazzlingly appeared before us, the largest was, of course, the
Philippines. Only the superficial eye could look upon this adventure as a 'forcible annexation'; to the thoughtful, our moral
obligation to acquire the islands was becoming daily more imperative. It became even more so with the reports from abroad
which seemed to indicate that Germany was anxious to relieve us
of it, for it is a singular fact that nations are seldom more ready to
sacrifice themselves upon the altar of duty than when some other
nation shows signs of a readiness to make the sacrifice for them.
The mere suggestion that the Germans might assume our 'unexpected' burden in the Far East drove us to a renewed speed in
getting it upon our own backs. We had taken the Philippines; our
moral responsibility to provide the Filipinos with a government
was clear. The case was incontrovertible — except for two inconvenient facts. The first was that we had not taken the Philippines. The second was that the Filipinos did not want a government. Under the benevolent neutrality of Admiral Dewey, they
were rapidly providing one for themselves.

The truth was that Admiral Dewey was just a trifle obtuse. Even by the end of June he was still cheerfully encouraging the insurgents to fight our battles for us and reporting that 'in my opinion these people are far superior in their intelligence and more capable of self-government than the natives of Cuba, and I am familiar with both races.' By the end of May they had cleared the whole of Cavite Province of the Spaniards and were practically at the gates of Manila. In the middle of June the Admiral looked on without alarm as Aguinaldo formed a civil government — this at a moment when we were assuming that the despatch of our troops was equivalent to a conquest, and Mr. McKinley was taking up in cabinet the problem of what customs tariffs and internal revenue should be applied to the islands. But there were other minds more alert than the Admiral's. Consul Williams was careful to avoid attending the meeting called by Aguinaldo in order to form his government. The Consul hoped soon to report that 'this magnificent insular empire has become a part and parcel of the United States of America.' And when, in the long course of the Pacific mails, Mr. Pratt's account of the manner in which he had invited General Aguinaldo's coöperation in the freeing of the islands arrived at the State Department, its shocked officials were moved to instant action. Secretary Day [1] himself immediately indited a letter to the Consul which should put the record straight:

To obtain the unconditional personal assistance of General Aguinaldo ... was proper, if in so doing he was not induced to form hopes which it might not be practicable to gratify. This Government has known the Philippine insurgents only as discontented and rebellious subjects of Spain, and is not acquainted with their purposes.... The United States, in entering upon the occupation of the islands as a result of its military operations in that quarter, will do so in the exercise of the rights which the state of war confers, and will expect from the inhabitants... that obedience which will be lawfully due from them.

This letter went off on June 16. But as yet there were few people in the United States who grasped the fact that in making an armed intervention in Cuba we had declared war upon the native

[1] Mr. Day had long been Secretary of State in fact. He had become so in name as well when, upon the outbreak of war, the aged Secretary Sherman realized that events had passed beyond his hands and gave up his office. Mr. Sherman resigned on April 25, the day of the formal declaration by Congress.

population of the Philippines. Nor was it thought wise, for the present, to explain the matter to the Filipinos. They were proving most useful to Admiral Dewey; their efforts, he found, were of 'material importance' in protecting his Marines at Cavite.

The Spaniards meanwhile had been making some rather feeble motions toward a defense of the islands. The Minister of War had even suggested, with an awe-inspiring disregard of geography, that Cervera's squadron might be withdrawn from Santiago, despatched to the Philippines to destroy Dewey, and should then, 'once its mission in the Philippines is accomplished, return to Cuba without loss of time.' Though he referred the plan to the Governor-General of Cuba, that official's veto was scarcely necessary. There was, however, a collection of vessels remaining in Spain, either obsolete or as yet uncompleted and consequently of small military value. The Madrid cables were now filled with talk of the despatch of some kind of squadron to the Far East *via* Suez, and there was a good deal of marching and countermarching in the Spanish dockyard towns. It was not taken very seriously in the United States, but it served to sharpen our determination to make good our hold.

Then the Hawaiian resolution was at last reported out of the House Foreign Affairs Committee (where 'Czar' Reed had been doing his best to smother it) and on June 11 the debate began. A map of the Pacific and a huge globe were set up in the open space before the Speaker's desk, and were 'surrounded all afternoon by members of the House studying the geography of the Pacific. Mr. Shafroth of Colorado, with tape in hand, made repeated measurements of distances on the globe and appeared to be trying to convince other members that Hawaii is of no consequence to the United States.' But most of them preferred to listen to Chairman Hitt of the Foreign Affairs Committee, whose 'luminous' and powerful address clearly explained the necessity for annexation.

Even now the opposition was not wholly stilled. At the Founders' Day exercises of the Lawrenceville School a once familiar voice was being heard again through the deepening June sunshine. 'Never before in our history,' the solemn warning fell from Mr. Cleveland's lips, 'have we been beset with temptations so dangerous as those which now whisper in our ears alluring words of conquest and expansion and point out to us fields bright with the glory of war.' And at the Omaha Exposition Colonel William Jennings Bryan was already embarking upon the difficult task of extricating his party from the trap into which its enthusiasm for freeing Cuba had led it; and endeavoring to reconcile the Bryanite ardor for war with an enlightened anti-imperialism wherewith they could once more assail the Republicans. Then there was a great meeting at Boston, held in Faneuil Hall itself, at which resolutions against a war of conquest were passed and the ringing voice of Mr. Moorfield Storey was heard putting embarrassing questions:

Why should Cuba with its 1,600,000 people have a right to freedom and self-government and the 8,000,000 of people who dwell in the Philippine Islands be denied the same right?... But it is said that there is a war necessity, or that we need indemnity. Can we exact our expenses from the enslaved people whom we intervened to help? Is Porto Rico more indebted to us than Cuba? Is the commandment 'Thou shalt not steal' qualified by the proviso 'unless it is necessary'?

But the answer was already on its way — in the shape of the American troopships. On June 18, General Aguinaldo at Cavite issued his declaration of independence, and proclaimed a provisional dictatorship to pave the way to a republic. A few days later he prepared a dignified statement to the governments of the world, announcing in unmistakable terms his aims and his ambition for the freedom of the Philippine people. In so far as that people could be said to have political aspirations at all (and they were not wholly negligible), General Aguinaldo at this time was undoubtedly their representative. But for the Philippines there was no Teller amendment; and on the 30th of June the transports bearing the first contingent of the American army of occupation steamed in past El Fraile and came to anchor in Manila Bay.

The Philippine expedition had duly paused at Guam, just long enough to inform the startled governor that a war had broken out and that what he took for a visit of courtesy was in reality an annexation to the United States; while in Washington the War President was watching the Hawaiian resolution go easily through the House and on to the Senate where opposition would not be serious. God was almost too good.

V

The Divine benevolence was less immediately apparent, however, to the 815 officers, 16,072 enlisted men, and 89 newspaper correspondents of the Fifth Army Corps, now pursuing a snail-like course toward Santiago de Cuba. Since June 14, General Shafter's expedition, loaded aboard thirty-two densely packed, stuffy, and badly found coastal steamers, had been crawling westward along the north coast of Cuba over a shining and placid sea. It comprised (in its final form) two divisions and an independent brigade of infantry, a division of dismounted cavalry, four batteries of field artillery, and a handful of auxiliary troops. The infantry force was made up of the eighteen regular regiments available, supplemented with the Seventy-First New York and Second Massachusetts, the two volunteer regiments which looked the least unreliable. It had originally been intended to take a third infantry division composed of volunteers, but the condition of the latter led to the substitution of the regular cavalry regiments to act as infantry (there would have been no room for their horses in any event). Of these there were five, and Mr. Roosevelt's Rough Riders were added to make up a full division of six regiments — all under the command of 'Fighting Joe' Wheeler, the little ex-Confederate cavalry general.

Thus organized, the Fifth Army Corps had set forth. Off Key West they had been picked up (after some delay and recrimination) by a naval convoy, and had turned in a long and straggling procession into the Bahama Channel. With an interminable deliberation the crowded vessels advanced across the burning and brilliant sea. The troops found very little provided to sleep on except the bare decks, and the air below so bad that sleeping was almost impossible. The water supply was for the most part foul; the food — the standard 'travel ration' hallowed by regulations — was wholly unsuitable for a tropical climate. The canned beef furnished spoiled when it was opened; the cooks did not know how to prepare it or had no facilities for doing so, and when it reached the men it was very bad indeed.

The arrangement whereby the chartered transports remained under the command of their merchant captains, who were responsible to their owners, soon appeared as a source of weakness.

The irritated naval vessels exhausted themselves in rounding up
and herding together the straggling troopships. On the first night
out a tugboat, upon which great reliance had been placed to assist
in the landing, simply deserted and was seen no more. The necessity for towing a water-schooner and landing lighters endlessly
delayed proceedings.

We travelled [Mr. Richard Harding Davis remembered] at the rate of
seven miles an hour, with long pauses for thought and consultation.
Sometimes we moved at the rate of four miles an hour, and frequently we
did not move at all.... We could not keep in line and we lost ourselves and
each other, and the gunboats and torpedo boats were kept busy... giving
us sharp, precise orders in passing through a megaphone to which either
nobody on board made any reply or every one did.

The vast armada was imposing, even though hardly military.
By day they wandered across the placid surface of the St. Nicolas
and Bahama Channels, cursing the heat or admiring the flying
fish. By night, although traversing a coast supposed to conceal
a number of hostile gunboats capable of making quick raids, every
vessel was brilliantly lighted up, while across the tropic waters
there floated the strains of the regimental bands 'banging out rag-
time music.' The lights showing 'from every part of the horizon
made one think he was entering a harbor'; and in spite of the heat,
the supposed gunboats and the very serious nature of their undertaking, they steamed cheerfully onward, confident that 'God takes
care of drunken men, sailors, and the United States.' It was
almost like an excursion, and almost as uncomfortable.

On board the Segurança, his headquarters ship, General Shafter
in a woolen uniform and an immense white sun helmet considered
his campaign. The problem of landing an untrained army upon
an exposed and precipitous coast in the face of hostile opposition
would have been difficult enough under any circumstances. General Shafter was compelled to study it amid the distractions of the
oppressive weather and the imminent presence (for the Segurança
was not a large ship), not only of his own and all the divisional
staffs, but of the foreign attachés, the Cuban generals, seven of the
war correspondents, the clerks, secretaries, colored waiters, five
hundred of the troops, and six rattling typewriters. All were
jumbled together in the narrow quarters, and the ship's 'social

hall' was the only headquarters office and meeting place they had.

The foreign military attachés cheerily explained to General Shafter the impossibility of his task. 'They talked most consolingly,' as he afterwards recalled. 'One, a French major, who was very friendly, said that it was certain to be a disaster'; while the General himself reflected upon the various invasions of Cuba which had been attempted by foreign powers during the preceding two centuries, and their uniformly calamitous results:

With knowledge of these previous expeditions before me you can imagine the feelings with which I entered upon that campaign. I have had yellow fever myself, and I knew just as well before I landed as I do now that within three or four or perhaps five weeks (it came sooner) that army would be prostrated with disease.... If I could get to Santiago before the men gave out well and good. If not, we were gone.... I determined to rush it.

Aboard the Segurança he put it a little differently to his staff: 'General Shafter... said we were a long way from the Civil War; that the country was no longer accustomed to hear of heavy losses in battle and would judge us accordingly; that he intended to get his army in position around Santiago and demand a surrender.' General Shafter, in spite of his unmilitary corpulence, seems to have been a man of some courage. Thus he formed his plan — it seems to have been about all the plan that he did form, but he stuck to it.

While he pondered, the seventeen thousand men of his command watched themselves borne slowly onward. 'The sea has been very blue,' Major-General Wheeler noted in his diary, 'quite as blue as indigo.' And again, 'The sky in the evening is perfectly beautiful, the stars very bright, and appear much more numerous than in more northern latitudes.' Presently the Southern Cross itself came up and looked at them over the velvet horizon, and many — how many, one wonders? — felt the strong, compelling grip of the great adventure upon which they had embarked. During the day they caught occasional glimpses of the high mountain peaks of Cuba itself standing silent and remote in the blue distance — the land about which they had all heard so much; that strange, romantic, and for some obscure reason important, island, with its queer Spanish place-names, sonorous and fascinating; with its memories of the old, high power of imperial Spain blending with the mystery and color of the tropics and tropic seas — the island which they had come to conquer upon the old trail of the Conquistadores. Half a century before a mystic exaltation had swept the common man of America through the steaming jungles and over the high ramparts of Mexico into the 'halls of Montezuma.' Now half a century later there was the same movement, the same restless and illogical stirring through our farms and cities. With Dewey we had reached out into the remote Pacific. The naval men for a month had been watching the exotic hills of Cuba. Up to this moment, however, it had all just been something one read about in the newspapers — it had been unreal until now, when at last the common man of the nation was looking again into battle, danger, and the deep thrill of tropic romance.

They had sailed on a Tuesday. The interminable week dragged itself away at last, and on Sunday morning, June 19, the leading ships were in the Windward Passage. In the course of the day they rounded the harsh, gray terraced flanks of Cape Maysi, with its long finger running into the sea. They found a breeze there, and were seasick in the crowded vessels, but next morning, June 20, they were off Santiago itself, huddled with their engines stopped some miles to the southward of the entrance. And looking away to the north, they saw at last the serene and lofty peaks of the Sierra Maestra, fresh in the morning sunlight.

About noon Sampson's chief of staff found the Segurança, came on board, and guided her up to the blockading squadron. Presently, the people in the headquarters ship found themselves among the gray men-of-war, rocking with their white windsails spread upon their long blockade. The naval men lined the rails and cheered them and the press boats hurried up — but behind the blockaders there arose, dark, formidable and ominous, the lofty shores which they had come to storm. They returned the cheers.

VI

The Navy had been awaiting them with an impatience considerably heightened by the rapid approach of the hurricane season.

In spite of Commodore Schley's fears over the coaling problem, the Navy had discovered that in Guantánamo Bay they had a near-by and ample harbor, sufficient for all their needs of shelter, coaling, and repair. Throughout the entire blockade, in fact, there was never any difficulty about refueling. But Guantánamo Bay was still some forty-five miles to the eastward of the Santiago entrance — too far away to cover it with certainty if a hurricane should come.

Its usefulness as a base, however, had already led the Navy to take a foothold there. Guantánamo Bay is a magnificent sheet of landlocked water, extending some fifteen miles inland from the coast. Its lower reaches were found to be entirely undefended; they were quite large enough to shelter the whole of the American Navy, and the fact that about halfway up there was an ancient fort mounting a few smooth-bores (and provided also with some submarine mines which would not explode) was of little consequence. But twelve miles inland from the bay shore, and some twenty miles from the sea, was the town of Guantánamo, garrisoned by a strong force of Spanish infantry. Small detachments from this force had been seen in the hills about the entrance, and as they were capable of annoying the ships it was decided, when a battalion of Marines arrived from Key West on June 10, to effect a landing.

The Marine battalion was put ashore the same afternoon. There was no opposition, and they established themselves comfortably on the east side of the entrance near a blockhouse which had previously been shelled by the Navy, then burned and abandoned by the Spaniards. They were still about twenty miles as the crow flies from Guantánamo and separated from it by the full width of the bay, but they had planted the American flag upon Cuban soil, and the Associated Press reported the occasion with the impressiveness which it warranted:

The invasion of Cuba by the American forces began today. Eight hundred Marines have pitched their tents about the smoking ruins of the outer fortifications of Guantánamo.... The main fort lies within the city limits and is yet to be reduced, but... American officers say it can be taken in fifteen minutes when desired.

Unfortunately, the Spaniards tried counter-attacking on the

afternoon of the 11th and again during the night and next day; the surgeon of the command and three men were killed and a number wounded, and there were banner heads in all the American newspapers. Although the Marine battalion was never seriously menaced, casualties of any kind had been so rare an occurrence that the Navy seems to have felt that it might have been rash, and it had an added cause for relief when on the morning of the 20th the Army at last came up over the eastern horizon, like a city afloat beneath a forest of masts.

Such was the situation when Admiral Sampson boarded the Segurança on the same afternoon in order to concert measures for the capture or destruction of Cervera. The Navy's ideas, which had already been communicated to General Shafter, were simple; they desired him to land his troops under the lofty Morro on the east side of the entrance and move directly to its assault. Having achieved this, they could easily drive the enemy from the Socapa battery on the opposite hill. The Navy could then sweep up the channel mines without molestation; steam into the harbor, and destroy Cervera with ease — and glory. But General Shafter must have surveyed the Morro with misgivings. Its picturesque and ancient battlements crowned a precipitous bluff two hundred and thirty feet high and rising so abruptly from the sea as to afford very little foothold from which to launch an infantry assault. Its moss-covered walls would have been valueless against high-powered artillery fire, but General Shafter had no high-powered artillery, and they presented a formidable obstacle to unprotected flesh and blood. It may also have occurred to General Shafter that by attempting the Morro he would be pouring out the lives of his own command in order to enable the Navy to win an easy triumph — General Shafter would get the onus for the losses and Admiral Sampson the honor for the victory. By following his own plan of surrounding the city (which lay four or five miles inland from the entrance) and demanding its surrender, not only should the losses be small, but the victory would be the Army's. As the Segurança steamed slowly east and west along the coast, General Shafter seems to have given no serious consideration to the Navy's wish for an attack upon the entrance forts.

There remained the problem of a landing place for the overland march to the city. Guantánamo Bay would have been the easiest point of debarkation, but it was forty-five miles away and the difficult and almost roadless character of the intervening terrain put it out of the question. At Daiquirí, eighteen miles east of Santiago, there was a beach with some slight shelter from the prevailing winds; at Siboney, ten miles east of the entrance, there was a somewhat better beach with somewhat less shelter. It was about all that offered on that side. Two miles west of the entrance there was Cabañas Bay, fully landlocked and giving access to the city over easy country, but it was very small and shallow and troops advancing from it would be under direct fire from the Spanish warships within the harbor.

After examining these places, the Segurança bore the General and the Admiral some twenty miles to the westward, in order to confer with Calixto García, the white-headed veteran of two insurrections who still held command of the insurgent forces in Santiago Province. General Shafter and Admiral Sampson were pulled ashore in a Navy gig; the staff, two of the military attachés, and the correspondents following cheerfully in their wake. The Cuban soldiers ran shouting into the water to welcome them; the problem of hoisting the three-hundred-pound Major-General up the cliffs to the insurgent camp was solved with a small white mule (though small he had, as the Cubans assured them, 'a stout heart') and the conference took place 'under a thatched roof of palm trees' amid a scene of 'wonderful tropical beauty.'

Beneath the camp the sea stretched in a motionless plain of dark blue, lying pulseless in the heat; overhead the mountains rose through a misty haze of heat to meet clouds of a glaring, blinding white.... It was all brilliant, gorgeous, and glaring.

While the correspondents and attachés looked on from a respectful distance or curiously examined the ragged Cuban soldiery, General Shafter formulated and announced his plan. General García advised the use of Daiquirí, and this was adopted. The landing was to be made there at daylight on the 22d. The Navy would bombard not only Daiquirí, but the various other possible landing places as well, and as a further feint five hundred Cubans would attack Cabañas Bay. Daiquirí, the insurgents said, was defended by only three hundred Spanish troops; to assist in forcing these out and to cover the actual landing, one thousand Cubans were to be massed behind that point. With these arrangements made, General Shafter returned to the shore and ultimately to his great fleet of transports. He found them in a characteristic position, drifting aimlessly and without formation all over the neighborhood, and he had some difficulty in rounding up his various commanders so as to give them their orders.

Preparations for the debarkation had been anything but elaborate. Before they started Mr. Long had jealously begged 'leave to inquire' how the Army intended to get itself ashore, pointing out that 'it is obvious that the crews of the armored ships and of such others as will be called upon to remove the Spanish mines and meet the Spanish fleet in action cannot be spared for other purposes and ought not to be fatigued by the work incident to landing of the troops.' In consequence, the harassed Quartermaster Department had provided what it hoped would be ample landing facilities — including three steam lighters, a tug, and two light-draft steamers, as well as the boats of the transports. Unhappily, one lighter broke down and never arrived, another was lost on the voyage out, and the tug, as has been said, deserted. Despite the fact that the Navy was not to be fatigued, its commanders on the spot, faced by the practical necessity of getting ashore the men who were to do the fighting, realized that it would be absurd not to utilize the naval equipment and personnel. Admiral Sampson agreed to lend all the steam launches as well as the pulling boats which he could spare, with crews to man them, while the actual operation was placed under the control of a naval officer, assisted by a naval beach-master on shore.

On the morning of the 21st there was wind, a choppy sea, and heavy rain — the first taste, as a matter of fact, of the rainy season. But it passed off in the afternoon; the sea fell calm and there was no change in the orders. Indeed, there could not be, for the transports were getting so short of water that a landing had become imperative. Before daylight on the 22d, the lighter vessels of the Navy were taking up their positions for the preliminary bombardment, and the excited men in the transports saw fires breaking out along the shore. They thought perhaps they were

GENERAL SHAFTER AND ADMIRAL SAMPSON ON THEIR WAY TO
CONFER WITH GENERAL GARCÍA

The General is mounted on his 'stout-hearted mule' and the Admiral wears a
white cap

signal lights, but they did not know. At last the day broke; the troops found their vessels huddled, in the customary confusion, before the beach at Daiquirí, and for the first time they looked directly at the place where they were to land — in the face, it was supposed, of hostile fire.

Daiquirí is scarcely even an indentation in a steep and exposed coast-line. An American firm, developing some iron mines in the hills behind it, had built out from the shore a large steel pier at which small steamers could be loaded. There was also a small wooden pier beside it and a shingly beach, but no other landing facilities whatever. In the open space beyond the beach there were a few shacks and tin-roofed huts put up by the mining company. The open ground, stretching away toward the distant mountains, offered space for re-forming the troops and establishing supply dumps and corrals, and was one reason why Daiquirí had been selected. But directly above the beach there rose a lofty hill, easily commanding the whole place as well as the seaward approach, and crowned — it could be clearly seen in the fresh morning light — by a Spanish blockhouse. Even three hundred determined defenders could have held the position long enough to convert the beach below into a shambles. Happily, however, our Army was quite ignorant of the possibilities of real war; and there was no one to be seen on the shore. There was no sign of life at all, except the smoke spiraling upward from the shacks and some ore-cars which had been set on fire.

About six o'clock the Navy boats began to come along in tow of the steam cutters, searching for the designated transports. At once the first difficulty appeared. The merchant captains of the transports were a law unto themselves, and being responsible to their owners for the safety of their vessels, could not be induced to come close in to a rocky and hostile shore. The commander of the U.S.S. St. Louis, one of the large trans-Atlantic liners which had been converted into auxiliary cruisers, was in charge of the landing operation. He took his ship in to within a mile and a half of the steel pier to give the merchant captains courage, but without much success; the transports persisted in staying well out to sea or even in vanishing altogether, and considerable time was wasted while our Navy steam launches gave chase to their respective quarries.

One transport, carrying six hundred troops which had been selected to lead the advance, could not be found at all, and well on in the afternoon four launches with eleven boats in tow were still 'vainly seeking her far out at sea.'

As fast as the transports were discovered and rounded up, the Navy put its boats alongside, and the troops tumbled into them with a willingness proportionate to their ignorance of the real nature of the job upon which their commanders were sending them. Something very like a holiday spirit seemed to dominate the occasion. Mr. Richard Harding Davis was one of the correspondents watching it from the deck of the Segurança:

Soon the sea was dotted with rows of white boats filled with men bound about with white blanket rolls and with muskets at all angles, and as they rose and fell on the water and the newspaper yachts and transports crept in closer and closer, the scene was strangely suggestive of a boat race, and one almost waited for the starting gun.

The scene was so very festive, in fact, that Mr. Davis seems to have overlooked the deadly seriousness of the attempt. It was at this moment, according to General Shafter's chief of staff, that a regrettable incident occurred which 'doubtless materially affected the future reputation of the General.' The General, Mr. Davis, and the chief of staff were standing together upon the promenade deck of the Segurança when Mr. Davis observed that the landing orders had been so drafted as to keep the reporters out of the first boats.

He was told that was true, but it did not indicate any unfriendliness to reporters.... Davis persisted in his argument and apparently did not realize the intense anxiety of our commander about the approaching landing, and the fear that concealed detachments of the enemy might shoot down our men as they approached in their open boats and while they were forming on the beach.

Finally Mr. Davis said he was not an ordinary reporter but a descriptive writer. At this the General's patience, never very long, gave way and he replied in a sharp tone: 'I do not care a damn what you are. I'll treat all of you alike.' Mr. Davis was offended at the abruptness of the reply, and never afterward, so far as I know, said a kindly word about General Shafter. It is thought several of Mr. Davis's friends sympathized with him.

Another journalist himself remarked that 'there are many

necessary evils in this world. Among others are newspapermen. From the moment of issuing that order pencils began to be sharpened for General Shafter.' Throughout, the Army lacked the Navy's tactfulness with the press, and its unfortunate commander had indeed prepared the grave of his own reputation, without even succeeding in keeping the correspondents back from the beach. One photographer smuggled his camera into the first boat and swam ashore himself; others got ashore in droves and were on hand from the beginning to write their critical accounts of the ensuing operations.

The process of capturing the transports and loading the troops had been going on for two or three hours — in full view of any one who cared to observe it from the shore — before there seemed to be enough men ready to undertake the advance. It was not until after nine o'clock that the first brigade of Lawton's division appeared to be fairly well embarked and it was not until 9.40 that signal was made to the Navy to begin its formal bombardment, while the steam launches with their strings of boats in tow solemnly formed up in readiness for their dash to the beach. For some twenty minutes thereafter Lawton's men bobbed up and down in the crowded boats, adding the qualms of seasickness to those of a natural excitement, while the Navy carefully laid down a barrage. Although this bombardment was duly carried out at all the possible landing places along the coast, the hope of concealing our real intentions from the enemy must by this time have seemed pretty slim.

The ineffectiveness of light-caliber naval artillery against well-constructed entrenchments was happily not so well understood in 1898 as it is today, and as the frame houses on the beach took fire or the dirt bounded into the air the execution seemed to the watchers in the ships to be fearful. The fire of the gunboats, according to the commander of the St. Louis, was 'heavy enough to drive out the whole Spanish army in Cuba had it been there'; and when presently somebody seemed to be waving a Cuban flag on shore, it looked all right. At about a quarter-past ten the Navy was requested to cease fire, and immediately thereafter the flotilla moved in under tow of the cutters, heading straight for the beach and for what to a modern commander would look like an inevitable holocaust.

But there was no holocaust. There was nothing at all. As the tows raced for the shore, not a shot was fired upon them. At about 10.25 the first boats touched the small wooden pier; the soldiers jumped to their feet, scrambled up with some difficulty upon the rather precarious planking, and arrived upon the soil of Cuba — without opposition of any kind. Except for the Cubans, Daiquirí was deserted. By what can only be another of those direct interventions of Providence which one seems to detect throughout the Spanish War, the enemy had evacuated the various landing places early that morning. What our men took to be signal fires were actually the flames from the buildings which they set alight as they withdrew.

For some mysterious reason the Spaniards had carefully thrown away their best — indeed, their only — chance. It is true that their forces were scanty; the great extent of exposed coast-line was difficult to cover; they were too short of ammunition to fritter it away in minor actions, and they probably had an idea even more exaggerated than our own of the effectiveness of naval fire. But even the few hundred men they had at Daiquirí on the night of the 21st might well have inflicted a terrible slaughter; while a skillful and resolute defense of the coast could have produced a disaster for the Fifth Army Corps that might have altered the course of the war. It seems at least doubtful whether our gorgeous political crusade would have stood up under the shock of a first-rate catastrophe; while if Shafter had been demolished there would have been almost nothing left that was capable of fighting. But the Spaniards forfeited the opportunity. It cannot be put down to a lack of physical courage, since both officers and men afterward behaved with bravery. More probably it indicated the profound hopelessness, the moral inertia, with which they regarded the whole issue. They were beaten before they began.

With the first boatloads upon the beach, the debarkation proceeded as rapidly as the distance of the transports (sometimes as much as four or five miles from the shore), the power of the steam launches, and the ingenuity of the men permitted. The troops piled ashore behind the launches, in the one available lighter, or even by pulling themselves in the rowboats. The steel pier was found to be so high as to be useless, and the swell made it difficult to spring from the boats onto the little wooden wharf; but the celebrated individual initiative of the American soldier overcame all obstacles and only two Negro troopers were drowned in the process. As was to be expected, that very individualistic soldier, Mr. Roosevelt, was at his best. The orders had placed the cavalry division well down in the list of precedence; but the lieutenant-colonel of the Rough Riders jumped to the conclusion that 'everything was being managed on the go-as-you-please principle,' so when a naval vessel came by under the command of an officer who had been Mr. Roosevelt's aide at the Navy Department, he immediately commandeered her. The Rough Riders gained at least an hour by the maneuver, and were early on shore. Theoretically, General Lawton was in charge of the advance; but 'Fighting Joe' Wheeler, who outranked him, got there almost as quickly. Observing the Spanish blockhouse on the hill, General Wheeler despatched some Rough Riders to hoist their regimental flag above it; General Lawton, it was clear, simply had no eye for publicity at all. The volunteers scaled the difficult height, and the American ensign fluttered out above the blockhouse.

The whole army — on shore, in the boats, and still lining the rails of the transports — saw it, and the whole army cheered. The troops, the Cubans, and the Navy people alike 'shouted and cheered again, and every steam whistle on the ocean for miles about shrieked and tooted and roared in a pandemonium of delight and pride and triumph.' It was a grand occasion.

Throughout the morning and afternoon the men arrived in a continuous stream. The animals for the artillery and the pack trains were landed by the simple device (it was later to bring down upon General Shafter the grave displeasure of the humane societies) of opening the cargo ports and throwing them into the water. Some headed out to sea and were lost, and it was ultimately found necessary to string them together by their halters and tow them in, but most made the trip in safety. Some headway was even made with the stores as well as with the men and animals, and when dusk fell at last and it was necessary to suspend operations, it was found that about six thousand men had been successfully got on shore.

So the swift darkness fell upon Daiquirí. In the middle of the afternoon, General Lawton had been ordered to push forward along the road to Siboney, and his leading regiments were bivouacking three or four miles to the westward. 'Fighting Joe' was making a private little reconnaissance of his own somewhere out beyond him, and all the way back into Daiquirí and about the beach the regiments were pitching their dog-tents and watching the tropic stars come out between the lofty fronds of the royal palms. As they settled into their blankets with the evening chill, the realization of the truth came over them. They were spending their first night in the field of war, in the near presence of the enemy. Whether or not they would ever spend another they did not know.

CHAPTER X

SAN JUAN HILL

I

GENERAL SHAFTER had but one plan — to get to Santiago and to get there as quickly as possible. He understood from the Cubans that the Spaniards had about twelve thousand men in and about the city, and it was known to be surrounded by a ring of entrenched lines protected by barbed wire. Of the enemy's precise dispositions, however, he had no knowledge, and the available maps were rather more than inadequate. But as for the route, there was only one. From the open ground behind Daiquirí it ran westward through a jungle to the beach at Siboney; there it turned inland, passed up over a gap in the coast range, and so into the rolling country behind, over which there was comparatively easy access to the city. This route was traversed by what was stated to be a 'wagon road,' but which probably was not; while the rolling ground behind the coast range was cut by numerous streams, commanded in many places by low hills and obstructed by patches of thicket and jungle, which in turn were separated by savannahs giving an admirable field of fire to the defenders. Over this uninviting terrain General Shafter now prepared to launch his force.

On the afternoon of the 22d, General Lawton had covered half the distance to Siboney. At daybreak next morning, he was pushing his men ahead, and by nine o'clock they had reached the collection of shacks which formed the town. There was a sudden rattle of Mausers from the thicket as the Spanish rear-guard slipped away. Nobody was hurt; but the American advance had for the first time heard hostile bullets whistling overhead, and at 9.20 General Lawton formally reported that Siboney had been 'captured.' His orders were to take up a strong defensive position, covering Siboney and its beach from molestation, and to hold it while the remainder of the army was landed and prepared for the real advance. In the course of the day the landing operations were switched from Daiquirí to Siboney, and during the next three days men, animals, and 'an immense amount of ammunition, food, and forage' were thrust ashore there through the surf without accident. Siboney — an almost unsheltered beach — was thereafter the main base of operations for the Fifth Army Corps.

The plan to reorganize the army and rest the animals, while Lawton held the gap through the hills from Santiago, was no doubt a sound one. Unfortunately, even General Shafter himself did not fully realize what an individualistic army he was commanding. Having entrusted the advance to Lawton, a reliable regular officer, and having taken the precaution of ordering the dismounted cavalry division (a somewhat uncertain quantity, since it was commanded by Fighting Joe, the volunteer Major-General, and included Mr. Roosevelt's *enfants terribles*) to keep well to the rear on the Daiquirí–Siboney road, General Shafter felt safe in remaining aboard his headquarters ship to oversee the difficult and delicate job of debarkation.

Such was the position when on the afternoon of June 23 General Lawton was alarmed to observe the arrival of Fighting Joe himself at Siboney accompanied by no others than Mr. Roosevelt, Colonel Wood, Mr. Richard Harding Davis (complete in a sack suit, a white puggaree, and tramping boots) and the Rough Riders, who 'in their anxiety to be well forward had reached Siboney by a forced march at night.' General Lawton had an unenterprising respect for orders and stayed where he was; but Fighting Joe (who was technically the senior) rode forth upon another private reconnaissance, in the course of which the Cubans told him that the Spaniards had retired and established themselves in a strong position two or three miles up the road.

'From the moment that the first soldier landed on Cuban soil,' according to one observer, 'there were not wanting evidences of a very natural but none the less deplorable rivalry between the officers and men of the several divisions composing the army corps for the honor of striking the first blow.' Returning to Siboney towards nightfall on the 23d, a strategic inspiration appears to have struck Fighting Joe. He perceived that under cover of darkness he could hurry his first brigade up, neatly outflank General Lawton, and by assaulting the Spanish position have the first battle altogether to himself, thus scoring a brilliant victory over the regular infantry. The Rough Riders went into camp in a 'beautiful cocoanut grove' beyond Siboney, ready to evade Lawton. Only half of the regular cavalry completing the brigade managed to get through; while Lawton's people succeeded in stopping a small dynamite gun upon which Fighting Joe was relying for his artillery support. That leader found, however, that he had with him the Rough Riders and one squadron each from the First and Tenth Cavalry, just under one thousand men in all. He decided that it was enough, and gave the orders for the advance next morning.

Throughout the night the men fought down their nervousness, the strangeness, and the hordes of those terrifying but quite harmless monsters, the land crabs, which infested the place with their obscene rustlings and scuttlings. Until an hour or two before dawn the troops were still coming ashore upon the beach just behind them under the naval searchlights.

It was one of the most weird and remarkable scenes of the war, probably of any war. An army was being landed on an enemy's coast at the dead of night, but with somewhat more of cheers and shrieks and laughter than rise from the bathers in the surf at Coney Island on a hot Sunday. It was a pandemonium of noises. The men still to be landed from the 'prison hulks,' as they called the transports, were singing in chorus, the men already on shore were dancing naked around the camp fires on the beach.... On either side rose black, overhanging ridges, in the lowland between were white tents and burning fires, and from the ocean came the blazing, dazzling eyes of the searchlights.

Fighting Joe's knowledge of the Spaniards' position was very sketchy, and his information as to their real strength uncertain in the extreme. Undeterred, however, by the thought of what would happen if he should be repulsed and thrown back upon the chaos at the beach, and filled with the old fire which thirty years before had made Wheeler's cavalry a terror to the Yankees, he went forward with his stratagem. After all, Lawton was a Yankee. Around five o'clock on the morning of the 24th, the squadrons of the First and Tenth Cavalry were knocked up and stole off through the clinging mists up the main road toward Santiago. A little later, the Rough Riders also got away. The regulars had General Wheeler. The Rough Riders had Colonel Wood, Lieutenant-Colonel Roosevelt, and (of course) the newspaper correspondents.

The Santiago road, which was taken by the regulars, leads northward up a broad valley, much obscured by thickets and jungle. A trail also ran parallel to it along the crest of the ridge forming the western side of the valley. The two converged at about the place where the Spaniards were supposed to be, and the Rough Riders were sent by way of the trail. The two columns quickly lost sight of each other behind the intervening jungle, and continued their respective ways through the brilliant woods and the beautiful morning sunshine. About 7.30 the regulars discovered the Spanish position — stone breastworks uncomfortably located upon a commanding hill which barred the way about half a mile ahead of them.

The column was deployed into a skirmish line on either side of the road, where they waited, somewhat uncertain as to what they should do next. Fighting Joe solved the uncertainty by trying a shot at the breastworks; the result was immediate and conclusive. A crackle of rifle fire leapt from the breastworks; there was the sudden, sharp, and sickening 'whit-whit' of the Mauser bullets clipping the foliage around them, and Fighting Joe, whose last experience of hostile fire had been with the muzzle-loading, single-shot muskets of the Civil War, discovered himself suddenly exposed to a volume of fire which astonished him. A man dropped very near him. The whole line was replying by this time as rapidly as they could. The question was answered. There was nothing to do but fight.

At about the same time the Rough Riders had run into the enemy on their own side. Colonel Wood had scarcely got his men deployed in the dense and often almost impenetrable undergrowth before heavy fire broke over them. They could not see the Spaniards; they could not see the regulars; they could see no more than a few of their own men at a time. The deep green jungle sloped away before them toward the depression separating them from the hill whence the bullets seemed to be coming. They could not tell just where they were or what was happening to them. Well down the trail Sergeant Hamilton Fish, the son of a distinguished New York family and a grandson of the Hamilton Fish who, as Secretary of State under Grant, had done so much to keep us out of a Cuban war twenty years earlier, was lying dead, shot through the heart. Captain Capron, the popular commander of the leading troop, was mortally wounded. Men were falling with a disconcerting rapidity; ugly wounds appeared with startling suddenness on the bodies and faces of comrades. It was hot, blind, a moment of stifling excitement. Wood had his whole regiment in the skirmish line, and there were no supports. But Lieutenant-Colonel Roosevelt had no qualms. As he leaped down the slope with his men, with the war correspondents in his wake, with the bullets clipping all about him, and with their high, dread whine in the air above, he knew that it was real war at last and that his supreme and crowded hour had come. Lieutenant-Colonel Roosevelt ran stumbling through the underbrush.

The regulars, on their side, were laboring under the disadvantage, not only of understanding what it was they were getting into, but also of being able to see it. Major Beach, acting as Fighting Joe's aide, began to wonder whether they had not been a trifle rash:

> The brigade commander very soon had his entire supports and reserves deployed, and from the heavy firing on our left we knew that Colonel Wood's regiment was likewise heavily engaged.
>
> After what seemed to be an interminable time and when our casualties were rapidly increasing, I said to General Wheeler, 'We have nine big regiments of infantry only a few miles back on the road. Let me send to General Lawton for one of them and close this action up.'

Fighting Joe hesitated. The brilliant outwitting of General Lawton would be damaged somewhat if he had to appeal to that officer to extricate him from its consequences, but things were getting serious and people were actually being killed. Fighting Joe gave his assent. When Major Beach summoned a courier, the man was too terrified to remember the message, and the Major had to scribble it down.

> The day wore on, dragged terribly in fact, and I for one was consumed with anxiety and apprehension as to the outcome of the fight, for our four hundred men were *not* advancing and we *were* piling up casualties; eight men killed and three officers and twenty or more men wounded. At that time, at our end of the line, with just one medical officer and one hospital

corps man to attend them, this was not pleasing to contemplate.... Time crawled, it did not fly; the sun seemed to stand still as in the days of Joshua of old, and it was too awfully hot and oppressive for words.

In the meanwhile General Lawton at Siboney had been listening to the firing. So had the troops, newspapermen, Cuban allies, teamsters, and every one else in the crowds milling up and down in the vicinity of the beach. In a few minutes a civilian packer drifted into the lines, shot through the neck and 'hollering,' "Come on, boys, help us out!"' Presently other wounded followed, and even, it is said, an unhurt officer proceeding rearward with unseemly haste and announcing that the cavalry had been ambushed and was being cut to pieces. Soon a litter arrived, bearing Mr. Edward Marshall, a correspondent of the New York *Journal*. Mr. Marshall, like Mr. Davis, had been with the Rough Riders; he was shot through the spine. He was suffering the tortures of the damned, but as he came through he was singing, with astonishing pluck, 'a song which was popular then, called "On the Banks of the Wabash Far Away."' To the waiting troops it must have been lugubrious, and as the Siboney correspondents scribbled their first stories and rushed them to the telegraph station which had been established, they reflected the prevailing atmosphere of gloom. General Lawton sent off an infantry regiment on the double.

But honors, after all, were more or less even. Just as the head of this column came into the sight of the anxious regulars on the firing line, the Spaniards suddenly broke from their entrenchments and departed. As they went, General Wheeler, laboring under a pardonable confusion in the excitement, shouted, 'We've got the damn Yankees on the run!' and so gave to the war one of its famous incidents and buried yet more deeply the last scars of Appomattox. The regulars swept forward in pursuit; at the same time the Rough Riders, who had managed to join up with them through the jungles, advanced on their side, and together the two detachments gained the breastworks, victory, and the headlines. Lawton's assistance had not really been necessary after all; they had scored a fair beat and it had taken them just an hour. But it had been a bad one, and Major Beach was astonished to learn that it was not the middle of the afternoon.

Such was the history of the battle of Las Guásimas — an action which was not only unnecessary (for the Spaniards had decided upon a withdrawal anyway) and which seriously embarrassed the plan for the main advance, but which cost sixteen men killed and fifty-two wounded. The publicity, however, would have forestalled any criticism; Mr. McKinley directed that his thanks be sent for 'the gallant action'; Mr. Roosevelt (curiously enough, since his rôle had been a comparatively minor one) was immediately being mentioned in the highest circles for promotion to a brigadier-generalcy, and General Shafter was forced to compliment Fighting Joe upon his strategy.

As Mr. Roosevelt put it to his friend the Senator:

Well, whatever comes, I shall feel contented with having left the Navy Department to go into the Army for the war; for our regiment has been in the first fight on land and has done well.... Our regiment furnished over half the men and over half the loss. Young [Mr. Roosevelt's brigade commander who had been with the regulars] did well. So did Wood.... The Spaniards were in a very strong position. I thought they shot well.... The smokeless powder made it very hard to place the men who were shooting at us; and our men at times dropped thickly when we could not tell where to fire back. Shafter was not even ashore! The mismanagement has been maddening. We have had very little to eat. But we care nothing for that as long as we got into the fight.

But Mr. Roosevelt was always a singular lieutenant-colonel. If the camp gossip can be believed, General Lawton himself flatly told Fighting Joe that 'this was no political campaign, but a military campaign; that he (Lawton) had been given command of the advance and he proposed to keep it, even if he had to post a guard to keep other troops to the rear.' But Fighting Joe was the senior, and the two divisions pushed together over the ridge at Las Guásimas to find themselves looking westward over a broad valley to the housetops of Santiago, some five or six miles away. There they took up position; while General Shafter, instructing Fighting Joe 'very positively' to stay where he was and attempt no more battles, devoted himself to the task of getting the rest of his army up to this new jumping-off place.

The strictly military consequences of the Las Guásimas action were somewhat mixed. The adventure had indeed secured the approaches to the city and removed all danger of interference with the landing beaches; but by extending the line of communication, it added greatly to the already very serious difficulties in the way of organizing the service of supply. Many of the privations which the troops were later to suffer — and for which General Shafter was to be condemned — might be traced in part to the individualistic strategy of Fighting Joe. But throughout the history of the Spanish War it was the non-military consequences which were of primary importance, and those of the Las Guásimas skirmish were to be profound. Mr. Roosevelt (assisted by the correspondents' irritation with the commanding general and their consequent need of some other hero) had entrenched himself firmly in the minds of the people; and it is not straining the facts too far to say that this hurried hour in the bush above Siboney was largely instrumental in giving us our next President of the United States. Mr. Roosevelt had reason to be content with having left the Navy Department.

II

The wide basin upon which the arriving troops now looked down — stretching from the steep slopes of the coast range at their left hand away to the mountains some eight or ten miles distant upon the right — presented military difficulties of an embarrassing kind. The Santiago road, which traversed it, was barred about three miles away (and about a mile from the inner defenses of the city) by a lofty ridge or series of ridges, known collectively as San Juan Hill. The country was so thickly covered with jungle and thicket that Fighting Joe had to scatter the arriving brigades about in isolated open patches in order to find room for their camps. While the road itself, upon which they had to depend for their supplies and which offered the only avenue of advance, turned out to be a rather bad track, so narrow in many places that two wagons could not pass, and inextricably involved in the windings of the little San Juan River, the bed of which it followed. Shortly after the skirmish the first rain broke over the valley; thereafter there were violent showers nearly every afternoon, the river and the road frequently became indistinguishable, while the troops, alternately scorched, drenched, and chilled by the sharp air at night, began to regret the blanket rolls they had thrown away in the advance and which had been appropriated, along with anything else not nailed down, by their Cuban allies.

The Santiago campaign very soon developed into the Tampa embarkation all over again. The divisions having been sent forward, it appeared that the expedition's pack trains were inadequate for supplying them. Before the wagon trains could be used, the wagons had to be got ashore and be put together and the harness unearthed. Once they were sent off, they immediately congested the road to a point at which it became nearly impossible to get them back again. Or else they broke down in the mud-holes and stopped all wheeled traffic entirely. The incompetence of some regimental officers who had failed to draw rations when directed left their men without anything to eat at all; while the individualistic efforts of others to remedy matters by capturing mule trains and raiding the bases on their own account did not lessen the growing confusion. The road was jammed; while the problems of unloading, landing, sorting, and forwarding the various stores from the desperately inadequate beaches soon assumed gigantic proportions. It was found, for example, that although the regimental medical officers had come ashore with their troops, they had left their chests and supplies in the transports and these had to be painstakingly collected. On June 29 there was a touching despatch from Fighting Joe, the Major-General commanding the cavalry to the adjutant-general of the Fifth Army Corps.

Colonel Viele, First Cavalry, reports that the wire nippers pertaining to his regiment were left aboard the Leona. These nippers are very necessary in our work here and I request that the bearer be furnished a launch to transport him to the Leona for the purpose of getting the nippers.

But if Colonel Viele mislaid his nippers, General Shafter himself managed to mislay one divisional commander, complete with his staff and a whole brigade of infantry. On the 22d, General Kent had been sent with the brigade to show his transports off Cabañas as a feint to cover the real landing; the unfortunate general was simply forgotten there, and it was not until three days later and after search had been instituted that anybody remembered the orders and he was recalled.

But one can only feel that General Shafter's burdens were

heavy, when one finds him forced to contend, at the very apex of the confusion, with such important instructions direct from Mr. Alger as the following:

The parents of Hamilton Fish and one or two others are very desirous of recovering the bodies of their boys. Is it possible to do so? Were any of them embalmed? I ask this because Senator Platt thinks young Fish's body was embalmed. How could heavy caskets be got to place of burial if parents should wish to remove the bodies?

Yet in spite of the innumerable distractions and difficulties of his position, General Shafter clung to his original intention to push on to Santiago at the earliest possible moment. The fear of disease and of hurricanes, the tenuousness of his communications both by sea and by land, alike impelled him to as early an action as possible; and on the 29th of June he had so far subdued the chaos at Siboney as to be able to move his headquarters from the coast to the advanced line and to prepare the assault. The reconnaissance of the ground ahead of him had been anything but thorough, the troops themselves were scarcely prepared for an attack upon entrenched positions, and in supply they had barely been able to keep abreast of consumption so that there were no reserves accumulated. But General Shafter determined to advance.

The enemy had already been observed throwing up entrenchments along the San Juan crests, where the road passed over them into the city. He also had about five hundred men in a fortified position at the village of El Caney, lying some two miles to the northward of this road, upon a road leading from Guantánamo. This force would be on the flank of any attack delivered against San Juan, and would also obstruct any encircling movement around toward the northern and western sides of the city. General Shafter particularly desired to extend his lines in that direction, both to intercept enemy reënforcements which were known to be fighting their way eastward from Manzanillo and to cut off the city's water supply, which was derived from the mountains through a pipeline entering from the north. He concluded that the proper course was to detach one of his three divisions to attack El Caney, at the same time launching his remaining two in a frontal assault against San Juan Ridge. He anticipated that a couple of hours' time at the most would be sufficient to drive in the

El Caney garrison, and that the division detached for the task could be brought up nicely on the flank of the Spanish main position in time to polish it off in conjunction with the frontal attack.

However admirable this conception may have been, it was seriously weakened by the fact that the terrain offered almost no roads over which to execute it. A narrow track ran northward to El Caney; it was bad, but there was open ground before the village for maneuver. The only known access to the San Juan position, however, was down the Santiago road — enfiladed by the Spanish entrenchments, and enclosed in jungles which offered no opportunity for deployment until the column had crossed the stream bed of the San Juan River and was directly under fire from the hills. By contrast, from this point onward there was no cover at all; a wide savannah led up to the foot of the steep slopes which would have to be climbed by the attackers. Artillery preparation would have been difficult even had there been any real artillery force; but the total for the whole army corps was just four light batteries. It was not an easy assignment.

But the entire army still retained a cheerful confidence in the inaccuracy of the enemy's marksmanship and his disinclination to serious fighting. Reassured by the results at Las Guásimas, no one expected anything but 'an easy and well-nigh bloodless victory,' and the only anxiety was to be certain of a share in the glory. General Shafter was already nearly prostrate under the intense heat of a climate in no way suited to an elderly general officer weighing one seventh of a ton, and he wanted to get along with the job. On the morning of June 30 (nearly a week had elapsed since Las Guásimas and the people at home were again impatient), he rode out along the Santiago road as far as it was safe and secured, from El Pozo Hill, a wide view of the field of action. It looked all right. General Shafter returned to his headquarters tent, summoned his divisional commanders, and informed them that the attempt would be made next morning. General Lawton, with his infantry division and one battery of field artillery, would take El Caney. As soon as he was well engaged, the dismounted cavalry would lead the way down the Santiago road (this ensured a prominent position for the Rough

Riders), cross the San Juan River, and deploy to the right. General Kent's division would follow in their wake and deploy to the left; the two together would charge the rifle pits upon the ridge. A second battery was to be posted on El Pozo Hill by way of artillery support; the remaining two were to be held 'in reserve.' It is a utilization of artillery which vividly suggests how far we were from the experience, not only of 1918, but even of 1865.

At about three in the afternoon the regiments were informed that they were to advance, and at about four o'clock they moved out into the trail simultaneously and started forward — as rapidly as the congestion which very naturally resulted would permit. Against the possibility that somebody might get wounded, the entire army corps possessed three ambulances. They had no extra rations and of course no way of getting any forward after the action had commenced. One brigade quartermaster, seeing that battle was impending, went to corps headquarters, browbeat a mule train out of them, led it all the way back for a raid on Siboney, and finally rejoined his command with the rations at 4.30 next morning. He left a supply for subsequent contingencies, but 'Colonel Roosevelt later appropriated the dump.'

Few, however, paused to worry over such details. The headquarters camp was crowded.

After a week of inaction the army, at a moment's notice, was moving forward and every one had ridden in haste to learn why. There were attachés in strange uniforms, self-important Cuban generals, officers from the flagship New York and an army of photographers.

There was also rather more than an army of reporters, while the general atmosphere of a magnificent county fair was heightened by the sudden apparition of the 'war balloon,' the great pride and triumph of the Signal Corps, ascending (under the control of three or four soldiers on the ground) in the lengthening sunlight of the afternoon.

So the sunlight lengthened and was snuffed out over San Juan Ridge, and the troops were still pouring onward down the Santiago trail as the mists came up out of the bottom-land and the moon arose through the exotic foliage. At midnight Lawton's division was halting to get some sleep well up the road to El Caney, while

Kent's people and the cavalry division were bivouacking around the base of El Pozo Hill and Grimes's battery was in readiness to mount it next morning and open fire. Some of the inquisitive climbed the hilltop for a last view. 'Three miles away across the basin of mist we could see the street lamps of Santiago shining over the San Juan hills. Above us the tropical moon hung white and clear in the dark purple sky pierced with millions of white stars.' They awaited the morning in a mood of happy anticipation.

III

Lawton permitted his men a bare four hours' sleep and a breakfast of 'cold water and hardtack' before setting them in motion once more. At sunrise he had his lone battery in position on a hillside some two thousand yards from the village, while his regiments, deploying through the rising mist, were looking for the first time upon the position they had come to take. It was formidable. The little collection of shacks was surrounded by a ring of entrenchments strengthened with blockhouses and in some places with barbed wire, while beside it there rose abruptly a small conical hill, surmounted by a stone fort. About seven o'clock the battery opened fire. The battle had begun.

Unfortunately, as the minutes dripped steadily away it showed no signs of progressing. It was observed that the fire of four light field guns, of a pattern already obsolete even in 1898, was singularly ineffective to silence well-protected infantry. The sharp crackle of the Mausers ran along the trenches, answered by the deeper popping of Krag-Jorgensens from the troops extended in the high grass. But nothing happened, except the biting whip of the bullets, a tightening in the throat, thirst, a growing heat as the sun climbed up behind them, and, presently, a casualty. Then another, and another. Lawton extended his lines in an encircling movement. Oddly enough, the Spaniards not only stayed where they were; they continued to shoot. And now and again they hit. The tall palms continued to wave gently in the burning sun; the grass was stifling; it was impossible to see that our fire, for which there was no target except the trenches, was having the slightest effect. Our advance was slow and costly. 'Every line of our approach was commanded by Spanish earthworks, and the damage we were able to inflict upon them was very small and insignificant indeed in comparison with the losses we had to suffer.' The morning was wearing on.

Captain Grimes, 'who had the bespectacled air of a professor,' had in the meantime got his battery into place on El Pozo, and at eight o'clock, with the sound of firing well developed from El Caney, he had opened up upon the blockhouses and entrenchments distantly visible on San Juan Hill. The immediate effect of this was regrettable. Congress had neglected to provide our artillery with the modern smokeless powder, and as the first great clouds of white smoke billowed forth from El Pozo, the Spaniards very naturally took them as a target for their own artillery. The cameras recording the 'first shot' were still clicking and an interested crowd of people from the regiments below was just gathering upon the hill to see what was going on, when the first answering shell sang over the battery and burst on the slope behind it, extinguishing a number of Cubans and wounding several Rough Riders who were in the farmyard below. It was not observed that the fire of Grimes's battery was effective except, by drawing reprisals, against our own people, and at about 8.45 the artillery preparation ceased.

General Shafter had remained behind in his headquarters tent, both because it was more central to the action and, perhaps, because the oppressive heat had already made it difficult for him to move. Colonel McClernand, his adjutant-general and representative, was directing matters at El Pozo. Colonel McClernand was seriously alarmed by the continued sound of firing from El Caney. Two hours at the most had been allowed for the reduction of that place, and an hour and a half had already elapsed. Fearful lest the enemy might reënforce El Caney and thus disrupt the arrangements, the Colonel ordered Kent's division and the dismounted cavalry to advance, thus launching the famous assault upon San Juan Hill. It was a little before nine o'clock on the morning of July 1. The day was a Friday.

The precise, and much controverted, details of what followed are difficult to reconstruct. Some ten or twelve thousand men plunged together into a narrow trail — barely wide enough in many places for the passage of a column of fours — which was hemmed in for most of its length by a tropical jungle, crossed by fords, and steaming in the heat under a mounting sun. Beyond a general idea that the enemy was powerfully entrenched along a ridge a mile and a half ahead of them, their commanders were ignorant of the situation and supplied with orders of an inconvenient vagueness. The traffic congestion which had accompanied every move of the Fifth Corps since its organization immediately ensued. Kent's division began by getting tangled up with the cavalry, and the Rough Riders (now commanded by Mr. Roosevelt, Colonel Wood having been advanced to command the brigade) were temporarily left behind. Kent's swearing infantrymen were 'halted and pushed into the bushes to allow the Rough Riders to pass by us, presumably to give them the first chance at the Spaniards.... Richard Harding Davis in full khaki regalia was with them.' The Rough Riders caught up; their division pushed onward, followed by the war balloon in tow of four enlisted men and containing Colonel Derby of the Engineers riding in splendid isolation above the scene. Kent went down into the defile in its wake, and the whole command was lost to the view of the watchers at El Pozo Hill, swallowed up under a sea of green above which there arose only the delicate stems of the scattered palms and the majestic and swaying bulk of the balloon, accurately delineating the advance.

To the troops crowded into this stifling trough through the jungle it seemed that they had scarcely left El Pozo when they first began to hear the terrible whistle and plunk of the Mauser bullets. There was a growing tension. The Spaniards observed the advancing balloon (it would have been difficult to have missed it) and naturally opened with shrapnel, which raked the road. The heat, sweat, and excitement increased; men began to fall, while the troops, jammed in column, could not have returned the fire even had they been able to see where it was coming from.

Then they even ceased to go forward. General Sumner (who because of an illness of Fighting Joe was now commanding the cavalry division) decided that he needed orders and halted his column; and for nearly an hour the men simply waited, while staff officers galloped frantically up and down, while shrapnel continued to burst above them from time to time, and they were afforded an opportunity to observe in all its details what a man looks like when he gets killed. They could observe also that it was now as impossible to retreat along the congested trail as it was to advance. The infantry behind them were in a similar situation; they were receiving the full effects of the Spanish attention to the balloon; they knew only that there was a block upon the road, that something had gone wrong, and that they were getting hurt. And time — ages of time — was passing.

No one seemed to know anything; losses were beginning to mount up; hours had elapsed since they had started from El Pozo. Finally somebody told Sumner to get on with it, deploy his troops to the right of the road and make the attack. At about the same time General Kent, exasperated at the delay, had himself galloped up to the head of the column. Presently he found General Sumner near the last ford; the jungle fell away at this point, disclosing the open meadow ground and beyond it the steep slopes of San Juan Hill, crowned by the crackling rifle pits. It was obviously a bad place, but it was the first opportunity for deployment. There was a consultation of generals (fortunately it did not occur to the Spaniards that we would use our divisional commanders for advance reconnaissance and the chance to decapitate the American army was lost) and Sumner got his men into a column of twos so that the infantry could be brought up the trail beside them. At the same time he started his division (led by the Ninth Cavalry, a colored regiment, followed by the Sixth and Third) up the stream bed to the right, where they still had the cover of a protecting screen of foliage. Kent rushed back to hurry along his leading brigade, consisting of the Sixth and Sixteenth Infantry and the Seventy-First New York. In column of twos or sometimes in single file the infantrymen pushed rapidly forward, jostling the dismounted cavalrymen and themselves trampled by the aides, couriers, and general officers, toward the ford which before nightfall was to become still another 'bloody angle' in our military annals.

As the Sixth Infantry had come up beneath the balloon, Colonel Derby (who despite the heavy fire he had been drawing down upon the unhappy soldiery beneath had himself remained quite unharmed) had leaned from the basket and hailed the ground:

'Is there a general officer below?' No answer. 'Is there a field or staff officer down there?' No answer. 'Is there any officer?' 'Yes, quite a few.' Then came this information from heavenward: 'I see two roads in front.' 'Where do they lead to?' was asked. Answer: 'I can't tell.'

One of the roads, however, was seen to be a hitherto unsuspected trail leading off toward the left and looking as though it might give a second access to the meadow. When the frantic Kent came thundering to the rear to hasten his men, he was informed of this discovery — the sole, and costly, triumph of our effort at aerial reconnaissance — and instantly decided to make use of it. The Sixth and Sixteenth Infantry were already hurrying along up the main road; the head of the Seventy-First New York was near the fork where the trail turned off. Kent diverted the regiment down this trail, with orders to reach the meadow and form up on the left of the other two regiments of the brigade as they extended their skirmish line down from the main road.

The Seventy-First New York was the only National Guard regiment in this action — the Second Massachusetts having been sent with Lawton to El Caney — and with the exception of the specially enlisted Rough Riders it was the only volunteer unit present. It had been chosen for the expedition because it was among the best of the state troops; but the quality of the state troops has already been indicated. Only five weeks before, its colonel was officially reporting that nearly one third of his men had never fired a gun, and how many of the others had ever succeeded in hitting anything is not recorded. While alone among the regiments on the scene it labored under the appalling disadvantage of being equipped with the old black-powder rifles, which could not be fired without setting up a plain target for the enemy. Yet by the fortunes of war it was this raw command which, after having been kept waiting for hours in a nervous jam upon the road, now found itself leading the way down an unknown trail under a 'galling fire' from an unseen enemy, and at the direction of officers who gave every indication of a large ignorance as to what they were doing.

The first battalion of the Seventy-First New York may not have been heroes, but one can only feel that they were men of discretion. At this point they came to the sudden conclusion that they were tired of the war. According to General Kent, who was at the forks of the road, 'the leading battalion of this regiment was thrown into confusion and recoiled in disorder on the troops in rear. At this critical moment the officers of my staff practically formed a cordon behind the panic-stricken men and urged them to again go forward. I finally ordered them to lie down in the thicket and clear the way for others of their own regiment who were coming up behind. This many of them did.' It was, indeed, a critical moment; but General Kent, faced with what at any instant might have developed into a complete and irreparable disaster, maintained a splendid poise. His second brigade, under Wikoff, was approaching, and he immediately sent it on down the side trail. Pointing to the brushwood, now thickly decorated with the recumbent forms of the unhappy Seventy-First, he said: 'Tell the brigade to pay no attention to this sort of thing, it is highly irregular.'

Thus cautioned, Wikoff's leading regiment, the Thirteenth Infantry, sprang down the pathway.

The men of the 71st [said its official report] were lying flat on the ground along the underbrush bordering the road with their feet toward the middle of the road. This made considerable of an obstruction to our passage and compelled us to move in single file. From the remarks they made to us all along the line as we passed them at a run, I inferred that they were in this prostrate formation for the purpose of avoiding exposure to bullets.

The inference was correct; and with all the congestion, heat, noise, blood, and dropping fire of that narrow corner, one can hardly blame them. But although many of the Seventy-First's men gallantly joined in with the regulars as individuals, and although the regiment as a whole soon recovered its morale, it had earned a black mark which the censorious publics who hadn't been there could not afterward forgive. The National Guardsmen had only one consolation. The balloon, the cause of all their woes, was at last being punctured by the Spanish fire; and shortly after the discovery of the trail, it sank gently down, to the immense relief of the army on the ground. Colonel Derby stepped out uninjured, and the aerial phase of our War with Spain was over.

THE 71ST NEW YORK GOING INTO ACTION, JULY 1, 1898

THE GROUND OVER WHICH THE AMERICANS CHARGED TO TAKE
THE BLOCKHOUSE ON SAN JUAN HILL

Showing the lagoon through which the cavalry division passed.
The Santiago road crossing the picture can be seen faintly.
Kettle Hill is behind the camera and to the right.

It was now well past noon. For the previous hour or so General Shafter, ill with the heat and the uncertainty at his headquarters tent behind El Pozo, had been a prey to a deepening anxiety. The firing at El Caney continued in unabated volume; that from San Juan swelled into an ever deeper and more ominous orchestration, and it was clear that the Spaniards, contrary to all expectation, were fighting. A battle which should have been over hours before gave no indication of even making progress. A reporter discovered the commanding general, his great bulk encased only in shirt-sleeves and trousers, standing before the telephone tent 'talking so energetically that the back of his head rolled up in wrinkles,' but talking what seemed to be 'common-sense.' Couriers and aides were constantly dashing up or away; the news appeared to be uniformly bad. The sun was directly overhead; it was intolerably hot, and when the reporter and a 'kinetoscope man' chose this moment to find out from the General 'what the next move would be,' they were not successful.

There was no next move to make. General Shafter had already despatched a brigade — his sole reserves — to assist Lawton at El Caney, and still nothing had happened. The actual position at this time was that the five thousand-odd men of Lawton's division were lying in the high grass (the Second Massachusetts had been withdrawn because of the smoke from its obsolete ammunition), firing from three sides, but without appreciable effect, into the entrenchments which the five hundred Spanish defenders obstinately refused to vacate. Kent and the cavalry division were still pouring down the road, debouching at the end under heavy fire and trying to find cover from which they could return it; while on both sectors commanders were beginning to see the end of their ammunition supply, and the totally inadequate hospital personnel, in hastily established and unsheltered dressing-stations, was putting up an heroic struggle against the rapidly mounting casualty lists. General Shafter could have had no very clear idea of what was going on, but he saw that something had to be done, and at two o'clock he sent off a note to Lawton:

I would not bother with little blockhouses. They can't harm us.... [You] should move on city and form the right of line.

Thereafter he could only wait; while the message itself reached Lawton too late to change matters.

The leading regiments of the cavalry division had turned off the Santiago road to the right and the line was now being extended northward at right angles to the road. While the Sixth and Ninth Cavalry were in skirmish order in the meadow, the Tenth Cavalry (another Negro regiment) and the Rough Riders passed behind them up the stream bed, still for the most part under cover, endeavoring to join on the right of the line, while the Third and First Cavalry came crowding in behind them. The regiments soon became pretty thoroughly mixed up in the course of this evolution; they found barbed-wire fencing obstructing the open ground, while directly before them there arose, as an unpleasant surprise, a small hill standing well in front of the main ridge and occupied by Spaniards. The cavalrymen lay down; at any rate, they were at last able to shoot back, and for the first time the Americans began to return the hostile fire while their officers tried to get them in shape for an assault.

The infantry regiments were in much the same position on the south side of the road. The Sixth and Sixteenth Infantry had deployed along the front edge of the thicket; six hundred yards away the Spaniards on San Juan were pouring in their volley fire across the intervening meadow, while immediately in front of them a heavy barbed-wire fence, enclosing the field, stopped them. They tried to hack it away with their bayonets, for they had no wire-cutters; they thought of uprooting the posts, but found that the wire had been strung to tree-trunks. General Hawkins, their brigade commander, was walking up and down behind them — a tall and soldierly figure with white goatee and mustache, brilliant in the sunshine and fearlessly exposing himself. But his men were getting killed with a disconcerting rapidity. Farther away on their left the Thirteenth Infantry, followed by the rest of Wikoff's brigade, was breaking through into the meadow. Wikoff himself was already killed; Worth, who had replaced him, was badly wounded; a few minutes later Liscum, who replaced Worth, 'fell under the withering fire.'

It was nearly two o'clock in the afternoon; they were in a tight place, and there were no orders. The distant artillery on El Pozo

Hill had long since ceased to fire. Somewhere in the confusion there was a wild message from Fighting Joe (who had arisen from his sick bed and was wandering more or less at large over the scene) 'saying that General Sumner wished to know if General Shafter's orders contemplated attacking entrenchments.' A reply was sent, saying in substance that they did. Then there was an appeal from Lieutenant Miley, Shafter's personal aide who was in general supervision at the front: 'The heights must be taken at all hazards. A retreat now would be a disastrous defeat.' An order was sent off; no one knew whether it reached him or not. But by that time the troops had arrived independently at the same conclusion as had Lieutenant Miley.

It was impossible to go back over the crowded road; it was extremely unhealthy to stay where they were, and only one thing remained. Fortunately, it was just at this juncture that a battery of Gatling guns under Lieutenant Parker, which had been sent forward on a kind of general roving commission, arrived upon the scene. Their approach had been heralded by an explosion of cheering from the wretched Seventy-First New York — an 'outburst of ignorant enthusiasm,' as Lieutenant Parker severely reported, which drew the enemy fire and put many soldiers 'forever beyond the possibility of cheering.' In spite of this *contretemps*, however, he got up by the 'bloody angle' and gallantly put his guns into action. The effect upon the Spanish trenches was immediate; almost at once their occupants were seen to be scrambling up out of them and vanishing over the hill. Orders appear to have been shouted by a number of commanders, but the long lines of men sweating and dying in the grass did not wait for orders. They got up and ran for the ridge. 'It looked like a long distance to charge — four or five hundred yards it seemed — across the comparatively open terrain in front of us, but we charged.' They knew what was good for them.

The long and ragged line of blue-shirted figures was seen suddenly to be weaving forward across the field. Some of them stumbled and fell as they went; but they kept on, crossed the meadow, gained the first slope of San Juan Hill, and starting up it all at once discovered themselves under the cover of the hillside and thus safe from the hostile fire. The battle of San Juan was won — or it would have been, had it not been for the artillery.

The artillery on El Pozo Hill, unable to see what was going on beneath the sea of jungle which stretched before it, had been a more or less inactive auditor of the stirring sounds of battle. Now, as they at last caught sight of the little blue dots rising against the distant hillside, and realized that the attack was going home, it occurred to them that this was an opportune time to lend their assistance. The artillery opened fire. The official report of Captain Allen, of the Sixteenth Infantry, graphically describes the result:

The advance continued steadily and without a pause until we were on the steep slope near the crest, two thirds of the way up, when our artillery fire coming from our rear became dangerous.... Some shells struck the slope between me and the crest, but I urged my men forward and they were responding most nobly. We had seen the enemy leave their trenches and I was anxious to press home our victory. But at this time there arose at the foot of the slope and in the field behind us a great cry of 'Come back! Come back!' The trumpets there sounded 'Cease firing,' 'Recall,' and 'Assembly.' The men hesitated, stopped, and began drifting down the steep slope.... Precious time was lost. As for myself and my company, we reluctantly drifted back downward about twenty yards, and I hurled at the wretches below all the oaths I have learned in thirty years' life in the Army.

One gallant officer tried by waving his hat to convince the artillery of their error. He succeeded only in getting himself wounded. The advance halted on the hillside, and there was a hurried period of shouting, flag-waving, and contradictory orders before somebody finally succeeded in shutting off the artillerists. Then the infantry went up with a rush, arriving together in a jumble of various regiments upon the crest line; where, dropping into the abandoned trenches, they opened fire upon the white figures of the retreating Spaniards, now at last fully visible in the valley beyond. San Juan Hill was ours.

At about the time that the infantry started forward on the south side of the road, the cavalrymen on the north side also advanced against Kettle Hill, the outlying position which separated them from the main ridge. Mr. Roosevelt, finding himself with a collection of his own Rough Riders and some colored troopers from the Ninth and Tenth Cavalry, waved his hat and started forward; so, apparently, did others, but Mr. Roosevelt afterward could not recall the presence of any commander in his neighborhood save himself. Reaching the top, he found that a deep depression with a shallow lagoon at the bottom still intervened between him and the main position. Mr. Roosevelt, with his followers at his back, swept down, splashed through the lagoon and gained the opposite height. There they found some of the Tenth Cavalry who had got up before them. Mr. Roosevelt formed up everybody he saw and, noticing the infantry engaged away to the left, poured in a fire upon the flank of the retreating enemy. The cavalry, in a highly disjointed state, was coming up all around; together they advanced and established themselves finally along the crest, looking down upon the city of Santiago. The reputation so brilliantly begun at Las Guásimas was enormously enhanced; and as the newspaper despatches went off describing the heroism of the Rough Riders and their lieutenant-colonel, another military genius had been given to American history.

By this time it was about four o'clock, and the action at El Caney was still continuing. While the troops at San Juan fell to the task of digging themselves in, sorting themselves out, and trying to get up ammunition and rations, Lawton's people were still trying to close upon the stubborn village. They had nearly surrounded the place, but were impeded by barbed wire and the lack of cover, and it seems probable that the affair might have gone on indefinitely, despite the ten-to-one disparity of forces, had not the defenders begun to run short of ammunition. Along in the middle of the afternoon the Spanish fire began perforce to slacken, and the American lines were able to work in closer and closer; and before General Shafter's admonition not to 'bother with little blockhouses' was received, Lawton had already embarked upon his final assault. The Spanish commander, General Vara del Rey, at last ordered his men to get away while they could. He was himself killed shortly afterward. There was a last hurried scramble in the lengthening sunlight; the American lines went in, and at about quarter-past four the Twelfth Infantry stormed the stone fort which was the center of resistance.

Captain Lee of the Royal Engineers, the British military attaché who is better known to history as Lord Lee of Fareham, watched them go with astonishment. 'He asked me,' according to the report of a major of the Twelfth Infantry, 'whether it was customary with us to assault blockhouses and rifle pits before they had been searched by artillery; to which reply was made, "Not always."' But at any rate, we had taken El Caney.

Even that was not the full measure of the heroism of Lawton's regulars. They buried their dead in a wonderful tropic sunset and then, impelled by urgent messages from headquarters, set off down the El Caney–Santiago road, in order to reach and reënforce the right of our precarious line on San Juan Ridge. Presently, however, they ran into some Spanish pickets in the darkness, and Lawton feared to risk another action at night in unknown country. The men had slept only four hours the night before and had been fighting all day with nothing to eat, but Lawton faced them about, marched them back through El Caney, and around by the road they had come until they reached El Pozo. They halted for some rest and then pushed on, over the now terrible route which Kent and the cavalry division had used, coming up at last into the line about the middle of the following day. It was something of an achievement.

CHAPTER XI
THE NAVY'S FOURTH-OF-JULY PRESENT

I

IT was to seem in retrospect a brilliant victory. But as the darkness finally fell upon that long, that bloody and peculiarly trying day, a profound depression reigned in the American army. They had learned to their surprise that the Spaniards could both fight and kill. The units upon the ridge discovered, when they had time to count up, that they were mere skeletons, for the army had lost nearly ten per cent in actual casualties, to say nothing of the stragglers. While the scattered, exhausted, and decimated troops clinging to the hilltops in the chilly darkness had looked down and seen that the inner defenses of the city, strong with barbed wire, entrenchments, and gun positions, were still intact before them. They were cold, hungry, and their nerve was shaken; behind them from the long grass and the jungle there arose the moans of the wounded still awaiting attention from the desperately overworked hospital personnel, and through the night there were desultory counter-attacks, or what they thought were counter-attacks, upon their position. War, for the first time, had become real.

Toward sundown General Shafter had sent off an optimistic telegram to Washington; but as the hours dragged away, the anxious officials at the capital waited in vain for further details. The full picture of what had happened was only gradually dawning upon General Shafter. Many of the wounded were never discovered at all until a day or two after the battle; but already the wagons which had been sent up with ammunition and rations were coming back, loaded with injured men from the advance dressing-station under the bank of the San Juan River. It was a dreadful journey over a rocky and jolting road, and when the agonized bodies were at last turned out upon the ground at the field hospital established near the General's headquarters, there were neither the facilities nor the personnel to take care of them.

At the hospital the few medical officers present labored strenuously all night. The wounded from El Caney kept streaming in for several hours. Fortunately, it was a beautiful calm night with a bright full moon taking the place of artificial light, which was lacking. Most patients had to be accommodated on the sandy soil, with or without blankets.

The country, as General Shafter had observed, was no longer accustomed to hear of heavy losses and would judge them accordingly. As the hospital filled before his eyes, the dreadful truth began to come over him, and shortly after midnight another brief message went to Washington: 'I fear I have underestimated today's casualties.' Thereafter the General was silent, and the nerve-racked gentlemen at the capital had to rely upon the press despatches which, between the lines, were sufficiently alarming.

General Shafter had actually thrown away 1475 men, killed and wounded, in the course of the day, and he had gained nothing save a precarious hold upon the outer line of the city's defenses. As the night wore on it was even doubtful whether he had gained that. The crowd milling about at headquarters was already nervous, and in the course of the evening an alarming note arrived from Fighting Joe, who as senior divisional commander present, had taken charge at the front:

A number of officers have appealed to me to have the line withdrawn and take up a strong position farther back, and I expect they will appeal to you. I have positively discountenanced this, as it would cost us much prestige. The lines are now very thin, as so many men have gone to the rear with wounded and so many are exhausted, but I hope these men can be got up tonight.... We ought to hold tomorrow, but I fear it will be a severe day.

The commanding general, ill with fever and with apprehension, was forced to his cot. He hardly knew whether he had achieved a victory or suffered a disaster.

The troops held through the night and managed to dig in to some extent, but during the next day (July 2) they were kept under a dropping fire and continued to suffer losses. The rather curious experiment was tried of sending artillery into the front line to keep down this fire. The experiment was not a happy one. The guns were emplaced in front of the trenches, and since the morning mist concealed all objectives they were simply discharged into the void, with the fuses cut to zero. The result of this hopeful procedure was instantaneous. The mist might conceal the enemy, but nothing could conceal the clouds of smoke emitted every time a round was fired. As the Spaniards replied with rifle, shell, and shrapnel, the gun crews ingloriously disappeared into the trenches behind them. 'Only with time and effort could the gun detachments be collected and driven back to the guns, yet this was accomplished, and in a short time a desultory fire was again opened, the usual target being the vacant world in front.' The battery commander was wounded in the midst of this peculiar scene; but 'order,' as a participant puts it, 'was finally restored,' and our fire became fairly regular before somebody had sense enough to withdraw them.

In the meantime the commanding general had realized that he was in a position of the utmost gravity. The remaining defenses were much stronger and more strongly held than those on San Juan; there was no way of taking them save by frontal assault, but to have attempted it might have ended in the disintegration of his army. At the same time the fear of disease and the possibility of a hurricane which would cut off his line of communications imperatively urged him forward. At this juncture one resource occurred to him — the Navy, which had been peacefully enjoying the scenery and the sea air (varied by an occasional innocent bombardment) while the Army undertook the real work of the naval campaign. Early on the morning of the 2d, General Shafter came to what seems a not unreasonable conclusion, and despatched a message to his colleague Admiral:

Terrible fight yesterday…. I urge that you make effort immediately to force the entrance to avoid future losses among my men, which are already very heavy. You can now operate with less loss of life than I can.

Even though the real weakness of the harbor defenses was not fully known, this request might seem to have had some justification. But unfortunately, from the moment when the Army had neglected to fall in with the Navy's ideas of how the land campaign should be conducted, a certain strain had begun to develop between the sister services. The Navy's reply was upon a note of surprised reproof. General Shafter was severely reminded that it was 'impossible to force entrance until we can clear channel of mines — a work of some time after forts are taken possession of by your troops.'

The military correctness of this position ought to have been enough for him; but the General was faced by the vivid prospect of having to order his men against strongly prepared positions without artillery support, and he replied with asperity: 'I am at a loss to see why the Navy cannot work under a destructive fire as well as the Army.'

Such ignorance evidently pained the naval arm. Clearly General Shafter had overlooked both the great principles of Mahan and the fact that while men, who are easily replaceable, may be sacrificed, the risking of ships, which cost money, is another matter. Admiral Sampson sat down to explain with patience why the Navy, unlike the Army, could not work under a destructive fire:

Our trouble from the first has been that the channel to the harbor is well strewn with observation mines, which would certainly result in the sinking of one or more of our ships if we attempted to enter the harbor, and by the sinking of a ship the object of the attempt to enter the harbor would be defeated by the preventing of further progress on our part. It was my hope that an attack on your part of these shore batteries, from the rear, would leave us at liberty to drag the channel for torpedoes.

Thus was still another example provided of the curious (if often overlooked) truth that fighting ships are generally very much too valuable ever to do any fighting. One is inclined to sympathize with General Shafter. Our Navy was so overwhelmingly superior to the Spanish that the loss of even a heavy ship could not have affected the result, while if one had sunk in the channel it would merely have accomplished what Mr. Hobson had tried and failed to do with the Merrimac. There was a danger that a ship midway in the entering column might be sunk, thus blocking a part of the fleet inside beyond reach of help from the rest. But it is still hard to understand why the Navy could not have attempted, at least, a mine-sweeping operation by the lighter vessels. Considering the known weakness of the batteries and the experience of the Merrimac, which had got well inside before even her own crew (to say nothing of the Spaniards) had been able to sink her, the Navy seems to have been lacking in energy. They had been there for a

month, but had not even tested the possibility of clearing the
channel. Yet the best which General Shafter could get on that
anxious Saturday afternoon was the promise that the Navy would
experiment with countermining, a work 'which is unfamiliar to
us,' and would 'require considerable time.' General Shafter, poor
man, had no time.

But Fate was to accord him a curious revenge. Admiral Sampson incautiously arranged to visit him upon the following morning
to discuss the matter in person.

As dusk fell on July 2, there was a council of war at El Pozo,
held in the open with sentinels posted (it was a necessary precaution in that army) 'to keep all at a distance.' The General was ill,
and so weak that he reposed his great bulk upon a door taken from
its hinges from a neighboring farmhouse, while his commanders
stood about him and gave their conflicting views. He told them
he would take the blame, whatever happened, and the conference
broke up. At the same hour the War President, Mr. Alger, and the
Secretary of Agriculture were sitting over the cables at the White
House in a state of only less intense anxiety. No messages came.
The minutes ticked away through the ominous silences of midnight. The day had been filled with 'foreboding rumors' and the
newspapers had been reporting the heavy losses, the illnesses of
the higher commanders, and stories of yellow fever among the
troops. It was four in the morning before they finally broke up;
and still there had been no word. Mr. Alger, before going home in
'the gray of dawn,' paused to send off a moving appeal: 'We are
awaiting with intense anxiety tidings of yesterday'; and supplemented it next morning: 'I wish hereafter that you would interrupt
all messages that are being sent to the Associated Press and others,
and make report at the close of each day.'

Sunday morning, July 3, broke upon the cold and nervous
troops along San Juan Ridge. War was still an intense and dire
reality; and the brass bands, the shouting crowds, and the patriotism were very far away. For one eminent military man war had
suddenly become very real indeed; it was at this dark moment
that Mr. Roosevelt himself was shaken into a singular and most
unmilitary appeal. In the stress of his emotion the lieutenant-
colonel of the Rough Riders turned, not to his commanding

officers, but to the more familiar recourse of political influence. His letter read:

DEAR CABOT:

Tell the President for Heaven's sake to send us every regiment and above all every battery possible. We have won so far at a heavy cost; but the Spaniards fight very hard and charging these entrenchments against modern rifles is terrible. We are within measurable distance of a terrible military disaster; we *must* have help — thousands of men, batteries, and *food* and ammunition. The other volunteers are at a hideous disadvantage owing to their not having smokeless powder. Our General is poor; he is too unwieldy to get to the front.

It is not suggested that Mr. Roosevelt was personally frightened, but again one seems to understand why Mr. Roosevelt was not asked to take the field when, in 1917, we entered a real war.

But the early hours of that morning were filled with the atmospheres of gloom. General Shafter had been revolving the situation, and before seven o'clock he had summoned his adjutant-general and dictated a tentative despatch for Washington:

We have the town well invested on the north and east but with a very thin line. Upon approaching it we find it of such a character and the defenses so strong it will be impossible to carry it by storm with my present force and I am seriously considering withdrawing about five miles and taking up a new position.... I have been unable to be out during the heat of the day for four days, but am retaining the command.

There were many other pessimistic details. Colonel McClernand dutifully took them down and the message was sent off.

McClernand, however, did not belong to the defeatist party, and he believed that after a little rest nothing more would be heard of the idea of falling back. He had already strongly urged the view that if they only held on the city would fall naturally into their hands:

Fortunately, about an hour later the General's remark, previously mentioned as having been made on the transport, about placing his army around the city and demanding a surrender recurred to me. Returning to him I said: 'General, let us make a demand on them to surrender.' He was still ill and lying on his cot. He looked at me for perhaps a full minute and I thought he was going to offer a rebuke for my persistence... but finally he said: 'Well, try it.' I went under a tent-fly that served for my office and wrote the demand of 8.30 A.M., addressed to the Commanding

General of the Spanish Forces, Santiago de Cuba.... He was told that unless he surrendered we would shell the city.

As a result of this curious incident, at the moment when Shafter's message proposing a retreat was arriving before the startled officials at Washington, his ultimatum demanding a surrender on pain of bombardment had already been delivered to the Spanish commander, General Toral. The whole line had seen the flag of truce which bore it; the firing had died away and in the ensuing quiet the frayed nerves had pulled together. As the mists rolled up out of those beautiful valleys, giving place to the hot placidity of a Sunday forenoon, the terrors and defeatism of the past two days began to evaporate likewise. There was a better feeling in the trenches and at headquarters. The people at Siboney, looking out across the brilliant surface of a dead calm sea, observed the reassuring outlines of Admiral Sampson's flagship approaching under easy steam for the conference which had been arranged the evening before. In the pleasant sunshine on the beach horses were waiting, saddled and ready to bear the Admiral up into the hills to General Shafter's headquarters. It was a peaceful scene.

But throughout that long Sunday in Washington there was no peace. The General neglected to inform his superiors of his surrender demand, but his message suggesting withdrawal arrived just before noon, to scatter consternation among the statesmen. It was obvious that a withdrawal now would have the gravest repercussions among the home public; it would be a political no less than a military disaster. All day the War Department was thronged by 'people prominent in political and private life, all anxiously inquiring for news.' It was the hottest July weather that Washington had known for fifteen years. Throughout a dreadful afternoon the President sat with some of his cabinet and military advisers at the White House, 'anxiously discussing the unhappy message of General Shafter' or rushing off telegrams announcing the immediate despatch of all possible reënforcements. It was noticed that Senator Mark Hanna was also present to lend his counsel. But there was no news. The hours wore on, and as the late summer twilight fell over the streets of Washington, it seemed that the whole country had sensed the depression. It was the eve of the national holiday; but the cables remained ominously silent.

Night fell. There had been no news. It was the darkest hour of our War with Spain.

But had they only known it, even as their gloom was deepening the day was being saved — by the Spaniards. It was along in the middle of that Sunday morning that an aide galloped up to El Pozo with astounding information; and it was about the same time that the men in the advanced trenches heard, some miles away over the hills by the harbor entrance, the sound of heavy cannonading. No news had gone to Washington because our commanders had been too busy and too excited to send it.

II

At the time that General Shafter was dictating his 'unhappy message' in the mists of El Pozo, the people in the blockading squadron had been coming on deck to another routine Sunday in their tiresome vigil. It was a beautiful day; the early mist burned off to leave a hot and glasslike calm, with the columns of smoke standing in graceful pillars upon the still and lovely air. It was 'one of those summer days when not the slightest breath of air stirs the leaves of the trees, when not the smallest cloud is visible in the skies, when not the slightest vapor fills the atmosphere, which was wonderfully transparent.' Amid this placid beauty the fleet resumed the usual small businesses of the day. It was lying, as always, in a wide semi-circle around the harbor entrance; Morro Castle formed its center and the radius was about four or five miles. Commodore Schley in his armored cruiser Brooklyn lay nearest to the shore upon the west, but rather farther out than usual. Then came the battleships Texas and Iowa, so placed that both of them could look up the narrow gut which formed the harbor mouth. Then came the battleship Oregon, already famous for her long run around Cape Horn; then Sampson's flagship, the armored cruiser New York, well around upon the eastern side of the arc; and finally, the battleship Indiana. Two converted yachts, the Vixen and the Gloucester (Mr. J. P. Morgan's Corsair), were stationed close inshore at the western and eastern ends of the semi-circle.

Presently the flagship New York made ready to depart upon her mission to Siboney, seven or eight miles away to the eastward.

Shortly before nine her engines were rung ahead; the customary signal 'Disregard motions of commander-in-chief' was hoisted, and she left the line. Commodore Schley was informed of her departure; it may have induced a bitter thought. The Commodore, the martial hero of that Chilean war which had never happened, had been smarting for a month under the orders of a former junior. Sampson had first been promoted Admiral over his head and then, after that rather unlucky business about the hunt for Cervera, had been placed directly in command over him. For one who had begun the war as the commander of an independent squadron, this was rather pointed. But as the flagship departed on her errand, the Commodore could at least reflect that he was temporarily the senior officer present.

The crews of the other ships watched the New York growing smaller in the distance, and then turned to the customary Sunday morning muster, the men steeling themselves to withstand not only the routine inspection and Divine service, but the Articles of War, which were habitually read to them on the first Sunday of the month. Officers and men had put on their clean white uniforms, and in the captain's cabin of the Iowa, 'Fighting Bob' Evans, the other Chilean hero, was just finishing his after-breakfast cigar.

It was at this moment that a general alarm rang through the ship.

Captain Evans leapt to his feet and dashed for the companion ladder. Just as his head came even with the deck, he heard his own ship fire a signal gun; looking out, he saw, coming down the channel bow on under a full head of steam, the Maria Teresa, flagship of Admiral Cervera. Resplendent in the brilliant sunshine, with a new coat of paint, with the smoke pouring from her funnels, a 'bone in her teeth,' and the great blood-and-golden battle-flags of Spain at her mastheads, she was heading directly for the American fleet and the open sea. Behind her, in the narrow passage between the gray heights of the Morro on the one hand and the Socapa Hill upon the other, there swung successively into view the Vizcaya, the Cristóbal Colón, and the Almirante Oquendo. And behind them in turn were the Furor and Plutón, Cervera's much-dreaded torpedo-boat destroyers. The Spanish fleet was coming out.

Before Captain Evans reached the bridge the signal that the enemy was emerging — in all the American ships it had been kept bent on and ready for the past month — had been hoisted and the Iowa's engines had been rung full speed ahead. Similar signals were fluttering from the mastheads of the other vessels; while all, acting upon the curiously simple standing orders of Admiral Sampson, were preparing to rush forward in a converging 'charge' upon the harbor mouth. Throughout the fleet the men were tumbling down the ladders to their battle stations; the fire-room crews were outdoing themselves in their efforts to crowd steam upon the boilers, while, as the ships slowly gathered headway, impatient navigating officers took notes to see who was leading in the rush.

But amid all the hurry and excitement a wonderful, an incredible truth was dawning rapidly upon a martial figure on the bridge of the Brooklyn. The supreme moment had come at last, and Admiral Sampson, by a just irony of fate, had gone to Siboney! Commodore Schley was, clearly, in command.

A moment later and the highly supererogatory signals, 'Clear ship for action' and 'Close up,' were being displayed from the Brooklyn. In the enthusiasm of the moment some of the captains may have read them; they could hardly have affected events, with all the ships doing their best to close up already, but at least they asserted the Commodore's right to the glory for anything which might follow. About 9.35 the Maria Teresa opened fire at long range. Some miles away, near Siboney, the people in the New York heard it. Admiral Sampson looked back, and plainly saw the distant silhouette of the Spanish flagship emerging from the entrance. Admiral Sampson, too, perceived that the great moment had arrived and that he was not there; and as the New York's helm was spun over and a surprised engine-room force ordered to do everything humanly possible to make speed, General Shafter, the innocent cause of the Admiral's absence, was avenged.

The tantalized Admiral and his officers watched the four Spanish armored cruisers emerge one after another from the entrance, turn westward, and vanish down the coast amid the thunders of the artillery, veiled in a mounting cloud of powder-smoke punctuated by the viperish flicker of the gun-flashes.

III

The heroic solution of a sortie had not been adopted by Admiral Cervera upon his own judgment. With the debarkation of Shafter's army he had come to the conclusion that it was already 'absolutely impossible for squadron to escape,' and, considering its naval rôle at an end, had put ashore his crews to assist in the land defense of the city. From the safe distances of Havana and Madrid, however, the idea of simply sitting down and permitting the squadron to fall into our hands by capture had no attractions. Even before the assault on San Juan, the Captain-General of the island was exerting pressure upon Admiral Cervera to attempt an escape — less for any military reason, since once the squadron got out it would be as helpless as before, than because 'if we should lose the squadron without fighting the moral effect would be terrible, both in Spain and abroad.' The Admiral convened a board of officers, took their views, and made a gloomy and remarkable reply:

The absolutely certain result will be the ruin of each and all of the ships and the death of the greater part of their crews... I, who am a man without ambitions, without mad passions... state most emphatically that I shall never be the one to decree the horrible and useless hecatomb which will be the only possible result of the sortie from here by main force, for I should consider myself responsible before God and history for the lives sacrificed on the altar of vanity and not in the true defense of the country.

It was a realism which did not appeal to political superiors who had their own reputations to take care of. The Captain-General argued at length that a sortie, especially at night, might easily succeed; while Madrid rather curtly told the pessimistic Admiral to 'avoid comments.' But Cervera remained obdurate, and continued to speak with embarrassing frankness about 'useless hecatombs.' Finally, on June 28, he was explicitly ordered to watch for an opportunity to go out; and should none offer, he was commanded to go out anyway, when the fall of the city seemed imminent. Admiral Cervera once more bowed his head; and so matters stood when the American land attack was delivered on July 1.

If General Shafter had been dismayed by the results of that experiment, he had spread a far deeper dismay in the minds of his opponents. When the rifle-fire died away that evening, it left a situation, very frequent in war, in which either side might have scored a smashing victory had it only known how badly it had frightened the other. In spite of their terrible barbed wire, the Spaniards were actually in much the worse position. Their ammunition was short. There was no food left in the city save rice, and very little of that; there was no possibility of getting additional supplies, and any reënforcements that might break through would only intensify the famine. The conviction of failure which had oppressed the Spanish commanders from the beginning now deepened into certainty. There was a curious scene that night in Cervera's flagship as he once more convened his captains and laid before them the question of whether the time had arrived when the capture of the city was inevitable. If so, their orders to go out had become mandatory. Solemnly they declared that the time had come, and appended their signatures to what they, like their Admiral, assumed to be the order for their own execution. Late that night Cervera made one last, despairing effort to wriggle out on the plea that a sortie might 'look like flight.' It was disapproved from Havana. Next day the crews were withdrawn from the shore defenses and reëmbarked and the boilers were lit off.

In view of what actually happened, one must feel that Cervera was too pessimistic — or too much impressed with the efficiency of the American Navy. Had he attempted a night sortie, he might well have escaped with most if not all his ships amid the confusion that would almost certainly have resulted, for our knowledge of fleet tactics at the time was most rudimentary. But the channel through which he had to pass was a difficult one even in the daytime; while the American vessels were in the habit of closing in during the night and they kept the entrance illuminated with searchlights. The squadron had steam up by Saturday afternoon, but the Admiral decided to wait for daylight.

Early next morning, Captain Concas of the Teresa went down to the harbor mouth to make a last reconnaissance; he noted the position of the ships and the fact that the Brooklyn, lying farther out than usual, had left a considerable gap on the western side of the arc. He returned to make report, and it was decided that they would slip out westward along the shore toward Cienfuegos.

They had a chance of outpacing our heavy battleships; but the Brooklyn was a fast cruiser, and would be close in their path. Admiral Cervera gallantly resolved to engage and if possible ram her with the Teresa, while the other three were to try to get away under cover of this attack. The final orders were issued; the council broke up; and presently the watchers on the shore heard the rumble of the winches as the anchors were brought up; they heard the devoted crews giving a final cheer for their Admiral as the battle-flags were broken out and the ships took station in line ahead; and they watched the little squadron pass down the bay and disappear behind the point. Only then did they realize that the berths where the vessels had for so long been swinging were empty — there was nothing left but a sheet of placid water.

In a few minutes the flagship had rounded Smith Key and come out into the upper end of the long, narrow entrance channel. Some miles away, framed between the twin bluffs which had for so long protected them, they saw at last the gray hulls of the waiting battleships. The Teresa held her course; her consorts followed steadily in her wake. A few minutes more and the flagship had passed out between the hills into the open sea. Already the smoke was pouring in startled clouds from the funnels of the American vessels; already they were gathering way in their charge upon the emerging squadron. But the Teresa held onward — they could not turn west until they had cleared El Diamante, a hidden shoal lying well offshore. An absolute silence reigned, save for the pounding of the engines and the throbbing of their hearts. Presently the pilot spoke: 'Admiral, the helm may be shifted now.' Cervera gave the order; the wheel was put over and the Teresa's bow swung to the westward. A moment later Captain Concas asked permission to open fire; the Admiral assented, and the clear notes of the bugles rang through the ship.

My bugles [said the captain afterward] were the last echo of those which history tells were sounded in the taking of Granada; it was the signal that the history of four centuries of greatness was ended....

'Poor Spain!' I said to my beloved and noble Admiral, and he answered by an expressive motion, as though to say he had done everything to avoid it, and that his conscience was clear....

The second gun of the deck battery was the first to open fire, and brought us back to this reality, too dreadful to allow us to think of other things. Giving the cruiser all her speed, we poured out a frantic fire.

Pandemonium ensued. One by one the three other cruisers came up to the Diamond Bank in her wake and swung to the westward. Each, with an astounding punctilio, slowed at the turn — the most dangerous point — to drop her pilot, for the pilots were civilians. Then the American gunners began to hit; there was a mêlée of rushing ships and powder-smoke, and a few minutes later pursuers and pursued alike were racing westward under the lofty Cuban coast-line, the sea and the inland valleys reverberating to the thunders of the cannonade. Cervera had got out.

It is clear that Admiral Sampson's naïve plan of action — to rush in and sink the Spaniards in the channel mouth — had failed. Exactly what happened in the next few minutes was obscured at the time by the powder-smoke and has been clouded ever since in the darker fogs of a famous controversy. Admiral Sampson was not present to alter his dispositions; but in the tensity of the moment it apparently did not occur to Commodore Schley to do so. Our joyously converging ships were already in danger from each other's cross-fire; while the Brooklyn, charging up in a northeasterly direction, found herself almost head on to the Teresa, and the closest of all our vessels to the Spanish fleet. The Teresa swung to ram, but then fell off and broke westward with her consorts. The Brooklyn might have turned with them, but it would have brought her still closer alongside. Instead, her helm was suddenly put down hard to port; she swung in a wide circle to starboard away from the enemy and toward the east and south, finally coming around until she was on a parallel course with the Spaniards, but considerably farther out. To Admiral Sampson, a distant spectator, and to later critics, this seemed to be running away from the enemy; it had the disadvantage also of losing time and involving the Brooklyn with our own fleet. It carried her directly across the course of the Texas, now forging up in a smoke-cloud of her own; and it was only through a casual rift in this cloud that the Texas saw the Brooklyn looming ahead — so close that the former went full speed astern on both her engines to avoid a collision. It is impossible to say just how imminent this collision really was, but at any rate the Texas was stopped dead in the water at a moment when speed was of the utmost importance. Another unlucky incident had been added to Commodore Schley's already vulnerable war record.

However, the American fleet eventually got itself more or less disentangled and streaming down the coast, while Commodore Schley, once more remembering that he was in command, hoisted the signal 'Follow the flag,' an order which was already being obeyed to the best of our captains' ability, since the flagship happened to be the nearest to the Spaniards. For a few bad moments it seemed rather doubtful whether we should overtake them. Most of our battleships had been four or five miles to the south or east of the entrance at the beginning of the action, and were being left behind. Even the Brooklyn was well astern of the leading Spanish ship, and the Brooklyn had only half her power available.[1] Behind her the battleship Oregon was forging up (her commander had kept all his boilers lighted against such an emergency); but the Texas was already out of it, and the rest of the squadron was spread out behind, the press boats tearing along in a frenzy of excitement on the wings, while far in the rear Admiral Sampson's New York was laboring to catch up with the fast-vanishing battle.

And in spite of everything Admiral Cervera might conceivably have got away had it not been for one fatal weakness in his own ships. Their decks were of wood. In the whole course of the action no one of the four was vitally injured in hull or machinery, but our first hits set them on fire. The wind of their own motion quickly converted their upper works into so many furnaces, and their devoted gunners found themselves serving their almost useless batteries with the deck-planking burning away under their feet.

The Teresa, receiving the brunt of the American attack as she led the squadron out, must have been on fire a very few minutes

[1] Both the Brooklyn and the New York were built with their engines in line upon the shafts, the forward engines being uncoupled for ordinary cruising speeds and the after ones alone being used. To couple the engines for full-power work took fifteen or twenty minutes. In both flagships the engines were uncoupled at the beginning of the action; at first they did not have enough steam on the boilers for the forward engines and thereafter there was no time to couple them. The curious result was that the only two ships in the American squadron whose speed was theoretically equal to that of the Spaniards were able, when the crisis came, to use only half their power.

after she had started westward. A shell cut an auxiliary steam line; the ship was suddenly filled with live steam, and lost speed. Another wrecked her water mains and it became impossible to fight the fire. Captain Concas was wounded. Some of their own light-caliber ammunition stored on deck began to explode in their faces; the whole center of the ship was a mass of flames and they found they could not reach the magazines to flood them. To avoid further loss of life the Admiral soon ordered her helm put up, and she ran for the shore, 'a towering mass of smoke ascending from her stern' and the whole interior an inferno. She was beached and abandoned about six miles west of the Morro, the Admiral himself swimming ashore in his underclothes and trousers.

A few minutes later, the Oquendo brought up just beyond her. The Oquendo was the fourth ship in the column; as the Teresa had received the fire from our leading vessels, the Oquendo had received the weight of it from those rushing up in pursuit. Her decks and cabins were soon blazing fore and aft; there was fire in the after torpedo room and in the ammunition-handling rooms, where some seamen were struggling valiantly to save the magazines by putting wet bedding over the hatches. One of her own guns burst, demolished the crew and blinded the gunner; the ammunition hoists were shot away, and a shell landed on her fore turret, putting it out of action. Fighting Bob Evans in the Iowa was helping to pound her to pieces. 'She rolled and staggered like a drunken thing,' he remembered, 'and finally seemed to stop her engines,' but presently went ahead again. 'As I looked at her, I could see the shot holes come in her sides and our shells explode inside of her.' Her interior was a furnace; most of the gun crews were dead or wounded and it was useless to continue. As she took the beach, the flames burned away the flag halliards and the ensign came down. A few minutes later, Captain Lazaga died, apparently of heart failure, while they were trying to get the wounded off in the two boats which remained to them.

The two destroyers — uncertain quantities which had caused some trepidation in our fleet — had emerged at about ten o'clock in the wake of the Oquendo. They met an even quicker death. They came out just in time to receive the concentrated fire of the fleet rushing past in pursuit of the cruisers, and it 'simply overwhelmed them.' A large shell was seen to land in the Furor; there was a cloud of smoke and steam, but the frail boat kept on. The converted yacht Gloucester had been posted especially to deal with the destroyers; presently she got a signal to go in and she tore them to pieces with her light guns while the rest of our fleet passed on. The destroyer crews stuck to their batteries gallantly, but they had so little training, or were so much shaken, that they did not land a single hit even though the Gloucester closed to six hundred yards. About four miles west of the Morro, the Plutón was run upon the rocks and blew up; the Furor went out of control and began to steam in circles. Her fire ceased entirely and some one was seen to be waving a white rag on board. The Gloucester sent off a boat to investigate. 'They found a horrible state of affairs.... The vessel was a perfect shambles. As she was on fire and burning rapidly, they took off the living.' Presently there was a series of explosions; the Furor flung up her bows and disappeared. The Gloucester went on. Around the next point she came suddenly on the Teresa and Oquendo still burning upon the beach. The Gloucester boldly stood in, and at great risk to themselves from the exploding magazines, her people assisted in taking off the wounded and rescuing the survivors on the beach from our Cuban allies. Mr. William Randolph Hearst, in the flagship of his press squadron, gallantly aided in the work.

But two of the cruisers were still alive. The Vizcaya, the second ship in the column, had been covered by the Teresa and had taken little injury at the commencement of the action. But her bottom was badly fouled and she could not make speed. The Brooklyn soon overhauled her, and presently the Oregon and the Iowa were within range. They failed to stop her, but they smothered her batteries and set her on fire. It was enough. She could make no effective reply. The guns jammed; often they could not get the breech-blocks to close, the firing mechanism would not work or the ammunition would not go off. In one gun they had eight misfires in a row; in another seven. Captain Eulate was wounded in the head and shoulder and had to withdraw temporarily. The Teresa and Oquendo had long since died behind them; and the Brooklyn was landing repeated hits in their upper works. Fires were breaking out everywhere, and the water mains had been shot away. Yet it was not until nearly noon and they were some fifteen miles west of the Morro that their last gun was put out of action. Captain Eulate made a final effort to ram the Brooklyn, but it was useless. Then a steam-pipe burst. Then something else happened — they thought it was one of the forward boilers going up, but it was probably the explosion of one of their own torpedoes, which broke up the whole bow of the ship. Captain Eulate summoned the inevitable council of war. It was agreed that they had done all they could, and she was run in and grounded upon the rocks near Asseraderos, where a month before General Shafter had climbed the hills upon the stout-hearted mule. As she touched, the fire arose in a great column above her smokestacks; the ammunition began to explode and her side armor was red-hot. Luckily they discovered that they still had one small boat which would hold water in which to ferry the wounded ashore. They believed that they got off all who remained alive. Behind them the chase passed on down the coast. The Colón, the fastest of the four and still uninjured, was still running for her life.

So the Vizcaya, also, died. But not without one triumph. It was a shell from one of her guns which, passing across the Brooklyn's forecastle, decapitated a seaman standing on the deck. Save for one other man who was wounded, this was the sole casualty in the whole American fleet. Some men standing near by made to give him an immediate burial in the sea, but Commodore Schley from the bridge stayed them with a splendid gesture. 'No!' he exclaimed, according to his own account, 'do not throw that body overboard. One who has fallen so gallantly deserves the honors of Christian burial!' In the Spanish squadron there was less chance to be heroic. 'Don't cheer, boys,' cried Captain Philip of the Texas as his ship went by the burning wreck of the Vizcaya, 'the poor devils are dying!' When the Iowa came up, Fighting Bob observed that it was useless to try to overtake the Colón; he stopped his engines and sent off his boats to rescue the Vizcaya's crew alive from the fire and from the insurgents who were probably behind the beach. Captain Eulate was hoisted overside in a chair, 'covered with blood from three wounds, with a blood-stained handkerchief about his bare head.'

As the chair was placed on the quarter-deck, he slowly raised himself to his feet, unbuckled his sword belt, kissed the hilt of his sword, and bowing low gracefully presented it to me as a token of surrender.... I instantly handed it back to Captain Eulate.... As I supported the Captain toward my cabin, he stopped for a moment just as we reached the hatch and drawing himself up to his full height, with his right arm extended above his head, exclaimed, 'Adios, Vizcaya!' Just as the words passed his lips the forward magazine of his late command, as if arranged for the purpose, exploded with magnificent effect.

The Colón by this time was far out of range; the firing died out upon the hot noontime air, and a profound stillness succeeded. In the natural course of events the American squadron had by this time been restored to order. The Brooklyn was still well in the lead. Astern of her was the Oregon, which had been able, because of her commander's foresight in keeping his boilers lit, to maintain a better speed through most of the action than the armored cruisers. Next came the Texas, and, considerably farther astern, the flagship New York, still desperately endeavoring to catch up with the battle, and passing one after another the blazing wrecks in whose destruction she had been unable to participate. The Iowa and the light vessels had stopped to succor the wounded; the Indiana had been ordered back to guard the harbor. On the beach the fires slowly burned out, and the race passed westward.

The Colón had gone inshore of her consorts, concealed by their smoke, and had cleared the action almost untouched. It was past noon, and to her officers it seemed that the pursuers were falling astern and the race nearly won, when she suddenly came to the end of her scanty stock of good fuel and the engine-room force had to turn to the inferior coal making up the rest of her supply. Steam began to go down, and the speed fell. About one o'clock the Oregon tried a ranging shot with her thirteen-inch guns; it fell short, but she tried again and presently a column of water sprang into the air beyond the Colón's bows. She was within range. The Colón's own heavy guns were in Genoa, and even her secondary battery could not be trained far enough aft to bear. Her disheartened commander gave up the fight on the spot. He was already some fifty miles from Santiago and he might at least have kept on until the Americans had begun to hit. But about a quarter-past one the helm was put up and the Colón headed for the shore. The Americans held their fire, and a few minutes later the last of Cervera's squadron ran hard and fast aground, not far from the place where twenty-five years before the filibuster Virginius had been captured by the Spanish Navy. When the American boarding officers arrived some time later, they found 'Commodore Paredes and Captain Moreu in the cabin taking a plate of soup, and the crew quietly standing about.'

The naval battle of Santiago was at an end. But an almost equally famous battle was just beginning. It was perhaps half an hour after the Colón had grounded and after the Brooklyn's captain had gone aboard to receive her surrender that Sampson in the New York finally caught up with his action. He was greeted by a significant signal from Commodore Schley's flagship: 'We have gained a great victory. Details will be communicated.' It apparently took some minutes for the full import of this message to sink into the Admiral's mind, but when it did, the reply was curt: 'Report your casualties.' The burning question of who was entitled to the glory for the battle of Santiago was fairly posed; and while Captain Philip in the near-by Texas was improving the moment with a Divine service of thanksgiving, a curious scene was being enacted between the two commanders.

'It is to be regretted,' as the Commodore afterward wrote, 'that no word of congratulation, so much valued by men and officers on such occasions, issued from the flagship.' After a pause the Commodore tried again with a hopeful 'This is a great day for our country.' The only reply from the outraged flagship was the hoisting of an answering pennant. The Brooklyn's captain, now observed to be coming away from the surrendered Spaniard, was summarily ordered to report aboard the New York instead of to the Commodore. The Commodore recalled that when he himself presently went to make report, the crews of all the ships there, except the New York, 'manned the rail, shouting in tumultuous huzzas that fairly shook the air. It was a tribute of confidence, an expression of approval in the very smoke of battle that cannot be dimmed or diminished by envious disappointments shown afterwards.' But on board the flagship the atmosphere of envious disappointment was already only too manifest; for his egregious subordinate's effort to take the credit on a technicality must have seemed to the Admiral an act of unparalleled impudence. Admiral Sampson received the Commodore with a chill formality, and the tension was only relieved when a sudden report that another Spanish ship had been discovered off Santiago made it possible to despatch the Commodore in pursuit.

The report, of course, turned out to be a mistake. There was a stranger, but she was a sight-seeing Austrian man-of-war; and although the enthusiasm of our victorious ships, combined with the similarity of the Austrian to the Spanish flag, nearly resulted in her destruction, the Commodore perceived in time that he had been sent off on a false alarm. But it had brought him within reach of the cable station; the Commodore saw a golden opportunity, and he hastened to prepare a telegram to Washington, reporting the victory and carrying the delicate implication that he had won it. Even here, however, the Admiral forestalled him; the officer bearing the telegram reached the cable station just behind one of Sampson's officers, and the Commodore's telegram was not sent. In the Admiral's, the Commodore was not even mentioned. Commodore Schley resigned himself to bitter thoughts upon the ingratitude of Admirals, and the foundations of the Sampson-Schley controversy — which was to shake the nation for years to come, which was to embitter both officers through the remainder of their lives and which was to be the means, incidentally, of revealing a good many details concerning our naval efficiency which might otherwise have escaped the light — were adequately laid.

The Commodore greatly endeared himself to the public by including in his official report the generous, if a trifle artful, statement that the victory 'seems big enough for all of us.' But considering the wretched condition of the Spanish ships, the peculiarity of our tactics, and the low percentage of hits at short ranges, a later age may wonder whether there was such a great amount of glory for anybody. Only estimates of the actual loss among the Spaniards are available, but it seems that the total of killed and wounded, out of a complement of 2225 men and officers, came to about 400. A tragic coincidence restores one to a sense of proportion. Early on the morning following the battle, off the Grand Banks of Newfoundland, the French Line passenger steamer La Bourgogne rammed a sailing ship in a fog and went down with a loss of 571 lives. Nearly as many people were drowned in that one peace-time disaster as were killed on both sides in the whole course of the War with Spain. For days after the news came in, it filled our front pages almost to the exclusion of the war.

IV

That Sunday evening had fallen in Washington upon a city exhausted by the heat and the intense anxiety. The nervous little group was still waiting at the White House when at seven o'clock it was thrown into dismay by a dreadful telegram from General Shafter, retailing the first reports of the naval action, but implying that Cervera had escaped. They hung over the wires. Three quarters of an hour later, there was another despatch from the Army; it was more hopeful, but the wording was ambiguous. Still later in the evening, General Shafter remembered to inform his superiors that he had demanded the surrender of the city — on top of the morning's telegram about withdrawing, it left them in a state of considerable mystification, but 'the curtain of gloom was rising.' It was not until one o'clock in the morning that another telegram from Shafter fully confirmed the destruction of Cervera's fleet, and fifteen minutes later that still another came, containing the single triumphant sentence: 'I shall hold my present position.'

As yet there was no word from the Navy, but the curtain had lifted. At two o'clock on the morning of the Fourth of July, Mr. Alger walked homeward 'with the newsboys crying in my ears the joyful tidings of "Full account of the destruction of Spanish fleet!"'

At about noon next day, Admiral Sampson's message (the one which had just beaten the Commodore's) arrived:

The fleet under my command offers the nation as a Fourth of July present the whole of Cervera's fleet. It attempted to escape at 9.30 this morning. At 2 the last ship, the Cristóbal Colón, had run ashore seventy-five miles west of Santiago and hauled down her colors.

It was splendid, it was unbelievable, it was magnificent. And as the nation turned to celebrate its greatest Fourth of July since the moment, thirty-five years before, when the news of Vicksburg and of Gettysburg had arrived simultaneously upon the national holiday, the earnest statesmen perceived that the war, now, really was over. They had only to hurry to collect 'the outlying things,' as Senator Lodge had called them, before Spain should cave in.

CHAPTER XII
THE REWARDS OF VIRTUE

I

THREE days after our glorious annihilation of the decrepit squadron of Spain, Mr. Hay, doing his part as Ambassador at London, was writing home in his jubilation to the War President:

> We have never in all our history had the standing in the world we have now, and this, I am sure, is greatly due to the unfailing dignity, firmness, and wisdom you have shown in every emergency of the past year.

For how was it possible that the world could return any other verdict upon so brilliant an example of our true greatness as a nation? Even the gentle Henry Adams, passing a hot day with the Camerons under the shade trees of 'the fine old house of Surrenden Dering in Kent,' yielded to the intoxication and received the news of the 'destruction of the Spanish Armada, as it might have come to Queen Elizabeth in 1588.' Perhaps the world, enmeshed in the peculiar criminality of the international politics of a generation ago, could indeed do nothing but applaud the new arrival among the thugs. Mr. McKinley, at any rate, appealed with confidence to an even higher tribunal, and in a moving proclamation summoned his people to return thanks to God for the victories which He had so clearly bestowed upon them. And why not? The religious press even suggested quite seriously that Cervera's downfall might be regarded as a direct punishment for Sabbath-breaking — had he not come out just as the American crews were going to Divine service?

Relying upon such august auspices as these, it was perhaps only natural that we should turn with eagerness to gathering up the rewards of virtue. The earth indeed lay before us. General Miles even found time to suggest that we should snatch an opportune moment while waiting for transport fleets to 'take and occupy the Isle of Pines.' It was disapproved; but there was ample loot in other directions fully to occupy our energies. The Chicago

Times-Herald, an Administration paper, observed with a splendid frankness:

Our jubilation over Dewey's unparalleled naval achievement was weighted with apprehension as to our responsibilities and with fear as to possible complications with other powers. The belief was general that we had acquired through the unavoidable exigencies of war something we did not want.

But all this has changed. We find that we want the Philippines.... The commercial and industrial interests of America, learning that the islands lie in the gateway of the vast and undeveloped markets of the Orient, say 'Keep the Philippines.'

We also want Porto Rico.... We want Hawaii now.... We may want the Carolines, the Ladrones, the Pelew, and the Marianna groups. If we do we will take them.... Much as we may deplore the necessity for territorial acquisition, the people now believe that the United States owes it to civilization to accept the responsibilities imposed upon it by the fortunes of war.

One eminent editor was publishing an interview in which he laid the ethical foundations of empire upon a somewhat sounder, but even more comprehensive, plan.

There was not then [at the beginning of the war] the remotest thought among us of taking Cuba for ourselves.... But the sweep of war is like that of the whirlwind — no man can tell where it may reach. We have interfered to give Cuba a better government and we therefore stand morally responsible to the civilized world for the character of its government. The present insurgents may be able to establish one that we can afford to be responsible for; but if not, our responsibility continues.

It was a contingency for which the Teller amendment had failed to provide. Then on July 6, the last feeble opposition in the Senate to the Hawaiian annexation collapsed. Fifteen Democratic Senators went down with their flag flying; there was a scattering of Populists and a lone Republican with them, but a majority was all that was needed, and Hawaii became ours by a vote of 42 to 21.

The nation scarcely noticed in the press of great events. At Manila, Admiral Dewey was still waiting before Cavite, observing with some interest the peculiar manners of a visiting German squadron, but still confident that he could take the city at any moment that he received troops with which to hold it. The first small contingent, indeed, had actually been put ashore, and General Anderson was negotiating with the insurgents (who represented the principal danger against which the city would have to be held) until the rest should arrive. The plans for Porto Rico were already well advanced; the best of the volunteer regiments had been designated for its conquest, and the movement waited only upon the lingering uncertainty as to Shafter's army before Santiago. There were even wider horizons. The Spaniards had at last collected the semblance of a second squadron, and a fortnight earlier Admiral Camara had passed with it into the Mediterranean,[1] bound ostensibly for the Philippines in a gesture of extraordinary futility. Improbable as it was that Camara's ships could survive even the journey to the east, much less Dewey's reception when they got there, the move led to the designation of some of our heavy vessels as an 'Eastern Squadron' to be sent under Commodore Watson upon a raid into Spanish waters in order to bring Camara back again. The destruction of Cervera had now made possible the release of these ships for the adventure, and the pleasant prospect of collecting the Canary and Balearic Islands and perhaps even a mainland port or two now danced before our avid people.

Thursday, July 7, was a tremendous day. The rumors that Spain was about to sue for peace were already very strong, and it must have been with relief that the officials read the despatch arriving that morning, announcing that troops were actually ashore at Cavite. There was another council of war beneath the great maps in the White House, and the rather anxious problem of General Shafter, who had been reported ill and almost incapacitated upon his cot for days, was solved. General Miles was despatched to oversee matters, with the understanding that upon the fall of Santiago he could move on to his great project of conquest in Porto Rico. The same afternoon orders were cabled to Sampson to form Watson's squadron. Just at seven o'clock, after a long day, President McKinley 'by a ceremony of the simplest character' signed the Hawaiian annexation resolution, and the

---

[1] It inspired Mr. Hearst to issue a celebrated order to the European representative of the *Journal*, commanding him to sink blockships in the Suez Canal. Fortunately, this did not prove necessary, and a war between Mr. Hearst and Great Britain was thus averted.

cruiser Philadelphia was ordered to Honolulu to take possession. Later that night, General Miles once more sallied forth to war, in a special train over the Southern Railroad. This time, however, he was unaccompanied by his family.

At about the hour that Mr. McKinley was annexing Hawaii, an extraordinary scene was being enacted in the Cuban hills. Mr. Hobson and his Merrimac crew, exchanged for double the number of Spanish prisoners, passed through the American front lines and down the long and crowded road to the beach and the ships. The entire journey was one magnificent and spontaneous ovation for those heroic men. They had been received at the first moment with a reverential silence on the part of the uncovered troops; but the cheers soon burst forth, and followed the Army ambulance in which they rode all the way down to the beach — and even then echoed and reëchoed from the Cuban hills as the naval crews gave vent to their admiration, while Mr. Hobson, upon the flagship, described for an eager press the true details of the famous exploit.

It was all marvelous beyond words; but the most marvelous fact of all was just beginning to come fully home to the serious-minded gentlemen who conducted the real destinies of the nation. The nation may have been annexing territory; but the Republicans had annexed the war. When on July 8, Congress finally rested from its great labors and went home to prepare for the Congressional elections in the autumn, the Chicago *Inter-Ocean* summed it up upon a note of lofty austerity:

No legislative body ever deserved higher praise for rising to the demands of a great emergency. Party lines were wholly forgotten. Unfortunately that non-partisan attitude could not be maintained. In subsequent votes a good many Democrats fell from grace. But enough rose grandly above petty politics to make the record of this session eminently creditable....

The people will go to the polls November 8 to register their indorsement of the way the affairs of the nation have been managed by the party which they had put in power by their votes of two years before. The political problem is very simple because there is in fact only one issue before the whole country.

It was the truth. Too late, in fact, had the Democrats awakened to the situation into which their enthusiasm for Cuban liberties and the astute statesmanship of their opponents had maneuvered them. Colonel Bryan had developed what he hoped might be a solution for the dilemma — the Democratic Party, he was arguing, had been ready enough to urge a war for bringing freedom to the oppressed, but could take no part in a base 'imperialism' of conquest and annexation. But if the Democrats were naïve enough to suppose that the mere freeing of oppressed peoples was all that the country really wanted, or that anybody could be frightened by so attractive a bogey as imperialism, the Republicans knew better. Besides, just enough Democrats had joined in with the imperialist enthusiasm to weaken seriously Mr. Bryan's argument. The Republicans hardly paused to worry over the main results of the election which Mr. McKinley had once so dreaded, but turned their attention to more particular considerations. From his office in the Senate Mr. Lodge sent off a letter of cheerful prophecy to his patriot friend, serving the nation as lieutenant-colonel of the Rough Riders:

I hear talk all the time about your being run for Governor and Congressman, and at this moment you could have pretty much anything you wanted.... I think it by no means impossible that a seat in Congress could be brought about, and I think if you could be elected in your absence by the time you were to take your seat the war would be over and you would come back into public life in a great popular body with an immense enthusiasm behind you. Perhaps something still better than this will offer, but I know that you think as I do about the House and I think you would find it without much difficulty the road to the Senate.

Happy destiny!

II

In the meantime, however, the Fifth Army Corps was confronting the as yet unconquered city of Santiago. General Shafter had decided that he could maintain his position along San Juan Ridge; on the other hand, the demand for surrender, sent in on the morning of July 3, had been refused the same afternoon. And that evening, while our people were rejoicing over the naval victory, Colonel Escario's column of three or four thousand men from Manzanillo had slipped into the city. The Cubans who had been posted to intercept them had failed in their mission, and the strong lines were now heavily reënforced.

It was a peculiar situation. The destruction of the fleet had removed the only strategic reason for wishing to take the city, and General Shafter recoiled from the thought of throwing his naked infantry against its barbed-wire defenses, to the certain slaughter of a very large number of them, merely to secure an objective which had ceased to be of any military value whatever. On the other hand, it was obviously impossible, because of the moral effect, simply to pack up and leave. The remaining alternative — to wait until starvation had reduced the city — would expose the command to the danger of being cut off by hurricanes or destroyed by disease.

As one studies his solution for this dilemma, one feels that history has been unjust to the corpulent commander of the Fifth Corps. His errors as a tactician have been remembered and held against him. Much less attention has been paid to what his aide justly called 'the remarkable series of negotiations' now undertaken by General Shafter 'to induce General Toral to capitulate.' Save for a little desultory firing on July 10 and 11, there was to be no more actual fighting. But within a fortnight the city of Santiago, and with it the entire eastern half of Santiago Province as well, had fallen. Where another man might have risked a bloody assault (and many of his subordinates actually urged him to this course), General Shafter achieved the result by correspondence. The commander of the Fifth Corps was in reality one of those very rare generals for whom bloodshed is a necessary evil rather than a desired end; unlike Colonel Roosevelt, he regarded it as his business not to achieve personal glory by fighting successful battles, but to secure the larger purposes of warfare (to which battles are never more than an incident) with the greatest economy of life. General Shafter devoted himself to bluffing his opponent into surrender.

It is true that the first object of his higher strategy was not the Spaniard, but the Navy. Since the only effective naval force which Spain possessed had been obliterated, there seemed no reason why we could not now afford at least the risk of a ship or two. Moreover, since the General had accomplished his original mission by expelling Cervera from the harbor for the Navy's benefit, it seemed to him, not unnaturally, that the Navy might be willing to

reciprocate to save the Army from the difficulties in which it had
been placed as a result. On July 4, General Shafter renewed his
request to Admiral Sampson with a disarming frankness: 'Now, if
you will force your way into that harbor the town will surrender
without any further sacrifice of life. My present position has cost
me 1000 men and I do not wish to lose any more.' The Admiral,
however, received this communication with pain. It showed, he
reported, 'a complete misapprehension of the circumstances which
had to be met.' General Shafter, evidently, was still under the impression that fighting ships were supposed to fight. The Admiral
could not possibly entertain so gross a violation of theory.

The General applied direct to Washington in a barrage of telegrams: 'I regard it as necessary that the Navy force an entrance
into the harbor.' 'If the Army is to take the place, I want 15,000
troops speedily and it is not certain that they can be landed, as it
is getting stormy.' 'Sure and speedy way is through the bay.' The
arrival of these telegrams caused a crisis. It appeared that the
Secretary of War was actually as ignorant of the correct principles
as his general. Mr. Alger went direct to the President, and the
Navy had to summon no less an authority than Captain Mahan
himself to defend it from the dangerous heresy. 'I remember,' the
Secretary of the Navy wrote, 'a pretty scrimmage between [Mr.
Alger] and Captain Mahan in the White House when President
McKinley was present.... The Secretary of War was complaining
because we did not take the risk of blowing up our ships by going
over the mines at Santiago.... Mahan at last sailed into him, telling him he didn't know anything about the use or purpose of the
Navy, which rather amused the President, who always liked a
little badinage.' Unfortunately no amount of badinage would
overcome the fact that if the Army attacked, it would be slaugh-
tered. Mr. Alger was insistent; ignorant as he was of the use or
purpose of the Navy, common-sense seemed to demand that the
Army should not be sacrificed until the Navy had at least tried
what might be done. The Navy rejected this view; it would not
even risk its light ships in the channel for the curious reason that
if one of them were sunk there 'the harbor would be effectually
closed to us.' It was an *impasse*. There was nothing for it save
that Mr. McKinley himself, the constitutional commander-in-

chief of both services, should resolve the issue. The War President arose to the occasion; on July 5 supreme authority spoke — in an unusually characteristic decision:

General Shafter and Admiral Sampson should confer at once for cooperation in taking Santiago. After the fullest exchange of views they should determine the time and manner of attack.

Though he did not abandon all hope of extorting some action from the Navy, General Shafter thereafter turned his principal attention to the Spaniards, who proved to be made of less stern a metal. It was never necessary to proceed with Mr. Alger's suggestion that the Army take a couple of transports, armor them with baled hay, and open the channel for the Admiral. But the Army after all had a hardly less ingenious revenge. General Shafter's telegrams were published.

It drew blood immediately, for the public appeared to share the Army's ignorance of the principles of war. There was an angry message from Admiral Sampson:

Published telegrams of General Shafter, Herald of July 6, reflect on Navy.... I have been ready at any time during the past three weeks to silence works, to clear entrance of mines and to enter harbor whenever the Army will do the part which the proper conduct of war assigns to it.

The Admiral deplored 'the very unwise publication' of the telegrams and the 'invidious and false position' in which this had placed the Navy, but it was rather late by that time, and one more of those unhappy controversies which did so much to mar the glory of the Santiago campaign had been brought into the open.

Later on, after the capture of the city, it was possible to examine the harbor defenses. With the exception of four medium caliber guns that had been taken from the fleet, the forts were armed with muzzle-loading cannon, most of them cast in the eighteenth century and one bearing the disconcerting date of 1668. When the terrible mines were at last dredged up, 'the first series of three electrical mines, controlled from Estrella Cove, was found abandoned and but two of the other four... could be exploded.' Farther up there were four more contact mines; the naval officer detailed to the task of removing them thought that an entering vessel might have been sunk there, but even he had to admit that this was 'problematical.'

It is impossible to follow in detail the involved negotiations, conducted beneath the shade of a great ceiba tree standing midway between the lines, in which General Shafter finally convinced his opponent that he had no course save to surrender. Disappointed in the Navy, Shafter at one time was ready to let the Spaniards simply give up the town and march out into the bush (where they would have been comparatively harmless), but the idea was vetoed by a Washington thirsting for unconditional surrender. Even this was finally obtained, with the assistance of a queer, long-range bombardment by the Navy over the hills, and the remarkable promise to General Toral that if he surrendered, his army would be transported entire and free of charge to Spain. This proposal, according to General Shafter, had a curious result.

He asked me if that would embrace his entire command. Up to that time I knew nothing of his territorial command, and I said to him, 'What does your command consist of?' He replied, 'The Fourth Army Corps.' I said, 'Where is it?' He said, 'Eleven thousand five hundred men are here, 7000 are at Guantánamo (which was fifty-five miles from us), 3500 men at San Luis (which was twenty-five miles away) and about 1500 about twenty-five or thirty miles away.' I said, 'Certainly, it takes in everything.' I do not hesitate to say to you that I was simply thunderstruck that of their own free will they should give me 12,000 men that were absolutely beyond my reach. I had no earthly chance of getting them.

But all were ultimately surrendered. On the 11th, before this had been consummated, General Miles with the reenforcements arrived upon the scene. General Miles came filled with the intention of carrying out the plan so ardently desired by the Navy. He proposed to land his troops upon the west side of the entrance and proceed without delay to an assault upon the batteries. Fortunately, he paused long enough to get in touch with Shafter; he learned that the surrender negotiations were already far advanced, and the landing on the west was never made. General Miles, as General Commanding the Army, exercised a certain supervision over the rest of the negotiations, though it was difficult to see that he influenced them greatly. Perhaps not even a superman could have hastened the resourceful procrastination of a Spanish officer trying to evade a fate which he knew to be inevitable. General Toral spun the proceedings out to an exasperating length, and it was not until 5 P.M. on July 16 that the articles of capitulation were finally signed, sealed, and delivered.

It was time. The rains had been getting steadily worse. On the night of the 11th a great storm burst over the trenches.

Streaks of lightning would start ripping across the eastern heavens and rush like great trains of fire along the mountain tops, disappearing in the west. Then would come a stunning crack of thunder, until it seemed as if creation were tumbling into chaos.... The camp was literally swamped. ... That night is said to be known in the history of the Santiago campaign as 'the night it rained.'

The roads were becoming so nearly impassable that the supply problem was again of the most serious nature, while malarial fevers, and omens of the more dreaded disease which was to follow, were already sweeping the command. After the numerous false starts and references to Madrid, the capitulation was, however, achieved. On the morning of Sunday, July 17, just two weeks after the sortie of Admiral Cervera, General Toral saluted the Spanish flag above the city for the last time, hauled it down, and rode out with his staff and escort to make formal surrender of the city and of the army division of Santiago de Cuba. He was met by the American generals, with their staffs and escorts, between the lines, while in the rear the American troops were drawn up along their trenches, 'from which nearly every one had a full view of the ceremony.'

General Shafter rode up to General Toral and presented him with the sword and spurs of the Spanish general Vara del Rey, who was killed at El Caney. The Spanish troops then presented arms.... The American officers and their cavalry troop also presented arms, after which the Spaniards filed to the left and returned to the city.

There the Spanish troops stacked their arms at the arsenal, while the American generals solemnly rode into the city after them, passing through no less than four lines of defense, each 'consisting in an enormous mass of barbed iron-wire, stretched across the entire length of the road. They were not merely single lines of wire, but pieces running perpendicularly, diagonally, horizontally and in every other direction.' The American officers reflected with thankfulness upon the terrible consequences had they been compelled to attempt those lines in an infantry assault unsupported by effective artillery.

When we reached the palace we were met by all the officials, civil governor, archbishop, consuls, etc. At about eleven o'clock we were invited to a lunch and then marched out to the Plaza, where thousands of the populace, Spanish and Cubans, had congregated to witness the ceremony. As the clock in the Cathedral opposite commenced striking the hour of noon the United States flag was hauled to the masthead.... At the same moment twenty-one guns were fired and the band of the 6th Cavalry struck up 'Hail Columbia!' The 9th Infantry, which was drawn up in the Plaza, presented arms to the American colors and the Eastern Province of Santiago... was surrendered to the prowess of American arms.

Thus did Fighting Joe describe that historic occasion. But there was one incident which General Wheeler omitted to record. As the officers upon the roof of the palace were preparing to hoist the Stars and Stripes, Mr. Sylvester Scovel, the correspondent of the New York *World*, observed that the photographers were training their cameras to record the scene. If the victory was due to the prowess of American arms, it was hardly less due to the prowess of the American press; and in a flash Mr. Scovel saw the news beat which the *World* would score if the photographs of the raising of our flag should display the *World's* correspondent prominently in the foreground. He scaled the roof. Unfortunately, the officer in charge penetrated his strategy and ordered him down. He would not go. The officer leaned over the parapet and appealed to General Shafter, standing in all his monumental dignity in the square below. 'Throw him off!' shouted the General, and two troopers were despatched to the roof to do it. Mr. Scovel saw them coming and got down, but, justly incensed at this display of military autocracy, he advanced upon the General and protested 'in a loud voice while the General and his staff were standing before the assembled troops, ready for the formal raising of Old Glory.' 'One word,' according to the General's account, 'led to another,' until Mr. Scovel suddenly launched a blow. Fortunately it missed; but it was only by a hair's breadth that the commanding general of the

CITY AND HARBOR OF SANTIAGO DE CUBA

AMERICAN AND SPANISH OFFICERS SHAKING HANDS AFTER THE
CAPITULATION OF SANTIAGO

Fifth Corps, in the very hour of his triumph, escaped the indignity of being punched upon the nose by a newspaper correspondent. In his wrath the General ordered that Mr. Scovel be held *incomunicado*; and since there was no very obvious place of detention available, an inventive subordinate put the *World* correspondent upon a pedestal (from which the statue had been removed) and two troopers with fixed bayonets kept him there in the blazing sunshine until somebody remembered him and he was transferred to a 'moss-grown calabozo.'

In all these ceremonies, it will be noted, the Navy did not participate. It was not — exactly — an oversight. Admiral Sampson had early informed the General that he expected to be represented in any negotiations for the surrender of the city. With guile the General agreed, promising to let the Admiral know the proper time at which to send in his representative. But, curiously enough, what with the difficulty of communication and the evasiveness of the Spaniards, it never seemed possible to send this warning until, upon the day of the capitulation, the General telegraphed: 'Enemy has surrendered. Will you send some one to represent the Navy in the matter?' When the Admiral's chief of staff arrived post-haste upon the scene, he found that it was all over. The capitulations had been duly signed — by the Army — and when he demanded the right to append his signature, he was informed, in effect, that as the Navy had left the job to the soldiers, the soldiers intended to take all the credit for it.

It was most unfortunate. Within Santiago Harbor there was still one small gunboat and a number of Spanish merchantmen. The Navy immediately claimed them, not only because they fell within the naval province, but in order to collect the prize money on them. General Shafter calmly announced that the Army had taken the place and the ships were his. The Admiral (though a trifle embarrassed by the lack of reference books) appealed to precedent. General Shafter said that he would speak to the Secretary of War about it. 'But that, of course,' as Admiral Sampson reported, 'could have no bearing upon what I considered my duty in the matter.' Consequently, as soon as the Spanish flag had been hauled down, the Admiral 'sent prize crews on board the gunboat Alvarado and to the five merchant steamers in the harbor.' To his pained surprise, he found the Army with fixed bayonets already in possession.

The situation was getting tense. Lieutenant Marble, who had been sent to cut out the Alvarado, resorted to base stratagem. He simply informed the Army officer in charge that it had all been arranged and that the Army was to turn over the gunboat; this they innocently did. By the time they had learned from General Shafter ('he was exceedingly wroth') that there had been no such arrangement, Lieutenant Marble and his prize were already steaming cheerfully down the harbor. A tug was hastily armed and despatched in chase, but the Alvarado outdistanced her and reached Guantánamo, which was naval territory, in safety.

But it had given the alarm. General Shafter (the surrender ceremonies were still scarcely over) cabled instantly to Washington for authorization; on the back of the answering cable he scribbled 'Take possession at once of all the shipping in the harbor and hold it subject to my order,' and sent the blank itself to the commander at the waterfront. Lieutenant Doyle, the naval officer who had been sent to get the merchant ships, found himself powerless in the presence of superior force.

Admiral Sampson addressed to his military colleague a request that these men be removed, and reminded him of the correct precedents in terms of the utmost severity. It had no effect. It had worse than no effect.

Early on the morning of the 18th [the Admiral reported], I received from the senior naval officer in the harbor a paper sent him of which the following is a copy: 'Santiago, July 17, 1898. Lieutenant Doyle can keep his men on the ships for the night, and in the morning one of the tugs will get up steam and transfer him with his officers and men to their respective ships. C. McKibbins, Brigadier General Commanding.'

It was an insult which left the Admiral very nearly speechless with rage, but he had strength enough left for a really excoriating communication:

I will not enter into any expression of surprise at the reception of such a paper.... I am unable to recognize the authority of the Secretary of War over my actions. I have telegraphed to the Secretary of the Navy and await his instructions.

In the event of a difference of opinion between the Departments, the question will, of course, be decided by the President of the United States; until then, my prize crews must remain in charge, and I have so directed.

'It is to the credit of General Shafter,' as Mr. Alger later said, 'that he did not reply to Admiral Sampson's letter in the same spirit in which that communication was written.' For the Admiral had been in error — his prize crews were not in charge; and the Army was. Not long after, the Attorney-General rendered an opinion that the ships were not subject to prize-law, anyway, so that when the Army finally turned them over to the sister service, it was but an empty victory. And even this was to be reft away; for a few weeks later a shortage of transports developed, and the Navy was ordered to give the steamers back again. That unspeakable 'paper' went unavenged.

But already the Army had something far more serious to think about. As early as July 9 there were three cases of yellow fever — or what they thought was yellow fever — at Siboney; and the news and the symptoms spread rapidly through the command. Just before the surrender, the Twenty-Fourth Infantry, a colored regiment supposed on that account to be immune from the terrible disease, was ordered to Siboney to assist the small staff at the base hospital in stemming what had become a deluge. Many were never to return. For with the fall of the city and the relaxation of the tension, malarial and yellow fever swept the Fifth Army Corps like a scythe; and within a few days the command was reduced to an army corps of prostrate invalids.

III

Meanwhile, on the other side of the world the war for Cuban freedom was taking on an increasingly anomalous appearance. On July 1 (at the moment that Shafter's men were preparing for their assault on San Juan Hill) the first Army contingent was being landed upon the soil of the Philippines. On the same day General Anderson, their commander, had an interview with General Aguinaldo, who had already proclaimed himself dictator-president of the Philippine Republic and was the commander of its ragged but quite genuine armies. General Anderson was grieved to note that 'the insurgent chief,' as he called him, 'did not seem pleased with the incoming of our land forces, hoping, as I believe, that he could take the city with his own army, with the coöperation of the American fleet.' Up to this time we had been glad to accept the services of the insurgents; with the arrival of our army, however, there was clearly no further necessity for the forces of the Philippine Republic, and General Anderson decided that he would prepare for the capture of the city by the army entirely on its own account. Unfortunately, he had with him a bare twenty-five hundred men in the first contingent, while General Aguinaldo estimated his own forces at fourteen thousand. The situation was very delicate, and General Anderson neglected to make his intention clear to the patriots. Instead, he entered into a most cordial correspondence with their commander.

But while General Anderson was addressing General Aguinaldo as 'your excellency' and expressing his desire 'to have you and your people coöperate with us in military operations against the Spanish forces,' Consul Williams, from his torrid quarters in the U.S.S. Baltimore, was painting for the edification of the State Department a splendid vision of empire. He spoke of the 'fabulous natural and productive wealth of these islands.' 'Now is the time to start,' he exclaimed. 'Those who come early will reap great rewards and serve patriotic purpose at same time.' There were no bounds to Mr. Williams's acquisitive enthusiasm:

Each American concern will be a commercial center and school for tractable natives conducive to good government on United States lines. Spanish or native language not essential.... Let natives learn English. I hope for an influx this year of 10,000 ambitious Americans and all can live well, become enriched and patriotically assist your representatives in the establishment and maintenance of republican government on these rich islands so extensive in area as to form an insular empire.

Unfortunately, the situation in the early days of July was complicated by a factor far more ominous than the possible aspirations of the 'tractable natives.' Dewey's victory over the Spanish fleet had attracted the usual collection of war-vessels of miscellaneous powers, bent upon sight-seeing and upon the dangerous habit of 'protecting national interests' that was prevalent at the time. The English and French officers had shown themselves both courteous and friendly, but since the 17th of June there had been present a full squadron of German ships, under the command of a Vice-

Admiral who was neither, and of an unnecessary formidability.

The peculiar conduct of Vice-Admiral von Diedrichs has never been quite adequately explained. Feeling between the United States and Germany had been bad for some years, and by this time almost the whole of the American press was convinced that the Germans had designs upon the Philippines. As it happened, the American press was right; but one would have supposed that this very fact would have led the German statesmen to enjoin an even greater caution upon their naval representative on the spot. All the chancelleries that summer were heavily charged with the atmospheres of highway robbery. In March, Germany had extorted the Shantung lease from China and Russia had replied with the acquisition of southern Manchuria, while England was signing up for Wei-hai-wei on the very day that General Anderson came ashore at Cavite. In Berlin our Ambassador was being told that 'the German Government clearly regards the emergency in the East as one from which she must gain something or lose prestige with Europe and even with her own people.' But even German diplomats could hardly have wished to trust the event to the powers for irritation of an Admiral on the other side of the world from them.

Admiral von Diedrichs, however, was extremely irritating. He got in the way of Admiral Dewey's patrols, resented his blockade regulations, annoyed him with searchlights at night, carried on communications with the Spaniards, and behaved in other ways with an exasperating provocativeness. Admiral Dewey bore it with an admirable patience, but by the early days of July it had become so obvious that our wardrooms were whiling away the hot evenings in debates as to whether the Germans were acting under orders or out of plain, bad-mannered stupidity.

Our own press was cheerfully convinced of the nefariousness of the German intentions, and was cartooning the still youthful Kaiser with a ferocity which was to be prophetic. Though our editors did not know it, the German Emperor had actually gone so far as to instruct his Ambassador in Washington that it was 'one of the main tasks of German policy not to allow any opportunity to slip by for the acquisition of maritime footholds in eastern Asia,' and a nebulous proposal for dividing up the islands among the powers, or perhaps even for establishing a German protectorate over them, had been going the rounds of the Foreign Offices. Even so the German statesmen probably did not contemplate a war. They were ready to intervene (like us) in the 'interests of humanity' or to 'protect German rights,' but were scarcely planning an assault upon Dewey. And though the merest hint that Germany proposed to tell us what we should do with our captured islands was enough to fire our jealous publics with rage, the fact remains that we had not yet captured them. Our people overlooked the circumstance that Admiral von Diedrichs had very nearly as much right to the Philippines as Admiral Dewey; our sole conquest embraced a very small territory surrounding the Cavite Navy Yard, and inasmuch as the United States was fighting for freedom and had not yet declared whether it even intended to take the islands or not, the German eagerness to gather up whatever might be left lying about when the 'emergency' was over was perhaps not so entirely criminal as it seemed.

But the situation was already tense enough, when Admiral von Diedrichs suddenly descried one of those 'interests of humanity' which he was present to protect. In the early days of July, General Aguinaldo informed Admiral Dewey that his insurgent troops had taken the shores of Subig Bay, but had been prevented from capturing the Spanish naval post on Grande Island, at the entrance, by the presence of the German man-of-war Irene. The German Admiral had all at once become concerned (precisely as our own officers became concerned when they thought of Aguinaldo's taking Manila) over the possible inhumanity of the insurgent's methods of warfare, and with a happy thought he had despatched the Irene to defend civilization at Subig Bay. As soon as he was informed of this outrageous interference, Admiral Dewey sent the Raleigh and the Concord in her wake; they entered Subig Bay cleared for action, but as the Irene saw them coming around one side of Grande Island, the Irene herself hastily departed around the other. The way having thus been cleared, Grande Island was taken — not, however, by the insurgents, but by the Raleigh and the Concord.

The brief telegram in which Admiral Dewey reported this incident arrived on July 13. There was a wave of passionate resentment. The New York *Times* was splendid in the declaration that 'we... acknowledge no overlord to tell us how far we may profit by the excellence of our gunnery and the valor of our troops.' The Detroit *Tribune* did point out that 'the Monroe Doctrine does not apply to the universe,' and Mr. Godkin's *Evening Post* tried to explain that even if Germany should seize one of the Philippine Islands, it 'would be an act of war against Spain, not against the United States.' But such voices were drowned. The Atlanta *Constitution* exclaimed:

Americans resent any kind of arrogance, but when it is displayed by a despot whose lunatic reign has excited the contempt and indignation of all who believe in human liberty, the feeling goes deeper.... Who knows but the Imperial war-god of Germany may cause to be fired the shot that will be the signal of a conflict the result of which may be indirectly to redeem all Europe from the fraudulent government of kings and emperors.

But it passed away. Even as Dewey's telegram was arriving, Mr. Hay in London was having a reassuring conversation with the German Ambassador, and was writing home to Mr. McKinley that 'you can now make war or make peace without danger of disturbing the equilibrium of the world.' As a matter of fact, the Germans had got no support among the chancelleries for their polite buccaneering expedition, and they were already realizing, perhaps, the extent of the proprietary interest which we were developing for the Philippines. Admiral von Diedrichs was content to be good, and not long thereafter the German squadron was withdrawn. The resentment cooled, and when Germany finally snaffled the Caroline Islands out of the Spanish wreckage, nobody minded. But the fact that the Germans might have pirated the islands was the final and convincing reason for our doing it ourselves. It made it, more than ever, a moral obligation.

At Manila the interest shifted back from the Germans to the insurgents. On July 15, General Anderson ferried his command across the bay from the base at Cavite to an entrenched position near Pasay, about three miles south of the city, his left resting upon the long beach and thus under cover of the naval guns. Before him there stretched a broken country of rice-paddies, swamps, and bamboo thickets, crossed by raised causeways carrying the roads up to the ancient and moss-grown walls of the city.

But intervening between General Anderson and those picturesque battlements there were the lines of General Aguinaldo's insurgents. The task of euchring them out of the scene was now begun.

Two days later, the second Army expedition (thirty-five hundred men under General F. V. Greene) arrived in the bay. It was debarked at Pasay, and it made matters considerably easier. A sharper tone appeared in General Anderson's correspondence with the 'insurgent chief' — 'General Anderson wishes you to inform your people that we are here for their good and that they must supply us with labor and material at the current market prices.' On July 22, Anderson was pointing out to his colleague in arms that 'your fine intellect must perceive... that I cannot recognize your civil authority.' But the fine intellect was strangely obstinate. It replied with a letter upholding by implication the existence and reality of the Philippine Republic and tactlessly requesting that American troops should not be put ashore upon the Republic's territory without written notice, because, 'as no formal agreement yet exists between the two nations, the Philippine people might consider the occupation of its territories by North American troops as a violation of its rights.' The American officials began to wonder whether they had not put too high an estimate upon the intellectual capacities of the Filipinos. Consul Wildman at Hong Kong began to find Aguinaldo 'childish,' and 'far more interested in the kind of cane he will carry or the breastplate he will wear than in the figure he will make in history.'

Admiral Dewey, who a month before had entertained so high an opinion of the Filipinos' capacity for self-government, now considered that Aguinaldo was getting a 'big head.' On July 25, Mr. Wildman addressed the Filipino commander in a fatherly tone:

Do not forget that the United States undertook this war for the sole purpose of relieving the Cubans from the cruelties under which they were suffering and not for the love of conquest or the hope of gain. Whatever the final disposition of the conquered territory may be, you can trust to the United States that justice and honor will control all their dealings with you.

The Consul later testified that he did not regard this ingenious communication as a 'pledge'; unhappily, Aguinaldo was not sufficiently childish to regard it as one either, and it did not help matters. On the 26th, Admiral Dewey cabled home:

Situation is most critical at Manila. The Spanish may surrender at any moment. Merritt's most difficult problem will be how to deal with insurgents under Aguinaldo, who has become aggressive and even threatening towards our Army.

But General Merritt, the commander-in-chief, had arrived the day before with the third Army expedition, and we now had present a force of nearly eleven thousand men. General Merritt immediately put a stop to the correspondence with Aguinaldo, resolving not to renew it until he should be in a position to 'enforce my authority in the event that his pretensions should clash with my designs.' Through their subordinate officers, however, the insurgents were persuaded to leave their trenches in front of our own position. Our troops were moved into them, and on the night of July 31 they came for the first time under the fire of the Spaniards, occupying the trenches opposite. At Manila, as Mr. McKinley later put it in his message to Congress, 'divided victory was not permissible.'

IV

But the sands were already running out; whatever we were still to do had to be done quickly, for it was evident to everybody that peace could not be staved off much longer. On the south coast of Cuba, General Miles, with the volunteer regiments he had brought down as reënforcements, was in a fever of impatience to be off upon his great Porto Rican conquest, while at home the War Department struggled against the lack of transports, the difficulties of geography, and the comparative inaccessibility of General Miles himself, to organize and coördinate his expedition for him. It was all very much complicated by the appalling condition of the Fifth Army Corps. General Miles had preserved his reënforcements from infection by keeping them in the transports; but they were not enough by themselves, and it was apparent that the Fifth Corps was useless for further service.

Since General Miles had been prevented by his impatience from going back to the United States and starting afresh, it became necessary to launch the Porto Rico expedition direct from several home ports, to rendezvous actually upon the hostile territory. General Miles, the War Department, and the local commanders at Tampa, Charleston, and Newport News plunged into a maze of telegraphy, from which they finally emerged on July 18, when General Miles cabled for authority to start immediately with the three thousand volunteers he had available. He proposed to land near Cape Fajardo, the northeast corner of Porto Rico, and there establish a base to which volunteer troops could be sent direct from the United States to join him. There they would be within easy reach of San Juan, the capital of the island and the center of its resistance. On the same day the desired authorization was cabled back, with specific and significant instructions 'that, on your landing on the Island of Porto Rico, you hoist the American flag.' There was not a moment to lose. On the same day — the day after General Shafter's triumphant entry into Santiago — the Spanish Government took its first step, through its Ambassador at Paris, to initiate peace negotiations under the good offices of France.

There were no moments to lose, but moments were lost all the same. The first result of this decision was a 'tedious delay' devoted to negotiations with the Navy as to the character of convoy which it would consent to furnish. Agreement, however, was at last reached even with the Navy, and on the evening of July 21, General Miles left Guantánamo with his three thousand men for Cape Fajardo. The War Department duly despatched the transport fleets from Charleston and Tampa for the same destination, and rested in the cheerful consciousness that it had done its part.

From this it was abruptly wakened on July 26 by newspaper despatches from the Associated Press correspondent, announcing that General Miles had landed at Guánica, on the southwest coast of the island and almost diametrically opposite to the point toward which the defenseless transports from the United States had been directed. Mr. Alger expressed his stupefaction in another barrage of telegrams; he finally learned that General Miles had suddenly changed his whole plan of campaign while in mid-passage. Instead of marching upon San Juan by the short route from Cape Fajardo, the General had decided to sweep triumphantly through the island, beginning at the most distant point (separated from the capital by a difficult mountain range) and spreading his conquering armies throughout its entire area. The General later advanced a number of reasons for this change of plan. One was that, since the press had of course announced the original destination to the world, he would probably find it easier to land somewhere else. He did, in fact, pretty well outgeneral the press — only one of the newspaper boats succeeded in keeping up with him and it was not until three days later that the rest arrived. Whether or not it was necessary to outgeneral the Spaniards, and whether the possible battle he evaded at Cape Fajardo would have been any worse than the battle he would have had to fight to gain the mountain passes on the interior route, are points that were left unanswered by the sudden end of the war. But aside from these military considerations, it is not wholly impossible that another motive weighed with General Miles. In an assault upon San Juan he would have had to accept the Navy's assistance; in a conquest of the interior, the glory would belong exclusively to the Army. 'Marching across the country,' as he explained to Mr. Alger, 'rather than under the guns of the fleet will have in every way a desirable effect on the inhabitants of this country.'

At any rate, no harm was done. The transport fleets were found and diverted. The landing at Guánica was effected practically without opposition on the 25th; the landing at Ponce, made by General Wilson on the 28th, was not only unopposed, but executed to the enthusiastic 'vivas' of the populace. Ponce, a few miles east of Guánica, was the principal town of the southern half of the island, and General Miles had determined to make it his base. The Navy had reconnoitered it the evening before, and first thing on the following morning had sent in a detachment which received the formal surrender of the helpless Governor. When General Wilson arrived later in the day, the American flag was flying from the port office and the city hall. By a peculiar appropriateness the hands which had raised it over both these edifices were those of a midshipman under temporary appointment — Naval Cadet G. C. Lodge, the son of the scholar in politics who had labored so long and so earnestly to make this happy consummation a possibility.

The Puertorriqueños, at any rate, received the event without qualms. As our conquering heroes came ashore, 'the several thousand people who were waiting for General Miles on the wharves and housetops and swamping the small boats in the wake of his gig shouted "vivas" and shrieked and cheered.... Later in the day General Miles and General Wilson received the homage of Ponce from the balcony of the alcalde's palace. Nothing could have been more enthusiastic or more successful than their open air reception.' Even so, General Miles did not hesitate to make the situation clear. That same day he issued a proclamation to 'the inhabitants of Porto Rico,' free from the ambiguities which had so complicated the course of events in the Philippines:

The first effect of this occupation will be the immediate release from your former political relations, and it is hoped a cheerful acceptance of the government of the United States.

It was all the same to the Puertorriqueños. They cheered themselves hoarse.

It was not a moment, not a moment too soon. Eight days before, the Spanish Government, now thoroughly alarmed, had telegraphed its Ambassador in Paris, urging haste in the peace negotiations if they were to save some fragments of their colonies out of the catastrophe. On the 21st, the French Government had authorized M. Cambon, its Ambassador at Washington (to whom Spain had entrusted her affairs), to present the Spanish note asking for peace. The note itself reached Washington on July 22, while General Miles was still at sea, but there was a regrettable delay. M. Cambon discovered that the Spanish diplomatic cipher had been entrusted, not to his office, but to the Austrian Minister; that official unhappily was out of the city and the despatch could not be decoded. Four days were lost in this way; even so, the despatch was delivered to the American Government on the 26th. It was the day after the capture of Guánica, the day before the capture of Ponce, and the day after General Merritt had arrived in Manila to take command. The note sought to learn from the President of the United States the basis upon which 'might be established a political status in Cuba and might be terminated a strife which would continue without reason should both governments agree upon the means of pacifying the island.'

The break had come; the moment had arrived. But, with Miles still organizing his campaign at Ponce, with no definite news at all from the Philippines, the War President confronted the event in an unhurried mood. The heat in Washington was severe, and Mr. McKinley suggested to his cabinet a trip down the Potomac in a lighthouse tender. In the privacy of her cabin 'the letter was then read, and a discussion ensued lasting several days, which proved to be the longest in which the McKinley cabinet ever engaged.' The great difficulty was, of course, the Philippines. A despatch from Anderson had already told them of the formation of Aguinaldo's government. Mr. McKinley could not make up his mind. They first prepared a draft note proposing to relinquish the whole group to Spain, with the exception only of a naval base. But it did not satisfy them. The Secretary of Agriculture wished to keep the entire archipelago in order to evangelize it; the Secretary of the Interior wanted to keep it because 'he saw a great commercial opportunity.' On the other hand, the Secretary of State, Mr. Day, stood out for a naval base only, and he was powerfully supported by the Secretaries of the Navy and the Treasury. The President himself was struck by the uneasy thought that, once the islands were in our possession, 'the people would never be satisfied if they were given back to Spain.' It seemed highly probable. In the end the solution came with a happy and characteristic inspiration of the President's. 'His own decision,' says his biographer, 'was to keep all the islands, at least temporarily, and await developments.' On the 28th there was a reassuring cable from Miles:

Spanish troops are retreating from southern part of Porto Rico.... This is a prosperous and beautiful country. The Army will soon be in mountain region; weather delightful; troops in best of health and spirit; anticipate no insurmountable obstacles in future results.

By the 30th, the statesmen were ready for a final discussion. While they were sitting, Admiral Dewey's despatch announcing that Manila might surrender 'at any moment' arrived, and when the cabinet arose in the early afternoon, the draft of the American reply had been completed. Ambassador Cambon was summoned; he was closeted in a long conference with the President, endeavoring to soften the blow as much as possible. But the summer shadows lengthened over the White House lawn outside, as inexorable as our purpose. At about half-past five on July 30, M. Cambon left the Executive Mansion, taking with him the best that he could secure. It was the day upon which Prince Bismarck died at Friedrichsruh.

We had informed Spain of our terms. They were: The relinquishment of all sovereignty over and title to Cuba and the immediate evacuation of the island (we made no promise as to our own evacuation); the cession by Spain of Porto Rico, of all her other islands in the West Indies, and of one of the Ladrones to be chosen by ourselves, as war indemnity (we stated that as a mark of 'signal generosity' we would 'not now put forth any demand for pecuniary indemnity'); and finally the famous and marvelously ambiguous stipulation that 'on similar grounds the United States is entitled to occupy, and will hold, the city, bay, and harbor of Manila pending the conclusion of a treaty of peace which shall determine the control, disposition, and government of the Philippines.'

It was duly placed upon the cables for transmission to Madrid.

Three days before, Ambassador Hay at London had found time to send off one of his witty little notes, to the colonel of the Rough Riders:

It has been a splendid little war; begun with the highest motives, carried on with magnificent intelligence and spirit, favored by that fortune which loves the brave. It is now to be concluded, I hope, with that fine good nature which is, after all, the distinguishing trait of our American character.

At Madrid they did not think so.

But in the happy clime of Porto Rico there was no doubt about its being a splendid little war. General Miles could scarcely compress his enthusiasm within the bounds of official language. 'At least four fifths of the people hail with great joy the arrival of United States troops.... They are bringing in transportation, beef cattle and other supplies.... Volunteers [the creole troops or guerillas in Spanish service] are surrendering themselves with arms and ammunition.' So far there had been no fighting to speak of, the skies were smiling, the only shortage was a shortage of American flags with which the populace might celebrate its annexation. A

'A SPLENDID LITTLE WAR'
Battery B, 4th U.S. Artillery, shelling Coamo, Porto Rico, August 8, 1898. Note the impenetrable clouds of smoke

supply of one hundred flags was forwarded to meet the difficulty.

Troops were also arriving. General Brooke with three volunteer regiments was diverted to land near Guayama, in the eastern end of the island. He found the difficulties of debarkation hardly less serious than they had proved to be at Santiago, but he managed to get ashore, and on August 5, after a skirmish in which he suffered a loss of four men 'slightly wounded,' he occupied the town. The next day General Miles at Ponce was ready to initiate his conquest; a regiment of infantry and two batteries of field artillery were ordered to advance around the western edge of the island, while the commander prepared to launch his main advance over the splendid macadamized road which, crossing the central mountain range, divided the island and led down into the capital city of San Juan.

So we had already turned into the month of August. Having devoted the three months from the latter part of April to the latter part of July to the preliminaries — the destruction of the Spanish fleet and the raising, training, and despatch of our volunteer armies — it was only now that we were entering upon the main business of the war. But the peace negotiations were already far advanced. The Spanish Ministry had spent a tortured week with Mr. McKinley's terms. From the beginning they had, of course, entertained no hope of victory. With the end of Cervera's fleet the question had become mainly one of internal politics — as to whether the Government had done enough to show that it had done all that was possible and could thus evade the domestic consequences of defeat. All that now remained was to bring the war to as speedy an end as possible and to save, by diplomacy, as much out of the wreckage of the Spanish colonial empire as they could. Cuba was clearly gone; they might as well throw Porto Rico and Guam after it in the hope of staying a ravening fate. But for the Philippines they had hopes — Mr. McKinley, after all, was so very vague. In the first days of August, M. Cambon was loyally wrestling with the War President; he secured the doubtful assurance that 'up to the present nothing against Spain has been settled *a priori* in my own mind,' but it was clear that the President, true to the habit which Sr. Dupuy de Lôme had noticed so long before, was holding the door through which he might take possession of the Philippines firmly open behind him. On August 7, the Madrid Government brought itself to face the facts and despatched a reply in which they accepted the stated conditions. Upon the same day Admiral Dewey and General Merritt were sending in a joint note to the Spanish commander at Manila, informing him that active operations against the city would begin in forty-eight hours.

The Spanish note of August 7 accepted our terms, but with one reservation. It pointed out, with an embarrassing truth, that 'the ground on which the United States believe themselves entitled to occupy the bay, the harbor, and the city of Manila cannot be that of conquest,' since Manila had not been conquered. As for the remainder of the archipelago, the whole of it was still 'in the power and under the sovereignty of Spain.' Therefore, while acceding to the third condition, the Spanish Government stipulated that it would regard our occupation of the islands as a 'guaranty' only, and that Spain would not renounce her sovereignty. She would leave it to the negotiators 'to agree as to such reforms which the condition of these possessions and the level of culture of their natives may render desirable.' The Spanish Government still clung to our own original theory of the war as one to improve the condition of oppressed peoples.

The note, transmitted through Paris and M. Cambon, was not in the hands of the President until the afternoon of August 9. In the meantime there had been no news from the Far East. But in Porto Rico everything was going swimmingly. On the 8th, General Miles had cabled that he needed no more troops sent to him, and his four columns — one under Brooke at Guayama, one under Wilson headed north on the military road from Ponce, one under Henry sent out to cross the mountains farther to the west, and the last under Schwan despatched around the western edge of the island — were moving out. In a beautiful and exotic country, under a smiling climate, amid a friendly populace, with almost no opposition and with, at last, a happy absence of newspaper correspondents (of the hundred or more in Cuba less than a score had reached Porto Rico), the National Guardsmen tasted their first experience of war. Another skirmish at Guayama cost General Brooke only five more slightly wounded, while in an elegant operation, which cut off part of the Spanish rearguard on the San Juan

road, only seven of General Wilson's men got hurt, 'none fatally.'
The western command was also to engage in one or two skirmishes,
but nowhere did the fighting promise to be of a lethal character.

Indeed, the War Department's only worry was to meet the sudden torrent of communications now pouring in from every part of
the country, urging that this, that, or the other volunteer command be despatched instantly to the front. As the peace negotiations rendered it increasingly improbable that there would be any
more fighting, these requests came down in an avalanche upon the
devoted head of Mr. Alger; Senators, Governors, eminent politicians, and leading citizens entreated, begged, recommended, or
even peremptorily demanded that the local heroes be given their
opportunity upon the field of battle. Every form of pressure appears to have been exerted:

'Minnesota boys at Chickamauga impatient to go to front. Can you
not befriend them and place them where they may face the foe? Their
sires fought and fell at Gettysburg.' 'Please send 5th Missouri to Porto
Rico. My son Ralph lieutenant Company F. That regiment anxious
to join expedition.' 'I am much disappointed that Colonel Cook's
regiment is not provided for, in view of your statement to me that his
promotion cannot be expected unless he goes to the front, and Arkansas
is anxious for a brigadier.'

Occasionally there was even greater frankness: 'Confidentially,
may I suggest that state and national politics are being complicated here, seemingly by whims of Regular Army officers who appear to be gratifying personal ends. Seventh California been repeatedly promised, and each time new excuses intervene.' And
there were many more. Upon the scene of action General Miles
was no less confident than the politicians of the triumphant result
of his campaign. There was only one alarming moment, when the
General was assailed by a sudden fear of treachery. It was not,
however, the Spaniards whom he suspected. It was the Navy. On
August 10 there was a nervous cable, 'personal and confidential'
to the Secretary of War:

I am fully convinced that Sampson sent orders to the commander of
this fleet, soon as Army leaves south coast, to take his fleet, go round to
San Juan, and demand the surrender of the capital, or bombard the city
and not to waste ammunition on any of the batteries. First: To bom-

bard a city containing innocent women and children would be a violation of the first order of the President. Second: It is an interference with the work given the Army by the President. I ask that any such action be suspended.... The control of all military affairs on the land of this island can be safely left to the Army.

But if this bloodthirsty and nefarious plan for depriving the Army of its glory was ever actually entertained by the sister service, there was to be no time in which it could be carried out. Whatever honor there was in the conquest of Porto Rico was to remain with the Army alone.

V

But already it began to seem dubious whether there was to be any honor for anybody. A war conducted in the full view of an army of newspaper correspondents, trained to the censorious appraisal of politicians and public affairs, could hardly be fought without criticism; while the editors who had mobilized their talents for the direction of operations could scarcely be expected to endorse the manner in which the military men had carried them out. And in our War with Spain there was only too much ground for attack. Even amid the patriotic harmonies of the early days there had been subdued rumblings, a presage of the storm. With the approach of peace and the relaxation of the patriotic pressure the storm broke; our proud and unbridled press turned upon the heroes whom it had just been manufacturing with a righteous violence, and already the reputations were swaying before the blast that was ultimately (and one is bound to feel somewhat unjustly) to uproot and scatter all but the toughest of them.

The delays, the inefficiencies, the want of material, and the prevalence of politics in our mobilization period had not passed unnoticed. The opposition press had commented with severity upon the gross political favoritism which appointed incompetents to command. In June there had been a bad moment when Mr. Poultney Bigelow had suddenly unburdened his soul concerning conditions at Tampa; Mr. Richard Harding Davis, still in a patriotic mood, had rebutted the attack. 'This,' he had observed, 'is no time to print news of such a nature.' But dreadful stories were already going the rounds about privation in the Southern concentration camps, about lack of uniforms, equipment, and even of food. They were exaggerated, however, and it seems improbable that there was any great amount of actual suffering. By really heroic efforts the War Department did manage to bring a fair degree of order out of the general chaos; it was impossible to conjure up tropical uniforms or modern rifles and ammunition out of nothing, but rations were ultimately provided on an ample scale and the militia regiments were slowly instructed how to draw and prepare them.

Then Shafter departed upon active service, taking the correspondents with him; the interest shifted, and, besides, it was 'no time to print news of such a nature.' At Camp Thomas, Chickamauga, at Camp Alger, across the Potomac from Washington, and at the various camps in Florida, the militia regiments were left more or less to their own devices. The newspapers scarcely noticed a new situation which now rapidly began to develop. In the National Guard regiments discipline was extremely lax. The elected officers had little control over their men, and knew nothing about how to take care of them. The consequences were inevitable — typhoid and dysentery.

From the beginning of July typhoid and dysentery began to appear at all the camps. At Chickamauga there were heavy rains. The camp had been located in an open forest with the intention of protecting it against the southern sun; the result was that the place would not dry out between one rain and the next. The soil was non-absorbent; the whole camp was soon pretty well flooded and sanitation became impossible. The hospitals began to fill; while the troops, finding themselves getting no nearer to the front, sank into a mood of inertia, disgust with the military life, and black depression. In the meanwhile the same diseases had appeared in Florida, and the Fifth Army Corps seems to have carried the germs with them to Santiago. During the three weeks of exposure and exertion which led up to the capture of the city, with scanty and monotonous food, unsuited to the climate and often bad, the health of the command had been surprisingly good. But the first signs of yellow fever had already developed in the last week of the 'siege,' and when the emotional strain of actual service passed with the fall of the city, the entire command was prostrated with a dreadful suddenness.

From the beginning yellow fever had been the one great dread alike of the politicians and the military commanders. Now it seemed to have struck. The first attempts to keep its presence secret were of course quite futile; and the news spread terror through the Fifth Corps. It spread an even greater terror through the officials at Washington, who were not only responsible for the well-being of the troops, but who were to find themselves at once under the severest kind of pressure to prevent the awful infection from being brought back to the United States. On July 14, Mr. Alger had cabled that 'the troops must all be put into camps as comfortable as they can be made and remain, I suppose, until the fever has had its run.' It was not a pleasant prospect for the Fifth Army Corps.

Only on July 22 they got their first fresh meat since their departure from Tampa five weeks before. Next day the inspector-general of the cavalry division was reporting the heavy sick list:

A more varied diet is urgently needed; beans and rice, even, owing to limited transportation have not been regularly issued, and since leaving transports the command has been living on hard tack, bacon, sugar and coffee.... The surgeons report about 90 per cent [of the sick] as malarial fevers, the rest ordinary camp diseases — no serious cases but the men uniformly appear weak, enervated, tired — need as near absolute rest as possible, and change to a cooling and nourishing diet.

The food came in, but conditions only grew worse. Yellow fever was actually not very prevalent — there was great uncertainty in diagnosis — but the malarial fevers rapidly got to the point at which a third of the entire corps was disabled at the same time, and, before they were finally relieved in August, from sixty to ninety per cent must have been on their backs at one time or another. The death list, though not heavy, continued to grow. One of the ablest of the surgeons later said that there was a difference of opinion as to the real cause and nature of the catastrophe. 'Mine is that yellow fever and malarial fever were never widespread and that most of the sickness... was the result of improper diet, over-eating and intemperance in a tropical climate.' However that may have been, the mentally depressing effect of malaria and dysentery are well known. The whole camp sank into a 'wretched condition'; it entertained the darkest forebodings and became nervously sorry for itself. By July 27 the total sick list stood at 4122, of which 3193 were set down as fever cases; there were 822 new cases that day and only 542 returned to duty. Two men died. The next day Mr. Alger cabled his decision that the command would be moved north to Montauk Point, Long Island, but only 'as soon as the fever cases subside.'

In the midst of this disaster the commanding general, in spite of his three hundred pounds, acted with a firmness and common-sense which did not characterize either his superiors, his subordinates, or the newspaper correspondents. He pointed out that, as most of the fever cases were mild, the situation was not yet serious, even though it threatened to be. He accepted it as his duty to remain until a relief could be sent to guard the Spanish prisoners of war; at the same time he urged that the troops be got home as soon as possible. He endeavored to isolate all the yellow fever cases at the hospital at Siboney, and on medical advice he tried the expedient of shifting the troops into new camp-sites from time to time to escape infection. It soon had to be abandoned; the men were already so enfeebled that the effort of moving merely ran up the sick report. The attempt was made to start the convalescents homeward. The first result was angry protest from the ports to which the transports were directed, who feared infection, but much worse was to follow. Through somebody's blunder the first of these ships was sent off without an adequate supply of fresh water, while with the great shortage of medical personnel and supplies against which they were struggling, the vessels could not be given a full hospital staff and equipment. They were supposed to carry only convalescents; but tropical fevers were not well understood by anybody at the time. Fever continued to rage on board, a number of the patients died on the voyage North, and when the transports finally arrived they were in a deplorable condition.

It needed only the imaginative efforts of the sensational press to convert these ships into atrocities of incompetence. The Army officials were denounced as 'criminals' and the term 'hospital ship' was readily converted into 'horror ship.' On top of this, the dislike which the correspondents in Cuba had formed for General Shafter was now breaking forth. Mr. Richard Harding Davis had abandoned his patriotic scruples and was sending home despatches denouncing an expedition, 'prepared in ignorance and conducted in a series of blunders,' in a manner calculated to give the greatest aid and comfort to the enemy. Others were ably seconding him; but Mr. Davis, who had been a war correspondent in the Greco-Turkish War, spoke with the authority of an expert. On their own account the newspapers were beginning to wonder whether war was quite all that it was cracked up to be. Mr. Pulitzer's biographer has a frank passage:

By this time the cost of conducting the fleet of tugs and voluminous cables had wiped out the *World's* profits. Dealers failed to cut their orders between battles and the paper was swamped with returns. Mr. Pulitzer lost interest in war and turned to urging an early peace.... The troops suffered severely in the tropic summer and Mr. Pulitzer... urged their prompt recall. 'Make your demand to send the soldiers home stronger,' he wrote W. H. Merrill [his editorial director]. 'The cry for investigation is secondary. The instant, urgent necessity is to break up the pest camps and disband the volunteers. There is not the slightest reason nor the slightest necessity for this immense army. The Navy has force enough to take care of remote contingencies.'

Mr. Pulitzer had suffered from very bad luck. He had hired Stephen Crane as a war correspondent, but the sole despatch of value which resulted was one which incautiously told the truth about the conduct of the Seventy-First New York at San Juan. It 'imperiled the paper.' It was immediately seized upon by Mr. Hearst as a slander upon the heroism of New York's sons. Mr. Pulitzer tried to escape by starting a fund for a war memorial to the Seventy-First and the New York men in the Rough Riders, to be erected upon the battlefield; even that was unfortunate, for Mr. Roosevelt, hearing of it, announced that no Rough Rider could sleep in the same grave with the cowardly dead of the Seventy-First, and the *World* ultimately had to return the money. Then there was Mr. Scovel's dramatic, but most damaging, interruption of the surrender ceremonies. The war, says Mr. Pulitzer's biographer, 'was far from satisfying the owner of the *World*. He never wanted another.'

Even Mr. Hearst was having his troubles. Shortly after the conquest of the city, three of his correspondents had conceived the brilliant idea of placarding its streets with posters headed 'Remember the Maine!' This attempt to perpetuate war passions in a place filled with a surly Cuban population surrounding the large force of disarmed Spanish prisoners (and with our own troops in no condition to suppress disorder) seemed to General Shafter so outrageous as to deserve 'death.' The punishment which he did mete out was possibly even more severe; he ejected the journalists from the island, thus at one blow depriving Mr. Hearst of all representation at the scene of action. Mr. Alger seems to have been alarmed at this temerity and cabled a series of nervous protests: 'The New York *Journal* people are in great trouble.' 'The *Journal* has been doing good work.' 'The New York *Journal* is in terrible distress.' But the General remained obdurate.

It is no wonder that our press turned to denunciation of the officials and measures which it had devoted the preceding three months to patriotically extolling. The real conditions in the volunteer camps were now discovered; the typhoid epidemic was bad enough in fact, but the newspapers exaggerated it with terrible effect. In his animosity toward General Shafter, Mr. Davis made a noble effort to bring forth General Miles as the true hero of the war and the Porto Rico campaign as a model of military efficiency; but the public would not take Porto Rico seriously, and criticisms and recriminations for the Santiago expedition filled the front pages. The Army, of course, received the brunt of the attack, and the Navy, which was loudly praised in order to produce an even blacker contrast, might have come out of it very well. But the controversy between the partisans of Admiral Sampson and of Commodore Schley as to which was entitled to the glory of Cervera's destruction was already developing, to sully even the great naval victory. The clamor, arising in a steady crescendo, would have been enough to wreck any peace negotiations with a nation less thoroughly convinced of defeat than the Spanish; while the gentlemen at Washington, already realizing the effect which this unanticipated assault might have upon the fall elections, seem to have been reduced to a state of serious alarm.

Peace negotiations or not, it was clear that something would have to be done about the Fifth Corps. A camp was prepared for them at Montauk Point — then an isolated and almost uninhabited area suitable for quarantine — but still Washington dared not order them home. In the meanwhile the newspapers, carried back to Santiago, informed the troops of how badly they were being treated, and the morale sank even lower. The dread of yellow fever was so unreasoning that naval commanders flatly disobeyed orders in their anxiety to keep Army personnel off their ships, sometimes even repelling authorized boarders by force of arms.

It was to end in one of the famous incidents of the war. On the 1st of August, Mr. Alger had at last screwed his courage to the point of authorizing the despatch of 'some of Wheeler's dismounted cavalry' to Montauk, provided that 'great care' was taken to include no one 'infected with fever.' On that day there were 4239 on sick report, 689 new fever cases and only 679 returned to duty; 15 men died of various diseases, one of them being 'malarial fever and despondency.' Since nearly every one seemed to be more or less infected with malaria, the Secretary's cautious authorization was not of much use. On August 2, General Shafter cabled urgently:

> I am told that at any time an epidemic of yellow fever is liable to occur. I advise that the troops be moved as rapidly as possible whilst the sickness is of a mild type.

The response, after 'full consideration with the Surgeon General' (and also with the President), was that it was 'deemed best' to move the command up into the mountains behind Santiago, where it was believed that yellow fever could not exist. A railroad led up into the hills from the city. When the yellow fever had disappeared, the command would be brought North.

The decision was received in Santiago with consternation. Washington had failed to grasp the psychological situation now ruling there. Moreover, the railroad was temporarily out of commission, and had so little rolling stock that it would have taken a month in any event to move the command by that means. To march the troops into the hills had become an impossibility. 'We are all aghast!' one officer noted in his diary. 'The idea, the absurd idea, of marching far up into the mountains has given us the horrors, and lack of confidence in our Washington administrators.' By this time they were really close to a state of panic, convinced that the Washington politicians were about to sacrifice them to yellow fever out of deference to the exaggerated fears of the seaboard constituencies. General Shafter summoned a council of his divisional and brigade commanders.

It was evidently decided to make the representations as strong as possible, in the hope of blasting the Washington authorities into action. On the afternoon of August 3, Mr. Alger received from General Shafter a long cable:

This move [to the hills] is practically impossible.... In my opinion there is but one course to take, and that is to immediately transport the Fifth Corps and the detached regiments that came with it to the United States. If it is not done, I believe the death rate will be appalling. I am sustained in this view by every medical officer present. I called together today the general officers and the senior medical officers and telegraph you their views.... This movement should begin tomorrow and be completed before the 15th.... Only course left open for the preservation of this army. There can be no danger to the people at home.

According to Mr. Alger, the gravity of the situation which this portrayed came to him as a complete surprise. He was, at any rate, shocked into immediate action; the same evening orders were sent off to move home to Montauk all troops not required for duty, and promising transports as 'rapidly as possible.' In the small hours these orders were reiterated: 'You will begin the movement at once, using the ships you have to their limit.' Mr. Alger felt, perhaps with reason, that he had met an emergency with promptness and courage.

But next day he was to receive a disagreeable shock. One of the officers who had attended General Shafter's council the afternoon before had been Mr. Roosevelt — now promoted to the command of his brigade. Mr. Roosevelt, perhaps because he was a politician himself, was especially alarmed at the danger of being sacrificed by the politicians. He seems to have felt, moreover, that this was a crisis calling for extra-military action, and he reverted once more to those political arts with which he was more familiar. General Shafter's telegram was, of course, a confidential official document. Mr. Roosevelt, however, prepared another and stronger statement of the case in the form of a letter to General Shafter, while the other commanders, fired by this example, drew up still a third document couched in language even better calculated to frighten Mr. Alger. There is some discrepancy in the accounts of what followed. According to General W. C. Brown, at the time a captain in the cavalry division, Mr. Roosevelt took him aside after the council of war had broken up and explained what had taken place:

The War Department authorities, he said, might pigeon-hole the official views of the division and brigade commanders, but if he could get a statement of the situation into the newspapers he was confident that such pressure would be brought on the Administration that they would be obliged to bring us North. He realized fully the gravity of the step being taken, but laughingly added that he did not fear any danger of being court-martialed for it.

Mr. Roosevelt gave his own letter to the correspondent of the Associated Press; the general officers' letter, entrusted to Colonel Wood, found its way to the same destination. The result was that Mr. Alger, to his shocked surprise, read them both in the newspapers next day — some hours after the orders which Mr. Roosevelt was endeavoring to extort from him had already been issued. Through the genius of Colonel Roosevelt the world, including the Spanish Government, was informed at the most delicate moment in the peace negotiation that the only really effective military force we possessed was prostrate. Above the signatures of its own general officers they read the declaration that:

This army must be at once taken out of the island of Cuba.... The army is disabled by malarial fever to such an extent that its efficiency is destroyed and it is in a condition to be practically entirely destroyed by the epidemic of yellow fever sure to come in the near future.... This army must be moved at once or it will perish.... Persons responsible for preventing such a move will be responsible for the unnecessary loss of many thousands of lives.

'This alarming and sensational paper [the 'Round Robin'] was ... published in every important newspaper throughout the United States on the morning of August 4. It struck the White House with the force of a thunderbolt. The President saw it for the first time in the newspapers and was justly indignant.' General Shafter was at once queried as to why he had permitted it to be made public in a manner that amounted to a dangerous military insubordination. General Shafter replied that it 'was given out, as I have since learned, before it reached me.... It was not until some time after that I learned their letter had been given to the press. It was a foolish, improper thing to do, and I regret very much that it occurred.'

Some years later, Mr. Roosevelt rather airily explained that the whole thing had been instigated by General Shafter and his officers; that they had included him in the council of war because they wanted him to use his political influence and because he was not a regular officer whose career would be damaged by doing so; and that General Shafter had himself been responsible for the publication. 'Both the letter and the Round Robin were written at General Shafter's wish,' Mr. Roosevelt declared, 'and both were published by General Shafter.' This, of course, amounted to charging General Shafter with disingenuousness if not actual falsification in an official report to his superiors. But by that time General Shafter was dead.

At all events, Mr. Roosevelt, whatever his part in the proceedings, was not court-martialed. Indeed, the results were most happy. Spain, fortunately, was through and the 'alarming and sensational paper' had no effect upon the diplomatic negotiations. Moreover, since the orders to recall the command had been issued only a few hours before the publication of the letters, the nation naturally assumed that the recall was the result of the publication, and that the resort to the newspapers had been a necessary expedient. Once more, as so often happened throughout his career, Mr. Roosevelt was either remarkably lucky or remarkably astute. He had neatly secured the credit for saving the Fifth Corps from extinction; he emerged as the shining hero of the episode and Mr. Alger, poor man, as the villain.

Three days later, the first transports were on their way (containing, incidentally, the Rough Riders); the effect upon the Fifth Army Corps was immediate; the sick lists dropped, and within a week General Shafter was reporting that while the yellow fever menace was grave for troops debilitated by malaria, it would be negligible for new and healthy regiments. In all, the troops in Cuba lost 514 men by disease — about double the number killed in action — in addition to 257 others who died after the command reached Montauk Point.

VI

The Spanish note of August 7, accepting our conditions, had been placed in Mr. McKinley's hands on the 9th — the day after the Fifth Corps had been started North. Though the conditions were accepted, the impolite reservation concerning our right of conquest in the Philippines presented an obvious loophole. Consequently, Mr. Day drew up a protocol repeating the exact language of our original terms, no more and no less, and submitted it on August 10 for signature. On the 11th, M. Cambon secured authorization from the Spanish Government to sign this definitive armistice in its name; and on Friday, August 12, at half-past four in the afternoon, M. Cambon and Mr. Day together, in the presence of Mr. McKinley, signed the instrument which ended the hostilities between the United States and Spain. Mr. McKinley immediately issued a proclamation, halting our armies and establishing the armistice, and it was cabled to all our forces in every theater of war. Three months and twenty-two days had elapsed since the moment when Mr. McKinley had unleashed Admiral Sampson's fleet from its moorings at Key West and had thus initiated 'armed intervention' in Cuba.

The proclamation was quickly telegraphed to Cuba, Porto Rico, and the various naval commanders on minor operations in West Indian waters. In Porto Rico it arrived dramatically on the morning of the 13th, just in time to stay the hands of General Wilson's gunners as they were on the point of opening fire upon Coamo. But there was one theater of operations which was beyond direct telegraphic reach. Half-past four on Friday afternoon in Washington is half-past five on Saturday morning at Manila. At the moment that Mr. Day's hand was tracing our signature upon the armistice, the American forces in the Philippines were advancing to the most singular of all the singular operations in our War with Spain.

Unknown to the statesmen in Washington, history, throughout the first week of August, was being made very rapidly in the Philippines. The wisdom of eliminating the insurgents had by this time become apparent to almost every one. Even Washington was now fully awake to 'the exceedingly embarrassing situation which confronts General Merritt through the officiousness of the insurgent chieftain, Aguinaldo. According to all accounts this young man's success has completely turned his head.' But General Aguinaldo was obstinately refusing to be eliminated. On August 1 he had armed himself with a solemn and formal declaration of the independence of the Philippine Republic, signed at Bacoor by his subordinate commanders, and had then turned to the difficult problem of circumventing the strategy of his liberators. His first effort was a remarkable letter to Consul Williams. He acknowledged in the most glowing terms the benefits, 'especially for me and my leaders, and, in general, for all my compatriots,' which Mr. Williams had assured him would result from a union of the Islands to the United States.

Ah! that picture, so happy and so finished, is capable of fascinating not only the dreamy imagination of the impressionable Oriental, but also the cold and calculating thoughts of the sons of the North.... You say all this and yet more will result from annexing ourselves to your people, and I also believe the same, since you are my friend and the friend of the Filipinos and have said it. But why should we say it? Will my people believe it?

General Aguinaldo concluded that his people would not. It was regrettable, but they were already entertaining the most 'unworthy suspicions' as to our motives, strange though that might appear. General Aguinaldo did not share these suspicions; but he intimated that they would render annexation quite impracticable.

I have full confidence in the generosity and philanthropy which shine in characters of gold in the history of the privileged people of the United States, and for that reason, invoking the friendship which you profess for me and the love which you have for my people, I pray you earnestly... that you entreat the Government at Washington to recognize the revolutionary government of the Filipinos.

It is improbable that Mr. Williams, judging from his own literary efforts, appreciated the finished irony in that communication; but he could appreciate at any rate that General Aguinaldo was going to prove a hard case. Needless to say, the Consul did not recommend the recognition of the Filipino Republic. Then, on August 6, General Aguinaldo tried another move. He published his declaration of independence; he published, also, an appeal to the powers for recognition. It was, of course, quite hopeless. But it was courageous, and it made it evident that the military problem was going to be very 'embarrassing' indeed.

Since July 31, when our troops had taken over the Filipino trenches, there had been intermittent firing between the American and Spanish lines, more or less for the look of the thing. For our relations with the Spaniards had long since ceased to be of a belligerent character. Admiral Dewey had not allowed the long weeks through which he had awaited the arrival of the Army to pass in idleness; he had in fact been improving them by a curious and decidedly friendly series of negotiations with the Spanish commanders within the city. Begun through the British Consul, they were continued after that official's sudden death through the Belgian Consul, M. Edouard André. The difficulty was not over the city; it was over the insurgents. Very early the Spaniards had intimated their willingness to surrender, but Admiral Dewey 'could not entertain the proposition because I had no force with which to occupy the city and I would not for a moment consider the possibility of turning it over to the undisciplined insurgents.' Now, however, the Army had assembled its eleven thousand men upon the scene and this latter necessity was obviated. While General Merritt in his dealings with the insurgents was busily 'mixing diplomacy with force,' as he put it, Admiral Dewey again addressed himself to the Spaniards. The results were most happy.

General Jaudenes, now in command at Manila, of course exerted the usual expedients of Spanish diplomacy for the embellishment of the record, and it seems probable that Admiral Dewey's and General Merritt's ultimatum of August 7 was issued to meet the desires of the hostile commander. It did not, at any rate, interrupt the negotiations. In the end, according to Admiral Dewey, there was no 'definite promise,' but 'General Jaudenes agreed that, although he would not surrender except in consequence of an attack upon the city, yet, unless the city were bombarded, the Manila batteries would not open upon our ships.'

Moreover, once the attack was begun, he would, if willing to surrender, hoist a white flag over a certain point in the walled city.... It was also understood that before this white flag was shown the Olympia should fly the international code signal 'DWHB' meaning 'Surrender,' and a sketch of the signal flags to be hoisted was given by M. André to General Jaudenes.

In accordance with these remarkable arrangements, the American commanders drew up their plan of attack. The Navy was to execute a bloodless bombardment in the general direction of the city. The Army was to advance upon the trenches opposite to them, but the orders were very explicit:

> If a white flag is displayed... the troops will advance in good order and quietly.... It is intended that these results shall be accomplished without loss of life; and while the firing continues from the enemy with their heavy guns, or if there is an important fire from their entrenched lines, the troops will not attempt an advance.

Our reason for this elaborate stage-management seems obvious. It would keep the insurgents out of the city; which would be impossible if there were to be a peaceful surrender and formal entry. General Aguinaldo appears to have appreciated quite well what was going on. When the final orders were being drawn up on the afternoon of August 12, he sent a staff officer to request our plan of attack. This request on the part of the allies whose coöperation we had invited was ignored. The General telegraphed angry protests; they were ignored likewise. Thus, at the moment when the American public was debating whether we could honorably 'give the islands back to Spain,' Spain was actually holding them for us against the native population; and, most curious of all, the Spaniards had entered into an effective though unofficial alliance with us to assist in the suppression of the patriots while we were concluding that our duty to these same patriots prevented us from leaving them under 'Spanish misrule.' It was very strange, very strange indeed, particularly as it had all come about through only the noblest of motives.

So it resulted that at the hour when the peace protocol was being signed in Washington, the American ships and troops were preparing, in the early morning mists on the other side of the world, to take Manila — from the insurgents. It was some hours later — about nine o'clock in the morning at Manila and about eight o'clock of the previous evening at Washington — that the fleet actually opened fire and the American troops went forward.

Unhappily, despite the perfection of the arrangements the execution proved to be faulty. In the accounts of the various commanders there is a noticeable lack of detail as to precisely what happened. A violent tropical rainstorm swept over them just as the advance started, and in the wet, the confusion, the difficulties of the rice paddies and bamboo thickets, it was hard to keep in touch. The first line of entrenchments was found to be vacant, in accordance with the schedule, but through the peals of thunder they soon heard an ominous sound — the roll of musketry fire. The American commanders knew that the action was to be bloodless, but it had been impossible to explain this to the forces of General Aguinaldo, or even to drive it home to our own enthusiastic militiamen. On the left the advance was up the wide beach; there were no insurgents in the immediate vicinity and matters could be more or less controlled. But on the right the way led up a single narrow road amid the rice paddies, where the troops soon got broken up and where 'many large bands of insurgents pushed forward on the flanks... sometimes crowding in with our troops in such a way that they had to be elbowed aside as they marched along.' When our own advance skirmishers came in sight of the enemy breastworks, 'they knelt and began to fire. Why they were firing was by no means clear, for we could see no Spaniards in the trenches and no shots were coming from that direction. A messenger was hurried off to put a stop to the fusillade.' But there was, of course, no way in which the insurgent fire could be stopped. At the village of Singalong, the right column came under an answering fire from the Spaniards; the troops soon found themselves briskly engaged, and as they were too ignorant to take cover behind the houses and walls they began to suffer casualties.

Meanwhile the rain passed over and the column on the beach went forward; but there were continued bursts of rifle-fire, no one knew very well what was going on, and it was nearly noon when the leading files came out into the open space beneath the enormous and hoary walls of the city. The white flag was duly flying and the battlements were crowned with Spanish infantry in full readiness to surrender, but the whole situation was very much confused. The foreground was filled with an indiscriminate assortment of retreating Spaniards, advancing Americans and insurgents; the hostile armies were doing their best not to hurt each other, but the patriot riflemen made it very difficult. By the time General Greene got up, the situation was exceedingly mixed, indeed, with

THE ADVANCE ON MANILA, AUGUST 13, 1898

U.S. Signal Corps troops laying the telegraph-line that was carried forward with
the leading troops and carrying flags to indicate to Dewey's ships
the position of the American line

WILLIAM, YOU'RE TOO LATE.

A CONTEMPORARY CARTOON .

troops of all varieties appearing suddenly around the corners from unexpected directions. At last somebody shouted from the walls to go around by the Puerta Real where somebody else would surrender the city, but before General Greene reached the gate, a 'carriage and pair with two men in livery came dashing out and a note was handed to the General.' It turned out to be from an American officer, Colonel Whittier, who, with the Second Oregon Infantry, had already got inside and appeared to be negotiating the surrender. It implored General Greene to stop the shooting. This was difficult. General Greene dashed in through the magnificent and picturesque old gateway to find the surrender proceedings for himself.

He ultimately discovered them going forward in the Captain-General's office. It must have been a peculiar scene. Colonel Whittier, Lieutenant Brumby of the Navy (representing Admiral Dewey), and the Spanish generals and admiral were earnestly drawing up the terms of capitulation, while some one said that General Merritt was already on his way ashore from the despatch boat whence he had been witnessing the action. General Greene, however, had no time for the admiration of this historic event. It looked all right, so he hurried back again to his troops outside the walls, and sending off detachments to stop the insurgent advance and prevent their firing any further upon the Spaniards, he set off for the northern side of the city, to secure it against the patriots who were coming up from that direction.

While the Army was fully occupied in these varied excitements, Lieutenant Brumby of the Navy calmly went to the citadel of Fort Santiago, hauled down the Spanish colors and hoisted the Stars and Stripes in their place. Manila appeared to be ours, and as the afternoon wore away, things seemed to get more or less straightened out. Our strategy had succeeded; the Americans were definitely on the inside and the Filipinos for the most part on the outside. That was the main point. But it had been a fairly close call, and the Spaniards themselves had been obliged to help us. As General Anderson reported:

On the north side of the Pasig River the Spaniards still held their own and kept out the insurgents from that direction, but on the south side the conditions were critical. The insurgents were excited and hostile.... It is even probable that some of the street firing upon our troops came from the Filipinos who had established themselves in Paco. About seven o'clock I received a message from the general commanding to get the insurgents out of the city if I could possibly do so. The best I could do at the time was to segregate the insurgent detachments by interposing our troops and placing artillery to command their positions.

Next day, however, General Aguinaldo was induced to send commissioners to discuss the matter. The Filipino leader was clear-headed enough to see that he had been beaten; he withdrew his command to try other tactics and the war was, for the time being, averted.

Altogether it had been an exciting day. When the figures were added up, it was found that we had lost in the operation five men killed and thirty-five wounded; it brought the total loss throughout our campaign against the Spaniards in the Philippines to eighteen killed and 109 wounded. But we really had, at last, captured Manila. The formal articles of capitulation were dated August 14 — two days after the War with Spain had come to its official conclusion. But it was not until August 16 that information of this fact arrived. Once more Admiral Dewey had cause to congratulate himself that he had cut the cable.

CHAPTER XIII
PEACE AND THE SENATE

I

THE war was over. It had all come true — all, with a suddenness, a brilliance, and a completeness beyond every possible expectation. We had shown the world. We had arrived. We had acquired a foreign policy almost as fatuous as the most elegant examples of monarchical Europe. We had seized a colonial empire in a manner entitling us to recognition by the very best diplomacies. Mr. Richard Harding Davis was reporting our imperial glories in a prose style that sounded almost like Kipling, while we, too, now boasted a flag upon which the sun never set — or practically never. Even the English were speaking to us just as if we had been equals.

It was miraculous. Our illustrated magazines were now decorated with views of the tropic beaches, the romantic palms, and the hoary citadels of our own 'possessions.' We had our own 'natives,' almost as picturesque and quaint as the Africans or Asiatics of other empires. In square miles our new domain might be a trifle small, but in geographical extent it left — as we pinned the little paper flags into the maps upon the farther shores of the Pacific — nothing whatever to be desired. Hawaii was ours; Porto Rico was ours; Guam, tiny but with a Polynesian glamour, was ours; the Philippines — well, the Philippines were practically ours, and even if we should decide to give them away again, it would be in an imperial gesture. And Cuba? Cuba was ours temporarily; under a pledge, of course, but there were those moral obligations, and nobody could as yet be sure of just what the future might bring.

In regard to Cuba, these triumphant weeks of August were witnessing a really remarkable reversal of opinion. Strangely enough, our first actual contacts with those heroic patriot armies whose cause we had espoused had left a most unfavorable impression. The failure of García's insurgents to prevent the entrance of Colonel Escario's relieving column into Santiago had been severely commented upon. We, too, began to discover that the insurgents, after all, composed only one element of the Cuban population. We, too, began to entertain serious doubts as to the Cubans' capacity for self-government. We perceived that it was necessary to go slowly. We faced the possibility that our military effort might be of long duration; and at all events, we saw clearly that we should have to assume for the present full and undivided responsibility for the government of Cuba.

At the fall of Santiago, General Shafter, though he had invited General García to take part in the ceremonies, had made it plain that the administration of the city would be continued in the hands of the Spanish officials and that the insurgents would have no part in it. Considering how often our writers and statesmen had insisted that the Cuban Republic was the real and effective government of the island, one can forgive General García for being both hurt and angry. There was an acrimonious correspondence; but García was of less heroic mould than General Aguinaldo, and the Cuban patriot ultimately faded from the scene. It was understood that he had gone to join Máximo Gómez, still exercising supreme command somewhere in the interior.

At about the same time an American Army officer in the west end of the island was making some curious discoveries:

It frequently came to my ears, through the fact that it was supposed I understood no Spanish, that the Cubans had no love for the Americans; that they expected after the present war was ended a conflict between themselves and the United States, and further they expressed a readiness to participate in such conflict when it did come.... As a whole I believe there is a feeling against us in all parts of the island.

General S. B. M. Young, one of Shafter's divisional commanders, was quoted in the terse conclusion that 'the insurgents are a lot of degenerates, absolutely devoid of honor or gratitude. They are no more capable of self-government than the savages of Africa.' And even among the editors who found this verdict too harsh, there was a growing doubt as to whether our duty would permit us to leave the Cubans to govern themselves.

But if this attitude toward our late allies may seem strange, the attitude toward our late enemies will seem even stranger. Stimulated by a natural impulse to emphasize the prowess of the foe whom we had defeated, a wave of sentimental enthusiasm for the Spaniards was actually sweeping the nation. The Spaniards — the cruel, blood-thirsty, contemptible Spaniards — were rapidly becoming national heroes. When Admiral Cervera was taken to Portsmouth, New Hampshire, to visit the prison camp where the men of his late command were held, he received 'a cordial reception from... the people of the city of Portsmouth, as well as those in the adjacent country, who flocked to see him during his visit'; and he attained, indeed, so enormous a popularity that a movement was actually set on foot to buy him a house in Florida as a testimonial from a grateful people.

In Santiago after the surrender, the American and Spanish troops fraternized in a spirit of mutual admiration for each other and mutual contempt for the Cubans. According to a Spanish officer, the Americans positively lionized the men of the Twenty-Ninth Battalion, who had held El Caney against such enormous odds. And finally, there is the celebrated letter addressed to the 'soldiers of the American Army' in which a Spanish private of infantry bade farewell, on behalf of himself and his comrades, to their conquerors:

You fought us as men, face to face, and with great courage, as before stated — a quality we had not met with during the three years we have carried on this war against a people without a religion, without morals, without conscience, and of doubtful origin, who could not confront the enemy, but shot their noble victims from ambush and then immediately fled.... With this high sentiment of appreciation, from us all, there remains but to express our farewell, and with the greatest sincerity we wish you all happiness and health in this land, which will no longer belong to our dear Spain, but will be yours. You have conquered it by force and watered it with your blood, as your conscience called for under the demands of civilization and humanity; but the descendants of the Congos and Guineas, mingled with the blood of unscrupulous Spaniards and of traitors and adventurers — these people are not able to exercise or enjoy their liberty.

It was no doubt read by our troops with a sympathy as lively as its own sentiments appear to have been heartfelt. It enjoyed, at all events, a wide circulation in the United States, for it echoed a suspicion which with many had been deepening into a certainty.

Indeed, our knowledge of Cuban conditions was progressing rapidly, and newspaper correspondents in Santiago were making still more remarkable discoveries:

The better class in Cuba favors the annexation of the island to the United States and a majority of the masses are ready and anxious to work and accept the shelter and protection afforded by an American protectorate; but they are influenced by a certain class of rabid orators and breeders of sedition and rebellion against anything smacking of law and order. This inflammatory class demands and urges the recognition of Cuba for Cubans.

Such is the educative value of war that after three brief months of it we were drifting into a point of view indistinguishable from that which in the mouths of the Spanish authorities had excited our derisive and contemptuous scorn. Of course, there was still the Teller amendment. But was even that obstacle altogether insuperable? American writers were not wanting to argue that, since it was merely a declaration by Congress, it could be withdrawn by another act of that body. And no less respected a voice than that of Mr. Joseph H. Choate was heard pointing out to the American Bar Association that 'the Government must not be held too rigidly to purposes and expectations declared before the commencement of the war and in utter ignorance of its possible results.... In war events change the situation very rapidly.' In this war they had changed the situation very rapidly indeed; and in Cuba, as in the Philippines, we seemed to be getting our enemies and our allies curiously mixed.

But for the time being everything was uncertain and nothing could be done. The captured garrison of Santiago was shipped home at our expense; General Wood became military governor of the city, and ten regiments of yellow fever 'immunes' (made up of recruits from the Southern States, many of whom as it turned out were not immune) were hastily got together and sent off to relieve the National Guardsmen in the island. In the meanwhile two commissions were appointed to arrange for the general evacuation respectively of Porto Rico and Cuba. In Porto Rico this was accomplished without trouble, but in Cuba the Spaniards made difficulties; the matter dragged along, and for the remainder of the year the island was permitted to relapse into 'a state of chaos.'

Mr. Atkins emerged from his temporary eclipse to urge upon the President, the Secretary of War, and the State Department the imperative need for immediately occupying the whole of the island and re-starting the wheels of its economic life. Cuba by this time really was in a critical condition; the destruction of industry and agriculture was now fairly complete, and with the insurgents adopting a most threatening attitude toward our meager forces and the whole situation in a state of greatest uncertainty, any sort of revival was out of the question. We had started out, of course, upon an intervention to relieve the miseries of Cuba; but now it was months before we really got around to the matter. There were so many other things to occupy our attention.

The most immediate was a sudden development at home of the utmost danger. The Republicans had annexed the war; unfortunately, it meant that they had annexed the warriors as well, and already by the middle of August 'a terrific storm of newspaper criticism pertaining to the conduct of Army affairs prevails in all parts of the United States.' For the party in power it was an unexpected peril, an assault from the rear that threatened to convert the whole brilliant episode, at the very moment of its success, into a disaster. The confident tone of a few weeks before vanished abruptly from the cogitations of the politicians as they faced the November elections. The Fifth Army Corps had landed at Montauk ragged and emaciated, and the death list continued to mount. The most vivid of the 'yellow journals' were Democratic; deprived of the Spaniards as a source of atrocities, they turned with only a greater avidity upon the Republican Administration, and they now described conditions at Montauk in terms of such dreadful exaggeration that a wave of horror and outrage filled the country. Except, perhaps, in the first days, the camp at Montauk was actually well organized and provided for, while our citizens deluged it with comforts and delicacies of every kind in a sentimental outburst over the supposedly suffering soldiers. Even so, the journalistic imagination, fresh from its training in Cuba, produced such frightful pictures that one parent, writing to protest against the 'cruel and horrible treatment inflicted on our own soldiers,' declared that he would not be surprised 'if the feeling should lead to a revolution of some kind.'

Even worse than Montauk were the Southern training camps, to which the press by this time had turned its full attention. Toward the end of July, the editors had begun to awake to the dangerous prevalence of typhoid at Chickamauga, at Camp Alger (unlucky association of names!) near Washington, and in the Florida camps. Toward the end of August, conditions were really becoming grave, and imagination was not needed to convert these camps into a shocking major scandal. On August 19, an Army inspector at Chickamauga was officially reporting that 'every precaution is being taken. But it is too late. The mischief has been done. This park as a camping place is incurably infected. Every breeze carries a stench.... The cases of typhoid fever have reached five hundred and the whole situation presages a general epidemic.'

Another called the place a 'pest-hole.' The public horror reacted, of course, upon the men, while the public's picture of conditions was in turn exaggerated by the resultant collapse of morale. With the coming of peace the volunteer regiments relapsed into their traditionally democratic methods and began to take votes upon the question of whether or not they wished to be demobilized. It produced an almost mutinous spirit and the authorities begged the War President to come and review the troops at Chickamauga in order to still the disaffection. The Inspector-General reported that the men had become 'morbid,' and that when the first regiments were sent home the others 'became more discontented than ever and began to importune their people at home and elsewhere, by private letters and by letters written to the press, to get their regiments mustered out also.' The results, in the press, need hardly be stated.

Against the memories which the Spanish War scandals have left behind them, the actual loss may not seem great. It must be remembered, however, that the typhoid and malarial fevers did not really begin to take hold until the end of the war, and that a far more serious catastrophe was probably averted (or concealed) through the early mustering out of the volunteers. As it was, in the period up to September 30, 425 men died at Chickamauga, 246 in the camp at Jacksonville, 107 at Camp Alger, and 139 in the camps near San Francisco from which the Philippine expeditions were despatched. Up to the end of 1898, the total of deaths in the American Army at all camps and in all theaters of war, was 5462 men and officers. Of these only 379 were killed in action or died of wounds. (The total battle casualties, including wounded, was 1983.) Compared to that figure, the loss through disease during the brief period in which the troops were under arms is sufficiently appalling. Yet it could have been much worse, considering the enormous handicaps under which the Army was obliged to work. The authorities pointed out, in fact, that it had been; for the percentage loss from disease was low compared to that of the opening months of the Civil War.[1]

Our fiercely sentimental public was not, however, in a mood for mere statistics; while the mass of statements, counter-statements, apologies, and controversies in which the responsible officials sought to exculpate themselves only supplied fuel for the flames. There were controversies between the Army and the Navy, between General Miles and General Shafter, between General Shafter and almost everybody, between the line commanders and the heads of the commissary and medical departments. And slowly the many blasts of criticism drew together and focussed upon the devoted head of Mr. Alger, the convenient and obvious target. The Administration itself shook beneath its responsibility for Mr. Alger; while the shrill voice of Colonel Roosevelt, now in the full limelight and in convenient reach of the reporters at Montauk, was heard high above the storm, damning the War Department and its head in the happy confidence that his own official career was associated with the Navy.

A Republican paper in Detroit (in Mr. Alger's state) could be severe against Mr. Roosevelt, especially as the shadow of the elections began to grow upon the horizon:

It remained for this mercurial and care-free firebrand to introduce into the public discussion of the war question in all its phases those excesses of partisanship which disgrace our political campaigns. He applied the torch of passion to the tinder of political partisanship, and the lamentable result is that yellow papers all over the country are assailing

---

[1] The maximum strength, reached in August, 1898, was 272,618. The total number who served up to September 30 was computed at 274,717, and the deaths from all causes up to that time at 1.059 % of that figure.

the authorities with a virulence and madness that are seldom equaled in the heat of political contests.

The political danger had, indeed, become so great that the War Department actually vetoed Mr. Roosevelt's plan for a triumphal parade of the Rough Riders (with Mr. Roosevelt, of course, magnificent at their head) up Fifth Avenue. But the nation was with the critics; it was set down to base intrigue by the scabrous officialism at Washington, and the tentative suggestion began to appear that Mr. Roosevelt should be nominated for Governor of New York.

All of this sudden and dreadful turn of affairs did, however lead to one of the most honorable of the War President's decisions Mr. McKinley himself escaped direct attack, but the assault upon him for retaining Mr. Alger in the cabinet was becoming bitter. The temptation must have been strong to throw the inoffensive Secretary to the wolves; but Mr. McKinley loyally resisted it. Instead, he adopted a more ingenious and more praiseworthy solution. Toward the end of September, on Mr. Alger's formal request, a commission of distinguished citizens was appointed to investigate and report on the conduct of the War Department. It addressed itself to the task of taking the most exhaustive testimony upon every phase of the entire episode. So thorough, in fact, was its search for the truth that it soon became evident that the commission would be unable to bring in its report until long after the November elections had passed.

Against this dark background of Army maladministration, the Navy — Mr. Roosevelt's Navy — shone with an added luster. It was not denied its triumphal procession. When Admiral Sampson's fleet appeared off Sandy Hook on the morning of August 20, it was 'met by a fleet of steamers, yachts and tugs loaded almost to the gunwales' with a citizenry giving expression to its joy 'in deafening huzzas and applause.' At the Narrows, in the upper bay, and in the Hudson River the men-of-war, as they passed northward in a splendid procession, were received with shrieking steam whistles, the ringing of bells, fluttering flags, and the cheers of a populace which lined every wharf end and filled every window.

Reaching Riverside Drive, the hillsides from the water to their tops were packed with enthusiastic people, women and children being clad in raiment of every variety of summer colors, which gave to the slopes the appearance of having been padded with flowers. The effect from the ships as they swung past was entrancingly beautiful in the bright sunshine of that beautiful summer day.

But a cloud, even for the Navy, was to fall upon the happy brilliance of that gorgeous homecoming. At Tompkinsville orders were awaiting the fleet whereby President McKinley promoted Admiral Sampson by eight numbers on the Navy list, and Commodore Schley, alas, by only six. Both officers were thus made permanent Rear Admirals, but whereas the conqueror of Cervera had outranked Sampson before the war, their positions were now permanently reversed; Admiral Schley ranked just behind the man who had been absent from the line on the day of battle. It was an injustice that rankled.

The nation for the most part took the side of Admiral Schley. Arriving at Washington a few days later, that officer was received, as he himself recorded it, 'by an almost countless multitude of his fellow countrymen, whose enthusiastic applause constitutes a delightful memory. After he was seated in his carriage and had reached Pennsylvania Avenue, a corps of bicyclists numbering over a hundred formed an escort on each flank of the vehicle as it was driven to the Shoreham Hotel.' But naval opinion ungenerously refused to endorse the popular verdict. As a result the newspapers assailed the Navy's bureaucratic inability to give honor where it was due; Sampson was freely described as a junior promoted through influence over the head of a better man, and as one who had then sought to attach to himself the glory which by accident had fallen after all to the other. Even Captain Mahan, with his immense prestige, was unsuccessful when he sought to recall the public to a better appreciation of the principles of naval warfare. The issue was seized upon by the opposition as another stick with which to beat the Administration; and in the bitterness which followed each side, of course, raked up every possible error or mistake committed by the other's hero. A display of the most discreditable vanities and jealousies was spread at large upon the record; ultimately in this matter, too, there was a court of inquiry, but it ended indeterminately enough to settle nothing, and such was the ferocity of the two officers' partisans that the controversy

was to divide America for a decade. Admiral Sampson died not
long afterward, his life probably shortened by the vilification to
which he had been subjected; Admiral Schley survived to have his
final years embittered by the failure of the court of inquiry to
sustain him.

In the meanwhile it did the Navy no good. Indeed, of all the
splendid reputations so finely flowering in our patriotic press during the opening days of the war only three were to survive the
wintry hurricanes of censure which followed. One was Theodore
Roosevelt's; one was that achieved by Mr. Richmond Pearson
Hobson, who had the good luck to be of junior rank; and the third
was that of Admiral Dewey, who had been out of reach of both
Washington and the newspaper correspondents. But upon the
last two Fate was to take an even more subtle revenge. With the
disappearance of all the other heroes, the praise and adulation
showered upon them arose to those heights of sentimental hysteria
which our press and people alone seem capable of attaining, and
the later reaction was to be correspondingly severe. When Admiral
Dewey at last got home, it was to encounter a wave of unbridled
enthusiasm too great for him, or perhaps for any man, to withstand; he collapsed under it, and his fame evaporated almost
immediately in a cruel ridicule. Mr. Hobson's was literally
smothered in the embraces of his countrywomen. The ladies
started a fashion of kissing him at his every public appearance;
and Mr. Hobson survived to be known as 'the most kissed man in
America' — though ultimately, as a member of Congress and an
ardent prohibitionist, he managed more or less to live it down.
And Mr. Roosevelt? For him a more extraordinary and inscru-
table destiny was reserved. Whether or not it will prove, in the
long perspectives of history, to have been a better one is a question
as yet unanswered.

II

On the 24th of August, the Navy's 'strategy board,' which had
sat at Washington throughout the war, was finally adjourned, and
on the same day the mustering out of the volunteer regiments
commenced. The war was over. The peace was yet to be begun.
When on August 26, Mr. McKinley announced the appointment

of the commission to negotiate peace there still remained the serious and delicate question of the future of the Philippines. However ready Mr. McKinley had been to undertake commitments in those distant seas, he had been very careful that none of the commitments should be final. The artful wording of the protocol provision had left every course open to us and had obligated us to none. The newspapers and leading men of the country were already plunged into a widespread debate in which every possibility and every combination of possibilities was discussed and advocated. Though the Republicans were naturally inclining toward the annexation side, and the Democrats were maneuvering more and more toward anti-imperialism, there were no clearly drawn partisan lines. Senator Hoar of Massachusetts, the venerable and respected colleague of Senator Lodge, was telling his countrymen that annexation of the Philippines would be a catastrophe endangering the whole spirit of Americanism. Staunch Democratic papers were urging the complete annexation of the entire group. The debate was in general conducted upon the highest plane. It was conducted, likewise, in a profound ignorance of the real situation in the islands and of the true character and aspirations of the Filipino people.

The fact that we still held nothing in the Philippines beyond the outskirts of Manila, and that to 'retain' the islands we would first have to conquer them from an organized and determined patriot government which had already declared its independence, was not fully understood. Indeed, even in the Far East the situation was muddied by the usual difficulty of discerning the real state of opinion amid a backward populace. General Merritt was reporting that the Filipinos were 'superior as a people' to what 'is generally represented'; that they had a force of ten thousand armed men surrounding the city and directed by leaders 'of education and ability,' and that they were 'resentful' and desirous 'of hostilities against American troops.' But at Hong Kong, Consul Wildman had discovered a group of wealthy Filipino families who were imploring him to cable Mark Hanna 'not to desert them and aid to obtain annexation of the Philippines to America.' In the Philippines, as in Cuba, there was undoubtedly the familiar division between the politico-military leaders who would benefit personally by independence and the wealthier native class whose interests were first in the maintenance of order. But when in September, Aguinaldo began organizing his native government, all classes joined with him in the effort.

In the meanwhile Mr. McKinley had already instructed Merritt and Dewey that there was to be no joint occupation of Manila by the insurgents, and our officers were endeavoring to secure the peaceable withdrawal of the patriots from their positions in the suburbs amid an atmosphere of growing tension. But our newspapers disregarded the danger, and dismissed the insurgents as semi-barbarous warriors of course incapable of making any effective resistance to American troops. Congress — perhaps it was fortunate — was not in session. And the cautious statesman in the White House continued, as he had decided, 'to await developments.'

His announcement of the peace commission, however, was not calculated to alarm the imperialists. Remembering the ancient difficulty of inducing the Senate to ratify peace treaties, the President established something of a precedent by appointing to the commission the chairman of the Senate Foreign Relations Committee, its next ranking Republican member, and its principal Democratic member. Mr. Day, the Secretary of State, was a natural appointee for the head of the delegation. These selections seemed to be more or less *ex officio*. The fifth and final choice, however, could be read as an indication of the President's intentions. It fell upon Mr. Whitelaw Reid, the editor of the New York *Tribune*. The *Tribune* was not only (in national affairs) the 'official' party organ; it had already given indication of its expansionist leanings, while its editor felt himself committed, by a signed article he had just published, to the retention of the islands. Mr. Reid's was a forceful and influential personality which could be expected to have considerable effect upon the decisions of the commission. And it also happened that Senator Davis, the chairman of the Foreign Relations Committee, was already identified as an imperialist if not a jingo; while Senator Frye, the Republican member, was one of the extremists. Mr. Day disliked the idea of taking the whole archipelago; but as Senator Gray was the only known representative of the anti-imperialist viewpoint on the

THE AMERICAN PEACE COMMISSION AT THEIR HOTEL IN PARIS
Left to right: Whitelaw Reid, Senator Gray, John Bassett Moore (secretary to the Commission)
Judge Day, Senator Frye, Senator Davis

commission, it seems fair to infer that by the end of August Mr. McKinley had already begun to make up his mind.

It is not to say that this lengthy process had been completed. The commissioners were summoned to Washington and entered at once into a series of exhaustive conferences with the President and his cabinet. Instead of issuing his instructions to the peace commission, the President asked their advice. With the storms of criticism raging over the Army, and with the divided state of the public mind over the Philippines, none could have failed to appreciate the great delicacy of the problem. Senator Hanna, coming East in September, heard that the Republicans were going to lose the House; and in Maine and Vermont, where early elections acted as barometers for the general election in November, the Republican majorities had been heavily cut. The peace commissioners actually turned out to be much divided, and except for Mr. Reid inclined toward taking only Manila, or only the northern islands at the most. On September 7, our Army commanders in Manila were reporting that 'insurgents have captured all Spanish garrisons in island and control affairs outside of Cavite and this city.' The obvious political danger of embarking upon a course that might involve serious military difficulties, or that the electorate might not approve, must have been considered. Yet there was the opposite danger that to 'give back' the islands might prove even more unpopular.

Still wider considerations loomed in the background. The English were urging us to take the islands for the sake of international comity in the Far East. The German attitude was not yet certain. And in the early days of September, Washington received information to the effect that, if we did not take the archipelago, it would be seized by Japan. It was this possibility, in the belief of one later student of the documents, which finally determined the President; for if we hesitated to permit the Germans to assume our 'unexpected burden' in the Pacific, we could not dream, of course, of allowing the Japanese to do so. On September 16, a long letter of instructions was issued to the commissioners. It sounded a familiar note:

It is my earnest wish that the United States in making peace should follow the same high rule of conduct which guided it in facing war. It should be as scrupulous and magnanimous in the concluding settlement as it was just and humane in its original action.

But should the Spaniards make trouble over our terms, it was pointed out that they could be clubbed into submission by reviving the demand for a pecuniary indemnity, which had been waived in the protocol. In other respects the protocol terms were to be insisted upon. The necessity for taking Cuba, not only on the grounds of humanity and civilization, but to assure peace near our own territory, was emphasized.

For the Philippines, however, it was obviously necessary to find some other argument:

The Philippines stand upon a different basis. It is none the less true, however, that, without any original thought of complete or even partial acquisition, the presence and success of our arms at Manila imposes upon us obligations which we cannot disregard. The march of events rules and overrules human action.... We cannot be unmindful that, without any desire or design on our part, the war has brought us new duties and responsibilities which we must meet and discharge as becomes a great nation on whose growth and career from the beginning the Ruler of Nations has plainly written the high command and pledge of civilization.

Incidental to our tenure in the Philippines is the commercial opportunity to which American statesmanship cannot be indifferent. It is just to use every legitimate means for the enlargement of American trade; but we seek no advantages in the Orient which are not common to all.

It seems a curiously romantic way of looking at the 'presence' of our arms in the Philippines. No matter; though somewhat self-contradictory this foundation was believed to be sound enough to erect our demand upon it:

In view of what has been stated, the United States cannot accept less than the cession in full right and sovereignty of the Island of Luzon. It is desirable, however, that the United States shall acquire the right of entry for vessels and merchandise belonging to citizens of the United States into such ports of the Philippines as are not ceded to the United States upon terms of equal favor with Spanish ships and merchandise.

It was a minimum demand; the maximum was left open. General Merritt, the instructions concluded, had been ordered to report to the commission in Paris in order to inform them of his own and Admiral Dewey's views on the whole subject. Thus armed, the commissioners sailed on September 17, enjoying the peculiar dual rôles of a diplomatic mission to enforce our policy and an investigating body to learn the facts and discover, if it could, what our policy ought to be.

Two days before, General Aguinaldo, in the country some twenty-five miles north of Manila, had formally opened the first Congress of the Philippine Republic, headed by a cabinet including the ablest men in the islands.

The occasion was one of great festivities; the town was thronged with thousands of people from the provinces and large numbers also from Manila, including prominent lawyers and merchants of the city. Several Americans, including the press correspondents, attended and were entertained at luncheon... and... warm expressions of friendship were interchanged.

The peace commissioners were in Paris by September 26. John Hay, polished, witty, and skillful, had come home to assume the Secretaryship of State in Mr. Day's place; the Philippine debate was still raging in the newspapers, while the autumn political campaign was deepening in a wild tangle of unpredictable crosscurrents. Prosperity was returning exactly to the schedule which its advance agent had promised. But in spite of everything, the free-silver issue was again raising its horrid head; Populists and silver men were going on the Western tickets, and Western conventions were repeating in their platforms the dreadful heresies of 1896 — just as if Mr. Hanna had never assembled his great majority to demonstrate their falsity. And popular though imperialism appeared to be, it was nevertheless coming under a steadily heavier sniping fire from the most formidable marksmen, while the War Department scandals threatened to turn all to dust in the mouth of an administration which up to that point had with reason regarded itself as under the special protection of an all-wise Providence.

In the important state of New York that generous prophecy which Mr. Lodge had made for his friend, the Colonel of the Rough Riders, had already been far eclipsed — so far eclipsed, in fact, that it was a trifle pointed. Two months before, the Senator had not taken 'much stock' in the suggestion that Mr. Roosevelt might be run for Governor of his state. But the crisis that year had found the local faithful in a badly divided mood. Mr. T. C. Platt, the elderly and very practical politician who ruled the Republican organization in New York, had for some time been anathema to the more refined minds of the 'better element.' At the very outbreak of the war, it had occurred to Mr. Platt that the conflict might provide him with a war hero for a gubernatorial candidate — one whose martial popularity would be sufficient to overcome these internal differences and so reunite the party. According to Mr. Platt:

> While division was acute between New York leaders as to who should be candidate for Governor, Roosevelt, covered with military glory, came back from Cuba. I sent Lemuel Eli Quigg to Montauk Point where the Colonel was camped with his spectacular troop.... Mr. Quigg found the Colonel more than pleased with the suggestion.

Mr. Roosevelt was not only the most popular of all the war heroes, but he was also sufficiently identified with the 'better element' to be the ideal man for Mr. Platt's discerning purposes. The Colonel made his pilgrimage to Mr. Platt's rooms at the Fifth Avenue Hotel, and in the nominating convention on September 27 the 'boss's' choice was ratified with all the precision of that machine system to which the Colonel was so much opposed. Mr. Platt, the Colonel believed, had responded to 'popular pressure' in bestowing the nomination. The two statesmen were later to differ as to whether it was in fact Mr. Roosevelt who annexed Mr. Platt or Mr. Platt who annexed Mr. Roosevelt, but at any rate the hero plunged with his customary enthusiasm into the battle, duly uniting the two wings of the Republican Party and spreading dismay among the boss-ridden corruptionists of the local Democracy. Mr. Roosevelt's personality, his expansionist views, his prestige as a soldier caught the attention of the country as well as of the state, and in this way the larger issues of the war were, through the exigencies of New York Republican politics, to be reflected in a contest which had nothing whatever to do with them.

But three thousand miles away at Paris the peace commissioners were already enshrouded in the loftier and far more elegant atmospheres of true statesmanship. M. Delcassé, the Foreign Minister of France, had formally received them, and on the following day had tendered them a luncheon at which they met the members of the Spanish commission with which they were to negotiate. Don Eugenio Montero Rios, president of the Spanish Senate, was at their head; the others were eminent as statesmen or soldiers. The luncheon set the tone. The actual discussions, begun upon October 1 at the Quai d'Orsay, were cast upon a plane of 'great courtesy which soon thawed into almost an appearance of cordiality.' The Spaniards, it is true, began with the tactless insistence that since we had taken Manila after the signing of the protocol, we should first restore it as a preliminary to any negotiations under that instrument. But this demand was sternly suppressed, and did not seriously ruffle the refined amenities of statecraft.

The management of *Le Figaro* got up a 'Five o'Clock' for both sides. The Coquelins took part, Renaud sang, there were Spanish songs and dances and finally Miss Loie Fuller supplemented her share in the programme with an amazing stump speech in which she appealed for the sending of the questions before the conference to arbitration!

The whole atmosphere could hardly have been more polished or more worthy of the great occasion. In fashionable and official Paris the peace conference actually became quite the rage. The Spaniards from the first seemed to adopt a tone of 'proud supplication.' It was the real thing, the world stage, at last.

On October 4, General Merritt, arrived direct from the Philippines, appeared before the commissioners, and thus for the first time the men in control of our policy came into personal touch with some one who had actually been on the ground. General Merritt was not, perhaps, quite as positive as some of the commissioners might have wished, and the long summary of his views which was at once cabled to Washington contained one or two rather weak passages:

Did not know that he could make out a responsibility [to retain the archipelago] by argument, but he felt it. It might be sentimental.... He thought our interests in the East would be helped by the cheap labor in the Philippines.

But upon the great question of being content with Luzon or taking the whole group, General Merritt 'did not think our humanity bounded by geographical lines.' To extend its benefits merely to Luzon would require, he thought, no more than about 20,000 or 25,000 troops.

General Merritt was only the first of a number of witnesses who were to be heard throughout the fall, as the inquiry into what we should demand in the Far East continued side by side with our negotiations with the Spaniards from whom we were demanding it. At the beginning, however, it was possible to leave the very delicate question of the Philippines in the background of the peace parleys. The Spaniards had conveniently started off by raising the issue of the Cuban debt; and here we felt ourselves upon solid ground. Spain proposed to transfer, together with sovereignty over the island, the financial obligations which she had contracted on behalf of her governments there and which had been secured for the most part on the island revenues. It was understood that they amounted in all to above $400,000,000. The proposal was firmly, almost indignantly, rejected. These debts, we stated, were in no sense obligations of the island, but obligations loaded upon it without its consent to meet the costs of putting down the aspirations of its own patriots in the Ten Years' War and the final insurrection. 'If... those struggles have, as the American Commissioners maintain, represented the hopes and aspirations of the body of the Cuban people, to crush the inhabitants by a burden created by Spain in the effort to oppose their independence' would be 'unjust.'

Any other attitude would not have been tolerated for an instant by the publics at home. And yet today the precise ethics of the position are not easy to follow. No doubt much of the Cuban debt was in speculative hands, and in hands very close to the Spanish Government, while it is true that its creation was a result of the losses and costs of the wars. But for thirty years we had been officially urging the Spanish Government to bend its every effort toward the suppression of these outbreaks; while at the time it was by no means certain that we ourselves were prepared to admit that the insurgent patriots 'represented the hopes and aspirations of the body of the Cuban people.' General García had been carefully excluded from any share in the governance of Santiago, and we never recognized the insurgent Republic as such either then or later.

But when it came to the debt, we insisted stoutly that the insurgent cause was 'so generally conceded to be just as to need no exposition,' and we were adamant. The discussion dragged through the first fortnight, the Spaniards making such desperate efforts to evade defeat that when the meeting of October 14 broke up 'long after dark,' the Americans were convinced that their opponents were 'looking for an opportunity to break up the conference, presumably with a view to an effort for European arbitration of some sort.' Sr. Castillo, the Spanish Ambassador at Paris, was not one of the official delegates to the conference, but he was an old personal friend of Mr. Reid, and he labored tirelessly with him to soften the iron surface of our rectitude.

'"You are in danger of an *impasse*," he would exclaim. "You are the only diplomat there. It is the duty of a diplomat to find some middle way, to avoid the absolute failure of negotiations, to accomplish something."' Thus adroitly did Sr. Castillo play upon what he must have known to be a peculiarly weak spot in Mr. Reid's armor. But it was in vain. As a peace-loving and idealistic people we were, of course, thoroughly committed to the principle of arbitration. But the idea of arbitrating the Cuban debt at this juncture outraged us no less violently than if we had been an ordinary predatory nation which, having all the might in its own hands, sees nothing to be gained by submitting to the adjudication of right or law. Arbitration, according to Mr. Reid's biographer, was obviously a mere subterfuge through which the Spaniards hoped to escape some of the proper consequences of defeat:

Reid found it perhaps the hardest contention of all to discuss with patience. The question of the Cuban debt was a thing which he couldn't consent to arbitrate under any circumstances, any more than he could consent to arbitrate a question whether we should or should not obey the moral law.

Those who do not have to seldom can consent. We were obdurate; but so were the Spaniards in their insistence that the debt question should be left to some kind of impartial determination which, 'pursuant to strict law and undeniable equity,' might at least decide how much of the debt could be properly charged to non-military expenditure in Cuba. We would accede to no such 'unreasonable and unprecedented' suggestion. We believed in arbitration; but it should, we insisted, come first for the purpose of avoiding a war rather than afterward as a means of mitigating the penalties of the vanquished. The superiority of our wealth, our man power, and our gunnery was ample proof of the justice of our cause. At the meeting on October 24, the issue came to its final crisis; the Spaniards were told in effect that further insistence upon our recognizing any part of the debt would terminate the negotiations. They retired to consider.

It was seen that a critical test of strength had come, and that upon the results the remainder of the negotiations would turn. On the night of the 26th, Sr. Castillo visited Mr. Reid at his hotel in a final effort to avert the calamity. There was a long conversation, but it was of no use. Late at night Sr. Castillo was forced to admit his failure; there was a strange and impressive scene which fixed itself in Mr. Reid's imagination:

By this time he had reached the door and was obviously greatly depressed. He said in saying good-bye: 'My dear friend, it is cruel, most cruel; pray God that you may never be likewise vanquished.' In return I expressed the most earnest conviction that it would only be adding to their misfortunes to break off the negotiations; assured him that he could hardly conceive what an unhappiness they would be bringing down upon Spain if they should persist in so unwise a course. Shaking hands again at the door, for perhaps a second or third time, I closed with the words — 'Do not break off'; and with every expression of cordiality but obviously with great sadness the Ambassador disappeared in the corridors of the hotel.

Thus Sr. Castillo retired down the long hallway, in the dead of night, until the shadows swallowed him. And as Mr. Reid watched that disappearing figure, it must have seemed to him that the greatness of the Catholic Kings, the majesty of Philip II, the glory of the Conquistadores, and the splendor of imperial Spain were vanishing likewise into the stuffy shadows of the modern age. The Spanish Ambassador — title of famous association! — put his silk hat upon his head, turned the plush-carpeted corner under the hall light, and it was all over. Pobre España!

III

At the next meeting the Spaniards yielded the point. Sr. Castillo had induced them to do so with the argument that they could get an equivalent elsewhere — which meant, of course, the Philippines — but at best they must have known that they were only whistling to keep their courage up.

The real issue over the Philippines was still not what we were in justice entitled to, but how much we should make up our minds that we wanted. Between conferences with the Spaniards the commissioners had been pursuing their researches upon the question. Commander Bradford of the Navy had appeared to give them an expert's opinion as to the desirability of taking the entire archipelago. They asked his reasons:

A.: The difficulties of defense, which I have already alluded to, and the fact that a whole loaf is better than half a loaf.

Q. [by Mr. Day]: That is, if one has a chance to take more, he better do it?

A.: Yes. All of these islands are very valuable.

Commander Bradford even expressed the firm conviction that the 'Pelews, Carolines, and Ladrones should all be acquired if we are to possess any territory near the China Sea,' and he left a solemn thought with the commission: 'Attention is called to the fact that there is nothing in all Polynesia remaining for any nation to acquire.' But even the technical expert was not blind to the higher things. He added his belief that 'we have incurred a moral obligation to take all of the islands, govern them, civilize the natives, and do the best we can with them.'

The dangerous attitude adopted by the Philippine insurgents in the early part of September had apparently passed; but on October 14, the day that Commander Bradford was testifying, there was a sudden and alarming cable from Washington transmitting the text of a message from Dewey:

It is important that the disposition of the Philippine Islands should be decided as soon as possible and a strong government established. Spanish authority has been completely destroyed in Luzon, and general anarchy prevails without the limits of the city and bay of Manila. Strongly probable that islands to the south will fall into same state soon.... The natives appear unable to govern.

Three or four days later, the commissioners learned that 'situation Luzon somewhat improved,' but it was obvious that affairs were serious. And in the United States the broad outlines of the anti-imperialism issue, obscured as they were in the fogs of local and personal politics, were emerging amid the various state electoral campaigns. Senator Lodge had 'had a troublesome time' with important Massachusetts politicians who were 'uneasy about taking any part in the Philippines,' but with 'a good deal of steering' had overcome the difficulty. His picturesque friend in New York was learning to his disgust that:

The Independents care very much less for honest government than they care to register themselves against my views of expansion and of an efficient Army and Navy. In addition to this, Algerism is a heavy load to carry.... In fact, taking it as a whole, New York cares very little for the war now that it is over, except that it would like to punish somebody because the Republican Administration did not handle the War Department well.

Mr. Pulitzer, for whom imperialism had become so 'distasteful,' was now training the heaviest artillery of the *World* against taking the Philippines, against the peace commission, and against the colorful Colonel. But these were not the only indices. The War President had once again applied his ear to the ground.

Throughout the middle of October, various cities of the nation had leapt with a sentimental enthusiasm into the organization of 'peace jubilees,' and Mr. McKinley had taken the opportunity which this offered to make, without derogation to the Presidential dignity, a 'swing around the circle.' From the 10th of October onward, he was speaking to loyal and enthusiastic audiences throughout the West and Middle West. When he had instructed his peace commissioners in September, it was with dubiety that he had authorized the taking of Luzon. Now he was, as that genial pacifist, Mr. Andrew Carnegie, observed, 'of course cheered when he spoke of the flag and of Dewey's victory,' and as those waves of patriotic applause broke upon him, the President began to see a new light. The conservative East might seem to be clinging to old-fashioned ideas of American policy and morals; but the untrammeled West, home of freedom and heir to a long tradition of territorial expansion, appeared to labor under no such ignoble restraints. They wanted it all.

Uncle Joe Cannon, that very practical man, later summed it up:

He returned to Washington convinced that there was no way out of it, and he would have to take over all the Philippines. It was either that or displeasing the West and running the risk of grave complications with some of the European powers and Japan.... He was a born leader; a man nature intended to be a leader of men.

The President was back in Washington on the 21st, and on the 25th he despatched a cable direct to the peace commission; asking their views and remarking that 'there is a very general feeling that the United States, whatever it might prefer as to the Philippines, is in a situation where it cannot let go.' On the same day the commissioners were cabling for instructions upon the same matter, submitting their opinions. Senator Gray alone was opposed to the whole idea of annexation, and his well-reasoned argument (which was, incidentally, to be borne out in many ways by history) was overwhelmed by the opinion written by Mr. Reid and signed jointly with him by Senator Davis and Senator Frye, urging the annexation of the entire group. Even Mr. Day thought annexation of Luzon, whether wise or unwise, had become inevitable through the actions of our military officers there.

In Washington the President's new mood had been received by some members of his cabinet with misgivings. The Secretary of the Interior, Mr. Cornelius N. Bliss, was so much alarmed that he even summoned his friend, Mr. Carnegie, to the capital to bring his heavier artillery to bear upon Mr. McKinley.

He said [Mr. Carnegie remembered]: 'You have influence with him. None of us have been able to move him since he returned from the West.' I... had an interview with him, but he was obdurate. Withdrawal would create a revolution at home, he said.

Thus, it appears, was Mr. McKinley's mind at last definitely made up, and that Far Eastern empire, into which he had advanced so tentatively and cautiously, finally decided upon. It is necessary to add, however, that Mr. McKinley's own and justly celebrated explanation gave very different reasons for the decision. It was over a year later, when the President had been receiving a delegation from the General Missionary Committee of the Methodist Episcopal Church (at the time in session at Washington) that he suddenly stopped them as they were turning to leave. The President said:

Hold a moment longer! Not quite yet, gentlemen! Before you go I would like to say just a word about the Philippine business.... The truth is I didn't want the Philippines, and when they came to us as a gift from the gods, I did not know what to do with them.... I sought counsel from all sides — Democrats as well as Republicans — but got little help. I thought first we would take only Manila; then Luzon; then other islands, perhaps, also. I walked the floor of the White House night after night until midnight; and I am not ashamed to tell you, gentlemen, that I went down on my knees and prayed Almighty God for light and guidance more than one night.

And one night late it came to me this way — I don't know how it was, but it came: (1) That we could not give them back to Spain — that would be cowardly and dishonorable; (2) that we could not turn them over to France or Germany — our commercial rivals in the Orient — that would be bad business and discreditable; (3) that we could not leave them to themselves — they were unfit for self-government — and they would soon have anarchy and misrule over there worse than Spain's was; and (4) that there was nothing left for us to do but to take them all, and to educate the Filipinos, and uplift and civilize and Christianize them, and by God's grace do the very best we could by them, as our fellow men for whom Christ also died. And then I went to bed and went to sleep and slept soundly.

Thus did Providence endorse Mr. McKinley's earlier view that while we were at war we should take what we could get and afterwards keep what we wanted. But though vouchsafing to the President this remarkable and curiously well-reasoned revelation, Providence completely overlooked the patent wisdom of vouchsafing a similar one to General Aguinaldo. At the moment that Mr. McKinley was receiving the vision, General Aguinaldo, according to a competent American observer, 'had assembled at Malolos a Congress of one hundred men who would compare in behavior, manner, dress, and education with the average men of the better classes of other Asiatic nations, possibly including the Japanese. These men...conducted themselves with great decorum.... The army, however, of Aguinaldo was the marvel of his achievements. He had over twenty regiments of comparatively well-organized, well-drilled, and well-dressed soldiers carrying modern rifles and ammunition.... The people in all the different towns took great pride in this army. Nearly every family had a father, son or cousin in it.'

But we were convinced by this time that it was our mission to civilize the Filipinos. The commissioners' request for instructions had barely reached the State Department before the President's reply was despatched:

> The information which has come to the President since your departure convinces him that the acceptance of the cession of Luzon alone, leaving the rest of the islands subject to Spanish rule, or to be the subject of future contention, cannot be justified on political, commercial, or humanitarian grounds. The cession must be of the whole archipelago or none. The latter is wholly inadmissible, and the former must therefore be required.

Yet to secure the archipelago without damage to our moral superiority was perceived to be something of a task. Two days later (on October 28) Mr. Hay supplemented these instructions:

> While the Philippines can be justly claimed by conquest, which position must not be yielded, yet their disposition, control and government the President prefers should be the subject of negotiation, as provided in the protocol. It is imperative upon us that as victors we should be governed only by motives which will exalt our nation. Territorial expansion should be our least concern; that we shall not shirk the moral obligations of our victory is of the greatest.... How these instructions shall be carried out... the President leaves to the judgment and discretion of the commissioners.

One may well believe that the commissioners regarded this assignment with some dismay. The Spaniards were slow to admit the altruism of our motives. 'The talk of old Montero [Sr. Montero Rios, the head of the Spanish delegation] is endless,' Mr. Reid privately reported to the President, 'and their capacity for producing long documents apparently increases.' Senator Frye was aware of an even more serious difficulty. He perceived that the Spanish commissioners were actually being pushed to the wall, and that the demand for the Philippines might rupture the negotiations. Strangely enough, the other powers, no less than the Spaniards, seemed incapable of appreciating the nobility of our self-sacrifice; even the London *Times*, the Senator noted, was raising its terrible voice against our position. And commanding though our situation might appear, the possibility of there being no treaty after all abruptly revealed our Achilles heel. Our army was demobilized; our people had already celebrated the peace; elections were at hand; the popular mandate for expansion in the Pacific was none too clear, and the resumption of the war on an issue of at least arguable morality might have had the most disastrous consequences. It is easy to understand why Senator Frye declared the securing of a treaty to be 'of vital importance to our country.'

It led Senator Frye to an inspiration. To avoid a crisis of such gravity might we not, he asked, 'agree to pay Spain from $10,000,000 to $20,000,000 if thus a treaty could be secured?' To throw Spain a few millions and call it square was indeed a remarkable idea, and it was in fact to prove the germ of the ultimate solution. For the moment, however, Mr. McKinley could hardly be expected to endorse such a novel proposal as that we should secure a peace treaty by purchase. The possibility that the Spaniards might not come to heel surprised him; he hoped that the situation was not so grave as the Senator painted it, and on November 1 directed that they proceed with the negotiations.

Our demand for the Philippines was formally presented on October 31, and on November 4 it was formally rejected. Mr. Reid believed the Spaniards to be playing for time in the familiar hope that the November elections would go against the Republicans; Mr. Day, however, and the Washington authorities addressed themselves to a telegraphic correspondence in which they sought rather desperately to bolster up the ethics of our Philippine claim. It was a difficult task; the precedents showed a perverse unanimity against us, and Mr. Day's was by training a legal mind. 'We have carefully examined all the leading text-writers and authorities,' he wrote the President, 'and find concurrence of opinion in the view that captures made after the execution of the agreement for an armistice must be disregarded and restored.' If the claim by conquest fell down, we had nothing but the protocol to go on, and the protocol itself gave us no right to annexation. Mr. McKinley boldly decided that we had conquered the islands by the naval battle of May 1 and in the assault on Manila had merely 'perfected' this achievement, but to the commissioners it seemed a rather tenuous argument for a nation as noble and unselfish as ourselves. The idea of claiming the islands as indemnity fluttered through the despatches; but here again we had tentatively renounced all indemnity except Porto Rico and Guam in the protocol. With the lingering uncertainty as to the nation's real attitude and as to the amount of capital which the Democrats might later be able to make out of the anti-imperialism issue, it began almost to seem as though we might have been too noble. But then at last the elections came.

The pessimists were wrong. Divine inspiration was right. What with the War Department scandals and the anti-imperialists the Republican majority in the House was severely cut, but it was not destroyed. While the Republican majority in the Senate, partly as a result of opinion and partly through the accidents of our constitutional system, was made safe 'for the next ten years.' In New York the colorful Colonel had gone in by 17,000 — a narrow squeak, but good enough considering the division in his own party and the handicaps of 'Algerism.' It was not only a victory for good government, but a powerful testimonial to the strength of the new philosophy of international relations. The peace commissioners applied themselves to their task with a renewed confidence.

By this time the full beauty of Senator Frye's inspiration was appearing to them. Even Mr. Reid was willing to grant an honorarium of twelve to fifteen million dollars, to be paid ultimately 'out of the revenues of the islands,' in order to get a treaty; and though Senator Gray still opposed the seizure, he saw that no treaty at all would merely result in our taking the islands by conquest. On November 13, definitive instructions were cabled by Mr. Hay:

Willing or not, we have the responsibility of duty which we cannot escape. You are therefore instructed to insist upon the cession of the whole of the Philippines, and, if necessary, pay to Spain $10,000,000 to $20,000,000.... The questions of duty and humanity appeal to the President so strongly that he can find no appropriate answer but the one he has here marked out.

On the day that Mr. McKinley took this final stand for humanity, General Otis, now commanding at Manila, was cabling that 'prudence dictates that all troops here and soon to arrive be retained.' Not only were the insurgents in control of Luzon, but by this time they were 'in full possession of Negros, Cebu, Panay all but city of Iloilo, and adjacent islands.' The Spaniards still held Iloilo, but they had been surrounded by the insurgents and 'doubts expressed of ability to hold out.' The revolutionary government was 'progressing,' but its real intentions were still of the utmost obscurity.

In Paris also the situation was obscure, while the autumn was deepening rapidly into winter and the leaves were falling along the boulevards. European opinion was most hostile to our Philippine demand, but there was no sign of actual intervention by the powers. The Spanish efforts at escape were inexhaustible; their memoranda became longer and longer still, until at last, on November 19, Mr. Day cabled that the commission was disposed 'to force this matter to an issue.' It had become evident that unless we made it possible, by offering some concession, for the Spanish commissioners to take home at least a shred of success, they would be facing a real choice between no treaty and a revolution; and if it came to that, they would undoubtedly choose to save the dynasty. The deadlock had to be broken; and on November 21 the commissioners availed themselves of the President's authorization. After reiterating all our claims and arguments, we again presented our demand for the cession of the Philippine Islands, but this time with an important addition:

The Government of the United States is unable to modify the proposal heretofore made for the cession of the entire archipelago of the Philippines, but the American commissioners are authorized to offer to Spain, in case the cession should be agreed to, the sum of twenty million dollars.

Sr. Montero Rios 'listened with a funeral face, puffing cigarette after cigarette in his perturbation.' We demanded a categorical reply within two days; Montero Rios exclaimed that he could reply immediately, but in reality he saw that acceptance was inevitable. He secured a postponement of some days, devoted to a despairing effort to bid up the honorarium or gain some other concession. It was quite fruitless. The matter was referred to Madrid and authorization secured. On November 28, the formal reply of the Spanish commissioners was read, amid 'a profound and painful silence':

The Government of Her Majesty, moved by lofty reasons of patriotism and humanity, will not assume the responsibility of again bringing upon Spain all the horrors of war. In order to avoid them it resigns itself to the painful strait of submitting to the law of the victor, however harsh it may be, and as Spain lacks material means to defend the rights she believes are hers, having recorded them, she accepts the only terms the United States offers her for the concluding of the treaty of peace.

'During the reading, the Spanish commissioners sat in their places with an air of mournful dignity. When it was finished, and just as the Americans were preparing to leave the room, the clouds that had been lowering over Paris all day cleared away for a moment, and a burst of sunlight illuminated the green table at which Ojeda, the Spanish secretary, was making his notes of the protocol. Reid happened to be standing at his side and expressed the hope that this meant good fortune for both countries. Ojeda replied: "No, everything is gloom around us."'

On November 30 they began at last to draft the definitive articles of the treaty. But there was more delay over the details; the Spaniards were still struggling to soften the blow. Nothing was definite when, on December 5, Congress met at Washington and the War President's victory message was read to them.

It was a long and splendid review of the events of that splendid year. From its opening sentence it breathed a new confidence, a sense of wider vision. Upon the many immediate problems presented by our acquisitions Mr. McKinley was still a trifle noncommittal. He did pause to prop up the tottering Teller amendment: 'As soon as we are in possession of Cuba and have pacified the island, it will be necessary to give aid and direction to its people to form a government for themselves. This should be undertaken at the earliest moment consistent with safety and assured success.' But the other islands were left until the treaty should be concluded, and on the one burning question — the fate of the Philippines — Mr. McKinley said nothing.

A clear suggestion, however, of the broader consequences to flow from our crusade for Cuban freedom could be read between Mr. McKinley's ringing recommendations. A prominent passage was devoted to the proposed Nicaraguan Canal, 'now more than ever indispensable,' in view of 'the annexation of the Hawaiian Islands and the prospective expansion of our influence and commerce in the Pacific.' The possibility of enlarging our markets in China was pointed out; so, oddly enough, was the appearance among the Chinese of a spirit of unrest and anti-foreignism which

gave Mr. McKinley a reason for 'disquietude.' In the Samoan
Islands a situation had arisen which would have to be watched.
We had at once and with cordiality accepted the invitation of the
Czar of Russia to a conference on disarmament, though our arma-
ments were so small that the matter could have for us 'no practical
importance.' But passing onward in his message, the President
declared that the importance of a permanent increase in our Army
was 'manifest,' while he gave his 'earnest approval' to the Secretary of the Navy's request for three new sea-going battleships, six
armored or protected cruisers, and six unprotected cruisers. More
than that, our merchant marine demanded aid and attention.
Spain had spent two million dollars a year in maintaining steamship services for her islands and we could not 'undertake to do
less.' Our territorial acquisitions, in fact, demanded 'the prompt
adoption of a maritime policy by the United States.'

Thus already had so much been accomplished by the Cuban
patriots — gentlemen, incidentally, who were already regarding
the results of our crusade in their behalf with the greatest misgivings. In Paris it could only stimulate our commissioners to
bring the long farce to an end. Even up to the last moment they
were afraid that the Spaniards might break off after all, but on
December 8, Montero Rios, under instructions from the Queen
Regent and Sagasta to get it over with, caved in and agreement
was reached. Two days later it was done; and by 8.50 on the evening of December 10, the treaty was formally signed.

Under its terms all claims for indemnity by either side, national
or private, were formally relinquished. Spain ceded to the United
States Cuba, Porto Rico, all other Spanish islands in the West
Indies, Guam, and the Philippine Archipelago. The theory upon
which the cession rested was not stated. But at the end of
Article III, which was the article relating to the Philippines, there
appeared a single paragraph, without explanation or elaboration:

The United States will pay to Spain the sum of twenty million dollars
($20,000,000) within three months after the exchange of the ratifications
of the present treaty.

That was all. So far as the record went, it was not a purchase
price. It was not a differential indemnity. It was not a payment
for the 'non-military' portion of the island debts which we had

refused to assume. It was not anything, in fact, which anybody might object to its being; and it had the ingenious effect of at once salving the Spanish honor, securing a treaty without reopening the war, and freeing us from the imputation that we had effected a 'forcible annexation' by conquest, which, as Mr. McKinley had so justly pointed out, 'by our code of morality would be criminal aggression' and not to be thought of. Unquestionably it was a device as admirable as it was original. The treaty was signed; there were speeches of the utmost magnanimity and politeness, and the conference broke up upon a note of cordiality and friendship which has subsisted in Hispano-American relations down to the present day.

The news was flashed to the world. The War with Spain was over. But there remained, as there always remains, the Senate.

IV

'We have beaten Spain in a military conflict, but we are submitting to be conquered by her on the field of ideas and policies.' Thus had that acrid college professor, Dr. William Graham Sumner, already proclaimed it, under his flaming title: 'The Conquest of the United States by Spain.' In the widespread press debate of the fall and early winter the sharp break which we seemed to be making with long-standing American traditions had not been overlooked; its significance had, if anything, been overemphasized by the enthusiasms of the new school no less than by the doubts of the old. We had come, the whole nation felt, to a turning-point in the national life; and there were those who, retaining their old-fashioned faith in a tradition which they felt to be an honorable one, hesitated at the course which seemed to be opening before us. Their voices were not popular, but they were resolute, and they appealed, above the glittering allurements of jingo patriotism, to the best impulses of the American character.

In the excitements of our dazzling achievement, in the crash of bugles and the tramp of marching men, these impulses had been silenced, but they had not been destroyed — and they were awakening now in a strong current of distrust for the fanfare and the flag-waving, a conservative dislike for these new paths and the prospect they offered of the militarism, the international

brigandage, the whole senseless and immoral pageantry of the
European 'autocracies' which we had so often contemned. The
cheers which had greeted President McKinley on his Western trip,
as Senator Hoar put it, were 'uttered by excited crowds,' but 'the
sober, conservative feeling which seldom finds utterance in such
assemblies, did not make itself heard.' And it was this feeling,
sensing in the new policies a violation of all that was best in the
principles and ideology of generations, that raised before the politicians of imperialism a last and possibly the greatest obstacle to
the attainment of their ends.

There could be little doubt that the majority was with them;
but to ratify a treaty requires a two-thirds vote in the Senate of
the United States. The horrid truth was facing them at last —
that one third plus one of the votes in the upper chamber would
defeat the treaty and bring down in ruins the whole splendid
edifice which they had so carefully erected. As early as December 7, Senator Lodge, the eminent member of the Foreign Relations Committee, was entertaining angry fears:

We are going to have trouble over the treaty. How serious I do not
know, but I confess I cannot think calmly of the rejection of that treaty
by a little more than one-third of the Senate. It would be a repudiation of
the President and humiliation of the whole country in the eyes of the
world, and would show we are unfit as a nation to enter into great questions of foreign policy. I cannot believe that the opposition, which is of
course composed of Southern Democrats, can succeed.

How closely those words were to be echoed by other statesmen
just twenty years later neither Mr. Lodge nor his friend could
foresee. The late Colonel of the Rough Riders answered in an
even more shocked alarm: 'It seems impossible that men of ordinary patriotism can contemplate such an outrage upon the
country.' Yet singularly enough, it was Senator Hoar, Mr. Lodge's
own colleague from Massachusetts and one of the last and most
respected survivors of Lincolnian Republicanism, who was to be
a leader in the outrageous attempt. The opposition was by no
means composed entirely of 'Southern Democrats.'

But precisely as was to happen twenty years later, the political
motive no doubt played a commanding part. The anomalous
position into which we had stumbled in the Philippines opened to

the Democrats their opportunity. The Democrats were, of course, committed as a party to the war in Cuba's behalf; but the Philippines, which had nothing to do with Cuba, which did not affect the peace or security of our own shores, and against whose inhabitants, above all, we now seemed on the point of waging a war of subjugation and conquest no different in principle from that which Spain had been waging in Cuba, offered the point for a deadly attack. From the opening of Congress, Democratic members began tearing the Philippine annexation to ribbons; for the fact that their protest was addressed to the better nature of the American people, and supported by some of the most conscientious men in the Republican Party, made it no less effective politics.

In the meanwhile the actual situation at Manila, dimly seen through the brief cables from our military commanders, was such as daily to provide the assault with more and more dangerous ammunition and daily to increase the anxiety of the Administration. We still held nothing save the city of Manila; Aguinaldo was still extending his authority through the islands and exciting 'public with cry for independence.' The wealthier classes in Manila, perceiving our real intentions, preferred immediate annexation and the reëstablishment of order to the long disaster of a hopeless war against us; but their influence over Aguinaldo, as well as Aguinaldo's real influence over the mass of the people, could not easily be gauged from the American headquarters within the city. The cables from General Otis varied in their tone almost from day to day. On December 5 he thought 'the insurgent government quite pronounced in asserting unqualified independence.' On the 8th he thought 'conditions improving and signs of revolutionary disintegration.' Nevertheless, General Otis still put his needs at twenty-five thousand men; and the necessity for seizing the important town of Iloilo before it should succumb to the insurgents, and for occupying the remainder of the archipelago as soon thereafter as possible, seemed to him urgent.

Washington must have realized that every moment of delay could only make subsequent occupation more difficult and more obviously a war of conquest over the Filipinos. But was it not already too late? Could we take Iloilo now without a fight? And if actual hostilities should be precipitated while the treaty was still unratified in the Senate, would not the consequences be disastrous? On the day after Congress convened, Senator Vest of Missouri had brought in an ominous resolution. It declared that 'the colonial system of European nations cannot be established under our present Constitution,' and that if we acquired new territory, it could therefore only be with the purpose of organizing it into states within the Union — a possibility which the imperialists dreaded almost more than a failure to secure ratification. Senator Hoar was tumbling in petitions and memorials by the dozen from all over the country, protesting against the acquisition of the Philippine Islands. And on December 10, the day the treaty was being signed in Paris, the Vest resolution was called up in the Senate and the debate begun. To Otis's request for authorization of a move upon Iloilo there was no immediate reply.

Congress was unable to wait for the formal presentation of the treaty. There was hardly any subject before it which did not sooner or later lead back to the great issue, and the pages of the *Congressional Record* throughout December were filled with it. Senator Gorman seized upon a debate over Army demobilization to proclaim that annexation of the Philippines 'will require and the next Congress will authorize a large permanent standing army, to me most abhorrent.' The House, of course, had no business with these great matters, but it did not hesitate to discuss them, and Mr. John Sharp Williams, then a youthful Representative from Mississippi, found in an agricultural appropriations bill the text for a fiery assault upon Philippine annexation. Mr. Williams exposed the hypocrisy of our 'moral obligation' with all the irony of a tongue that was to be famous for a generation. 'We are not bound to have the Philippines!' he exclaimed. 'Why, six months ago men who talk that way did not know where the Philippines are!' And the House responded with laughter. The argument that we had to take the Philippines in order to save them from misgovernment was laid bare in a memorable sentence: 'Who made us God's globe-trotting vice-regents to forestall misgovernment everywhere?'

Our Army of Occupation... will be confronted... with the huger problem of retaining in unwilling subjection 10,000,000 Filipinos... who have just emerged from a brave struggle for independence against Spanish tyranny, and who have announced to us and to the world that they did not free themselves from Spanish domination for the purpose of yielding their birthright of independence and ending it all by submitting to American domination.

It was exaggerated, perhaps, but it was telling. In the House, too, there was 'Czar' Reed himself, a pillar of Republicanism and profoundly antagonistic to the whole imperialist procession. In the breast of Senator Lodge he aroused feelings of the deepest pain:

Reed is terribly bitter, saying all sorts of ugly things about the Administration and its policy in private talks, so I keep out of his way, for I am fond of him, and I confess that his attitude is painful and disappointing to me beyond words. What a singular collection the so-called anti-imperialists are getting together — Bryan and Carnegie, Pingree and Cleveland.

But there was one rock of hope. Mr. McKinley, the Senator reported to his friend, 'has risen up during the summer to the level of the great events in a very striking way.' On the 20th, Mr. Lodge thought that they would ratify the treaty 'without trouble.'

Possibly the Senator was unaware of the growing danger in the archipelago. General Otis had been cautioned to send his cables in cipher. The General was becoming insistent on the occupation of Iloilo. The Spanish garrison there was still holding it for us, but the commercial interests were petitioning us to take over to avert disorder. At last upon the 21st, as Congress was approaching the Christmas recess, Mr. McKinley decided that he would have to risk it:

President directs that you send necessary troops to Iloilo to preserve the peace and protect life and property. It is most important that there should be no conflict with the insurgents. Be conciliatory but firm.

On the same day, feeling that something more was needed, President McKinley prepared a letter of instructions to Otis mainly designed to inform the Filipino people of our intentions in a manner which would break it to them as gently as possible. But on the 22d, General Otis was again optimistic and the letter was withheld. On Christmas Eve, Colonel Potter was despatched from Manila to Iloilo to confer with the Spanish commander and report upon the actual situation.

Christmas Day, 1898, came and went. In the hot streets of Manila it found our commanders in a mood of confidence, but of the greatest uncertainty; in Washington it found Mr. McKinley, imperfectly informed of what was really going on, facing what was perhaps the most delicate problem of the whole war. The letter of instructions was still held. But early on the morning of the 27th, another cable arrived from Otis. The Spanish commander had evacuated Iloilo on Christmas Eve, and Colonel Potter had been just thirty-nine hours too late. The insurgents had taken possession of the city on the 26th, and Potter had arrived to find Aguinaldo's flag flying above it. What would happen next General Otis could not tell.

The same evening the letter of instructions went upon the cables. The treaty had not yet even been laid before the Senate, but delay seemed no longer possible.

With the signature of the treaty of peace... the actual occupation and administration of the entire group of the Philippine Islands becomes immediately necessary, and the military government heretofore maintained by the United States in the city, harbor and bay of Manila is to be extended with all possible despatch to the whole of the ceded territory.

In performing this duty the military commander of the United States is enjoined to make known to the inhabitants of the Philippine Islands that ... the authority of the United States is to be exerted for the security of the persons and property of the people of the islands, and for the confirmation of all their private rights and relations. It will be the duty of the commander of the forces of occupation to announce and proclaim in the most public manner that we come, not as invaders or conquerers, but as friends....

In view of the obstinate fact that we had actually come both as invaders and as conquerors, and intended to remain as such, it was a difficult task for General Otis. But the instructions closed with a task more difficult still:

Finally, it should be the earnest and paramount aim of the military administration to win the confidence, respect, and affection of the inhabitants of the Philippines by assuring them in every possible way that full measure of individual rights and liberties which is the heritage of free peoples, and by proving to them that the mission of the United States is one of benevolent assimilation.

Two days later, General Otis was ordered directly to 'occupy all strategic points in the island possible before the insurgents get possession of them.' On December 30, the melancholy reply came back: 'All military stations, outside Luzon, with exception of Zamboanga, turned over by Spaniards to inhabitants, who may be denominated insurgents, with more or less hostility to United States.' There were large numbers of insurgents scattered through Luzon; there were about six thousand of them investing Manila, while the city itself contained 'large numbers of sympathizers who have threatened uprising.' Still, General Otis thought that the insurgent movement might break up, though he dared send no more of his troops from Manila.

Then on January 1 there was a report from the force which had been sent to take Iloilo. Its commander 'can take city with force at hand, but not without great loss of life among inhabitants and destruction of property. Merchants who petitioned for troops now ask [him] to avoid conflict. His troops in harbor close to city and he awaiting instructions.' It was New Year's Day of 1899, and, as had happened with nearly every important event throughout the war, again a Sunday. Congress would reconvene on Wednesday and the treaty would go before the Senate. The answering cable went back: 'The President considers it of first importance that a conflict brought on by you be avoided at this time if possible.' The flag of the Philippine Republic continued to float above the city of Iloilo.

Such was the state of affairs on the day when the treaty by which we were to 'retain' the archipelago which we had 'captured' from Spain was presented to the Senate of the United States for its approval. It was a profoundly ironic situation. The islands, in so far as they were being held at all, were being held practically in our name by the Spanish Army. The Governor-General, Diego de los Rios, was still holding out at Zamboanga in the large southern island of Mindanao. Another Spanish garrison was maintaining itself under siege in the town of Baler, Luzon, and we were without troops with which to reënforce it. The Spanish Army endeavored to the best of its ability to discharge its part of the bargain made at Paris and deliver the islands to us. As W. Cameron Forbes was later to write:

The loyal efforts of the Spaniards, unsupported from Madrid, to maintain the dignity and fulfill the obligations of their government during this long period of national humiliation merit the highest praise. Severe losses of life and property were suffered, and many acts of individual gallantry and collective bravery and fortitude occurred of which few have come to public notice.

It was not until April, 1899, that we despatched a naval force to relieve the garrison at Baler; and then the landing party was overwhelmed and its survivors captured. But the Spaniards held out until June, when Aguinaldo himself raised the siege as a tribute to their gallantry. It was not until May that we were able to relieve the garrisons in Mindanao, and General de los Rios was to serve as Governor-General until June. Thus the Spanish Army did its best to hand over the islands; but by the beginning of 1899 it had ceased to be within its power to do so. The Philippine clause of the treaty had become in fact, if not in law, a dead letter, and if we were to annex the islands now, it could only be by the subjugation of their people.

But in the United States all this was not fully known or fully realized. How far the situation had been misjudged is indicated by the fact that when the President's carefully considered letter of instructions arrived at Manila, General Otis did not dare to release it in full. He contented himself with issuing a 'conservative proclamation stating declared intention of President to ensure individual rights,' and promising the people 'most liberal form of government' in which they would have full representation and in which Filipinos would be appointed 'to civil positions of trust and responsibility.' The commander on the transports at Iloilo was less diplomatic; he published the President's letter in full. It fell like a blow upon the populace, many of whom, in Luzon, were literate; and drew an instant protest from General Aguinaldo 'in the name of God, root and source of all justice,... against this intrusion of the United States Government on the sovereignty of these islands.'

But on January 4 the treaty of peace with Spain had been transmitted to the Senate.

V

According to his biographer President McKinley had decided to keep the Philippines in order to give them a government 'solely in their own interests.... Such a vision as the President's could not come to a man of less faith in the essential goodness of the American people. It is not remarkable, therefore, that... the Senate should have hesitated.' It was not; and the hesitation was of a character already most alarming to the imperialists. Discussion of the treaty itself was promptly put into executive session, where it was safe from the scrutiny of public opinion, but Senator Vest's resolution and others like it were seized upon by the opposition as a means for getting its views before the nation. With the near approach of hostilities in the islands, the inconsistency of our whole adventure there offered better and better material, and the opposition used it with a terrible effect. The imperialist philosophy, Senator Hoar exclaimed, would make the United States 'a cheapjack country, raking after the cart for the leavings of European tyranny.' And to demolish the dogma that we could not 'haul down the flag' once it had been hoisted, the Senator quoted McKinley's declaration against forcible annexation with the barbed query: 'Who shall haul down the President?'

At Manila as the days passed the situation lost none of its tensity; General Otis still believed that the insurrection would collapse, but his cables were conflicting and confusing in the extreme. On January 8 he reported that a conflict at Iloilo would mean war throughout the archipelago. Mr. McKinley responded over his own signature:

Am most desirous that conflict be avoided.... Such conflict most unfortunate, considering the present, and might have results unfavorable affecting the future.... Time given the insurgents cannot hurt us and must weaken and discourage them. They will come to see our benevolent purpose.... We accepted the Philippines from high duty in the interest of their inhabitants and for humanity and civilization. Our sacrifices were with this high motive.

And no doubt by this time Mr. McKinley believed it himself. But in the Senate it was clear that even without a war it would be touch and go. So far the imperialists had left the public speechmaking to the opposition while they gathered the votes. But the crisis was deepening. On the 14th, Senator Lodge found time for a note to his friend:

The fight that is being made on the treaty is disheartening, and every day that it is delayed increases our difficulties in the Philippines and the danger of bloodshed. The Spaniards are filling the papers with false reports in the hope that the rejection of the treaty will throw back the islands to Spain, and the attitude of American Senators is helping them. It is not very easy to bear.

Behind the scenes Senator Lodge was doing the heavy work; a few days later he thought he could amass the votes necessary, but as matters stood the opposition was still strong enough to beat him. Fortunately, General Otis continued to be reassuring; but in the open sessions of the Senate the debate wound on, with Senator Platt of Connecticut left almost single-handed to stem the flood of opposition oratory. Something had to be done, and on January 24, Senator Lodge came to his colleague's aid with the first public defense of the treaty to which the statesman had condescended. Mr. Lodge did not attempt a lengthy argument: 'I want to get this country out of war and back to peace.... I want to enter upon a policy which shall enable us to give peace and self-government to the natives of those islands. The rejection of the treaty makes all these things impossible.' With the moment hourly approaching when we should begin to give the natives peace in earnest, though hardly self-government, the argument was perhaps more ingenious than frank. But Mr. Roosevelt, who found it difficult 'to speak with moderation of such men as Hoar,' thought it 'splendid.'

Thus January was running out. In Cuba we had at last managed to effect the Spanish evacuation and to establish our troops and authority at Havana; there had been some rioting and trouble, but a provisional government was beginning to take over and we were getting around to the problems of Cuban misery, which we had set out ten months before to solve. In Porto Rico there had been no difficulty. But in the Philippines, 'situation remains critical,' the cables announced, with 'threats to drive invader from the soil.' A civilian commission of inquiry, designed to facilitate our work of civilization, was being rushed out to the scene and with them six more regiments of infantry. From the cables one could make out very little as to what Aguinaldo's real intentions were; and in the Senate the situation was still most dubious.

And then a new, an unexpected factor appeared suddenly upon the scene. It was Mr. William Jennings Bryan.

This astonishing politician had arrived in Washington filled with a strategic inspiration. Mr. Bryan himself had been among the first to see the usefulness of the anti-imperialist issue, and the Bryanite wing in the Senate was strong enough to have defeated the treaty. But Mr. Bryan now proceeded to undertake a vigorous lobby among his surprised supporters in the Senate to induce them to give their votes for ratification. He told them that the Democratic Party could not hope to win the next Presidential election upon the silver issue, and that they must therefore preserve the issue of imperialism for use in 1900. To do this, he argued, it was necessary that the treaty be ratified, so that we should be in possession of the islands and the troubles they promised to bring with them when the election came round.

Some of his supporters heard this extraordinary program with amazement. 'I was so incensed,' declared Senator Pettigrew, 'by his effort to induce me on the score of expediency to change front that I finally told him that he had no business in Washington on such an errand; that his stand reflected on his character and reputation as a man.... Despite the vigor of my statement, I doubt if Bryan understood what I was driving at.' Others refused with an equal flatness to follow a course as obviously futile as it was unprincipled; but Mr. Bryan clung to the belief that 'paying twenty millions for a revolution' would be enough to defeat any party, apparently never grasping the fact that it would certainly defeat his own. Realizing that if the treaty once were passed, especially with the aid of Democratic votes, it would all be over with the Democrats, they besought him to go away, to get out, to leave it to the Senate. Mr. Bryan did finally depart for Omaha, but not before he had lined up enough votes to make defeat impossible. Mr. Carnegie, who was himself in Washington lobbying with an equal vigor against the treaty, sent a despairing telegram after him.

His reply was... better let the Republicans pass it and let it then go before the people.... One word from Mr. Bryan would have saved the country from disaster. I could not be cordial to him for years afterwards.

When the Senate rose on Saturday, February 4, Mr. Lodge and Mr. Aldrich, the imperialist leaders, had 58 sure votes in line; they needed 60, but there were four doubtful men 'to work on' and they felt confident that they could get at least two of these. The Senate recessed until Monday, when the vote was to be taken.

At five minutes past eight o'clock on the following morning (again it was a Sunday), the officials in the Navy Department were reading this despatch:

Secretary of the Navy, Washington:

Insurgents have inaugurated general engagement yesterday night which is continued today. The American Army and Navy is generally successful. Insurgents have been driven back and our line advanced. No casualties to Navy. In view of this and possible future expenditure request ammunition requisition doubled.

DEWEY

And a little later there was a flash from the Army:

Action continues since early morning. Losses quite heavy. Lines badly cut at first. Communication now satisfactory. Everything favorable to our arms.

The war — a war of conquest which was to flicker on for several years, which was to cost us as much in life and effort as the whole of the War with Spain, and which was to repeat in a kind of grotesque analogy almost everything which we had charged against the Spaniards since the 1895 outbreak in Cuba — had begun. At about half-past eight on the evening of the 4th, an insurgent patrol of four men had come within the territory we had marked out as our own. The American sentry, a Nebraska volunteer, challenged, and as they continued to advance, he fired. There was an answering volley from the insurgent blockhouse near by, and the general assault upon Manila was precipitated. But throughout the anxious night of the 4th–5th of February the attacks were beaten off, and during the next two days the insurgents were driven without serious difficulty. Manila was safe. Our casualties upon the first day, however, were estimated to come to over 175 men, and when the figures could be added up, it was found that in the first four days of their war the Filipinos had inflicted upon us a loss of 268 killed and wounded. This was to be real war. When the Senate met again on Monday, February 6, the 'peace' which Senator Lodge desired us to bring to the Philippines had already cost not only the lives of our own troops but those of some five hundred Filipinos.

A REGIMENT OF AGUINALDO'S INSURGENTS
'Superior to what is generally represented'

BEGINNING OF THE ACTION AT CALOOCAN, NEAR MANILA
FEBRUARY 10, 1899

The 3d U.S. Artillery (employed as infantry) is already engaged in the background. The American line lies behind the wall at the left; the Utah Battery in the foreground.

The vote was set for three o'clock. It occurred to the imperialists that the news of the Manila outbreak, coming just when it did, might act to favor ratification, so that the dangerous situation could be cleared up, rather than to prevent it. But the imperialists were mistaken. 'The line of opposition,' according to Senator Lodge, 'stood absolutely firm, to my great astonishment. I thought the news from Manila would have shattered it, but it did not, marvelous as it may seem.' By half-past two, however, one of the waverers of Saturday had been won over; at five minutes before three they got the second, and their sixty votes. One of the other two joined during the roll-call, and they knew that the treaty was ratified, with one vote to spare. The last obstacle had gone down; whatever might happen now, the nation was irrevocably committed — their amazing adventure had succeeded amazingly and the future lay before them. But it had been a narrow thing; and they owed it, by one of the singularities of history, to the baffling figure of Mr. William Jennings Bryan, who had thus delivered not only his party, but his country as well, into the hands of the skillful politicians of expansion and imperialism. It is not impossible that Mr. Bryan's inspiration will stand as one of the decisive factors in the history of the American people.

It was at any rate decisive in the history of the Democratic Party. The issue which Mr. Bryan had sought to preserve was of course destroyed, in so far as its effect upon the public went; and the party even today may be suffering for this gross forfeiture of its position as the exponent of a disinterested and upright sentiment which had stirred in the American people.

'It was the closest, hardest fight I have ever known,' Mr. Lodge wrote to his friend, 'and probably we shall not see another in our time where there was so much at stake.' Mr. Lodge was mistaken. But when, just twenty years later, that other came, Mr. Lodge showed that he had not forgotten the lesson which the amazing Bryan had taught him. For Mr. Lodge had learned how not to do it.

CHAPTER XIV

CONCLUSION

THE ratification of the Treaty of Paris brought the War with Spain to an end; the immediate events which followed belong rather to the War with the Philippine Republic, of which the Treaty of Paris was the beginning. The '*War* Treaty with Spain, not the Peace,' as that jocular pacifist and arms manufacturer, Mr. Andrew Carnegie, was wickedly to call it. Even in Cuba it seemed for a time as if it might almost be a war treaty too. Máximo Gómez, the Santo Domingan, was passing through the island to the enthusiastic acclaim of the populace, making speeches of an alarming character: 'The Americans have embittered the joy of the Cuban victors with their forcibly imposed tutelage, nor have they been able to soften the pain of the vanquished.' The Army of Occupation continued to entertain the lowest opinion of the Cuban patriots; there were riots and street fights, and in March, Mr. Atkins, back at last to survey the ruins of his estate near Cienfuegos, felt that a 'spark would start a blaze now that might be hard to put out.'

Perhaps the Teller amendment was in danger, what with General John R. Brooke, our Governor-General, at Havana in Weyler's chair, what with all the sanitation and school-teaching and anti-malarial studies we were carrying out so obviously for the Cubans' good, and what with our own increasing doubts as to their capacities for self-government. Perhaps it was in danger — but our commitment was too clear, our own sense of decency too strong, and our hands, besides, too full in the Philippines. Senator Platt of Connecticut was ultimately to solve the difficulty, and Cuba was to be admitted to limited self-rule — an act of fairly evident justice which, in the piratical times of thirty years ago, we were to pride ourselves upon as remarkable.

Into the many incidental difficulties which our new possessions were to cause us, into the curious conflict which cropped up at every turn between the idealism of our professions and the practical necessities of such matters as tariffs and representation and so on, it is impossible to enter. It is even less possible to enter into the broad consequences, ever widening in their effect, ever leading into still newer horizons, which are in some measure traceable to this strange episode. In March, with the treaty safely ratified, the gentle Henry Adams was able to sail with the Lodges 'to pass April in Sicily and Rome' — a happy vacation for the statesman who had made the war, concluded the peace, and already completed his popular history of the whole incident. Mr. Adams, a student of history himself, entertained no misgivings that brilliant summer:

In forty years America had made so vast a stride to empire that the world of 1860 stood already on a distant horizon somewhere on the same plane with the republic of Brutus and Cato.... The climax of empire could be seen approaching, year after year, as though Sulla were a President or McKinley a Consul.

And why not? Was not Mr. Kipling himself telling us to 'take up the white man's burden'? Were not the English enthusiastic, seeing us an imperial collaborator in the Far East? Was not our flag known, our name in the papers, our Navy building up, our Army being enlarged, and had we not snubbed the Kaiser himself?

That autumn Mr. McKinley's secretary found him one day in a happily pensive mood. It was all glorious, glorious beyond words. The Philippines, it is true, still rankled; Aguinaldo, obstinately refusing to be beaten, was killing our troops, prolonging the insurrection until it might after all serve Mr. Bryan's nefarious purpose, and worst of all was drawing the parallel between our position in the Philippines and the Spaniards' position in Cuba ever closer and more deadly. The official papers were explaining, precisely as the Spanish press had once explained, that the insurrection did not represent the people, that it was the rains which were delaying the decision, that it would be all over when fresh troops were sent out. The very words were those which we had so contemptuously flung back at the Spaniards in those idealistic debates so long ago. But what matter? This, of course, was all very different, for our assimilation was 'benevolent.' And no doubt we could make the Filipinos understand it sooner or later. There were larger considerations. If we had not taken the Philippines, Mr. McKinley told his secretary, 'we would have been the laughing stock of the world.' We had avoided that fate. There had been a better result from that *annus mirabilis*, flowing so strangely from an explosion of gunpowder in Havana Harbor. The President reviewed the whole history.

'And so it has come to pass,' he concluded, 'that in a few short months we have become a world power; and I know, sitting here in this chair, with what added respect the nations of the world now deal with the United States and it is vastly different from the conditions I found when I was inaugurated.'

The Philippines did rankle. The insurrection would, of course, end soon — but it did not end. It was not, said the *Review of Reviews*, 'the period of the year most favorable for marching.' The next few weeks would surely do the trick, and we had sixty-five thousand men (four times the number with which we had conquered Cuba) now in the islands or on the way. But the stalwarts of the old régime still vented their disgust in private. 'The folly of ignorance and rascality we are displaying in the attempt to conquer and have " subjects " would disgrace a trades union,' Mr. Godkin wrote in his bitterness to Mrs. James Bryce. But talking about the Philippine War rendered his language 'unfit for publication,' and he had therefore 'ceased to write about McKinley,' as he told another correspondent. 'Every one who believes in the Divine government of the world must believe that God will eventually take up the case of fellows who set unnecessary wars on foot, and I hope He won't forgive them.'

But the yellow newspapers had broken Mr. Godkin's heart. Others could watch with less bitterness the end of that old-fashioned morality to which they had clung. 'It is a matter of congratulation,' Mr. Carnegie wrote to Whitelaw Reid, 'that you seem to have about finished your work of civilizing the Filipinos. It is thought that about 8000 of them have been completely civilized and sent to Heaven. I hope you like it.'

'Czar' Reed was finished. He stayed by the party only long enough to see it through the crisis and then resigned the seat which he had held so long in the lower House, and went into a retirement from which he fired occasional shots. 'Thanks for the statistics,' he wrote to the clerk of the House Committee on Appropriations. 'I have got to hunt all over your figures even to find out how much each yellow man cost us in the bush. As I make it out he has cost $30 per Malay and he is still in the bush. Why didn't you purchase him of Spain F.O.B. with definite freight rate and insurance paid?' And then he turned to amuse his leisure with the composition of imaginary letters from General Weyler to Congress, in which the General asked that body to give him due credit as the originator of its methods in the Philippines.

But it meant nothing. Up to June 30, 1899, the Philippine War had cost us 225 men and officers killed and 1357 wounded (since its outbreak on February 4), but the enlistments for the crusade to bring civilization to the Filipinos were still going beautifully; while if the campaign did stultify somewhat our earlier nobility, that was only the more reason why Mr. Bryan would have difficulty in inducing the nation to admit it. Anti-imperialism could not now be a serious danger. In September, Admiral Dewey came home at last to an ovation greater, perhaps, than any which the nation had ever offered any hero. There was the fleet in the North River and the Victory Arch in Fifth Avenue and crowds cheering themselves speechless at the Admiral's every footstep. He reported, of course, to the President — the interview was on October 3 — and there survived a curious memorandum jotted down by Mr. McKinley during the conversation:

> 4000 followers
> 8 or 10 millions
> . . . .
>
> What is our duty?
>   Keep the islands permanently.
> Valuable in every way.
> . . . .
>
> Should we give up the Islands?
>   Never — never
> The stories of church desecration and
> inhumanity

'Should we give up the islands? Never — never.' We could not now, not for all the oratory of the Boy Orator of the Platte. Nor can one overlook a chronological accident that must have had its effect upon men's minds. It was the year 1899; as the year ran out, the century, too, was coming to its end, and it was like a sign and a promise — an invitation to open the marvelous twentieth century without regrets cast backward at the nineteenth. So Mr. Walter Hines Page, the young editor of the *Atlantic*, saw the vision in the year's closing weeks:

Of American life, as the century ends, the keynote is the note of joyful achievement; and its faith is an evangelical faith in a democracy that broadens as fast as social growth invites... [The Republic's] influence has broadened the thought of the Old World and is now felt in the Oldest World. It is liberalizing kings toward their uncrowning and softening class distinctions, and it is making all artificial authority obsolete.... It has now yielded material for a new period of constructive thought.

Perhaps the way in which American Infantry was making artificial authority obsolete in the Philippine jungles at that moment was rather curious — but who can say that Mr. Page was not right? Who could say so upon the dawn of the twentieth century? Not the American people.

So the sands ran out, weaving, interweaving as they ran, forming new channels, opening new possibilities. At Albany as the century turned, Theodore Roosevelt was working out his extraordinary destiny in difficulty and hesitation, dreaming of the Presidency, but ignorant of the strange chances which were to befall him and through him the nation. The spring of 1900 came and went; imperialism was clearly the Democratic issue, for free silver was dead amid prosperity and the Philippine War still dragged on. But we had at least broken up the Philippine Government and reduced the war to that guerilla status which had brought our intervention in Cuba.

No matter. As the delegates were going up to the Presidential conventions in the summer heat, new avenues were opening. The Boxers were out in China and a detachment of fifty American Marines had been sent on to Peking, along with troops of other powers, as a legation guard. And then one afternoon in June, a ruffle of shots echoed down a long, empty street in the Manchu capital, and as a French machine gun answered at four hundred meters the siege of the Peking Legations had begun. It was to center the attention of the world; there was to be a relief expedition, and American infantrymen were to loot the Forbidden City and stare at the Dragon Throne, while American diplomacy stepped in full confidence upon the world stage and by a process of 'bluff' settled a great matter of international affairs.

The conventions sweltered through a more torrid summer heat than even convention cities had ever known; Mr. Roosevelt emerged, flushed, angry, and disappointed, as a mere Vice-Presidential candidate; and in November the nation went to the polls. It went to pass its first full verdict upon the great series of events, upon the decisions which had been taken in its name and the policies to which its statesmen had committed it. The verdict was complete and unanswerable. The Democracy was routed, overwhelmed, and buried beneath the landslide, not to revive for another decade. The great terror of 1896 had at last been scotched; free silver was beyond reviving, and even Mr. Bryan would take eight years to recover. As Mr. McKinley read the returns, he must have felt that there could be no more complete a triumph of statesmanship, for what he had set out to achieve in 1896 had been brought to a brilliant and conclusive fulfillment. Around him those discerning younger politicians, who so long ago had decided that it might be well to go in for international relations, could have felt hardly less amply rewarded by the astounding work which they had wrought, the astonishing position they had taken in the minds and enthusiasms of their countrymen.

And yet —? Two years before Senator Gray, the Democrat upon the peace commission at Paris, had cabled home his solemn warning upon the Philippine adventure and the whole imperialist philosophy which it involved:

Policy proposed introduces us into European politics and the entangling alliances against which Washington and all American statesmen have protested. It will make necessary a Navy equal to largest of powers, a greatly increased military establishment, immense sums for fortifications and harbors, multiply occasions for dangerous complications with foreign nations, and increase burdens of taxation. Will receive in compensation no outlet for American labor in labor market already overcrowded and cheap, no area for homes for American citizens.... New and disturbing questions introduced into our politics, church question menacing. On whole, instead of indemnity — injury.... But even conceding all benefits claimed for annexation, we thereby abandon the infinitely greater benefit to accrue from acting the part of a great, powerful, and Christian nation.

On election night in 1900 some of that prophetic warning had already come to pass. Would the rest follow? As President McKinley sat in the White House that night, reading the returns so joyously pouring in upon him, did he perhaps seek to pierce the larger future which was to flow from his administration, and for which he knew he would be held largely responsible in the eyes of future generations?

One wonders if he did. Not a year away from that joyful evening was the bandaged hand in a line of handshakers, a piercing shock, and the acrid smell of powder-smoke. There was Theodore Roosevelt, President of the United States; and there was the Panama Canal, and the 'police power' in the Caribbean. Not four years away there was the Treaty of Portsmouth — Russia and Japan sitting down by the New Hampshire seacoast to settle the Far Eastern Question under our good offices. Six years away was Algeciras and American delegates at a general conference of Europe; eight years away there was Admiral Evans — 'Fighting Bob' himself — going around the world in command of a Navy second only to those of Great Britain and Germany, and going under the orders that he might have to fight Japan on the way. Sixteen years away there was preparedness and a naval building program 'second to none'; and in another year there was war — war this time in desperate earnest. Eighteen years away there was a tall figure standing in the white glare of a world's urgent necessity, a President of the United States representing everything that was the antithesis of what Mr. McKinley and his statesmen had represented, and advancing upon a larger and more terrible stage than Mr. McKinley could have conceived. Twenty years away there was Senator Lodge — older, white-haired, but still astutely managing another treaty fight as he, too, found himself the representative of ideas which had passed, of principles which were anachronisms, and of a cause which in its success was to break him as failure had broken Mr. Bryan. And thirty years away there was America, rich, powerful, commanding a greater economic and perhaps political strength in the world than any nation which had ever gone before — aloof, untrammeled, admitting no restraints upon the uses to which that power might be put. But after that?

Who knows?

THE END

BIBLIOGRAPHICAL ACKNOWLEDGMENT

BIBLIOGRAPHICAL ACKNOWLEDGMENT

THE foregoing book was undertaken rather as an essay in history than as history itself, and it makes no pretense to monumental scholarship. But throughout the effort has been to make no statement of fact not founded upon competent authority; quotations (save where the contrary is obvious) are from eye-witnesses, from contemporary newspaper files or from the voluminous published documents. The quoted press comment, however, has for the most part been taken from the *Literary Digest* or the *Review of Reviews* instead of from the original publications.

The standard work upon the Spanish-American War is found in Admiral French Ensor Chadwick's three solid volumes, 'The Relations of the United States and Spain.' The first of these is a scholarly study of the diplomatic backgrounds; the last two supply a complete history of the military operations, including the personal contribution of the author, who served as captain of the New York and Admiral Sampson's chief of staff. I must acknowledge my debt to these books, which I have used freely as guides. Since their publication in 1911, however, a good deal of additional material has been supplied in the memoirs and biographies of the chief actors. I am especially indebted to a collection of first-hand accounts of the Army campaign in Cuba issued in 1927 by the Society of Santiago de Cuba.

It may seem that I have stressed the satiric aspects of the war. This is true; and my defense is a belief that every war in modern times has presented precisely the same elements, though ordinarily they are concealed beneath the immense tragedy which war normally involves. Our War with Spain merely offered an opportunity to examine them in one case where that tragedy was not present.

PERIODICAL
  New York Tribune.
  New York World.
  New York Journal.
  Literary Digest.
  Review of Reviews.

OFFICIAL
  Congressional Record.
  Foreign Relations of the United States (various volumes).
  Compilation of Reports of Committee on Foreign Relations, 1789–1901.
    (vol. 7.)

Cuban Correspondence (Senate Doc. 230; 55th Congress, 2d Session).
Message and Documents, 1898. (4 vols.)
Correspondence Relating to the War with Spain. (2 vols.)
Proclamations and Decrees.
Treaty of Peace and Accompanying Papers (Senate Doc. 62, parts 1 and 2; 55th Congress, 3d Session).
Annual Report of the Secretary of War, 1899.
Report on the Census of Cuba, 1899.
Report of the Commission to Investigate the Conduct of the War Department. (8 vols.) (Senate Doc. 221; 56th Congress, 1st Session.)
Report of the Naval Court of Inquiry upon the Battleship Maine.
Proceedings of a Court of Inquiry in the case of Rear Admiral Winfield S. Schley. (2 vols.)

GENERAL

ADAMS: The Education of Henry Adams. 1918.
ALGER: The Spanish-American War. 1901.
Apuntes Históricos Sobre la Representación de Cuba en España. New York, 1877.
ATKINS: Sixty Years in Cuba. 1926.

BALLOU: History of Cuba. 1854.
BEER: The Mauve Decade. 1926.
BENTON: International Law and Diplomacy of the Spanish-American War. 1908.
BISHOP: Theodore Roosevelt and his Time. 1920.
BLEYER: Main Currents in the History of American Journalism. 1927.
BONSAL: The Fight for Santiago. 1899.
BURTON: John Sherman. 1906.
BUSBEY: Uncle Joe Cannon. 1927.

CABRERA Y BOSCH: Los Partidos Coloniales. Havana, 1914.
CALDWELL: The Lopez Expedition to Cuba. 1915.
CARNEGIE: Autobiography. 1920.
CERVERA Y TOPETE: Spanish-American War. (Navy Department translation.) 1899.
CHADWICK: The Relations of the United States and Spain. (3 vols.) 1909–1911.
CHAPMAN: History of the Cuban Republic. 1927.
CISNEROS: Story of Evangelina Cisneros By Herself.
CONCAS Y PALAU: Squadron of Admiral Cervera. (Navy Department translation.) 1898.
CORTISSOZ: The Life of Whitelaw Reid. 1921.
CROLY: Marcus Alonzo Hanna. 1912.

DAVIS: The Cuban and Porto Rican Campaigns. 1898.
DENNIS: Adventures in American Diplomacy. 1928.
DEWEY, D. R.: National Problems. 1907.
DEWEY, A. M.: The Life and Letters of Admiral Dewey. 1899.
DEWEY, G. W.: Autobiography. 1913.
Diary of a Spring Holiday in Cuba. 1872.

España y Cuba, Estado Político y Administrativo de la Grande Antilla.
Madrid, 1896.
EVANS: A Sailor's Log. 1901.

FISKE: From Midshipman to Rear Admiral. 1919.
FLINT: Marching with Gomez. 1898.
FLORES: La Guerra de Cuba. 1895.
FORBES: The Philippine Islands. 1928.
FUNSTON: Memoirs of Two Wars. 1911.

GANOE: The History of the United States Army. 1924.
GELPI Y FERRO: Situación de España y de sus Posesiones. Madrid,
1875.
GLEAVES: The Life of an American Sailor. 1923.
GÓMEZ: La Insurección por Dentro. Madrid, 1900.

Harper's Pictorial History of the War with Spain. 1899.
HEMMENT: Cannon and Camera. 1898.
HENDRICK: The Training of an American. 1928.
HIBBEN: The Peerless Leader. 1929.
HOBSON: The Sinking of the Merrimac.
HOAR: Autobiography of Seventy Years. 1906.
HUMBOLDT: Island of Cuba (with Preliminary Essay by J. S. Thrasher).
1856.
HUNT: Young in the Nineties. 1927.

JOHNSON: History of Cuba. 1920.
Commander J...: Sketches from the Spanish-American War. (Navy
Department translation.) 1899.

KENWORTHY AND YOUNG: Freedom of the Seas.

LATANE: America as a World Power. 1907.
LANG: Autobiography of Thomas Collier Platt. 1910.
LODGE: The War with Spain. 1899.
LODGE: Letters of Theodore Roosevelt and Henry Cabot Lodge. 1925.
LONG: The New American Navy. 1903.

Mayo: America of Yesterday, As Reflected in the Journal of John Davis Long. 1923.

McCall: Life of Thomas Brackett Reed. 1914.

McElroy: Grover Cleveland. 1923.

McIntosh: The Little I Saw of Cuba. 1899.

José Martí, Apuntes Históricos. Tampa, 1896.

Miles: Serving the Republic. 1911.

Miley: In Cuba with Shafter. 1899.

Millet: The Expedition to the Philippines. 1899.

Morales y Morales: Iniciadores y Primeros Mártires de la Revolución Cubana. Havana, 1901.

Mueller y Tejeiro: Battles and Capitulation of Santiago. (Navy Department translation.) 1898.

Ogden: Life and Letters of E. L. Godkin. 1907.

Olcott: Life of William McKinley. 1916.

Parker: Recollections of Grover Cleveland. 1909.

Peck: Twenty Years of the Republic. 1906.

Pepper: Tomorrow in Cuba. 1899.

Porter: National Party Platforms. 1924.

Quesada: History of the War for Independence. 1898.

Rea: Facts and Fakes About Cuba. 1897.

Reparaz: La Guerra de Cuba. Madrid, 1896.

Rhodes: History of the United States from the Compromise of 1850.

Richardson: Messages and Papers of the Presidents.

Ridgely: The Coast Guard Cutter McCulloch at Manila. (In United States Naval Institute Proceedings, May, 1929.)

Roosevelt: Theodore Roosevelt: An Autobiography. 1913.

Roosevelt: The Rough Riders. 1899.

The Santiago Campaign. 1927.

Sais de la Mara: Consideraciones Alrededor de Máximo Gómez. Havana. 1925.

Schley: Forty-Five Years under the Flag. 1904.

Seitz: Joseph Pulitzer. 1924.

Sigsbee: The 'Maine.' 1899.

Spears: The History of Our Navy. 1897–99.

Sumner: War and Other Essays. 1911.

Tetuán: Apuntes del Ex-Ministro del Estado. Madrid, 1902.

Thayer: The Life of John Hay. 1915.

TRUJILLO: Apuntes Históricos — Propaganda y Movimientos Revolucionarios Cubanos. New York, 1896.
TURNBULL: Cuba, with Notices of Porto Rico and the Slave Trade. 1840.

VARONA: De la Colonia a la República. 1919.
VIVIAN: The Fall of Santiago. 1898.

WATTERSON: Marse Henry. 1919.
WEYLER: Mi Mando en Cuba. 1910.
WHEELER: The Santiago Campaign. 1898.
WHITE: Autobiography. 1905.
WILSON: The Life of Charles A. Dana. 1907.
WINKLER: Hearst. 1928.

INDEX

Spanish names which include the article appear under initial of name, as: 'Caney, El.' Daily newspapers are under city in which published; other periodicals under name.

Sanguily, General Julio, 69–71

San Juan Hill, 276, 278–79, 282–91

San Juan, P.R., 204–06, 236, 336–37, 343–44

Sankey, Ira, 242

Santiago de Cuba, and insurrection, 1, 74, 75; and reconcentration, 76, 90–91; land defenses, 269, 293, 295, 325–26; approaches to, 276; sea defenses, 296, 323–24; condition after San Juan, 303–04; fall of, 321, 324–25; surrender ceremonies, 325–27; Wood as military governor, 364

Santiago Expedition, ordered, 238; embarkation, 241–48; sails, 249, 255–58; strength, 255; landing, 262–68; advance of, 269–71, 276–81; at Las Guásimas, 271–76; El Caney and San Juan, 281–92; after San Juan, 293–99, 320–21, 325; disease in, 329, 335, 345–48, 350, 353; return of, 349–53; at Montauk Point, 365

Santiago, naval battle of, 300–02, 305–14

Scandals over conduct of war, 344–45, 347–48, 365–68, 375

Schley, Admiral Winfield S., at Valparaiso, 19; commands Flying Squadron, 150, 203; and pursuit of Cervera, 230–36, 239; at Santiago, 300–01, 302, 306–07, 310, 312–13; and Sampson, 301, 312–13, 349, 369–70

Schurz, Carl, 160–61

Schwan, General Theodore, 342

Scovel, Sylvester, 326–27, 348

Second Infantry, 247–48

Second Massachusetts, 255, 285, 287

Second Oregon, 359

Second Wisconsin, 216

Segurança (ship), 256–57, 258, 260–62, 264

Seventh Artillery, 159

Seventh California, 343

Seventh Regiment, New York, 158–59

Seventy-First New York, 207, 212–13, 215, 247–48, 255, 284–86, 289, 348

Shafroth, Representative John F., 253

Shafter, General William R., appointed to Fifth Corps, 166; to make reconnaissance, 166, 174; to advance on Havana, 199, 208; ordered to Santiago, 238, 241; and Tampa embarkation, 242–48; plan of attack, 256–57; meets García, 260–62; and R. H. Davis, 264–65; plans advance, 269, 270, 278–80; at San Juan, 282, 287, 288, 289; after San Juan, 293–94, 295–97; proposes retreat, 297–98; demands surrender of city, 298–99; reports naval victory, 314; ill, 318; and surrender negotiations, 321, 324–25; and Sampson, 295–97, 321–23, 327–29; and Scovel, 326–27; and disease situation, 347–48, 350–53; and *Journal*, 349; and Round Robin, 352–53; Roosevelt on, 275

Shaw, Dr. Albert, 40

Sherman, John, alleges Spanish atrocities, 48–49; Secretary of State, 74; protests

reconcentration, 79, 89; and de Lôme letter, 99; resignation, 252 n.; also, 6, 24, 38, 45, 81, 135

Siboney, 261, 269–70, 271, 274, 299, 329, 347

Sigsbee, Captain Charles D., 93–94, 96, 100–06

Silver question, 8, 22, 24, 26, 34, 56–58, 77, 124, 375

Singapore *Free Press*, 182

Sixth Cavalry, 284, 288, 326

Sixth Infantry, 246–47, 284–85, 288

Sixth Massachusetts, 220

Sixteenth Infantry, 284–85, 288, 290

Skinner, Representative Harry, 49

Spain, attitude toward U.S., 49, 54; refuses to proclaim reforms in Cuba, 54; pledges partial reform, 66; Liberals alter policy of, 80–81, 87; pledges autonomy for Cuba, 87–88; permits American relief, 92; and Maine, 95, 96, 109, 113, 131; refuses to sell Cuba, 125; suggests guaranteed truce, 125–26; refuses to grant truce, 130–31; unconditional truce, 132, 135; granted, 137–38; severs relations, 144; declares war, 150; sues for peace, 336, 338–40, 341–42; signs armistice, 354; signs peace treaty, 388–91. *See also* under subject heads, etc.

Squire, Senator Watson C., 45

Stevens, Frederick L., Minister to Hawaii, 20–21

Stickney, J. L., 194–95

Storey, Moorfield, 254

Subig Bay, 186, 332

Sumner, General S. S., 284–85, 289

Sumner, Professor W. G., 77, 391

Tampa, 154, 165–66, 208, 213, 241–48

Teller, Senator Henry M., 143

Teller Amendment, text, 143; 174, 227, 317, 364, 389, 404

Tenth Cavalry, 271–72, 288, 290–91

Tenth Infantry, 242

Ten Years' War, 13–16, 23, 48, 378

Teresa (ship), 167, 301–02, 305, 306, 307–08, 309

Terror (ship), 204

Texas (ship), 300, 306–07, 311–12

Third Cavalry, 284, 288

Third Nebraska, 219–20

Thirteenth Infantry, 247, 286, 288

Thirteenth New York, 158

Thirty-Second Michigan, 245

Toral, General José, 299, 321, 324–25

Treaty of Paris, negotiated, 377–81, 385–86, 388–89; signed, 390–91; ratification of, 392, 398–403; Carnegie on, 404

Trocha, 35

Turpie, Senator David M., 50, 68

Twelfth Infantry, 291–92

Twentieth Kansas, 214